HISTORY OF THE CO[...]
OF GREAT B[...]

HISTORY OF THE COMMUNIST PARTY OF GREAT BRITAIN

VOLUME TWO:
1925–1927: THE GENERAL STRIKE

by

JAMES KLUGMANN

LAWRENCE & WISHART LTD
LONDON

Copyright © Lawrence & Wishart, 1969

Reprinted 1976
Reprinted 1980

*Printed and bound in Great Britain at
The Camelot Press Ltd, Southampton*

This volume is dedicated to the militants who led the great strike of 1926, and to the miners who fought on despite betrayal.

CONTENTS

Preface	9
I Prelude to the General Strike	11
Appendix I. Instructions for Embargo on Coal Movements, July 30, 1925	86
Appendix II. "Communists and the Labour Party": Communist Party Statement, October 1925	88
II The Party and the General Strike	91
Appendix I. Communist Party Executive Statement of January 10, 1926	200
Appendix II. Communist Party Statement on the Royal Commission Report on the Mining Industry	202
Appendix III. "All Together For the Fight!", Communist Party Executive Statement of April 23, 1926	205
Appendix IV. Communist Party Manifesto, of May 2, 1926	207
Appendix V. "The Political Meaning of the General Strike", Communist Party Executive Statement of May 5, 1926	209
Appendix VI. "Stand by the Miners". Communist Party Appeal of May 13, 1926	210
Appendix VII. "Why the Strike Failed". Communist Party Statement of June 4, 1926	212
Appendix VIII. The Preliminary Railway Settlement of May 14, 1926	218
Appendix IX. Communist Party's Statement on the General Strike, October 1926	219
III The Communist Party and the Labour Movement, May–November 1926	230

IV Against Imperialism and War, 1925–1926	289
Appendix I. Party Press and Publications on Imperialism, 1925–1926	328
Appendix II. Communist Party Executive Committee Resolution on China, October 1926	330
Appendix III. Congresses and Extended Plenums of Communist International, 1919–1926	333
V Communist Party Life and Organisation, 1925–1926	334
Appendix I. Communist Party Congresses, 1924–1926	359
Appendix II. Communist Party Leadership between the Sixth and Eighth Party Congresses	359
Appendix III. Young Communist League Leadership between Second and Fourth Congresses	363
Index	365

PREFACE

This second volume of the *History of the Communist Party of Great Britain* treats the period from the defeat of the first Labour Government at the end of 1924 to the end of 1926.

Originally I had planned that all this would be included in the first volume of the History, but, in the course of writing, it more and more seemed necessary to treat in detail the many-sided aspects of the General Strike of 1926, so important a chapter in British Labour History. The volume describes different aspects of the work and life of the Communist Party—struggles in the industrial field, relations with the Labour Party, the Party's role in the unemployed struggles, its international policy and actions of solidarity, especially its initiative in the "Hands off China" campaign. It analyses the changes in party organisation. It contains brief histories of the Young Communist League, the National Minority Movement and the National Unemployed Workers Committee Movement during the period 1925-1926.

But inevitably, the General Strike, its prelude, its brief but momentous days, the prolonged and bitter struggle of the miners which continued after the general strike had been betrayed, came to dominate the whole story of these two years. I have tried to work out in some detail the role of the Communist Party during the General Strike and to consider at some length the lessons which the Strike had both for the labour movement in general and for the Communist Party in particular.

Once again, an attempt has been made to write not an internal isolated history of the Party, but its history within the living context of the general labour movement.

I must warmly thank those who read and commented on the draft—R. Page Arnot, J. R. Campbell, R. Palme Dutt, Frank Jackson, John Mahon and Andrew Rothstein. But once again, I must accept full responsibility for the judgements made and for errors committed.

May I appeal to those who have memories of the period, particularly of the role of the Communist Party and its members during the General Strike and the Miners' Strike, to put them on paper or tape, and to let me have copies for the Communist Party library. May I appeal equally to those who have kept leaflets, pamphlets, internal Party documents, local bulletins of the Councils of Action, material of the Young Communist League, National Minority Movement and of the National Unemployed Workers Committee Movement, to let me have them or copies of them for safe keeping in our library. It was very hard in those two years of bitter struggle to preserve ordered libraries or neat files of documents.

I should like to thank those who have sent me comments, criticisms and information about errors or omissions related to the first volume of the History. May I ask that the same be done for Volume II.

I have now, jointly with Jack Cohen, begun work on the third Volume, which will cover the period from 1927 to (provisionally, a final decision has yet to be made) around 1932. The period includes the beginning of the great slump, the Second Labour Government, Mondism in the trade union movement, and also some hard-fought and bitter class struggles. It is a complex and difficult period of British labour history and of the history of the Communist Party in particular. It was a period of great discussion and at times of struggle within the Communist Party and the Young Communist League. We shall try to deal in detail with these inner Party discussions and also with the relations between the Communist Party of Great Britain and the Communist International, which are of a special importance in this period.

Again, we would be grateful for any memories or material which can help us in this work.

JAMES KLUGMANN

January 15th, 1969

CHAPTER I

PRELUDE TO THE GENERAL STRIKE

Seventh Congress of the Communist Party—International Trade Union Unity—Campaign for Unity Proceeds—Anglo-Soviet Trade Union Conference—Support and Hostility—Minority Movement—Capitalist Offensive—Challenge to the Miners—Communist Party and the Miners—Coalowners Attack—Miners Fight Back—The Coalowners Surrender—The First Round Only—Solemn Warning—The Capitalists Prepare—The Capitalist State Prepares—How Far does Labour Prepare?—Communists, Continued Warning—Second Conference of National Minority Movement—Scarborough: Positive and Negative—Communist Party and Labour Party—Liverpool—The Trial of the Twelve—Arrest of Welsh Miners—Solidarity with the Twelve—The Significance of the Trial.

SEVENTH CONGRESS OF COMMUNIST PARTY

The Seventh Congress of the Communist Party of Great Britain was held in the St. Mungo Halls, Glasgow, from May 30–June 1, 1925.[1] It was already clear that the British capitalists were preparing a far-reaching onslaught on working-class conditions and rights, that the British workers were unevenly prepared for the struggle, that whilst in some, primarily trade union, circles there was a militant feeling arising, in other spheres (for instance inside the Labour Party) the right wing were gaining ground.

It was necessary to sound the alarm, to warn, to work speedily for greater unity of the working class, to isolate those right-wing leaders, MacDonaldites and their trade union counterparts, who were preparing to retreat and to capitulate. And this, in many ways, was the central Congress theme.

The Party had not waited to issue its warnings. Nor had the National Minority Movement. The Labour Government had come under such

---

[1] See *Report of the 7th Congress of the Communist Party of Great Britain*, C.P.G.B., 1925, 207 pp. The Congress was welcomed to Glasgow by George Buchanan, M.P., then one of the followers of Maxton.

heavy capitalist attack precisely because a left-wing trend had been rising within the country and because the growing role of the Communist Party within this left movement was especially disturbing to the authorities.

Defeat of the Labour Government meant preparing the ground for a new attack on the workers—so the Party warned from the very moment the new Tory Government assumed office:

> "It should be apparent to even the meanest intelligence that the employing class is preparing a devastating offensive against the labour movement. . . .
>
> "The wage offensive is likely to be accompanied by an attack on the Labour movement itself. . . ."[1]

"Will the 'Left' Awake?" was the title of an article by J. R. Campbell in the first issue of the *Workers' Weekly* in the New Year, 1925.[2] 1925 would certainly be "a year of struggle" but there was

> "a noticeable difference between the preparation of the employing class and the working class. . . ."

The employers, Campbell wrote, were preparing "quietly and determinedly", but the workers, though they were putting new demands to their Union Executives, were "not preparing the machinery for action at all". They were leaving it all to their leaders. Could they afford to do that?

It was not by chance that it was particularly in the trade union field that the militant trend in the British Labour movement was manifested after the fall of the first Labour Government.

For one thing, within a period of general world capitalist restoration of partial stability, in Britain, the economic depression, which had begun in 1920, continued and worsened; naturally enough, from the employers' angle, this was expressed in an attempt to restore their own position at the expense of their employees.

In the second place, after the defeat of the Labour Government and after the experience of the sorry attitude of the Labour leaders in office to the problems of trade unionists, it was natural enough from

---

[1] *Workers' Weekly*, No. 94, November 21, 1924.
[2] J. R. Campbell, "Will the Left Awake?", *Workers' Weekly*, No. 100, January 2, 1925.

the workers' point of view that they should look to their industrial organisations, their trade unions, for defence.[1]

Thirdly, both in a number of individual unions, like the Miners' Federation where A. J. Cook replaced Frank Hodges as Secretary, and in the General Council of the T.U.C., there were in leading positions a number of union leaders who took a left line on a number of issues.

And finally, but by no means least, now that the most militant workers of all, the Communists, were being excluded from the Labour Party, it was precisely in the unions that their influence was most felt. To an extent the contrast between the increase of right-wing influence in the Labour Party and of left-wing influence in the unions was based on the role of the Communists.[2]

INTERNATIONAL TRADE UNION UNITY

One of the trade union issues on which the Communist Party in this period felt and fought most keenly was international trade union unity. Of course, the issue transcended the boundaries of trade unionism proper. What was at stake was working-class unity on a world scale. Its significance was revealed not only in the enthusiastic campaigning by militant trade unionists but in the bitter opposition of the capitalist press and of the most right-wing circles of European reformism.

"All capitalist newspapers," declared Harry Pollitt in his Chairman's Address to the opening session of the Seventh Party Congress (May-June 1925):

> "during the last six or seven months, have printed so many columns of good feelings for the old conservative trade unionists, and deprecated those elements in the unions who desire to see the unions of Great Britain and Russia come together. The bourgeoisie can see even clearer than many of our class that this question of international trade union unity is not a question of trade unionism pure and

---

[1] Note the remark of Ralph Milliband in *Parliamentary Socialism: A Study in the Politics of Labour*—"After the disappointments of 1924, the notion that the unions must look to their own combined industrial strength for the protection of their members had acquired a new measure of popularity." Chapter V, "The General Strike", p. 122.

[2] Ralph Milliband notes this point in the same chapter quoted above: "In the coalfields and in the trade unions generally, the National Minority Movement, led by the Communists and designed to bring about a broad alliance of militants within the Unions, was gaining marked support". Op. cit., p. 122.

simple, but is a class question, intended to rally the workers internationally on the basis of the class struggle to fight against capitalism.

"We welcome as a Party the coming together of these tremendous potential working-class forces of the world. . . ."[1]

The Party embodied its views on the role of, and struggle for, international trade union unity and, within this, for Anglo-Soviet trade union co-operation, in the Thesis on International Trade Union Unity adopted at its same Seventh Congress.[2]

At its Third Congress in 1924, the Red International of Labour Unions (R.I.L.U.) had proposed a Unity Conference with the Amsterdam Trade Union International, which the latter rejected. However, from the end of 1924 the British trade union movement, from within the Amsterdam International, began a major campaign to reverse this decision.

At the Hull T.U.C. in 1924, the British delegates gave an enthusiastic reception to a fraternal delegation from the Soviet trade unions led by Tomsky, Chairman of the Soviet T.U.C., and the General Council was invited to send a delegation to the Soviet Union.

On November 7, 1924, a British delegation of seven full delegates of the General Council, and a further three acting in an advisory capacity, proceeded to Russia.[3] It was a most representative delegation, including Herbert Smith, President of the Miners' Federation, Ben Tillett, the founder of the Dockers Union and a member of the General Council since 1922, John Turner of the General Council, John Bromley, M.P., a pioneer of railway trade unionism, Alan Findlay of the United Patternmakers' Association. A. A. Purcell, once a member of the Social Democratic Federation and of the Communist Party, pioneer of the Furnishing Trades Union, Vice-Chairman of the General Council, acted as chairman of the delegation, and Fred Bramley, then Secretary of the General Council, as its secretary.

In the course of the visit, the British delegates were able not only to study economic and political conditions in Russia, but to attend the Sixth All-Russian Trade Union Congress and to discuss the whole question of international trade union unity with their Soviet opposite

---

[1] *Report of 7th Congress of C.P.G.B.*, pp. 7-8.
[2] "Thesis on International Trade Union Unity" and "Appendix to Thesis on International Trade Union Unity", in *Report of 7th Congress of C.P.G.B.*, pp. 188-194.
[3] See "*Russia: the Official Report of the British Trade Union Delegation to Russia and Caucasia, Nov. and Dec. 1924*", T.U.C., 1925, 250 pp.

numbers. In a letter dated Moscow, November 17, addressed to Tomsky of the U.S.S.R. Central Council of Trade Unions, Fred Bramley summed up the large measure of agreement reached at these conversations.[1]

After recording its appreciation of the Russian trades unions' activity for international unity, the British delegation declared that it was prepared:

> "to take the responsibility of agreement with the Russian trade union movement, such agreement to make provision for the promotion of the following:
> (1) To request the Amsterdam International to agree to a free and unconditional immediate conference with representatives of the Russian Trade Union Movement.
> (2) To secure for the Presidium of the Russian Movement and the General Council of the British Trades Union Congress full power to act jointly for the purpose of promoting international unity."

This was reported on the delegation's return to Britain and the action was approved.

The publication in February 1925 of the British delegation's visit to Russia met with a barrage of attack from the capitalist press.[2] Typical comments were:

"Trade Unionists who were hoodwinked" (*Daily Chronicle*, February 28, 1925); "The delegates did not attempt to see through the camouflage" (*Daily Mail*, February 2, 1925); "Pictures to deceive the simple" (*Daily Mail*); "Red Whitewash" (*Daily Express*); "An Irrelevant Report" (*The Times*). Most of the continental social-democratic press either passed over the report in silence (for instance *Vorwärts* of the German Social Democratic Party, *Le Peuple*, central organ of the Belgian Labour Party, or *Le Peuple*, organ of the French C.G.T.) or, like the *Robotnik*, organ of the Polish Socialist Party, vied with the capitalists in abuse.[3]

But the attacks on the Report on Russia were comparatively mild compared to the thunder (or silence) which met the delegation's declaration on international unity.

[1] Letter quoted in full in *Report of Proceedings at the (Scarborough) 57th Annual Trades Union Congress*, T.U.C., 1925, p. 296.
[2] See "Reception of the Russian Report" in *Trade Union Unity*, Vol. I, No. 1, April 1925, pp. 11–12.
[3] *Robotnik*, March 6, 1925. See also Allen Hutt, *The Post-War History of the British Working Class*, Victor Gollancz, 1937, pp. 102–103.

CAMPAIGN FOR UNITY PROCEEDS

Despite the attacks from all directions, the campaigns on international unity proceeded within the British trade union movement.

The first full international discussion of the British proposals took place at the Council meeting of the International Federation of Trade Unions (I.F.T.U. or Amsterdam International) held at Amsterdam on February 5–7, 1925, at which A. A. Purcell presided and Fred Bramley, ardent protagonist of unity, represented the T.U.C. A British resolution proposing an "unconditional conference for informal discussion purposes" as preliminary to a mandatory congress,[1] was defeated by 13 to 6 with one abstention, and in its stead a motion passed expressing willingness to admit the All-Russian Council of Trade Unions *into* the I.F.T.U. on the basis of the latter's *existing* constitution, i.e. the very constitution on which the differences arose.

All the more reason, the Communist Party argued, for proceeding apace with negotiations for the formation of an Anglo-Soviet Trade Union Committee, which could become the prime mover in the campaign for international unity.[2]

Communists, militant trade unionists who at this moment included a number of the official leaders of the key British trade unions and of the General Council, and (though to a less extent) a number of militants in the Labour Party, joined in the campaign for unity.

Lansbury's Labour Weekly[3] appealed for international unity:

> "Trade Union disunity is working class suicide. The employers do not discriminate between Communists, Social-Democrats, and the other sections in enforcing a cut in wages or an increase in the hours of labour. When they make war they fling all our bodies into the carnage, with a sublime disregard for our varying theoretical opinions. Just as they do not discriminate in using us as wage-slaves or as cannon-fodder, we must not discriminate among ourselves in resisting and overthrowing their dominion."

In April, the first issue was published of a new monthly *Trade Union Unity*, edited by A. A. Purcell, Edo Fimmen[4] and George

[1] See Scarborough (1925) T.U.C. report, p. 297.
[2] See *Workers' Weekly*, No. 106, February 13, 1925, pp. 4–5: article, "Amsterdam I.F.T.U. Conference against International Unity".
[3] March 14, 1925.
[4] Edo Fimmen, a Dutchman, was one of the secretaries of the International Federation of Trade Unions from 1919–1923, and General Secretary of the International Transport

Hicks, with the subtitle "A Monthly Magazine of International Trade Unionism".

The campaign bore fruit. On April 6–8, 1925, an official Anglo-Soviet Trade Union Conference was held at the offices of the General Council in London.[1]

ANGLO-SOVIET TRADE UNION CONFERENCE

The Conference represented over five million British and six million Soviet trade unionists.

After statements from the two sides a *Joint Declaration on International Unity* was adopted. Having heard the report of Tomsky, the head of the Soviet delegation, the British delegation proposed that it should fight inside the I.F.T.U. for a new International Federation "of an all-inclusive character", which could not be developed "except by making full provision for variations in tradition, historic association and political differences in the various countries".

It was desirous that the I.F.T.U. should "call an immediate conference with the representatives of the All-Russian Council of Trade Unions"; but, and this was the important clause 3(b) of the British statement:

> "In the event of the Bureau of the International Federation of Trade Unions deciding that they are unable to convene a Conference as proposed above, the British Trades Union Congress General Council will undertake to convene a Conference and endeavour to promote international unity by using its mediatory influence as between the Russian Trade Union Movement and the Amsterdam Bureau."

The Joint Declaration,[2] setting out the reasons for national and international working-class unity, treated not only the necessity of struggle on economic and social issues, but emphasised the struggle against war:

> "There is but one power that can save mankind from being plunged into another universal catastrophe. There is but one power

---

Workers' Federation from 1914–1922. In 1925 he was a member of the General Council of the I.F.T.U. and a strong supporter of international trade union unity.

[1] See *Report of Proceedings of 57th (Scarborough) T.U.C.*, pp. 297–300, also *Trade Union Unity*, Vol. 1, No. 2, May 1925, pp. 26–29.
[2] See *Trade Union Unity*, Vol. I, No. 1, pp. 26–28.

which can defend the workers of all countries against political and economic oppression and tyranny. There is but one power which can bring freedom, welfare, happiness and peace to the working class and humanity. That power is the working class itself, if well organised, properly disciplined, self-devoted and determined to fight all who would oppose and prevent its complete emancipation. The working classes, if united nationally and internationally, would constitute an insuperable barrier to capitalist oppression and an unbreakable bond of peace and economic security . . . so long as the capitalist system continues there is a danger of war. The merciless struggle for supremacy between the conflicting vested interests of competing groups of exploiters will, as in the past, eventually provoke a new crisis plunging the workers of the world into another disastrous war. . . ."

This was a *joint* statement produced *jointly* by the Soviet trade union representatives and those of the General Council of the British T.U.C. It is not for nothing that this joint declaration was virtually ignored by successive General Councils that were to follow.

But it was an important declaration, and showed very clearly how far at this moment in history Communist and militant ideas were exercising an influence in the trade union movement.

Alongside the *Joint Declaration* was a *Joint Agreement*.[1] It covered the exchange of information and documents between the two movements, arrangements for the extension of contacts and, above all, the creation of a Joint Advisory Council consisting of "the Chairman and Secretaries of both bodies, together with three members each of the All-Russian Trade Union Council and the British Trades Union Congress General Council." The first paragraph of the Agreement explained that:

"It will be our aim to promote co-operation between the British T.U.C. General Council and the All-Russian Trade Union Council in every way that may be considered from time to time advisable, for the purposes of promoting international unity."

Paragraph four, looking hopefully to the future, stated that:

"As opportunities are provided, a further extension of joint contacts may be devised for the purpose of developing the closest possible mutual aid between the two countries."

[1] See *Trade Union Unity*, Vol. I, No. 1, pp. 28–29.

SUPPORT AND HOSTILITY

Once again the British capitalist press was up in arms.

The *Times* warned that the General Council:

"may cause irreparable injury to the Trade Unionism of the continent, which, though with difficulty, is maintaining a bulwark against the westward spread of communism among the workers."[1]

The *Daily Telegraph*:[2]

"The General Council, in fact, have sold the pass."

The "Liberal" *Daily Chronicle*[3] deplored the tendency of "some of these Trade Union leaders to break away from the saner Trade Unionism of this country and the continent."

The *Glasgow Herald*[4] considered the Joint Declaration and Agreement to be documents:

"which will be read with astonishment and dismay in socialist circles on the continent."

As indeed, in a number of cases they were, and not only on the continent.

"Any steps cutting us off from Amsterdam," bewailed Ramsay MacDonald, "are steps towards international disunity."[5] The results of the Joint Conference, could, alas, have been foreseen, deplored the Polish "Socialist" *Robotnik*,[6] "since on the British side it consisted of Bolshevik followers and sympathisers, with Purcell, Ben Tillett, and Bramley at their head. . . ."

About the same time as these laments of the capitalist and reformist press, the Communist Party of Great Britain was holding its Seventh Congress. The thesis adopted on *International Trade Union Unity* summed up the lessons of the campaign to date.

It called for the development of the Anglo-Russian Trade Union Committee into a Unity Committee which could carry on the campaign for international trade union unity.

It stressed the need for a *comprehensive, all-inclusive* trade union international:

---

[1] *The Times*, April 22, 1925. [2] *Daily Telegraph*, May 12, 1925.
[3] *Daily Chronicle*, April 8, 1925.
[4] *Glasgow Herald* quoted in *Trade Union Unity*, Vol. I, No. 2, p. 26.
[5] *Daily Herald*, May 4, 1925.
[6] *Robotnik*, April 21, 1925.

"(10). In realising international unity there must be no victors or vanquished. Unity must be realised not by one section imposing conditions upon the other, but by a world Conference of all trade union organisations which will lay the basis of a new trade union international. Within this trade union international there must be absolute freedom for every section to state its point of view in order to have that point of view considered by the movement generally."

In the months that followed the I.F.T.U. was adamant in its position. It would incorporate the Soviet Unions into I.F.T.U. on its *own* terms, it would *not* work for international unity. The British trade unions, for their part, remained adamant for unity.

The Scarborough (Fifty-seventh) Trades Union Congress (September 7–12, 1925), perhaps the most consistently militant T.U.C. ever held to date (1969), welcomed and ratified all that had been done by the British delegation to Russia, by the General Council, and by the Joint Conference.

Sam Elsbury of the Tailors' and Garment Workers' Union, then a member of the Communist Party, moved a resolution of appreciation of the General Council's efforts to promote international unity.[1]

Fred Bramley, the T.U.C. Secretary, spoke in moving terms of the need for unity.[2] He spoke too of what the British delegation to Russia, after and as a result of their visit, considered to be the correct working-class approach to the Soviet Union:

> "the Russian revolution was the first revolution in all history aiming at and securing the overthrow of economic exploitation. It is also the first great national experiment of working-class control, giving expression—at any rate under certain circumstances and from a certain point of view—to the resolutions we have passed at Trades Union Congresses for many years."

Russia, he continued, was a *socialist* Republic. The economic revolution which had taken place in Russia was the only one to receive "the universal condemnation . . . of the possessing and exploiting class of Europe". He drew the moral:

> "It appears you can cut off the heads of kings, you can abolish royal families, you can imprison your emperors—as they have done in Austria and in Germany—you can permit world wars leading to

[1] Report of Scarborough T.U.C., pp. 485–487.   [2] Ibid., pp. 482–484.

universal devastation and universal slaughter, and you can be forgiven and accepted into the comity of nations. . . . But if you disturb the landed interest of a country and abolish the exploitation of the wage-earner, deal with the factory exploiter, and get rid of the privilege, property, and power possessed by a minority, then you will have to face what Russia is now facing—isolation, boycott, and international persecution."

"We consider it our duty," he concluded, "to stand by the working-class movement of Russia." Tomsky, fraternal delegate of the Soviet Trade Unions to Scarborough, paid tribute to the aid of the British trade unionists in the fight for international unity:[1]

"When the Russian unions found that they were alone in the struggle for unity, they turned to the British Trade Union Movement, and their experience has told them they did right."

The British trade unions, he declared, "were the first to give a response, outside Russia, to their call for international trade union unity. . . . We have started the campaign together; let us finish it together."

This, alas, was not to be. Internationally and nationally, right-wing Labour attacks on the movement for unity were growing. The untimely death of Fred Bramley shortly after the Scarborough Conference was undoubtedly a factor in reducing the campaign in Britain. But above all, the fate of the campaign and of the Anglo-Russian Trade Union Committee was linked to other stirring and testing events that lay ahead.

MINORITY MOVEMENT

In the Party discussions on the trade unions which were frequent at this period, the questions of unity and militancy of the unions *at home* was always linked with the question of *international* trade union unity.

One of the particular contributions that the Communist Party made in this respect was the role of a number of its most leading members in developing the National Minority Movement (N.M.M.), the formation of which we examined in the last volume. When the Tory Government came into office the N.M.M. was actively spreading its influence in new geographical areas and fields of industry. The second meeting of its Executive Committee was held in London on

[1] Ibid., p. 478.

November 1, 1924,[1] and amongst those present with long experience in the industrial field were George Fletcher, Wal Hannington, George Hardy, Arthur Horner, Tom Mann and Harry Pollitt. Already a conference of railwaymen had been held in London, of general workers (in Glasgow), a conference of metal workers was being prepared in Sheffield, and the first preparations were in hand for a National Conference.

A Builders' Section of the N.M.M. was formed at the end of November.[2] A special folder was published in December greeting the developing unity between the British and Russian trade unions.[3]

In 1925 the Minority Movement leadership began to prepare the new National Conference which had been postponed to the end of January. The General Council of the T.U.C. rejected an invitation to attend,[4] but the furnishing trades union, N.A.F.T.A., agreed to send its Secretary, Alex Gossip, and the miners' leader A. J. Cook agreed to take the chair.

The N.M.M. celebrated the New Year with an "Open Letter to All Left-Wingers" warning that 1925 would be a year of capitalist offensive. It stressed once again that the role of the N.M.M. was *not* one of separation or division, that it sought *not* to split off support from the official British trade unions but to rally support for them and to strengthen their fighting capacity. The N.M.M. aims, it declared:

"at building up and strengthening the existing trade union organisations of the workers, and at getting these organisations to fight for the interests of the workers and to carry out the class struggle."[5]

The "Unity Conference" of the N.M.M. was held at Battersea Town Hall in London on January 25, 1925.[6] It was attended by 630 representatives from some 38 trade unions, 10 Co-operative Guilds and 34 Trades Councils, representing in all around 600,000 workers.[7]

---

[1] *Workers' Weekly*, No. 42, November 7, 1924.
[2] Ibid., No. 96, December 5, 1924.
[3] *The Minority Movement*, issued as Special Supplement No. 1 to the *Workers' Weekly* of December 5, 1924.
[4] *Workers' Weekly*, No. 100, January 2, 1925.
[5] Ibid., No. 101, January 9, 1925, "An Open Letter to All Left-Wingers from the N.M.M."
[6] Ibid., No. 104, January 30, 1925. This was sometimes referred to at the time as the "Second" Conference. But later it was the August 1925 Conference that became known as the Second Conference.
[7] In an internal report to the Communist Party I have seen the figure of delegates given as 567 and the number of Trades Councils represented as 29.

Fraternal delegates attended from India, Ireland, France, Germany and Czechoslovakia. In the absence of A. J. Cook, Tom Mann took the chair.

Resolutions were passed expressing solidarity with the Indian trade unions and the workers of the British Empire. Harry Pollitt reported on the Sixth Congress of the All-Russian Council of Trade Unions. An important part of the discussions centred around the resolution on International Trade Union Unity moved by Arthur Horner, leading Communist and militant Welsh miner, and seconded by Alex Gossip of the furnishing workers union (N.A.F.T.A.).

The discussions on *international* unity were closely related to the question of unity *in Britain*, including the problem of limited organisation of trade unionists in factory and workshop. This was reflected in the Resolution which, supporting the Anglo-Russian discussions to date and the proposals for an all-inclusive international trade union conference, stressed that:

> "this Conference, while pledging itself to wholeheartedly supporting this policy of the General Council, is also compelled to declare that unless we can establish real unity in our own ranks, all our desires for international unity will be of little use. Unity in our ranks can only be achieved when we have overcome the divisions caused by craft unionism and sectionalism. . . .
>
> ". . . this Conference calls upon the workers to start an immediate campaign for the formation of shop and factory committees which will unite all the workers without craft or sectional distinction, and thus make it possible to successfully face the great battles that now confront us."[1]

The whole tone of the Conference, its essential message, was one of warning of the need to prepare for the struggles ahead. It was not surprising that this should be the content of the message read to the Conference from A. J. Cook, the Secretary of the Miners.

He was not a member of the Communist Party. But he was an unashamed militant and revolutionary. "I am proud to be a disciple of Karl Marx and a humble follower of Lenin," he declared in his Address. But, above all, he called for unity and vigilance.

"We are in danger. A united enemy is knocking at the gate. . . . My slogan is be prepared."[2]

---
[1] Individual typed copy of resolution.
[2] *Workers' Weekly*, No. 104, January 30, 1925.

The warning came from the leader of the miners; it was the miners who were to lead the next important battle of British trade unionism.

CAPITALIST OFFENSIVE

The capitalist offensive against which the Communists and militants had so consistently warned was a general one; it was much more than a simple attack of the coalowners on the conditions of the miners. It was a reflection of the weakening position of British capitalism within the world system of capitalism. In particular it reflected the utter failure of two aspects of British foreign and economic policy—the Dawes Plan and the restoration of the gold standard.

The Dawes Plan fiasco followed from a deep contradiction in British capitalist policy, the contradiction between the desire to restore Germany as a strong "bulwark against Communism", and the effect of a strong *capitalist* Germany on British (capitalist) economy.

By 1925 the Dawes Plan for German Reparations[1] *had* succeeded to an extent in strengthening German reaction and, in this context, the drive of German capitalism for more production and export of coal. Now the result was seen in increasing competition, the increasing difficulty in exporting British coal. The Communist policy had always opposed the Dawes Plan. The Miners' Federation of Great Britain also opposed it strongly, not only because of German competition, but because the miners (rightly enough) considered that the reparations policy would harm the workers of both paying and recipient countries alike.

The restoration of the gold standard was also the fruit of a long-term contradiction in British capitalist policy. The centre of world capitalism had long passed to America. The restoration of the gold standard might seem, on the surface, to strengthen Britain's world financial position but, in Britain's weakened position, it was bound to lead to an increased burden of state debt and an all-out attack on wages.

The pound sterling had been forced off the gold standard at the outbreak of war in 1914 amid expressions of dismay by Britain's bankers. In 1924 a Committee (mainly of these self-same bankers) appointed by the Chancellor of the Exchequer had counselled return to gold. Now, in spring, 1925, the new Chancellor, Winston Churchill, hardly renowned for his economic aptitude, announced the return

[1] See Vol. 1, chap. III, pp. 281–359 *passim*.

to the gold standard which, he said, would "enable the pound sterling to look the dollar in the face". For the Governor of the Bank of England, Mr. Montagu Norman, gold, in the words of Lloyd George,[1] "might well be the only god to lead the nation out of the wilderness".

The battle to bring the pound back to the basis of gold was the most serious expression of the battle to maintain Britain's world position against the advance of American capitalism.

With Britain's relative economic weakness, and in the absence of any fundamental reconstruction at home, the attempt to return to gold inevitably meant in practice an attack on the workers, and, equally inevitably, at some future date, the breakdown of this gold restoration.

To those more economically far-sighted the effect on Britain's exports was easily calculable. J. M. Keynes quickly pointed out that Churchill's policy would inevitably produce an atmosphere favourable to the reduction of wages.[2]

British Marxists warned again and again about the fruits of the gold standard, as they had warned about the effects of the Dawes Plan:

> "The gold has come back to Europe—yes: but it has come back in reality as an added burden, and only apparently as a new life to capitalism; that is, it has increased and not diminished the gulf between America and Europe and the inequality of capitalism. . . .
>
> "On every side, in every country in Europe, the call is sounded to increase output, to cheaper output, to greater intensity of labour, to longer hours, to more economy of 'social' services, to lower wages, to more and more competitive effort. In England and Germany alike the challenge to the working class is proclaimed."[3]

This was the background of Prime Minister Baldwin's exhortation to the miners to help him to meet "the difficult situation with which the industry is confronted", and the ensuing famous dialogue in which he categorically declared:

> "all the workers of this country have got to take reductions in wages to help put industry on its feet."[4]

---

[1] Lloyd George, *The Truth about Reparations and War Debts*, 1932.
[2] J. M. Keynes, *The Economic Consequences of Mr. Churchill*, 1925.
[3] R. Palme Dutt, "Notes of the Month", *Labour Monthly*, Vol. 7, No. 3, March 1925, p. 146. The notes continued with a precise prediction that the collapse of the gold standard would follow at such time as the repayment of interest on the American loans, together with the weight of reparations and debts, outweighed the American advances.
[4] *Daily Herald*, July 31, 1925, quoted by Allen Hutt in his *Post-War History of the British Working Class*, p. 110.

CHALLENGE TO THE MINERS

No one was surprised that the offensive against working-class conditions should in the first place be launched against the miners.[1] The effect of the National Wages Agreement between miners and mineowners of July 1921 had been, in the words of R. Page Arnott:

> "that coal-mining, from being for a short time one of the best paid trades, fell to being one of the worst paid."

The decline, declared the Miners' Executive in spring 1923, "has been swift and well-nigh universal".

By mid-1923 the average wage per shift worked had fallen to less than half what it had been in the winter months of 1920–1921. There was, due to the fall in German competition, a short boom in the coal industry in 1923, but in 1924 this had ended, and the miners were once again fighting for their lives. It is not surprising, therefore, that they were, as we have seen, amongst the foremost in the fight for international trade unionism, and for unity at home; nor that out of the ranks of the miners came a number of outstanding Communists of the type of Arthur Horner of the Welsh[2] and Abe Moffat of the Scottish Miners,[3] and consistent support for the N.M.M.

The Triple Alliance had first been formed in 1914, and we have examined its breakdown in 1921. Now the question of an industrial alliance came under discussion again, particularly amongst the miners, and a resolution in favour of such an alliance was remitted to the Executive at their Conference in the summer of 1924.

When A. J. Cook became the Miners' Secretary, the issue became a very live one:

> "On one question of principle, the necessity of unity within all working-class bodies, Cook hammered untiringly. He had accepted it as a principle in the Miners' Minority Movement, of which he had been an ardent supporter."[4]

---

[1] The whole background and story of the capitalist offensive against the miners and the miners counter-offensive in June–July 1925 is splendidly given in R. Page Arnot's *The Miners—Years of Struggle*, chapter XI, "The Revival of 1924–25", from which I have drawn extensively.
[2] See Arthur Horner, *Incorrigible Rebel*, MacGibbon and Kee, 1960.
[3] See Abe Moffatt, *My Life with the Miners*, Lawrence and Wishart, 1965.
[4] R. P. Arnot, op. cit., pp. 350–351.

By the end of 1924 the Miners' Federation of Great Britain was actively furthering the campaign for such an industrial alliance. The return of the Tories to government made the miners more, not less, enthusiastic for unity. "Once again," wrote A. J. Cook in June 1925, "ringing through industrial areas of Britain in every mine, workshop and factory—is that blessed word unity."[1]

COMMUNIST PARTY AND THE MINERS

Not just as individual miners within the Miners' Union, not just as leaders or supporters of the N.M.M., but as a Party, and through the journals and declarations of the Party, the C.P.G.B. was warning of the coming offensive, and calling for support for the miners and their impending struggle. The *Workers' Weekly* defended A. J. Cook from the attacks by Philip Snowden in the *Weekly Dispatch*.[2]

It launched a campaign at the end of March for unity of action between the mining, metal, transport and railway unions.[3] It strongly warned against allowing the capitalists to take on the trade unions one at a time, beginning with the miners.[4]

"Their (the employers) general plan is to tie the workers up in a number of enquiries which will begin and terminate at different times and so make united action difficult."

It called for rank and file joint committees to press for and strengthen unity from above. It worked to heal the rift in the Fife Miners where two rival unions were now in being.[5] At the Seventh Congress of the C.P.G.B. (May 30–June 1, 1925) an emergency resolution on the Mining Crisis was moved by Arthur Horner, and again called for united support for the miners. The Congress voted:

"that only through working-class loyalty and working-class solidarity can the workers hope to improve their conditions, and make a successful fight against the attacks of the employers."

[1] A. J. Cook, "The Problem of the Hour—Is Unity Possible?", *Labour Monthly*, Vol. 7, No. 7, July 1925, pp. 410–411.
[2] *Workers' Weekly*, No. 110, March 13, 1925.
[3] Ibid., No. 111, March 20, 1925.
[4] Ibid., No. 113, April 3, 1925, p. 3, "How Rank and File Must Reply to Disruption".
[5] See R. Page Arnot, *History of the Scottish Miners* for background; also Abe Moffat, op. cit., chapter II. For Communist attitude see particularly statement of Political Bureau of C.P.G.B. in *Workers' Weekly*, No. 113, April 3, 1925. Whilst expressing the view that it was the leaders of the old union who were responsible for the split, the P.B. declared: "the split should be immediately liquidated by a unity conference of both the unions. Communists should work in both unions to further a unity conference".

It pledged to give the fullest support "to the miners in the crisis which now confronts them", and called upon all other working-class organisations:

> "to stand by the miners in whatever struggles their conditions drive them into."[1]

COALOWNERS' ATTACK

The situation very soon called for this pledge and this plea to be transformed from promise into practice.

On June 30, the coalowners gave notice to terminate the existing Agreement which had been in force since June 18, 1924. The notice was to run for the month of July and terminate at midnight on Friday, July 31.

On July 1, the Mining Association of Great Britain (the organisation of the owners) put forward proposals for a fresh wages agreement which meant in fact an immediate reduction in wages, the end of the guaranteed minimum wage and, in its place (Clause 4) what amounted to a guarantee of profits.[2]

The next day (July 2) the Miners' Executive recommended rejection. On July 3 the miners' delegates, at a special Conference held at the Kingsway Hall in London, unanimously endorsed rejection.

This was a decisive moment. All the most militant sections of the workers, including in a major role the Communist Party and the N.M.M., put support for the miners at the centre of their endeavours:

> "The miners' struggle is the central and supreme issue of the British working class at the present moment ... it would be criminal folly to imagine that the fate of other industries is not bound up with that of coal. ... To leave the miners to their fate would be class suicide."[3]

MINERS FIGHT BACK

The M.F.G.B., under militant leadership, turned to the workers centrally and in all parts of the country. On July 10 the full Executive Council of the Miners put their case before the General Council of

---

[1] *Report of 7th Congress of C.P.G.B.*, p. 20.
[2] For details of the owners' proposals see R. Page Arnot, op. cit., pp 362–366.
[3] R. P. Dutt, "Notes of the Month", *Labour Monthly*, Vol. 7, No. 8, August 1925, pp. 460–463. Written early in July.

the T.U.C. The General Council, also, as we have seen, under left influence, voted "complete support" for the miners and pledged full support "in their resistance to the degradation of the standard of life of their members". The General Council also agreed to appoint a Committee of Nine to "maintain continuous contact with the negotiations now taking place" and with power, if necessary, to summon a full meeting of the General Council.

Meanwhile, on a parallel plane, the M.F.G.B. were speeding up their work for the formation of an Industrial Alliance of Heavy Industry.[1] On July 17 a meeting was held of the unions concerned,[2] and it was very obvious that the sense of solidarity and readiness for combined action, so long preached by the left wing, was spreading fast.

The militant atmosphere of the Industrial Alliance meeting influenced in its turn the development of militant approaches in the General Council and in the key individual unions.

On July 20 the first delegate conference of the Transport and General Workers' Union (T.G.W.U.) opened with a Chairman's Address largely devoted to support for the miners, and the conference empowered the Executive (acting in consultation with the General Council) to call a strike if necessitated by developments in the coal dispute. Two days later the Miners' Executive (now also strengthened with a pledge for full support from the Associated Society of Locomotive Engineers and Firemen (A.S.L.E.F.)) refused any concessions to the coalowners and again turned to the General Council.

On July 24 a special T.U.C. was held to discuss problems of unemployment. Moving speeches on the mining position were made by Herbert Smith, the President, and A. J. Cook, the Secretary of the M.F.G.B. and a detailed document,[3] "The Joint Investigation into the Economic Position of the Mining Industry", was submitted to the Conference by the miners.

The miners are confident, the document stated:

"that their fellow workers will not expect them to accept degrading conditions of employment, or to assent to the retrograde step of reverting to the eight-hour day. . . ."

[1] A sub-committee to elaborate its constitution had been set up on June 14, 1925.
[2] M.F.G.B., the three railway unions, the transport and dock workers' unions, the Iron and Steel Trades Confederation, the Engineering and Shipbuilding Trades Federation, the Amalgamated Engineering Union, the Electrical Trades Union and the unions of boilermakers and foundry workers. See R. Page Arnot, op. cit., p. 372.
[3] Quoted in full in R. Page Arnot, op. cit., pp. 388–392.

The Miners' Federation felt assured, it concluded, that:

> "on this occasion, if a lock-out matures, it will not be left to a section to fight alone, but the struggle will be taken up, and the issue joined, by the whole Trade Union Movement:

The next day the T.U.C. agreed to put an embargo on all movement of coal in the case of a mineowners' lock-out, and, from that moment until the show down, the General Council remained in close and regular contact with the M.F.G.B. Indeed, during the whole last week of July with its welter of meetings involving miners, coalowners and, at times, Cabinet and Prime Minister,[1] the situation was dominated by the unity and determination of the trade union movement.

True, the Government and employers still bluffed and blustered. On July 29 Prime Minister Baldwin was "definitely" insisting to the miners "that the Government would not grant any subsidy".[2] But bluff could be called.

On July 30—a crucial day—the whole complex of meetings, offers and counter-offers continued. A special Conference of Trade Union Executives met at the Central Hall, Westminster, to receive a statement from the miners and a report of the special T.U.C. Committee which had now ratified the embargo.

The Conference in its turn ratified, and went further. It empowered the T.U.C. to give financial support and to issue strike orders. On the evening of that day last instructions were given for an embargo on all movement of coal to be put into force.[3] It was a firm, detailed, precise, almost military document of class war. It was signed by the nine members of the special Committee of the General Council, by the Chairman of the Council's Transport sub-committee, and by the leaders of the Associated Society of Locomotive Engineers and Firemen, of the National Union of Railwaymen, of the Railway Clerks Association, and of the Transport and General Workers Union. Never before had such a complete power for action been given to the T.U.C.

THE COALOWNERS SURRENDER

Never before had the Government been confronted by so united and militant a T.U.C. leadership. And the effect was instant. The Cabinet was recalled. Discussions continued up to and after midnight.

---

[1] Examined in detail in R. Page Arnot, op. cit.　　[2] Ibid., p. 371.
[3] See Appendix I of this chapter.

Early on Friday, July 31, the Government agreed to offer a nine-months subsidy in return for which the owners were to withdraw their notices, whilst during the forthcoming nine-month period a full enquiry, it was promised, would be made by a Royal Commission.

At 3.45 p.m. the Prime Minister met the special Committee of the T.U.C. along with the Miners' Executive. He officially notified them of his new terms. The "definitely no subsidy" had become an offer for a nine-month respite.

At 4 p.m. a short wire was despatched to General Secretaries of District miners' organisations:

"Notices suspended—work as usual.

Cook—Secretary."

On the same day the General Council of the T.U.C., in a letter to all affiliated unions and to all Trades Councils, drew the proper lesson:

"The manifestation of solidarity which has been exhibited by all sections of the Trade Union movement is a striking portent for the future and marks an epoch in the history of the movement."

A definite offensive by the coalowners on the miners, a definite refusal of the Government to grant a subsidy, both had been defeated by the definite unity of the trade unions and the definite pledge for an embargo on every movement of coal.

The name given to that day and that victory by the *Daily Herald* was "Red Friday". It was well chosen.

THE FIRST ROUND ONLY

A victory had been won, this was indubitable. Red Friday was and remains a red-letter day in working-class history. But, and it was a big but, the real issue was what was to follow.

It is difficult to convey the shouting headline anger of the British Tory press in the first days of August 1925. Some saw nothing but a cowardly retreat on the part of Baldwin and his Cabinet; others recognised the traditional strategy of the British ruling class—prudent retreat as prelude to a new offensive. But all reactionaries of every ilk agreed that a new offensive against the working class *must* be prepared.

Let the protagonists speak for themselves.[1] The Home Secretary,

[1] See in *Workers' Weekly*, No. 131, August 7, 1925, the various estimates of Red Friday published under the heading "Why the Owners Withdrew".

Sir William Joynson-Hicks ("Jix"), beat the war drum as usual, in private, in Parliament, in public too:

> "He said to them, coming straight from Cabinet Councils, the thing was not finished. The danger was not over. Sooner or later this question has got to be fought out by the people of the land. Was England to be governed by Parliament and by the Cabinet or by a handful of trade union leaders?"[1]

As usual, "Jix" pointed to the sinister hand of Moscow. "If a Soviet were established here . . .", he continued at Northampton, ". . . a grave position would arise." On the other hand, if people were prepared to support the Government . . then he said quite frankly, quite seriously, there would be for a time grave trouble in the land, but if the heart of the people were sound, they could stand it.

It is clear that, *already at this stage*, the British ruling class had decided to engage and crush militant trade unionism and Labour, but, in order to accomplish this, were trying to turn the issue from economics to politics. The support that they could not rally for reducing wages *might* be mustered under the banner of "defence of the Constitution". If the Constitution was to be defended from "subversive red agitators", then the Government could hope not only to win the support of the supremely "constitutional" Labour leaders, but also to find the pretext for massive use of "the state".

"Jix's" sparring partner, the Chancellor of the Exchequer, Winston Churchill, made this clear in the House:

> "In the event of a struggle, whatever its character might be, however ugly the episodes which would mark it, I have no doubt that the State, the national State would emerge victorious in spite of all the rough and awkward corners it might have to turn. . . . As the struggle widened, as it became a test whether the country was to be ruled by Parliament or by some other organisation not responsible by our elective processes to the people as a whole—as that issue emerged more and more, and with every increase in the gravity of the struggle, new sources of strength would have to come to the State or some action, which in ordinary circumstances we should consider quite impossible, would, just as in the case of the Great War, be taken with general assent and as a matter of course."[2]

[1] Speech at Northampton, reported in *The Times*, August 3, 1925.
[2] Hansard, August 6, 1925, quoted by R. Page Arnot in *The Miners: Years of Struggle*, p. 383.

But if popular assent was to be won for action by the Tory state against the "agitators", the unity that had obtained on the eve of Red Friday, the unity that had, indeed, made that Friday "Red", had in some way or other to be broken. This was the particular role, conscious or unconscious, or sometimes dimly somewhere between the two, of British reformism.

Many of the centre-socialists, I.L.P. variety, greeted Red Friday with genuine joy. But, often, even in their expression of joy, the danger could be perceived. Some wrote of the triumph of "Right and Justice", or of "Opinion". The Parliamentary Labour Party, in a resolution congratulating the General Council of the T.U.C., referred to its successful organisation of "trade union opinion". But the refusal to move coal, the detailed instructions on how virtually to paralyse British economy was something more than "mobilising opinion".

In the context of August 1925 expressions of joy without *warning* of future struggle and preparation to mobilise *struggle* rather than "opinion", meant, in fact, lulling, disarming the Labour and trade union movement.

If this was the role of what can be called the centre in the Labour leadership, the right wing, epitomised by Ramsay MacDonald, went much further. For them Red Friday was a disaster. Again to discuss at length how far such an attitude represents conscious betrayal is a waste of energy. Ramsay MacDonald, a thorough-going reformist (in this context "consistent" would not be an improper adjective), geared to proceed "within the framework of capitalism", was furiously indignant at militant trade union action that represented a real challenge to capitalism, and, at the same time, to reformism, reformist methods, reformist leaders. To him it seemed that the Government had surrendered to the "militants", the "agitators", the "reds", and, in so doing, had stabbed him, Ramsay MacDonald, in his oft-stabbed back. "The Government", he said, at the I.L.P. Summer School:

"has simply handed over the appearance, at any rate, of victory, to the very forces that some, well-considered thoroughly well-examined socialist feels to be probably its greatest enemy."[1]

"If the Government," he continued:

"had fought their policy out, we would have respected it. It just suddenly doubled up.

[1] *Manchester Guardian* report of August 4, 1925. The *Workers' Weekly* of August 7, quoting MacDonald, comments: "When will the Labour Party get rid of this man?"

"The consequence has been to increase the power and the prestige of those who do not believe in political action."

SOLEMN WARNING

It was only the militant wing of the Labour Movement which, in the midst of celebration, rightly estimated Red Friday. And it was no accident that the most solemn warnings to British Labour came on the one hand from the miners and on the other from the Communist Party.

"This is the first round . . . let us prepare for the final struggle" was the verdict of the miners' Secretary, A. J. Cook.[1]

The Miners' Delegate Conference met at the Kingsway Hall. London, on August 19. The Chairman, Herbert Smith, celebrated the victory, but as a victory of unity. The real battle was still to come:

"we have no need to glorify about a victory. It is only an armistice, and it will depend largely how we stand between now and May 1st next year as an organisation in respect of unity as to what will be the ultimate results. All I can say is, that it is one of the finest things ever done by an organisation."[2]

People are calling us "Bolshevists", the Chairman continued, but if what they had done was Bolshevism, he did not "mind being called a Bolshevist". Then once again he repeated *"it is only an armistice"*.

The *Workers Weekly* and the leaders of the Communist Party, summing up the lessons of Red Friday, made their warnings even sharper and more clearly.

The *Workers' Weekly* editorial, "After Red Friday",[3] summarised the Party's position. Firstly it was a victory, but a *partial* victory only:

"the withdrawal of the mineowners' demands for wage reductions is a victory for the working class, but it is a victory of limited extent. It leaves the workers economically where they were, i.e. in many cases with wages below the level of pre-war."

Secondly it was only a truce:

"What has been achieved is the imposition on the capitalist class of an unstable truce, which cannot lead to industrial peace, but only to renewed class conflict.

---

[1] Quoted in *Workers' Weekly*, No. 131, August 7, 1925.
[2] Quoted by R. Page Arnot, op. cit., pp. 383-384.
[3] *Workers' Weekly*, No. 131, August 7, 1925, p. 2.

"Behind this truce, and the industrial peace talk which will accompany it, the capitalist class will prepare for a crushing attack upon the workers. If the workers are duped by the peace talk and do not make effective counter-preparations then they are doomed to shattering defeat."

The economic situation, the loss of Britain's traditional monopoly and markets, the fruits of reintroducing the gold standard, would force the capitalists to act. And, therefore, the *Workers' Weekly* continued:

"the Government, acting upon the behalf of the capitalist class, is certain to prepare for a new struggle with the working class under more favourable circumstances than this time, and will endeavour to break the united front of the workers in order to make its attack successful."

R. Palme Dutt, summing up the balance of Red Friday,[1] issued again and again the same warning:

"If ever there was a 'settlement' that settled nothing, it is the Truce of July 31. . . . The Government has made it clear that it regards the present strategic retreat as only a preparation for a decisive conflict in the future, and that it still stands by the objective of a general reduction of wages. . . .

"The Royal Commission is once again, as always, only the smoke-screen for the preparation for a decisive battle. There is no escape from the future conflict."[2]

The need of the hour was preparation, preparation to meet and defeat the inevitable counter-offensive of capital. That demanded working-class unity, the ending of discrimination against the militant left, the isolation of the reformist leaders who were already preparing the great betrayal of May 1926.

The preparation for battle, alas, was far better comprehended by the employers and the Tories than (except for the militants and Marxists) by Labour and the working class.

---

[1] "Notes of the Month" in *Labour Monthly*, Vol. 7, No. 9, September 1926. (These notes had to be written soon after the events of end of July in order to be ready for press in mid-August.)

[2] See also warnings by W. Gallacher ("Is it a Workers' Victory?"), *Workers' Weekly*, August 7, 1965, and estimate of Harry Pollitt in *Serving my Time*, chapter XIII, "A Great Year, 1925".

THE CAPITALISTS PREPARE

All sections of British capitalism were agreed on the need for a "showdown" with Labour after due preparation. And all sections of capitalism proceeded, therefore, without delay, to prepare for the coming struggle.

On September 25, 1925, the press announced the formation of a body which called itself the "Organisation for the Maintenance of Supplies", and which quickly became known as the O.M.S. (O.H.M.S. would have perhaps been more appropriate).

Its aims were clearly set out in its first official communiqué:

"For many months past it has been evident that a movement is being organised to take advantage of a trade dispute, exceptionally difficult to solve, in order to promote a general strike...."

To combat this, efficient organisation was necessary and

"it seems, therefore, that the moment has come to announce publicly that such an organisation has already been constituted and is at work in many metropolitan boroughs, while steps are being taken to create corresponding organisations in all the principal centres of the Kingdom."[1]

If the organisation was already "at work" by the end of September, it must have been constituted immediately following Red Friday, if not before.

"The object it has in view is to register and classify those citizens of all classes and of either sex who are prepared to render voluntary assistance in maintaining the supply of food, water, and fuel and the efficiency of public services indispensable to the normal life of the community."[2]

Its object clearly enough was to *break* a general strike. But already at this stage the attempt was made to distinguish between "legitimate" strikes and large-scale *effective* strikes that would be "illegal" or "unconstitutional". It was a "nice" theory. Ineffective small-scale strikes would be permissible but as soon as they became embracing enough to be *really* effective they were to be "unconstitutional". The communiqué explained:

[1] Quoted by R. Page Arnot, op. cit., chapter XII, pp. 393–394. [2] Ibid.

"It (the O.M.S.) has no aggressive or provocative aims. It is not formed with any idea of opposing the legitimate efforts of trade unions to better the status and conditions of their members, and it is in complete sympathy with any constitutional action to bring about a more equitable adjustment of social and economic conditions.

"If however, in order to secure a particular end, an attempt is made to inflict severe privation on the great mass of the people who have no direct part in the actual dispute, this Organisation of Citizens, serving the interests of the general community, will place its entire resources at the disposal of the constitutional authorities."

The same initial communiqué announced the leadership.[1] The President was Lord Hardinge of Penshurst, ex-Foreign Office, ex-Ambassador, ex-Under-Secretary of State for Foreign Affairs, ex-Viceroy of India.

The Central Council included Admiral of the Fleet Lord Jellicoe, Major-General Lord Scarborough (Director of the General Territorial and Volunteer Forces, 1917-1921), Lieutenant-General Sir Francis Lloyd (Food Commissioner for London and Home Counties 1919-1920), Lieutenant-Colonel Sir Martin Archer-Shee, Lord Ranfurly, Lord Falkland, Admiral Sir Alexander Duff, Sir Lynden Macassey (for a period during the war, Chairman of the Government Commission for Dilution of Labour on the Clyde), and other simple English gentlemen who could be relied on to be "strictly neutral" on the side of the powers that be. The pattern seemed to be a leadership of retired (often half-pay) officials of the state, of whom even if one foot might be in the grave, the other was securely planted within the Establishment.

Sir Rennell Rodd, outlining the O.M.S. proposals, explained that there were five categories in which volunteers would be classified:[2]

(a) For "protecting the public services" and, if necessary, enrolling as special constables.
(b) For the railways, tubes, trams, handling of foodstuffs, etc.
(c) For drivers of vans, lorries, etc.
(d) For messengers in the event of telephone and postal services being involved.
(e) For clerical workers.

[1] See R. Page Arnot, *The General Strike*, Labour Research Department, 1926, pp. 50-52; *Monthly Circular of the Labour Research Department*, November 1925, p. 242.
[2] *Monthly Circular of the Labour Research Department*, November 1925, p. 242.

Local Committees, it was announced, had already been formed in 22 of the Metropolitan boroughs and were to be set up all over the country.

Although in the first announcement, at the end of September, the O.M.S. was presented as an "independent", "non-political" body, its direct connections with the Government and state was soon acknowledged by "Jix", the Home Secretary, in a letter to *The Times* of October 1:

> "I have known of the inauguration of this body for many weeks past; in fact, the promoters consulted me as to their desire to form some such organisation. . . . I told the promoters of the O.M.S. that there was no objection on the part of the Government to their desire to inaugurate the body to which you refer, that, if and when an emergency arose, the Government would (assume) the responsibility which is theirs, and theirs alone, but that it would be a very great assistance to us to receive from the O.M.S. or from any other body of well-disposed citizens, classified lists of men in different parts of the country who could be willing to place their services at the disposal of the Government. . . ."

The O.M.S. proceeded to organise, attacked by the militant Labour Movement in general, but accepted by the official Labour leadership. Amongst other activities it carried out the secret training of drivers behind the high walls of various factories whose owners allowed their premises to be used as testing grounds at week ends. Similar training was carried out in private enterprises after working hours for telegraph operators and telephonists.[1]

When the strike finally broke out "the O.M.S. effaced itself as an organisation and turned over its trained personnel to the Government".[2]

Though some liberals (*Manchester Guardian* for instance) deplored the establishment of the O.M.S., the Labour leadership by and large let it pass. The *Daily Herald* treated it not as an attack on labour but an insult to Mr. Baldwin the Prime Minister, thus helping to spread the illusion of the separation of O.M.S. and the state.

The "British Fascists" had already put the breaking of a general

---

[1] Colonel Romain, "La Lutte contre La Grève Générale en Angleterre", in *La Revue Hebdomadaire*, No. 6, 1926, p. 77.

[2] Wilfred Harris Crook, *The General Strike*, University of North Carolina Press, 1931, p. 301.

strike as a central point of their programme.[1] And, in effect, the President and Vice-President of their organisation (Brigadier-General Blakeney and Rear-Admiral Armstrong) and the majority of their Committee withdrew on the grounds that:

> "at the present moment effective assistance to the state can best be given in seconding the efforts of the O.M.S."[2]

Only the militants warned of the real nature of the O.M.S. The *Sunday Worker*, a left-wing united-front Labour paper (started on March 15, 1925), immediately denounced it as a fascist-type organisation directly linked with the Government.[3]

The view of the Communist Party put in the *Workers' Weekly* was that the O.M.S.

> "represents the most complete scheme of organised blacklegging and strike breaking yet devised, and is the most advanced form of Fascism yet reached in this country."[4]

THE CAPITALIST STATE PREPARES

It would be possible to show the O.M.S. as one in a line of a long history of strike-breaking organisations.[5] But whatever the variety and activity of such organisations in 1925,[6] attention must *mainly* be turned to the direct activity of the capitalist state itself. Here too the Government and State in the new measures were only continuing a long history of "emergency" Acts and organisations for use against the Labour Movement.[7] In the stormy days that followed World War I the emergency road transport system was organised by the

---

[1] See L.R.D., op. cit., p. 243. A circular of the "British Fascists" in the latter part of 1925 stated "it is not a strike-breaking organisation, but in the event of a General Strike designed to paralyse the country, it will most certainly co-operate wholeheartedly with the Authorities in the direction of safeguarding the food supply and of assisting to maintain vital services."

[2] See Crook, op. cit., p. 302; Hutt, *Post-War History of the British Working Class*, p. 115; and Milliband, *Parliamentary Socialism*, p. 125.

[3] See *Sunday Worker*, No. 29, September 27, and No. 30, October 4, 1925. The front page headline on the O.M.S. on September 27 was "Boss Class Gets Ready for the Big Fight".

[4] *Workers' Weekly*, No. 139, October 2, 1925.

[5] See *Monthly Circular of the Labour Research Department*, November 1925, "Strike Breaking Organisations", pp. 241–245; Crook, op. cit., chapter XI and *passim*.

[6] Other organisations in 1925 included "The National Citizens Union", "The British Empire Union", "The National Guard".

[7] See especially Crook, op. cit., *passim*, and George Glasgow, *General Strikes and Road Transport*, Geoffrey Bles.

Coalition Government at the time of the 1919 railway strike. In fact the Government attempted to form a "Citizens Guard", similar to that formed on the Continent in that year, and the notice went out the day before the settlement. 1920 saw the Emergency Powers Act (E.P.A.).

In 1920 an emergency organisation was worked out in a permanent form and was ready to go into action just before Black Friday. Early in January 1925, the railway companies issued a circular to their employees asking them to enrol in the transportation branch of the Army Supplementary Reserve. Similar steps were taken by the London General Omnibus Company and recruiting forms were also sent to the docks.[1]

Such recruits would be liable to be sent to any part of the country, to be called out by Proclamation, and *to be called out in aid of the Civil Power.*[2]

Now, after Red Friday, and with Joynson-Hicks at the Home Office, the whole organisation was rapidly developed. The main responsibility for the details was in the hands of the Home Office, and in particular its permanent under-secretary Sir John Anderson,[3] but "Jix" had his hand in it from the first weeks of his appointment.[4]

England and Wales were divided into ten "Divisions" each under a Minister acting as a Civil Commissioner, who would be assisted, if and when required, by a group of civil servants appointed in advance.

Each "Divisional" H.Q. had its own Civil and Road Commissioners, Coal, Finance and Food Officers appointed by the Ministry of Transport. There was a network of local Committees each with its own intricate organisation,[5] and to the ten "divisional" commissioners were responsible 150 Road Officers stationed at the local committees. London and the Home Counties formed an especially important area. The London Food Officer had some 102 Divisional Food Officers

---

[1] *Monthly Circular of the Labour Research Department*, November 1925, pp. 244-256.
[2] For eternal shame it should be noted that authorisation for this supplementary reserve was given in August 1924 *under the first Labour Government*!
[3] The normal training for Police Commissioners and high Home Office officers is a period in the Empire, so that after the experience of "putting down the natives abroad" the official is apt at "putting down the natives" at home. Sir John was joint under-secretary to the Lord Lieutenant of Ireland in 1920. After the Home Office (1922-1932) he was to enrich his "putting down" experience as Governor of Bengal, 1932-1937, returning, still more experienced, as Home Secretary, 1939-1940.
[4] "Within a few weeks of Joynson-Hicks' appointment at the Home Office, the business of improving these emergency plans was handed over to a Special Committee, of which he as Home Secretary was appointed Chairman." H. A. Taylor, *Jix, Viscount Brentford*, Stanley Paul and Co., 1933, pp. 193-194.
[5] See Glasgow, op. cit., pp. 31-32; Crook, op. cit., pp. 305-310.

under his control, usually a local borough or council official such as a Medical Officer of Health or a Town Clerk, but *not so* in a number of cases where there was a Labour majority on the council.[1]

The Divisional Officers had full powers under the Emergency Powers Acts, they could requisition, fix prices, order a policeman to make an arrest.

In a Circular,[2] dated November 20, 1925, from the Ministry of Health, local authorities were informed in general terms of all these arrangements. In December and again in January 1926 conferences were held on questions of transport and police between national and local officials. Two more conferences were held in March. The signal for the operation of the plans was to be receipt of a telegram from Whitehall containing the sole word "Action".[3]

HOW FAR DOES LABOUR PREPARE?

The Labour Movement's preparation for the coming struggle was as indefinite and ineffective as the employers' and Government's preparations were definite and detailed.

The right-wing leaders of the Labour Party and of the General Council adopted what Professor Wilfred Crook, the American historian of the General Strike, aptly termed a "studied attitude of unpreparedness". Studied is the word, it was not through ignorance. The leaders of the General Council indeed later openly acknowledged that they did nothing *because* the Government was doing something.[4] J. H. Thomas explained that it had been impossible to prepare "deliberately and calculatedly" for a General Strike because, amongst other things, "the other side would anticipate every move".[5] At the same discussions (the inquest on the General Strike held in January 1927), Walter Citrine equally avowed that:

"it was known that preparations had been made so elaborately by the Government as to make the possibilities of success much less than in 1925".[6]

[1] Crook, op. cit., p. 307.
[2] Circular 636 (England and Wales), Ministry of Health, November 20, 1925.
[3] Mowat, op. cit., pp. 295–296; Glasgow, op. cit., pp. 55–94 *passim*; text of Circular 636 in W. Milne-Bailey, *Trade Unions and the State*, pp. 24–78.
[4] See Ralph Milliband, *Parliamentary Socialism*, p. 127.
[5] T.U.C. General Council, *The Mining Crisis and the National Strike, 1926* (London 1927), p. 26.
[6] Ibid., p. 43.

Three days before the General Strike was due to begin (May 1, 1926), Ernest Bevin was to complain that no real preparations had been made before April 27.[1] Within the General Council it was tacitly assumed that some way out of the coal crisis would be found by the Samuel Commission and that some compromise would be reached.

In what could be called the centre of the Labour Movement there was much strong feeling about the impending struggle but little effort for practical preparations. The I.L.P. were, in the main, otherwise engaged, busy propounding theories of "the living wage".

In fact it was only the Communist Party and the organisations in which it had a strong influence that consistently called to action, for preparation, and that repeated almost to monotony the warning of the struggle ahead.

COMMUNISTS CONTINUE WARNING

The *Workers' Weekly* carried a regular "warning" in a frame showing how many weeks remained to prepare. For instance on August 28, 1925:

> 34 weeks to go
>
> Thirty-four weeks to go to what? To the termination of the mining agreement and the opening of the greatest struggle in the history of the British working class. . . . WE MUST PREPARE FOR THE STRUGGLE[2]

A type of warning made by Communists only was the constant repetition of the nature and role of the state and the danger in Britain of some sort of fascism. The kidnapping of Harry Pollitt at Edgehill by a group of fascists[3] in mid-March 1925, brought the incipient fascist activity from under the surface. The finding of the kidnappers not guilty by a middle-class Liverpudlian jury equally underlined that almost any form of action against "the reds" could be condoned under British justice. The Marxist press, in a way that now seems almost prophetic, but which was often enough mocked at the time, repeatedly warned against the danger of fascism in Britain and the world. As early as March 1925 the Political Bureau issued a warning about the actions

---
[1] *The Mining Crisis and the National Strike, 1926*, p. 10.
[2] *Workers' Weekly*, No. 134, August 28, 1925, p. 2.
[3] See Pollitt, *Serving my Time*, chapter XIII.

of the *British Fascisti* as they then termed themselves, and called on the Labour Party and T.U.C. immediately to

> "start an exhaustive enquiry into the strength of the Fascist movement, and bring forward as a result of that enquiry countermeasures which should be adopted by the Labour movement as a whole."[1]

We have seen already the *state* preparations made by the Government for the impending General Strike. Lack of understanding of the nature of the state, the acceptance of the reformist illusion of "neutrality" has always been one of the deepest weaknesses of the British Labour Movement, even in its militant sections. And therefore the Communist Party's direct warning of the role that the *capitalist* state would inevitably play, was a particularly important contribution, though at times the arguments were put in a way that were not sufficiently calculated to win over non-Marxists from their easy-going illusions.

"The machine of the State", wrote R. Palme Dutt:

> "is, in its cutting edge, always a machine of the exploiting class, whichever the phrase maker at the head of it. Despite all the fairyland of theoretical democracy, in actual practice the 'blessed constitution', through some twist, turn, accident, forgotten law, precedent, privilege or what not, always turns out against the working class in the moment of testing."[2]

In August the Communist Party sent a warning letter to Mr. Arthur Henderson for the Labour Party Executive (and a similar letter to the T.U.C.), stressing[3] particularly that the capitalists were preparing to use the armed forces to break any struggle of the workers and asking that the Labour Party should put the workers' case to the members of the Army and Navy—a proposal characterised (characteristically enough) by J. R. Clynes as a "hysterical demand for a campaign of sedition and disaffection among the soldiers and sailors".[4]

At the beginning of September when the Party was preparing a recruiting campaign (Red Week) there were strong rumours that the

---

[1] *Workers' Weekly*, No. 111, March 20, 1925. See also R. Palme Dutt in "Notes of the Month", *Labour Monthly*, Vol. 7, No. 7, July 1925.
[2] "Notes of the Month", *Labour Monthly*, July 1925, p. 393.
[3] *Workers' Weekly*, No. 133, August 21, 1925.
[4] Interview with the *Sunday Times*, August 23, 1925.

Authorities were preparing some or other form of action against the Party and its leadership, and a warning (also rather prophetic) was issued both to the Party membership[1] and to the T.U.C. Scarborough Congress.[2]

The explanation about the class character of the state and the preparation for more open use of the machinery of state against the Labour and trade union movement was continued by members and supporters of the Communist Party at the Liverpool Congress of the Labour Party at the end of September.[3]

SECOND CONFERENCE OF NATIONAL MINORITY MOVEMENT

The Party's activity in this post-Red-Friday period was not confined to general warnings. Wherever there were Communists in the trade union movement or Labour Party they did their best to press for a sense of preparedness for the coming struggle and for the greatest unity and solidarity of action.

Communist trade unionists were particularly active in preparing the Second Congress of the National Minority Movement which was held at Battersea Town Hall on August 29-30 with Tom Mann in the chair.[4]

This represented a considerable advance on the first conference of August 1924. Then some 271 delegates represented around 200,000 workers. Here 683 delegates represented around three-quarters of a million workers.

Two slogans gave the keynote to the Conference:

"Prepare for the Coming Fight"

"Solidarity Spells Success"

Preparedness was the essence of the address by Joe Edwards, Vice-President of the Battersea Trades Council, who welcomed the delegates. "Make no mistake about it," he declared:

[1] Circular, *Red Week and Possible Attacks on the Party*, signed A. Inkpin, September 12, 1925.
[2] *Sunday Worker*, September 13, p. 7.
[3] Gallacher's moving of reference back of paragraph on Recruiting in Executive Report (*Report*, pp. 194-194); Resolution on Secret Service moved by W. T. Colyer and seconded by Reg. Bishop (ibid., pp. 283-284); Resolution on the Pollitt Case (ibid., pp. 299-301).
[4] See *Final Agenda of the Annual (Second) Congress of the National Minority Movement, Battersea Town Hall, August 29-30, 1925*; and *Report of Second Annual Conference of National Minority Movement*, 32 pp. pamphlet published by N.M.M.; *Communist Review*, October 1925, J. R. Campbell, "From Minority to Majority".

"the truce will enable your bosses to prepare all the forces at the command of capitalism when the time comes next May to beat the miners and all the workers, unless we stand solidly together."

Preparedness was the keynote too in the Presidential Address by Tom Mann. The miners, he said, backed by trade union solidarity, had successfully held up the owners but:

"Still we have to ask ourselves
Are we prepared to meet the opposing forces when the next round begins . . . be prepared."

The Presidential Address included a number of specific propositions addressed to the Labour Movement. Tom Mann stressed the role of Trades Councils and called for the preparation of Councils of Action for the coming battles; he underlined the role of the National Unemployed Workers Committee Movement (N.U.W.C.M.) and criticised the inactivity of the T.U.C. with regard to the unemployed. He warned of the potential danger of the incipient fascist organisations ("I wish to make it clear that the Labour Movement does not pay sufficient attention to this new anti-Labour movement which is growing up before their eyes"); he expressed the need for solidarity with the workers of the British colonies.

Harry Pollitt, the General Secretary of the N.M.M., moved an important resolution on the "Aims and Objects of the Minority Movement",[1] seconded by Nat Watkins, a miner and secretary of the Miners' Minority Movement. The general Aims and Objects were followed by a more detailed Programme on such issues as wages, working hours, nationalisation, unemployment, housing, foreign policy, and an Organisational Programme.

The organisational proposals were directly connected with the needs of the hour. They included support for the formation of Workshop Committees, the reorganisation of the local Trades Councils "to make them become local unifying centres of the working-class movement in every locality", the affiliation of the N.U.W.C.M. and Trades Councils to the T.U.C., and the development of a General Council of the T.U.C.

"with full powers to direct the whole activities of the Unions and under obligation to the T.U.C. to use that power to fight more effectively the battles of the workers."

[1] *Report of Second Annual Congress of N.M.M.*, pp. 20-22.

This latter slogan may seem strange to later generations of militant trade unionists. At the time the left wing had seen at Red Friday what the trade union movement could achieve when it took strong action. They had seen a positive attitude of struggle from a number of prominent trade union leaders. They knew that a battle was preparing and they wanted a strong united "command" for the working class. Certainly the main emphasis at this time was on the need to strengthen the trade union movement "from below" by powerful Workshop Committees and Trades Councils. Moreover, it was quite clear that what was envisaged was a General Council that would use its powers to fight for the working class. But it can still be questioned whether this was a correct demand, whether it was correct to insist on full powers for the General Council to "direct the whole activities of the Unions" without even greater insistence that such powers would *only* be justified if it was certain that they would be used for and not against the militant working class.

The credential report is indicative of where at this period the N.M.M. exerted influence. There were delegates from over 40 Trades Councils, 126 delegates from metal workers' organisations, 103 building workers, 75 from transport, 72 from organisations of the general workers, 33 miners, 16 delegates from co-operatives and 45 from unemployed organisations. Though seven district trade union organisations were represented, there were only two delegates from trade union National Executives.[1]

The influence of the Communist Party and the National Minority Movement on the general trade union movement was certainly not a decisive one, but it was by no means small. And this was to be shown by the degree to which a number of the key approaches and policies of the Party and the N.U.M. were reflected at the Scarborough Congress of the T.U.C.[2]

SCARBOROUGH: POSITIVE AND NEGATIVE

The Fifty-seventh Annual T.U.C. opened at Scarborough hardly a week after the closing of the N.M.M. Conference. A number of the key resolutions before the Congress had been based on N.M.M. resolutions or put forward by trade unionists who were supporters

[1] N.A.F.T.A. and Chemical and Drug Workers.

[2] The direct influence of the Minority Movement Conference on the Scarborough T.U.C. is studied by J. R. Campbell in an article "From Minority to Majority" in *Communist Review*, Vol. 6, No. 6, October 1925.

of the N.M.M. It should be noted that more members of the Communist Party had been elected as delegates to Scarborough than to the previous T.U.C. The general atmosphere from the very beginning was militant.

The Conference opened with a stirring speech from the Chairman, A. B. Swales of the A.E.U. The time for conceding reductions in wages, he urged, had gone. He touched on the need for close collaboration with the Trades Councils, for international trade union unity, to eschew class collaboration. What was needed was unity and:

> "one of the lessons is that a militant and progressive policy, consistently and steadily pursued, is the only policy that will unify, consolidate and inspire our rank and file."[1]

He raised the issue of the role of the General Council:

> "Congress must give to the General Council full powers to create the necessary machinery to combat every movement by our opponents."[2]

He expressed solidarity with the Indian workers, the people of China and Mexico,[3] and even raised the question of the state by declaring that what was needed for foreign relations was a "Labour Diplomatic Service".[4]

It was on the issue of the powers of the General Council that, in fact, the main Scarborough debate took place, a debate that followed on directly from the similar discussions inside the N.M.M.

A resolution moved by the delegate of the National Union of Vehicle Builders[5] called for the powers of the General Council to be increased to allow it "to levy all affiliated unions", to call for a stoppage by an affiliated organisation or part thereof in order to assist a union defending a vital trade union principle, and also to arrange with the Co-operative Wholesale Society (C.W.S.) to make provision for the distribution of food and other necessaries in the event of a strike or other action in preparation for a strike.

An amendment was tabled immediately (by the delegate of the London Society of Compositors) that would have had the effect of watering the resolution down.[6] A. J. Cook of the Miners strongly supported the resolution.[7]

[1] *Report of Proceedings at the 57th Annual T.U.C., Scarborough, September 7–12, 1925*, p. 67.
[2] Ibid., p. 68.　　[3] Ibid., pp. 71–72.　　[4] Ibid., pp. 73–74.
[5] Ibid., p. 380.　　[6] Ibid., p. 382.　　[7] Ibid., pp. 384–385.

"It was because on July 31st there was an organisation ready to act without considering any constitution that the miners received help. . . .

"Be realists, my friends. Realise that it is only power that counts . . . this resolution gives this power . . . where can you get protection without united action."

He spoke as a "realist" and from experience when he called for a closer link with the Co-operative movement:

"you are going to have a struggle, and you know that an army fights on its belly, and we have no right to lead men into a strike unless we are prepared to feed their wives and families."

Apart from Cook none of the other prominent left trade union leaders came out in support of the resolution, but the big guns of the right swiftly moved into opposition. The Rt. Hon. J. H. Thomas opposed.[1] Ernest Bevin of the Transport and General opposed.[2] And so did the Rt. Hon. J. R. Clynes of the National Union of General Workers in a textbook classic of reformism. "I do not fear, on this subject", he said, "to throw such weight as I have on the side of caution." He continued:

"*I am not in fear of the capitalist class. The only class I fear is our own.*[3]

"I think, therefore, it will be better not to divide the congress by insisting on a vote on this question, but that these proposals should be withdrawn and *that we should put our trust in our leaders.* . . ."

To reach a compromise, and the decision to compromise was a sure sign that all was not militant at Scarborough, the resolution and amendment were referred to the General Council who were to report later to a Special Conference of Executives.[4]

Another important and indicative debate was on "Trade Union Aims",[5] moved by G. E. Joseph of the militant Tailors and Garment Workers Union and seconded by Harry Pollitt, as delegate of the Boilermakers. This too, was in the direct line of the Minority Movement discussions. It opened:

---

[1] *Report of Proceedings of the 57th Annual T.U.C.*, pp. 386–387.
[2] Ibid.
[3] Ibid., p. 387. My emphasis in respect for a classic.
[4] Ibid., p. 395.   [5] Ibid., p. 437.

"This Congress declares that the Trade Union movement must organise to prepare the Trade Unions in conjunction with the Party of the workers to struggle for the overthrow of capitalism."

It warned against the various schemes of co-partnership and continued that the Congress:

"considers that strong well-organised shop-committees are indispensable weapons in the struggle to force the capitalists to relinquish their grip on industry, and, therefore, pledges itself to do all in its power to develop and strengthen workshop organisation."

It was the factory committees that Pollitt particularly emphasised:[1]

"no scheme of amalgamation, either on industrial lines or one big union could become effective if they could not unite at the point of production the people in the workshops, mines, ship yards and factories. . . ."

Most of the right-wing leaders had been committed to vote for this resolution by the decision of their delegations, and although James Sexton, M.P., of the Transport and General, denounced it as "a thinly veiled attempt to pledge this Congress to the principles of Communism" (an indirect compliment to the Communist Party), it was carried by 2,456,000 votes to 1,218,000, a fairly considerable majority.[2]

Militant resolutions were adopted on international trade union unity,[3] on the Dawes Plan (after a strong speech by Harry Pollitt), on China, and on imperialism. These latter we shall examine later in connection with foreign and colonial affairs.[4]

All in all Scarborough was a very militant Congress. It is extremely important to note that nearly all the left-wing resolutions were defended by the militant wing around the Communist Party and the National Minority Movement. This is important because it shows that in a favourable objective situation, when through their own experience the mass of workers were learning both the need to struggle and the effects of struggle, the majority of the T.U.C. could be won for the policies put forward by the Marxists and the militants, provided they *were* put forward, and put forward well and strongly, as men like Pollitt knew how to do.

But all was not rosy at Scarborough. The well-known left trade unionists apart from A. J. Cook, and Swales in his Presidential Address,

[1] Ibid., pp. 438–439.
[2] Ibid., p. 441.   [3] See pp. 20–21.   [4] See pp. 297–298, 309.

were conspicuous by their silence before the attacks of the right wing.

Moreover, although the *general* resolutions adopted were admirable in tone and content, things were far less positive when it came to *specific* measures to prepare for the impending battle.[1] Future general was far more militant than present particular. The resolution proposing the reaffiliation of the Trades Councils to the T.U.C. was ruled out of order. The issue of the powers of the General Council was referred back to the Council itself. And the newly elected Council marked a definite turn to the right, with the return of J. H. Thomas after two years' absence. It was, incidentally, the first occasion on which Ernest Bevin was elected to the General Council, but this was not yet Bevin the pathological anti-Communist.

Both the strength and weakness of Scarborough were well appreciated by Communists at the time. Pollitt considered it the most militant to date in the history of the T.U.C.[2]

He noted the growth of a left trend in the T.U.C., "a growing revolutionary opinion which no intrigues or appeals to constitution procedure could stifle", a force that was now "organised under the leadership of the National Minority Movement", but he equally noted the serious shortcomings—the failure of Congress to give an organised lead to the fight against unemployment, the failure to give support to the seamen's strike, and, above all:

> "The reluctance of the left wing of the General Council to come out openly and fight the right wing on every possible occasion, for there could be no doubt that the right wing leaders, as represented by Messrs. Thomas, Clynes and Cramp, had very effectively marshalled their forces and were organised to take up the battle whenever an opportunity presented itself. . . ."

When, in his stirring opening remarks, A. B. Swales warned that "many of our good comrades who in the days gone by taught us to believe there was no remedy other than the abolition of capitalism, seem afraid now that the system is collapsing, and appeal for a united effort to patch up the system with the aid of the present possessing class", there was a loud roar of approval from the delegates. But remember the words of Clynes—"The only class I fear is our own". There were many militants at Scarborough, but there were no small

---

[1] See Allen Hutt, *Post-War History*, p. 118.
[2] See Harry Pollitt, "The Scarborough Conference" in *Labour Monthly*, October 1925, reprinted in *Selected Articles and Speeches*, Vol. I, pp. 18–23, Lawrence and Wishart, 1953.

number of right-wing officials, leaders in their unions, who *did* fear above all the collapse of the capitalist system and saw as the main enemy their own—*working*—class. A centre section was silent. And a number of trade union leaders, who were indeed "left" as regards the past and even "left" as regards the present in so far as their *feelings* were concerned, had no theory, no consistent outlook to oppose to the reformists, and were doomed, therefore, given the relative weakness of the Communist Party at that time, to be submerged by reformism, to sink, if you like, in its swamp.

Thus it was that though, as Pollitt put it in his autobiography, "the T.U.C. had reached the high-tide of militancy", the Liverpool Conference of the Labour Party that followed it, as he also put it, "served as a mouthpeace for MacDonaldism."[1]

Indeed, there is a close connection between the advances at Scarborough and the defeats at Liverpool.

The high point of the left offensive at Scarborough was *immediately* followed by the most intensive right-wing offensive at Liverpool. As Red Friday led to the capitalist preparation for the showdown of the General Strike, so Scarborough led to the MacDonald-Thomas answer at Liverpool. And one of the aspects of the Labour movement that this most clearly revealed was that the trends so strongly militant in the industrial fields were by no means at the same level in the political field.

COMMUNIST PARTY AND LABOUR PARTY

The Liverpool Labour Party Conference was to be a victory for those who saw as the main enemy the militants in the working class. It was a victory for anti-Communism. But before we examine it we have to take up again the thread of Communist-Labour relations where we left it in the preceding volume of this history[2]

At the 1924 Labour Party Conference, as we have seen, resolutions were carried by large majorities rejecting the affiliation of the Communist Party to the Labour Party and deciding that no Communist Party member be eligible for endorsement as a Labour candidate for Parliament or local authority.

A third resolution, stating that no member of the Communist Party be eligible for membership of the Labour Party, was carried only by a narrow majority of 1,804,000 to 1,540,000.

[1] *Serving my Time*, chapter XIV, "The Communist Party on Trial".
[2] Vol. I, pp. 309 ff.

Already at the 1924 Conference a number of delegates raised questions on the application of this third resolution and the Conference Chairman stated "that any interpretation of the resolution carried must be made by the Executive Committee of the Party".[1]

The Executive Committee appointed a sub-committee to consider the operation of the resolution and, as a result, a statement was issued on February 7, 1925, saying that:

"the logical interpretation of the third resolution would exclude members of the Communist Party from membership of the Labour Party as individual members, as delegates, and as affiliated members. It was agreed, therefore, that further information should be collected throughout the year from affiliated bodies, and that the sub-committee should continue in being to consider this information and report further to the National Executive in order that a definite recommendation may be made to the next Annual Conference of the Party for giving proper effect to the decision."[2]

Later the sub-committee made a further report which was accepted by the National Committee, who recommended two resolutions to be put before the forthcoming Liverpool Conference:[3]

(a) No member of the Communist Party shall be eligible to become a member of any individual section of any affiliated local Labour party, or be entitled to remain a member.

(b) The National Executive also desires to intimate to the Conference that in its opinion affiliated Trade Unions can only act consistently with the decisions of the Annual Conference in its relation to the Communists by appealing to their members when electing delegates to national or local Labour Party Conferences or meetings, to refrain from nominating or electing known members of non-affiliated political parties, including the Communists.

When reporting these resolutions in the annual "Report of the Executive Committee" to be submitted at Liverpool, the ominous words were added:

"should these resolutions be adopted by the conference, the National Executive has decided that they must be consistently administered

---

[1] "Report of the Labour Party Executive Committee 1924–1925", in *Report of the 25th Annual Conference of the Labour Party*, Liverpool 1925, p. 38.
[2] Ibid., p. 38.   [3] Ibid.

by constituency and local parties in the appointment of their officials."[1]

What all this meant in reality was that the *nearer* the movement approached a decisive struggle with capitalism, the more right-wing Labour became ready to capitulate; the more shaky capitalism became, the more they rushed in to firm it up; the nearer they came to the decisive battles, the more their main enemy became those who wanted the working class to fight; the more a united Labour movement was reached the more the right wing was intent on breaking that unity—and that in the first place meant "casting out" the Communists from the Labour Party.

During this whole period the Communist Party was not idle and tried, at times with considerable success, to strengthen the feeling for unity and to develop a pressure inside the trade unions and Labour Party branches against the official demand for Communist exclusion. It would seem, however, that the Communist Party's efforts were more consistent in the trade union field than in the field of the Labour Party, that there was a certain degree of neglect to develop a struggle *inside* the Labour Party by the Communists and militants who were at that time still members. At times the extremely (and correctly so) vigorous attacks on the right-wing Labour Party leaders and their reformist outlook were allowed to weaken the common struggle and ties of friendship with the normal rank-and-file members of the Labour Party.[2]

But this was a weakness only, *not* a deliberate policy. In fact, following the 1924 Labour Party Conference, the Party continued to work for unity and against this final split in the Labour Party. It fought to maintain full rights of membership in the Labour Party.

At the end of January 1925, Albert Inkpin wrote to Henderson, Secretary of the Labour Party, on behalf of the C.P.G.B. that there was great resistance within the local Labour Parties against the expulsion of Communist members and that, in fact, no large town Labour Party had done so.[3]

Discussions held within a whole number of local Labour Parties in ensuing months were to confirm this; and of course this was particularly true in the traditionally militant working-class areas.

---

[1] Ibid.
[2] This is reflected in the resolutions and discussions at the Seventh (Glasgow) Congress of the Party, May 30–June 1, 1925.
[3] "Open Letter to Labour Party E.C.", in *Workers' Weekly*, No. 105, February 6, 1925.

The Rhondda Borough Labour Party, for instance, held a special conference towards the end of February and considered the question of Communist–Labour relations.[1] On the affiliation of the local Communist Party to the Rhondda Borough Labour Party the vote was *for* 12,090, *against* 5,668. On the endorsement of Communist Party members as Labour Party candidates, 11,367 voted *for*, 4,437 *against*. On the question of the right of individual Communists to Labour Party membership, the Conference unanimously voted *for*. A letter from the National Labour Party agent condemning the acceptance of affiliation of local N.U.W.C.M. branches was rejected by a vote of 15,379 to 1,312. Similar decisions, even if not so sweeping, were reported from Lancashire and Scotland.[2]

A Political Bureau statement of end-March again called for resistance to all attempts to expel Communists from the Labour Party.[3] "Against the Policy of Expulsion," the statement ran, "the Communist Party stands for the maintenance of the Federal principle of the Labour Party." The C.P.G.B. May Day Call again stressed the need for unity— "Make May Day 1925, a landmark in the march towards Unity...."[4]

In May and June both Lansbury's *Labour Weekly* and the more militant *Sunday Worker* reflected in editorials and correspondence columns a desire for Labour–Communist unity on the part of rank and file and local Parties. Something like a left-wing movement was arising, mainly from below, but still very dispersed and spontaneous.

At the end of August a strong appeal for left-wing unity and against any policy of excluding the Communists from the Labour Party was made by a considerable body of leading figures in the trade unions and Labour Party. Signatories included from the unions: J. Bromley, M.P., A. A. Purcell, M.P., A. J. Cook (Miners), A. B. Swales (A.E.U.), Fred Potter (T.G.W.U.), Alex Gossip (N.A.F.T.A.), and from Labour Party and I.L.P. George Lansbury, M.P., James Maxton, M.P., Campbell Stephen, M.P., Margaret and G. D. H. Cole, H. N. Brailsford, J. F. and Winifred Horrabin from the N.C.L.C., David Kirkwood, M.P., John Wheatley, M.P., Neil Maclean, M.P., George Buchanan, M.P., Tom Johnston, M.P.[5]

---

[1] See *Workers' Weekly*, No. 108, February 27, 1925.
[2] See, for instance, *Workers' Weekly*, No. 115, April 17, 1925, pp. 2 and 4; *Sunday Worker*, May 24, 1925 (re Battersea Labour Party).
[3] *Workers' Weekly*, No. 112, March 27, 1925, p. 4.
[4] Ibid., No. 117, May 1, 1925.
[5] For further lists of signatories see *Workers' Weekly*, August 28, p. 1; September 4, p. 1; September 11, p. 1; *Sunday Worker*, August 30, p. 2, and September 20, p. 7.

They called for the rescinding of the resolution that would bar Communists from individual membership of the Labour Party. They called for unity:

> "The critical times we are passing through demand the closest solidarity of all the forces engaged in the struggle against capitalism. . . . Anything that makes for division in the ranks must be avoided.
>
> "A campaign against any section of the workers because of their 'extreme' views will only make for distrust, dissension and disruption. The long list of local Labour Parties, that appears in the preliminary agenda of the Labour Party Conference, makes it clear that the attempt to exclude the Communists has not met with the approval of large and important sections of our rank-and-file, and that a continuation of this policy will lead to very bad results in the Unions."

They concluded their appeal:

> "In issuing this statement we are prompted by the sole desire of keeping the movement free from internecine strife, so that it may be able to stand strong and solid against any attacks that may be made upon it."

Something like a hundred local Labour Parties supported it.[1]

As week by week the Liverpool Labour Party Conference grew nearer, and as the campaign for unity (with all its weaknesses) grew more articulate, the heavy guns of the capitalist press began to thunder their warnings. The resolutions *must* be carried.

The *Observer* pressed:

> "If these resolutions are carried, Labour will have nailed its colours . . . to the Parliamentary mast. Its break with the Minority movement in the Trade Unions will be complete."[2]

Sir Alfred Mond remonstrated (addressing the Liberal Club at Glasgow)[3] that Labour leaders "must decide whether they wished to be regarded as responsible statesmen or not"; and in sorrow and in anger he asked them "how much longer they were going to tolerate the canker which was eating at their hearts".

---

[1] See *Workers' Weekly*, No. 138, September 25, 1925, for figures of local Labour Parties, trade unions, M.P.s opposing one or other or all the various discriminatory measures against the Communists.

[2] *Observer*, September 7, 1925.

[3] Quoted in *Sunday Worker*, September 20, 1925, p. 3.

The "Thunderer" itself pointed the way:

"The forthcoming Labour Party Conference must obviously attempt a reconciliation of the two attitudes which may be more or less successful. The only sure step to maintain the Party's unity and likewise its credit, is the ostracism and condemnation of Communism."[1]

Or again on the opening day of Liverpool:

"The future of the Labour Party—even its existence as a party of power in the councils of the state—depends upon the resolutions of the Executive being made effective not only in the local Labour Party organisations but throughout the Trade Unions as well. . . . This would be more than a Party achievement. It would be a definite gain for England."[2]

What capitalism wanted was indeed only too obvious. Perhaps there could be no greater compliment paid to the small Communist Party of that date than the repeated demand from all sections of British capitalism for the exclusion of the Communists from the Labour Party and (if possible) from the trade unions. Left Labour's defence of unity, alas, was not nearly so clear and consistent as capitalism's call for a split.

As for the right-wing Labour leaders themselves, MacDonald and company did not need warnings or threats or bribes. To "oust the Communists" was their highest ambition.

LIVERPOOL

The world did not have long to wait to discover the "tone" of Liverpool. From the first moment of opening it was the opposite of Scarborough. It was a conference of anti-communism. Just as Swales in his Presidential Address opened the T.U.C. at Scarborough in an atmosphere of militancy and struggle, so C. P. Cramp of the railwaymen opened the Labour Party Conference in an atmosphere of defeat and division.[3]

Labour must, he declared, "recognise" the class struggle, but the fundamental task was a "creative" one. "In our practice as a political

---

[1] *The Times*, quoted in *Workers' Weekly*, No. 138, September 25, 1925, p. 2.
[2] *The Times*, September 29, 1925.
[3] *Report of the 25th Annual Conference of the Labour Party*, Liverpool, September 29–October 2, 1925, pp. 172–177.

Party we do actually transcend the conflict of classes; we direct our energies to constructive work and ask for the co-operation of all classes."[1]

He defended the record of the recent Labour Government, turned his wrath against the left and their "glib phrases about a workers' State or mere denunciation of capitalism", denounced "revolution" which for his purpose he neatly identified with violence, and eulogised at length the Dawes Plan.

The Presidential Address was hardly concluded and the Report of the Arrangements Committee hardly adopted, when William Gallacher, speaking as a delegate of the Paisley Labour Party, moved reference back of that section of the Report dealing with the handling of the resolutions on the Communist Party. He attacked the proposal that, under Standing Orders, resolutions on affiliation of the C.P.G.B. and banning of Communists as Labour Party candidates could not be discussed at Liverpool, or rather only if the Liverpool Conference rejected the two resolutions proposed by the Executive.[2]

Much had changed, he argued, in the year that had passed since the preceding Conference:

> "Would the Standing Orders Committee say that whilst there might have been a change of outlook in the Labour Party in the country during the year they would not allow that change of outlook to express itself?"[3]

Henderson opposed, and the reference back was defeated by 2,954,000 to 321,000.[4] The trend of the Conference was already visible.

Without delay, after one or two minor issues had been dealt with, Conference passed to the main issue—the two Executive Resolutions on the Communist Party.[5] The two parts of the Resolutions ((a) and (b)) were discussed separately and Harry Pollitt, as the Boilermaker's delegate, moved the reference back of section (a), the eligibility of Communists to join the Labour Party.

Pollitt referred to the original basis upon which the Labour Party had been founded—an all-in comprehensive movement of which the trade unions formed a major part. How could Communists be excluded

[1] Ibid., p. 173.
[2] Standing Orders laid it down that "when a general policy or principle has been decided it shall not again appear on the Agenda for a period of three years".
[3] Ibid., p. 180.
[4] Ibid., p. 181.
[5] This debate is in *Report of 25th Annual Conference of Labour Party*, pp. 181–189.

from the Labour Party when the main basis of the Labour Party was the affiliated trade unions, he asked. For:

> "if the Communists were members of the Trade Unions paying the political levy ... then the Unions, in the last analysis, were going to decide who were the proper people to represent them either at the Local Party Conferences or at the National Conferences."

The Labour Party had been formed, continued Pollitt, as a comprehensive body open to Socialists of different approaches and opinions. "He could mention four members of the Executive Committee who had admitted to him privately time and time again that they did not believe socialism could ever be obtained by constitutional democracy." The resolutions were directed against Communists only, they were a measure of discrimination:

> "If the movement and the Labour Party was wide enough to include in its ranks those who could go to the Isle of Wight with Lord Inchcape, or to Balmoral, then it ought to be wide enough to include the others."

The demand to exclude the Communists, he continued, did *not* come from the local Labour parties or from the active rank and file members. On the contrary! The bulk of the speaking engagements of Communists like himself

> "came from local Labour Parties and Trades Councils who were anxious to have the Communists in their localities doing the pioneer work. If they were good enough for that, they were good enough to be within the Labour Party as a whole."

Why, he asked, such great pressure to remove the Communists? MacDonald and his colleagues wanted to conciliate capitalists and Conservatives, to show that "they had once and for all cleared out the Communists bag and baggage". But would this make the capitalists more lenient to Labour? "Not a bit of it!"

He warned, very solemnly, that if these resolutions were voted *it would be the right wing, the Executive Committee, who were responsible for the split.*

Pollitt was ably seconded by another leading Communist, Aitken Ferguson of Glasgow, speaking as delegate of the Glasgow Trades and Labour Council, who in the course of his speech made the prophetic warning of the consequences of excluding from the Labour Party active Communist trade unionists whilst admitting men who had never been in the unions like Lord Haldane and Sir Oswald Mosley.

The reference back was supported by Ben Turner (Woollen Textile Workers), one of the few leading trade unionists who found the courage in the hostile atmosphere of Liverpool to support a militant line. He opposed "a heresy hunt". It was against the spirit of the pioneers. While not a Communist, and actively opposed to ideas like that of "the dictatorship of the proletariat", he thought the Executive proposals for exclusion "a very dangerous policy".

It was supported too by Joe Vaughan, delegate of the Electrical Trades Union, and by Will Crick of the Rusholme Labour Party, who stated that in his Branch their experience of Communist membership was very favourable, that he was also a President of a Branch of Bevin's union (T.G.W.U.) where "they had worked with members of the Communist Party in the utmost harmony . . . the Communists had been their most loyal members".

But it was opposed not only by Ernest Bevin but by Ramsay MacDonald, at the height of his loquacious emotional eloquence, who, supported by suitable applause, worked it up and up. He paid tribute to Bevin's speech. It was "realistic", it "dealt with experience". Of course he, Ramsay MacDonald, was not against opposition:

> "As Mr. Bevin assured you, he and I have a little bit of a row occasionally. Why not? *Provided we are in the same spirit, holding the same view*" (my emphasis J.K.).

All the local resolutions were "machine-made". He returned to his earlier point:

> "Division on certain policies held by men with the same spirit, certainly within the same Movement; but with different philosophies, different outlooks; no. . . ."

And so to the peroration:

> "I say again, 'God defend the side that is right!' I believe we are right."

Whether it was God or some more mundane factor, when the vote was taken the reference back was defeated by 2,870,000 votes to 321,000. Conference passed on to debate section (*b*) on the Executive demand that trade unions should refrain from nominating or electing Communists to local or national Labour Party conferences.

The reference back was moved by a non-Communist, Emanuel Shinwell, delegate of the Marine Workers. He called for a more consistent attitude: if the left wing were to be barred, what about the right wing? Conference was trying to dictate to the trade unions, instruct the Boilermakers not to send Pollitt and the E.T.U. not to send Vaughan. Even W. J. Brown (Civil Service Clerical Association) supported the reference back and John Bromley (Locomotive Enginemen) always a champion of unity, spoke very strongly indeed. In adopting section (a), Conference, he said, had adopted "a very foolish resolution". He opposed a heresy hunt inside the unions, the next step in which would be an attempt to exclude Communists from the unions. And with feeling, as a non-Communist, he warned:

> "in spite of the love and respect he had for the Movement—and he had done his share in building it up over a period of twenty-five years—if he came to the Conference with one or more colleagues—he had had as many as three out of five, elected by the rank and file, who were Communists—and if they were asked to leave he would leave with them, because they were his people, and if his Union elected them they had a right to be there."

When Bromley concluded the debate, Arthur Henderson had already spoken. He said, if this were possible, less than Ramsay MacDonald. But the pressures were on, the whips were whipping, with a few honourable exceptions the non-Communist left remained silent, the card vote was taken, and though support for the reference back increased a little, it was still heavily defeated by 2,692,000 to 480,000.

With the vital anti-Communist resolution easily adopted, the right wing could proceed to the discussion of the resolution on "Labour and the Nation" which virtually removed from the Labour Party programme what rudiments of socialist conceptions remained within it. The title itself—"Labour and the Nation"—represented a step back from the 1918 "Labour and the New Social Order".

The objective outlined in Section Five of the resolution was vague enough:[1]

> "a co-ordinated policy of National Reconstruction and Reform which seeks, by Parliamentary means and in progressive stages, supplemented by the increasing control of industry by those engaged therein, to develop the material and mental resources of the nation

---

[1] *Report of 25th Annual Conference of Labour Party*, p. 218.

in order to secure for all manual and mental workers the reward and security to which their activities rightly entitle them."

But the speech in which Ramsay MacDonald formally moved the Resolution on behalf of the Executive made even its vague and woolly wording seem solid and almost socialistic. Socialism, said MacDonald:

"is the idea of the political state acting more and more in co-operation with the industrial state, not in rivalry, not by suppression, not by substitution, but in co-operative harmony."

What this meant no one could know, except that the conceptions of class struggle adopted by the T.U.C. at Scarborough were abandoned, the conception of the social ownership of the means of production, distribution and exchange was dissolved into a sea of verbiage, and the state was conceived of, not as an instrument of class power, but as something vague, amorphous, and unconnected with class.

An Amendment that would have meant setting up a series of committees to decide what to nationalise and how to nationalise it, proposed by delegates from local Labour Parties, was quickly brushed aside.

The only serious opposition to *Labour and the Nation* came, once again, from Communist delegates and a group of militants from the local Labour Parties. Aitken Ferguson (Glasgow Trades Council and Labour Party) proposed an amendment (which was in fact diametrically opposed to the original resolution) calling for a "vigorous struggle for the overthrow of the capitalist class and the establishment of the rule of the working class".[1] This amended resolution had first been adopted by the Glasgow Trades Council, a body which included fifteen local Labour Parties and thirty I.L.P. branches. It explained that real democracy was not possible within capitalism; that the growing resistance of the colonial peoples and loss of Britain's industrial monopoly inevitably meant a concerted drive by the employers against living standards; that it was essential to end imperialism and replace capitalist economy by socialist economy, i.e. "the social ownership of the means of production which only a Workers' Government can introduce".

This counter-resolution to *Labour and the Nation* can probably be criticised with some justice for the doctrinaire character of its language and for its insufficient link with the great struggles that lay immediately ahead. But it had the merit of directly challenging the whole drift of the Labour Party under the leadership of MacDonald and his right-

[1] Ibid., p. 221.

wing colleagues, who were in fact, under the camouflage of a verbal fog, replacing a programme that at least contained the germs of socialism with an acceptance of capitalism.

Aitken Ferguson drew attention to the capitalist offensive, to the capitalist character of the state. C. J. Moody (Richmond Trades Council and Labour Party), seconding the amendment, emphasised that the "reconstruction and reform" envisaged in MacDonald's resolution was reform *within* the system of capitalism.

J. H. Thomas, defending the Resolution,[1] was confident that the real enemy was not the capitalists but the unwillingness of the workers "to trust their leaders". In any case, who wanted to be tied down by a programme? If you adopted a programme you were likely to have to revise it or adapt it:

"He was concerned in asking the Miners' leaders, the Transport Workers' leaders, and the Textile Workers' leaders whether they had not been faced, when dealing with programmes, no matter how they had been drafted or what they contained—when they were in the boardroom and had been faced with the necessity of arriving at an immediate decision, they were told they wanted to betray their men because they had had the courage to adapt themselves to the circumstances and face the facts as they were at that particular moment."

Harry Pollitt, who always endeavoured to follow Thomas in debate, did his best to demolish the Executive Resolution and defend the amendment.[2] In particular, he spoke of the significance of imperialism and the problems of British imperialism.

But the Amendment was heavily defeated[3] and the original resolution "declared carried by an overwhelming majority".[4]

The contrast between Liverpool and Scarborough was reflected equally in the resolution on "Labour Policy for the British Commonwealth of Nations",[5] moved on behalf of the Executive by J. R. Clynes. It was a virtual apology of Empire. The discussion on this resolution and on those concerned with India, Egypt and China we shall examine later.

Ernest Bevin, moved a resolution on "the Labour Government":[6]

---

[1] *Report of 25th Annual Conference of Labour Party*, pp. 222–223.
[2] Ibid., pp. 223–224
[3] By 2,844,000 to 206,000.
[4] *Report of the 25th Annual Conference of the Labour Party*, p. 224.
[5] Ibid., pp. 228–229.
[6] Ibid., p. 244.

"This Conference is of opinion that in view of the experience of the recent Labour Government, it is inadvisable that the Labour Party should again accept office whilst having a minority of Members in the House of Commons."

The resolution, undoubtedly, reflected discontent with the dismal record of the first Labour Government. More revealing than Bevin's opening was the speech of John Bromley.[1] Before the Labour Government, he explained, he was "enthusiastically and wholeheartedly in support of it." But experience had changed his attitude. Unwilling to fight yet desirous to retain office, "the Party was inclined to compromise with the people who had power to displace them". The experience of the Party in office, he declared:

"was that they had continually to compromise, and that they thereby lost the fighting chance which those that voted for Labour candidates intended to give them."

In essence a Party in a minority holding office was nothing but a coalition Government, to which he was strongly opposed.

Even more revealing than the dissatisfaction with the experience of the Labour Government was the line of defence of that Government taken up by J. H. Thomas and above all Ramsay MacDonald at the height of his most oozy-eloquence.[2] For generations to whom MacDonald is unknown and almost unbelievable, passages deserve record. "When they and he were dead," he told the assembled delegates:

"and when their children were dead, and when a more remote succession of generations read of the old twentieth century, he did not think it was flattering the Labour Government or flattering the Party if he said they would then be loud in their praise when they read that, in the year 1924, the men from the pits, the men from the factories, and the men from the fields, coming into office with a minority and as a minority, and for the first time breaking the record in that respect, accomplished as Labour Ministers a work that would be enshrined in the records of the British people."

The resolution, if adopted, would "tie the hands" of the Labour leaders. "No leader could fight if he was tied in that way." Conference should not deal with hypothetical eventualities. They should "keep to

[1] Ibid., pp. 246–247.   [2] Ibid., pp. 249–250.

the grindstone of reality", and decide on such problems as and when they arose.

By 2,587,000 votes to 512,000 the resolution was lost, and another victory chalked up to the right.

It was a victory of the right-wing leaders that was instantly and uproariously hailed as a victory for the capitalists, the employers, the Tories. It was a victory for profit, for investment. On this there was no doubt:

"There was a much better tendency in the Stock Exchange, not a little due to the decisive defeat of the Communists at the Labour Conference" (*Daily Telegraph*, October 1, 1925).

"Stockmarkets were decidedly better. There was a more cheerful feeling round the House, begotten, it was said, of the satisfactory developments at the Labour Conference at Liverpool and the overwhelming defeat there of the Communist elements" (*Daily News*, October 1, 1925).

"Investment, evidently, is greatly relieved by the testimony afforded at the Liverpool Congress to the fact that the Reds are not going to have things their own way" (*Financial Times*, October 1, 1925).

But it was *The Times* leader "From Words to Deeds", on the morrow of the Conference decision to exclude the Communists, that gave what may be called the ruling-class directive. It was not enough to rejoice, it was time to act:

"The Party has made a great and welcome affirmation. . . . But these resolutions do not end the matter. . . . The declaration of the Conference will in due course have to be transformed into acts . . . the main difficulty is in dealing with the Communists in the Trade Unions. It is a comparatively simple matter to expel a handful of Communists from a local Labour Party or even to expel one or more of such bodies which have renounced the Party principles. But a Trade Union cannot be called upon—such is the constitution of the Labour Party—to expel its Communist members. It can only be instructed in the inconsistency of belonging to the Labour Party and sending Communists to represent it in the Party meetings. . . .

"The Liverpool Conference has enunciated a principle, so far so good. A policy must follow. *Communism must not only be condemned; it must be cast out.*"[1] (My emphasis J.K.)

[1] *The Times*, October 1, 1925.

The Times was echoed by MacDonald. "The National Executive," he wrote, "after the Liverpool decisions, will no doubt put its foot down heavily upon offending parties."[1] Or again: "Liverpool has laid down the charter, and those who are not to respect it had better clear out."[2]

A few days later J. H. Thomas joined in with a *Weekly Dispatch* article "Smash the Reds or they will smash us".[3] At the Conservative Party Conference early in October, Baldwin announced to delegates incensed at the Government's "capitulation" the preceding July, that proceedings against the Communist Party were under consideration. "The decisions of the Liverpool Conference," wrote R. Palme Dutt, "constitute a direct invitation to the bourgeoisie to begin the attack."[4] Within a fortnight of Liverpool the logical step was taken. Twelve leaders of the Communist Party were put under arrest.

That the Liverpool Conference was a big victory for the right-wing Labour leaders in the Labour Party and the trade unions, a big victory of the small but powerful group around MacDonald, Thomas, Clynes and company, was painfully obvious. To the mass of members of the various Labour organisations the real significance and dangers of Liverpool were not so obvious. Even some of those looked upon as on the left utterly failed to appreciate its consequences. "It has been a very good Conference spoiled by the outrageous acoustics of a very large hall," was George Lansbury's weighty judgement.

On the whole it was left to the Communists to give a real analysis of the Liverpool Conference and to give a due warning as to what it involved. It was a "liberal" Conference, said Pollitt.[5] He stressed the fact that it was the relatively small group of Communists and their sympathisers at Liverpool who alone put forward an "alternative working class policy":

> "True we were weak numerically, and from a debating standpoint we possessed none of the acts of the theatrical or moving picture professions but our policies are on record as the only organised attempt to challenge the liberal leaders now in control of the Labour Party."[6]

---

[1] Quoted by R. Palme Dutt in "Notes of the Month", *Labour Monthly*, November 1925.
[2] Ibid. [3] *Weekly Dispatch*, October 11, 1925.
[4] "Notes of the Month", *Labour Monthly*, November 1925. (Written at the beginning of October before the arrest of the Communist leaders.)
[5] *Labour Monthly*, November 1925. [6] Ibid.

He stressed the complete silence of the non-Communist left who allowed MacDonald "to ride roughshod over them".[1] This was indeed a significant aspect of the Conference. The left-wing trade union leaders, some of whom had taken a prominent part at Scarborough, failed completely to fight in the harder conditions of Liverpool. An important lesson might be learned, a lesson which history teaches the hard way to successive generations of workers. Within a trade union movement, on relatively restricted trade union issues, a left militant wing without a scientific outlook or ideology can sometimes lead the movement to provisional success. But militants without a socialist ideology are powerless when confronted with Labour leaders with a strong reformist or, if you like, a capitalist ideology. Socialists who lack science, socialists of the heart or sentiment or instinct only, quickly become the prisoners of right-wing dazzlers, experts in reformism of the MacDonald type. To defeat reformist ideas, a scientific socialist Marxist ideology is essential. At Liverpool, the influence of Marxist ideas was still relatively weak. "Revolutionary political understanding," wrote R. P. Dutt, at the time,[2] "is still lacking. In consequence the reins of leadership remain in the hands of the old and experienced reformist leaders. . . ."

The Executive of the Communist Party, following Liverpool, issued a statement *Communists and the Labour Party*.[3] It underlined the contrast between Scarborough and Liverpool. It issued a call for action to meet the blows of the employers which Liverpool made all the more inevitable:

> "Form Factory Committees to secure unity at the bottom! Send delegates from the factories to the Trades Councils, and thus consolidate your forces locally! Insist on the formation of the Workers' Alliance under the Supreme authority of the General Council! Meet the threat of organised strike breaking and capitalist violence by insisting on the right to tell your brothers in the Army and Navy that they must not scab on the workers, and by forming your own Defence Corps against the O.M.S. and the Fascisti!"

It offered unity in struggle with all ready to resist the inevitable capitalist attacks, and called for increased membership and activity of the Communist Party.

[1] *Labour Monthly*, November 1925, p. 643.
[2] "Notes of the Month", *Labour Monthly*, November 1925.
[3] *Workers' Weekly*, No. 140, October 9, 1925. For full text see chapter IV, Appendix II.

But whatever Communists and militants might do to stem the Liverpool defeat, the Labour Party Conference had issued an open invitation to the Government to strike at the Communist Party. As Harry Pollitt was to write in his autobiography:

". . . The Liverpool Conference contained the germ of the abject sell-out of 1931. . . .

"The hoisting of the white flag at Liverpool was the signal to the Government to intensify its anti-working-class drive, and the blow was not long in coming. . . ."

On October 12 came the arrest of the twelve Communist leaders.

THE TRIAL OF THE TWELVE[1]

On Wednesday, October 14, 1925, some 30 or so detectives raided both the national and London offices of the Communist Party, the young Communist League, the National Minority Movement and rooms used by the staff of the *Workers' Weekly*. The raids continued roughly from 5 p.m. on the Wednesday to mid-day the following day. Eight leading Communists were arrested: Tom Bell, Editor of *Communist Review* (the Party's theoretical monthly), J. R. Campbell, Ernie Cant (Secretary of the London District of the Party), William Gallacher, Albert Inkpin (the Party's Secretary), Harry Pollitt (at that time Secretary of the National Minority Movement), Bill Rust (Secretary of the Young Communist League) and Tom Wintringham (Assistant Editor of the *Workers' Weekly*). Some days later the arrests were extended to four further Communist leaders[2]—Wally Hannington, leader of the organisation of the unemployed, the N.U.W.C.M.,

---

[1] The fullest accounts of the arrest and trial of the twelve Communist leaders are contained in the *Workers' Weekly* and the *Sunday Worker*. There is useful material also in the *Daily Herald*. In his autobiography, *Serving my Time*, Harry Pollitt describes his arrest and period in prison and quotes in full his defence speech. J. J. Murphy describes his arrest and imprisonment in *New Horizons*, chapter XIII. The three defence speeches at the Old Bailey, made by Harry Pollitt, J. R. Campbell, and W. Gallacher, were published verbatim as 2d. pamphlets by the C.P.G.B. under the general title *Communist Party on Trial*. A selection of the documents alleged to have been seized by the police in their raids and used by the prosecution was published as Cmd. 2682 in 1926 under title of *Documents Selected from those obtained on the Arrest of the Communist Leaders on the 14th and 21st October 1925*. A brief summary of the background, arrest and trial by James Klugmann was published in *World News*, September 10 and 17, 1960, under title of "The Trial of the Twelve".

[2] *Workers' Weekly*, No. 142, October 23, 1925.

Arthur MacManus, J. T. Murphy, and Robin Page Arnot.[1] Almost the whole Political Bureau was thus arrested (eight out of ten).

The raids were not confined to the different offices. The homes of the arrested were also ransacked. From offices and homes the police seized virtually tons of material. A witness reported the raid at 16, King Street:

> "Each room had its plain-clothes guard—there are twelve rooms counting cellars and attics.[2] Not a stamp, not a matchbox, could escape. Every visitor to shop or office was detained. A solemn stillness reigned and over all loomed the Chief Inspector Parker like the spirit of God moving upon the face of the waters."[3]

Every scrap of paper seemed to the raiders to be suspicious, sinister, if not directly seditious. Correspondence of a purely personal nature was seized, and even the works of a certain Herbert Spencer and the novels of Anatole France. Busts of Lenin, Zinoviev and other Russian Bolsheviks were "arrested" and carted away, and even a mysterious metal sphere later revealed as a toilet accessory.[4] Whole editions of the *Workers' Weekly* were seized and held for over 24 hours.

The arrested 12 were charged:

> "With having on divers days since January 1st, 1924, unlawfully conspired together to utter and publish seditious libels and to incite divers persons to commit breaches of the Incitement to Mutiny Act, 1797 against the peace of our Lord, the King, his Crown and dignity."[5]

Preliminary hearings took place at Bow Street over a period of three weeks during which Sir Travers Humphreys, for the Prosecution, made particular efforts to prove the illegality of the Communist Party. "The persons concerned" in the trial, he said, "are prosecuted as

---

[1] The British Special Branch sent a man over to Brussels to include R. Palme Dutt in the "haul", and he was arrested on November 5. However, with the aid of the head of the Brussels bar, the Belgian authorities got tied up in legal complications. Dutt had been charged with conspiracy against King Albert, which under Belgian law prevented his extradition. Eventually, with the help of international solidarity, the charge was dismissed.

[2] For puzzled contemporaries—there are more rooms today because in the war years 27, Bedford Street was acquired and joined to the offices at 16, King Street.

[3] *Sunday Worker*, October 18, 1925, p. 5.

[4] For historians—the King Street lavatory ballcock.

[5] *Workers' Weekly* No. 143, October 30, 1925.

the leaders and principal executive officers of two illegal organisations."[1]

The Political Bureau of the Party discussed the best methods of conducting the defence and decided that a number of the arrested comrades should defend themselves. In these preliminary hearings, therefore, whilst Sir Travers Humphreys and Mr. Percival Clarke, instructed by Mr. C. Wallace, appeared on behalf of the Director of Public Prosecution, Sir Archibald Bodkin, who was present in court at the opening, Sir Henry Slesser, M.P. and Mr. Arthur Henderson, Jnr., instructed by Mr. W. H. Thompson, defended Arnot, Cant, Hannington, Inkpin, MacManus, Murphy and Wintringham, whilst Bell, Campbell, Gallacher, Pollitt and Rust defended themselves.

Sir Travers Humphreys, having affirmed the illegality of the Communist Party and the Young Communist League, argued that *all* persons who disseminated Communist doctrines (or more specifically the doctrines that the defendants called communism) were liable to be prosecuted for sedition.[2] Communism, he declared, and this was perhaps the most central feature of the Prosecution's case, hails from Russia. It was illegal, first, because it sought "to overthrow the constituted Government of this country and establish forms of Government by force". The second basis of its illegality, he argued, "involves the creation of antagonism between different classes of His Majesty's subjects". And thirdly, it was illegal "because it involves the seducing from their allegiance of the armed forces of the Crown".

Defending seven of the arrested, Sir Henry Slesser made his main case the argument that the Communist Party was as lawful as any other political party. J. R. Campbell spoke for those not defended by Slesser, followed shortly by Bell, Gallacher, Pollitt and Rust.

The reference, said Campbell,[3] by the counsel for the Prosecution to the C.P.G.B. and Y.C.L. as "two illegal organisations" was "more an expression of political hope than of legal fact". It was foolish to cite class war as a proof of the illegal activity of the Communists, because it was not the Communists who *created* the war of classes, but the class war was implicit in capitalist society. It was not incitement to mutiny for workers to discuss political questions and points of view with soldiers drafted to their areas, nor was it seditious to state that workers and soldiers were "class brothers". To argue that the C.P.G.B. was Russian-controlled because the office of the International was in the U.S.S.R. was as illogical as to argue that the League of Nations and all

[1] Ibid. [2] Ibid.
[3] Ibid., No. 145, November 13, 1925.

its members were Swiss, because its headquarters were at Geneva. The counsel for the Prosecution, said Campbell, had provided no proof whatsoever of conspiracy. The various quotations used to prove the Prosecution's case against Communism were selected from speeches and writings taken out of context and often out of date. Some of the extracts from statements of the Communist International had long been superseded by more recent Congress decisions, and in any case had been published years ago (and been in the possession of Scotland Yard) without any action being taken.

Rather revealing were the replies of the witnesses for the Prosecution, under the skilful cross-questioning of the Communists who were defending themselves.

Detective-Sergeant O'Connor admitted, examined by Campbell, that his notes of a speech by Hannington were taken at a meeting organised by the T.U.C. and the Unemployed:

> "The meeting was not a Communist meeting. I took notes of other speeches by Mr. Ernest Friend, Mr. Sam Marsh, M.P., Mr. A. Wall, Mr. Jack Jones, M.P. and Mrs. Young, a member of the Edmonton Board of Guardians."[1]

Pressed further by Campbell, the detective-sergeant reluctantly admitted that his eight-year experience of noting political meetings had been somewhat one-sided:

> "I frequently take notes at meetings. . . . I don't think I have ever taken notes of a Conservative or Liberal M.P.'s speeches. . . . I've not recently been to a Conservative meeting to take notes."[2]

Examined by Gallacher:

> "I don't attend meetings unless detailed to do so."[3]

Detective-Sergeant Kitchener was forced to admit he had been put on to study Communist documents for sedition *well after* the arrests had been made. Detective-Sergeant Kitchener will go down in history for another classic admission about the Marxist theory of the state:

> *Campbell* (cross-questioning): Do you consider that it would be seditious for the Labour Party to tell the soldiers its point of view in a labour dispute?

---

[1] Communist Party Records and *Workers' Weekly*, No. 145, November 13, 1925.
[2] Ibid.   [3] Ibid.

Witness (Kitchener): It all depends on the point of view. (Laughter in court.)[1]

The preliminary hearings ended on November 11. The magistrate, Sir Charles Biron, declared that a *prima facie* case had been made out against the accused, and they were committed for trial at the Old Bailey.

The Old Bailey trial opened on Monday, November 16, 1925. The defendants were granted the right to bail and to be seated. The charges had now been slightly altered. "The prisoners at the bar," recited the Clerk:

> "are charged on an indictment containing three counts. The first of which charges that on days between the first of January 1924 and the 21st October 1925, they together conspired to publish and utter seditious libels and words.
>
> "The second count charges them all with conspiracy to commit breaches of the Incitement to Mutiny Act, 1797.
>
> "The third count charges them all with conspiracy to endeavour to seduce persons in His Majesty's forces, to whom might come certain published books and pamphlets, to wit, the *Workers' Weekly* and certain other publications mentioned in the indictment and to incite them to mutiny."[2]

All pleaded not guilty. Again the Central Committee of the Party had decided that two lines of defence should run concurrently. Sir Henry Slesser would undertake the legal defence of nine of the accused, naturally concentrating on the *legal* aspects of the case. Meanwhile, J. R. Campbell, William Gallacher and Harry Pollitt would defend themselves and carry out an open *political* defence.

The Attorney-General, Sir Douglas Hogg, opened the case for the Prosecution, once again along the lines that the Communist Party of Great Britain was "Moscow-controlled", that it was trying to subvert the armed forces, that it aimed at civil war, though even he had to admit that the Prosecution could find little evidence to support its claim that the Party was "financed from Moscow".

It is interesting to examine the motley collection of documents the Prosecution alleged it had seized in the various raids, and on which it,

---

[1] *Workers' Weekly*, No. 144, November 6, 1925.
[2] *Workers' Weekly*, No. 147, November 27, 1925, and Tom Bell, *The British Communist Party, A Short History*, Lawrence and Wishart, 1937, pp. 108-109.

to no small extent, claimed to base its case. A selection of these "documents" was published later by the Government.[1]

The capitalist press had been busy working up an atmosphere of "red-scare", "sinister figures from Moscow", "international atheistic agents", "bloodstained and bloodthirsty reds". Despite the fact that it is theoretically illegal to make comments which might in any way prejudice or influence a jury's verdict, Jix himself, on the night of the first arrests, had boasted at a meeting of an amateur dramatic society:

> "I believe that the greater part of the audience will be pleased to hear that warrants have been issued and in the majority of cases have been executed for the arrest of a certain number of notorious Communists."[2]

Lord Rothermere's *Evening News* immediately after the arrests published a cartoon depicting the accused in a motor-car, complete with whiskers and bombs, captioned "Mutiny and Sedition" (which cost the newspaper a fine of £100—chicken feed) and a leader boldly entitled "Well Done Jix!"

Read in that context it can be understood that the counsel for the Prosecution could present his motley collection of documents as evidence for sedition. Examined in a cooler context, the main crimes that emerge from the odd letters to and from the Communist International, R.I.L.U., etc., and the varied reports of fragments of them, were of the use of a somewhat sectarian language which was indeed, it must be admitted, a considerable weakness at the time; and of negligence in leaving documents concerning Communist activities, apt to be apprehended by MI5, so loosely about in the various offices.

A transcript copy of undated manuscript shorthand notes for a letter to Bennett, a representative of the Communist International (at times in Britain), spoke of an allocation of £16,000 to the Party for the year 1925, of which £4,000 had been allotted towards the cost of running the *Sunday Worker*.[3] Another document spoke of an allocation of £5,000 for the year 1924.[4]

From other documents there was evidence that the R.I.L.U. Head Office had promised to the British Section a grant of £150 a month for a period, and that the International Red Aid was receiving the help of

---

[1] *Communist Papers—Documents selected from those obtained on the Arrest of the Communist Leaders on the 14th & 21st October, 1925*, H.M.S.O., Cmd. 2682, 1926.
[2] *Daily Herald*, October 16, 1925.
[3] *Communist Papers*, Document 30, pp. 62–63.   [4] Ibid., Document 25, p. 57.

Prelude to the General Strike

some British Communists in conveying assistance to Bulgarian comrades suffering under a peculiarly atrocious white terror.[1]

There were some documents concerning problems of organisation, the essence of which had long been published in open documents of the Communist International and the C.P.G.B. There was some evidence, of which the Communists of Britain could well be proud, that the C.P.G.B. was trying to help the Communists and national revolutionaries of China, Egypt, India, Morocco and Ireland, and that Ralph Fox (later to be killed as a member of the International Brigade in Spain) had gone to Moscow to work on colonial affairs in the Communist International. There were some fascinating pieces for the historian.[2]

Once again, the Defence counsel and Pollitt, Campbell and Gallacher were able, by acute cross-questioning, to reveal both the bias of the witnesses themselves, almost all of whom were members of the special department of the C.I.D. (though not those who appeared at the preliminary hearings who had been tactfully withdrawn) and the bias or the normal practice of the capitalist state.

---

[1] I expect that one day in a socialist world, when all relevant documents are available, it will be shown that in the first few years of the Communist International some of the money collected from its sections *was* sent out to its sections. This was *not* a Russian subsidy though naturally the Russian section was the largest single source of dues and donations. It will be shown that British Communists *at a very early date* opposed this practice except for Parties struggling under conditions of terror and illegality, and the practice was very soon dropped except in just such circumstances. At a time when the C.I. was considered as a *single* international organisation with a *single* world leadership, the practice was normal enough, and had been the general practice of the international movement long before the formation of the Communist International; but experience shows in my opinion that whilst international solidarity is always essential in a revolutionary movement, in conditions of legality each revolutionary movement should provide its own finances.

[2] For instance a "sinister letter from Bucharin":

Comrade MacManus!

Sinowjeff and myself go to Caucasus overmorrow. Will you with us? Wi kan not understand as necessary differences in the english party without the language. Wenn you kan not, you must recomand to us one english comrade for this task. This is 'conditio sine equo non' of our effectiv work in the english question.

Excuse my for this analphabetical letter,

Yours, BUCHARIN.

Or the ingenuity of MI5 in deciphering the angry comments of Clemens Dutt in a letter to the General Secretary of the C.P.G.B. and which on second thoughts he had carefully erased.

Or the official Home Office definition:

"*Stickers*: (*a*) Small white adhesive labels on which was printed anti-militaristic propaganda. (*b*) Small red illustrated adhesive labels on which were printed 'Join the Communist Party' slogans."

Detective William Rogers of Scotland Yard admitted that, though he was well experienced at watching King Street, he had, as yet, no equivalent experience of watching Conservative or Liberal premises. A bank official called by the Prosecution admitted that there was no evidence of money from Russian sources being paid into the Communist Party's account. Then there was Detective William Hastings who was asked by Harry Pollitt why, at the Young Communist League office at Great Ormond Street, he represented himself as a Communist:[1]

> *The Witness*: They regarded me with some suspicion. . . . We must do as we are told, and at times we have to represent ourselves as something even if we do not say we are such.
> *Pollitt:* If I went to Scotland Yard and reported myself as one of you, what would happen to me?
> *Mr. Justice Swift:* I do not think that is a question witness can answer.

Persistent and judicious examination of witnesses revealed that some of them had been instructed to "dig up" evidence for the Prosecution and discover seditious passages in Party pamphlets and periodicals after the arrests had been made; that police agents had been taking notes at meetings, watching Party offices, following Party members and hiding under Party platforms; that they were perfectly aware that letters of Communists were frequently opened; that a number of police agents had represented themselves as Communists as "camouflage" to obtain information; that the "burglary" at various offices in October 1924, previously considered to have been a fascist raid, had in fact been undertaken by the police; that none of the witnesses could produce any tangible evidence of "plot", "conspiracy", "secret meeting" or underhand financial transaction.

Sir Henry Slesser, for the Defence, concentrated on the legal case—the absence of evidence of sedition and incitement to mutiny. Pollitt, Campbell and Gallacher concentrated on a political answer to what was so plainly a political prosecution.[2]

Why had the Government launched this trial, asked Pollitt; and answered:

---

[1] *Sunday Worker*, November 22, 1925.
[2] *The Communist Party on Trial—Harry Pollitt's Defence*, C.P.G.B., 2d. *The Communist Party on Trial—J. R. Campbell's Defence*, C.P.G.B., 2d. *The Communist Party on Trial—Wm. Gallacher's Defence and Judge Rigby Swift's summing up*, C.P.G.B., 2d.

"The Government were in difficulties as a result of the mining crisis last July and were compelled to make a settlement as a result of a threat of direct action by the trade unions. The Party to which we belong has been the only party to propagate a certain doctrine of united action, and because the Government did not feel strong enough to attack the trade unions directly, we are to be made the cat's-paw in order to satisfy the diehard section of the Conservative Party, who were compelling the leaders of that Party to attack the Communist Party...."[1]

It was the Liverpool Labour Party Conference, said Pollitt, that gave the Government the immediate go-ahead:

"... they found that at the Liverpool Labour Party Conference we were expelled from the Labour Party, and they thought that, seeing we were isolated ... seeing that the official movement had in its own way disowned us, then was the time of attack...."[2]

The Prosecution, contended the accused, had been trying to work up an anti-Communist scare. The conception of Communism put forward by the Attorney-General, said Campbell:

"is the conception of revolution and revolutionary activity that one gets in the pages of popular lady novelists who write hair-raising stories about the French Revolution under the impression that the French Revolutionaries were revolutionary Socialists, whereas the fact is that they were respectable middle-class citizens whose views on private property were not dissimilar to those held by members of the Conservative Party."[3]

Pollitt and Campbell dealt with the eternal accusation of "alien" or "Moscow" gold:

"Members of the jury ... I am confident that you will agree that there has never been any case of political persecution in this country in which the Government of the day did not endeavour to justify that persecution by exactly the same sort of talk of alien gold as the Prosecution has had to indulge in during these proceedings. When Lloyd George opposed the Boer War, the newspapers said that he was in receipt of Boer gold; when John Redmond was sponsoring the Home Rule agitation in Ireland, it was Yankee gold which was endeavouring to undermine the Constitution of the British Empire.

[1] *Harry Pollitt's Defence*, p. 8.   [2] Ibid., p. 7.   [3] *J. R. Campbell's Defence*, p. 3.

When Mr. Ramsay MacDonald took an attitude which was thought to be unfair towards the War, it was German gold that was endeavouring to undermine and sap the foundations of this great nation.

"And now that a new political party has come along giving expression to ideas and to opinions and to politics which are no new thing, but which represent traditions going far back into the history of the working class movement, now, for want of argument . . . they again resort to 'alien gold'."[1]

William Gallacher explained the essential sources of the Party's expenditure, estimated by the Prosecution at around £12,000–£14,000 per year—bookshops, press, dues, donations, etc.[2] And he spoke of the real amounts of money paid as wages to these "sinister international agents":

"You have evidence that my home is in Paisley. . . . You have evidence that I was in charge of the Parliamentary Department. That means that I have been working about the headquarters at King Street as the man in charge of the Parliamentary Department. You have evidence that we are paid £5 per week, from £5 to £3 10s 0d. £5 per week! You will understand if you think it over that it will be necessary for me to send half of that up to Paisley to my home and that I have £2 10s. 0d. a week to carry on in London."[3]

Hired by the Third International to commit assorted monstrous crimes for £2 10s. 0d. per week! Gallacher's defence and the Prosecution's accusations against the Third International and the C.P.G.B. inevitably bring to mind the similar charges against Marx, Engels and the General Council of the First International.[4]

J. R. Campbell, in the course of his defence, described what had, in fact, been published by the *Workers' Weekly* with regard to the men in the armed forces.

---

[1] *Harry Pollitt's Defence*, pp. 4–5.
[2] *William Gallacher's Defence*, pp. 5–7.   [3] Ibid., p. 16.
[4] Marx at times felt bitter at these accusations. He writes in *A Reply on the First International* (August 1878); "The Council in its published report to the Congress of Basle (1869) ridicules the huge treasure with which the busy tongues of the European police and the wild imagination of the capitalist had endowed it. It says: 'if the people, though good Christians, had happened to live at the time of nascent Christianity, they would have hurried to a Roman bank there to pry into St. Paul's balance'." A similar reply to the various wild accusations was given by Engels in his financial report to the Hague Conference of the First International in 1872.

In each of the issues of July 31, 1925 and August 7, 1925, there was an article which stated:

> "I say, you soldiers, sailors, airmen and all workers. The Communist Party stands for—formation of soldiers and sailors committees. Right to join political parties and attend meetings. Right to join and form Trade Unions. No troops to be used against strikers. Immediate pay increases for rank and file. Sailors pay to be equal to merchant service. Equal leave for men and officers. Right to wear 'civvies' on leave. Shorter service periods and eight-hour day. Full T.U. rates for soldiers in Government workshops. Men's Committees to control rations, etc. No compulsory Church attendance. Increased pensions and widows pensions. Boys not to be sent on active service. Abolition of all reserve forces. Workers! Tell any soldiers and sailors you know about this programme, and help to fight against capitalist warmakers."[1]

He quoted other passages that had been used by the Prosecution in the endeavour to prove incitement to mutiny. Campbell argued that the aim of the *Workers' Weekly* was to bring before the members of the Forces the political ideas of the Party and, at the same time, to appeal to the general public to work for the improved lot of the men in the forces. Such agitation, along with the appeal to the soldiers not to let themselves be used against strikers, was, he argued, completely legitimate.[2]

It was Pollitt, above all, who in his defence insisted on the open, public, *political* character of the Communist Party. It was the capitalist press and the Prosecution that was trying to conjure up the image of a secret conspiratorial underground group:

> "What does conspiracy conjure up in the minds of the lay people not in the legal minds? Dark corners, secret meetings, hole-and-corner mutterings. . . . But we are a perfectly legal political Party which has been pursuing the tenor of its way since its formation in 1920, and if what we are saying now is wrong, it was wrong when the Party was formed."[3]

And he ended thus his defence.[4]

---

[1] *J. R. Campbell's Defence*, p. 17, and in relevant numbers of *Workers' Weekly*.
[2] Ibid., pp. 17–27.
[3] *Harry Pollitt's Defence*, p. 14.
[4] Ibid., pp. 31–32.

"I say the Party is a political Party carrying out its political ideas. ... I would like my last appeal to you to be this: to remember while you are endeavouring to arrive at your verdict—what was the nature and the circumstances of the Act of 1797 under which you are trying us. Believe me, members of the jury, this cause to which we belong, this Party, this Communist International of which I am an accepted member, and proud to acknowledge the fact, is now a permanent factor of current political life; that the ideals for which we are to be convicted here are ideals which have inspired and will inspire more and more in the future, millions of the very best in the working class. ...

"... Progress can be hindered and can be retarded, but it can never be stopped. Communism today is a general political issue which cannot be wiped out by political theory, by persecution or repression."

Mr. Justice Rigby Swift, summing up, made one interesting avowal. The Prosecution had pointed out, he said, that about £14,000 had been paid into the Defendants' bank in the previous 12 months, but:

"*There was very little evidence that it came from Russia.*"[1]

None of the accused, however, had much doubt that the verdict would go against them. "We all knew the British legal system too well," wrote Pollitt, later, "and especially did we understand the character of the Tory Government that had ordered our arrest."[2] "We were quite confident," wrote J. T. Murphy, "that we were going to prison before ever we saw the jury; it was to us so obviously a political trial and part of a larger manœuvre outside the court that we thought of the proceedings only in their effect on the outside public."[3]

The jury were absent a mere twenty minutes and returned a verdict of "Guilty". The judge, passing sentence, reiterated the illegality of the Party: "You are members of an illegal Party carrying on illegal work in this country."[4]

Five of the accused—Gallacher, Inkpin, Hannington, Pollitt and Rust, all of whom had previous (political) convictions—were sentenced to 12 months. The judge then turned to the others:

"You remaining seven have heard what I have had to say about the society to which you belong. You have heard me say it must be stopped. ...

[1] *Judge Rigby Swift's summing up* (published at the end of *Gallacher's Defence*), p. 22.
[2] *Serving my Time*, chapter XIV.
[3] J. T. Murphy, *New Horizons*, p. 212.   [4] *Judge Rigby Swift's summing up*, p. 24.

"Those of you who will promise me that you will have nothing more to do with this association or the doctrines which it preaches, I will bind over to be of good behaviour in the future. Those of you who do not promise will go to prison."[1]

One by one, beginning with J. T. Murphy, and ending with Tom Bell, the judge asked: "Will you be bound over?" One by one each of the seven accused answered: "No, I will not", and was given six months and hustled below.

ARREST OF WELSH MINERS

Within a few weeks of the imprisonment of the 12 Communist leaders another directly political trial opened at Cardiff and at Carmarthen. This time it was not Communists who were in the dock but militant miners, members of the South Wales Miners' Federation, working in the anthracite mines of the Amman Valley.[2]

The arrests and trials arose from a militant strike of the anthracite miners which took place in July and August 1925. As the collieries involved were in Glamorganshire as well as Carmarthenshire, the trials were divided between Cardiff and Carmarthen, but the main ones took place at the latter.

In all, 167 miners were tried over a three weeks' period at the Carmarthen Assizes. The first batch of 19 prisoners were charged that they:

"On July 29, 1925, in the County of Carmarthen, unlawfully and riotously assembled to disturb the peace, and then did make a great riot and disturbance to the terror of His Majesty's subjects."

This trial, too, bore all the hallmarks of class justice. Writing in the *Sunday Worker*, Ben Griffiths, General Secretary of the Mining Clerks' Guild, commented on the Carmarthen jury:[3]

"The grand jury is composed of the aristocratic big guns of the county—mainly of the landed proprietor class—and has Colonel

---

[1] Ibid., p. 24.
[2] For account of the trial see *Sunday Worker* of December 6, 13 and 20, 1925. See also reference in *E.C. Report* of First National Conference of International Class War Prisoner's Aid (I.C.W.P.A., British Section), held at Nine Elms Baths, Battersea, December 12, 1926, and George Lansbury's "The I.C.W.P.A. at Work", a speech to the I.C.W.P.A. International Executive in Moscow, July 29, 1926.
[3] *Sunday Worker*, December 6, 1925, p. 1.

F. Dudley Williams-Drummond, C.B.E., estate agent to Lord Caudor, as its foreman.

"There are also two colonels—three majors, a captain, a knight, a parson and an agent for a local lady with big income from royalties. These are to try trade union fighters."

Of the 167 tried at the Carmarthen Assizes over a three weeks' period at the end of November and the first half of December, 50 were sentenced to terms of imprisonment ranging from 14 days to 12 months. One of the prisoners, Evan Llewellyn, got a total of 17 months on different counts.

To many of the public it seemed clear that the trial of the Welsh anthracite miners was part of the same political offensive as the trial of the Communist leaders, and this was reflected in the fact that in many areas the campaign of solidarity was carried out at the same time for Communists and miners together.

The Government's attack on the 12 Communist leaders aimed to behead the movement, to remove from action the most militant leaders of the workers before the coming show-down, to separate the militants from the masses. The right-wing Labour anti-Communist attack at Liverpool had, roughly, the same objective.

SOLIDARITY WITH THE TWELVE

In fact the instant show of solidarity from almost all sections of the Labour Movement for the arrested Communists showed that, to some extent, the attack had the opposite effect of what had been intended.

This immediate and generous solidarity coming from many people who were far from Communists and had, often enough, crossed swords with the Communists, was shown already on the question of bail. George Lansbury immediately, on the first news of the arrests, offered to help with bail. The list of those who finally went bail at the preliminary Old Bailey hearings is revealing.[1] It includes H. N. Brailsford, Editor of *The New Leader* (MacManus), Richard Coppock, Secretary of the National Federation of Building Trades Operatives (Rust), A. J. Cook, Secretary of the Miners (Tom Bell), George Hicks, Secretary of the Amalgamated Union of Building Trade Workers (Murphy and Pollitt), Susan Lawrence of the L.C.C. and the Women's Section of the

---

[1] *Workers' Weekly*, Nos. 142 and 145 of October 23 and November 13, 1925; *Sunday Worker*, November 8, 1925; also various papers of the trial.

Municipal and General Workers (E. W. Cant), John Scurr, M.A. of the Poplar Board of Guardians and Editor of the *Socialist Review* (Wintringham), Bernard Shaw (Gallacher), Miss Madeleine Symons, Women's Section of the Municipal and General Workers (Arnot), the Dowager Countess of Warwick (Albert Inkpin), and Colonel Josiah Wedgewood, M.P., former member of the Labour Government (Campbell and Hannington). Amongst other volunteers for going bail were the Earl de la Warr, Lord Arnold, John Wheatley, M.P., C. P. Trevelyan, M.P., George Lansbury, Professor H. B. Lees Smith, M.P. of the Union of Democratic Control, Robert Williams and Ben Tillett.

Sir Charles Biron, the Bow Street magistrate, admitted bail in £100 per prisoner. "Are you worth £100?" he asked Bernard Shaw. "Well," replied Shaw, "I do have that much money."

The list of those standing surety at the main Old Bailey trial was equally representative.[1]

Naturally the Communist Party devoted all possible energy to the defence of and solidarity with its arrested leaders, but very quickly a whole organisation of solidarity began to grow up with extremely representative support inside the Labour Movement. The main organisation in the campaign was the International Class War Prisoner's Aid (British Section), or as it was usually known, the I.C.W.P.A.

The I.C.W.P.A. (British Section) first came into existence at the end of 1924, devoting its energies at first to help for the victims of oppression, fascism, white terror in such countries as Poland, Bulgaria and Italy, and in the colonial countries of the British Empire like Ireland, India and Egypt. The original secretary was Wal Hannington.[2]

Prior to its formation there was no national organisation in Britain whose regular activity and responsibility was solidarity with persecuted members of the international working class and national liberation movement, and with their families and dependants.

When the arrest and trial of the Communist leaders and of the

---

[1] See *Sunday Worker*, November 18, 1925. There attended to stand surety: Earl de la Warr, Lord Arnold, Miss Susan Lawrence, Miss Madeleine Symons, John Wheatley, M.P., C. P. Trevelyan, M.P., George Lansbury, M.P., Professor H. B. Lees Smith, M.P., John Scurr, M.P., Colonel Wedgewood, M.P., Robert Williams, Chairman of the Labour Party, George Hicks, Ben Tillett, A. J. Cook and Richard Coppock.

[2] The most detailed information on the origins of the I.C.W.P.A. (British Section) is in the *E.C. Report to the First National Congress*, held at Battersea, December 12, 1926, under the chairmanship of William Lawther of the Durham Miners (15 pp.), and in *The I.C.W.P.A., a Speech Delivered in Moscow* by George Lansbury, I.C.W.P.A., November 1926, 28 pp., 2d. Much information on its early activities are in *Workers' Weekly*, *Sunday Worker*, *Lansbury's Labour Weekly*.

anthracite miners came at the end of 1925, the I.C.W.P.A. immediately began a campaign of solidarity, formed a "Free Speech and Maintenance Fund", of which the aim, at first, was to collect money for the legal defence of the prisoners and later to support their dependants. The general, more political, campaign proceeded under the I.C.W.P.A. (British Section) directly.

The Free Speech and Maintenance Fund was extremely representative, with John Bromley in the Chair, George Lansbury, Treasurer, H. B. Lovell, Secretary, and a Committee including A. A. Purcell, A. J. Cook, George Hicks and the Rev. H. Dunnico.[1]

Over £3,000 was collected very rapidly, most of which was expended on legal costs and maintenance allowances for the prisoners' dependants. The Miners' Federation accepted responsibility for costs and maintenance in connection with the anthracite miners, but a token sum of £100 was given by the Committee towards this support. Protagonists of the "Moscow Gold" approach would do well to study the many unions, Labour Party and I.L.P. Branches that sent in subscriptions.[2]

As soon as the verdict of the trial of the Communists was announced, protests came flooding in. Within a couple of days the Executive of the Miners, the London Trades Council, 70 or so Labour M.P.s were demanding the prisoners' instant release. In January 1926, a National Petition campaign was promoted by the I.C.W.P.A. and by the end of February 300,000 signatures had been collected and the Petition presented by S. Saklatvala, M.P. to Parliament on February 24. In the same month a printed Bulletin, *The Prisoner*, was published and widely circulated. The Communist Party, meanwhile, had printed and widely distributed the three defence speeches of Pollitt, Gallacher and Campbell.

Conferences of solidarity with the Communists and anthracite miners were organised up and down the country[3]—Plymouth, Barrow, Sheffield, Manchester, East London, Liverpool, Coventry, Cardiff, etc. The character of the meetings, rallies, demonstrations became more and more representative and militant.

---

[1] A General Committee of around 60 contained many of the leading names of the Labour Party, T.U.C., I.L.P. and Communist Party, including H. N. Brailsford, W. N. Ewer of the *Daily Herald*, Neil Maclean, M.P., Tom Mann, James Maxton, Rev. Conrad Noel, R. W. Postgate, G. D. H. Cole, R. H. Tawney, Ben Tillett and Ellen Wilkinson.
[2] Some funds were collected *directly* by the Communist Party. For instance at February 5, 1926, the figures were £2,348 collected by the I.C.W.P.A. and £493 by the C.P.G.B.
[3] See *E.C. Report to First National Congress of I.C.W.P.A.*, pp. 8–10.

On December 12, 1925, over 600 delegates (representing around 800,000 workers) met under I.C.W.P.A. auspices at Essex Hall, in the Strand, London, with A. J. Cook in the Chair. Speakers included George Lansbury, Colonel Wedgewood, Helen Crawfurd, and Marjorie Pollitt, Harry Pollitt's wife, already at that time a moving speaker.

February 7, 1926, became the "Release the Prisoners Day" with meetings in support of the imprisoned Communists and miners in many parts of Britain (Sheffield, Burnley, Edinburgh, etc.). In London 15,000 assembled on Clapham Common and marched to Wandsworth Gaol where the Communist leaders were imprisoned. Marches to the gaol were held almost weekly.

On March 7, 1926, the I.C.W.P.A. organised a huge solidarity rally in London's Albert Hall, hired in the personal name of Lansbury as it could not be got hold of in the name of the I.C.W.P.A. This, George Lansbury declared later,

> "was one of the biggest meetings ever held in London. It was at that meeting that I got the whole audience to stand and repeat after me the slogans for which the Communists were sent to prison. To call upon the workers not to go into the capitalist army or navy or air force, for no worker to join the military, and for those who were in the military or navy not to fire on their comrades who are workers".[1]

A. A. Purcell, seconded by George Hicks, proposed the resolution demanding the release of the Twelve and of the Ammanford miners.

A week later, an enormous demonstration marched again from Clapham Common to Wandsworth Prison, the crowd chanting, cheering and singing loud enough to be heard by those still within the walls.[2] Contingents assembled from Battersea, Bethnal Green, Deptford, Erith, Finsbury, Greenwich, Holborn, Poplar, St. Pancras, Stepney, Streatham, etc. Communist and Labour women had organised a "Don't Shoot" tableau and the demonstrators again solemnly repeated the call to the men in the forces made by George Lansbury the previous Sunday:

> "We call upon all soldiers, sailors and airmen to refuse under any circumstances to shoot down the workers of Britain, and we call

[1] George Lansbury, *The I.C.W.P.A.*, p. 11.
[2] Ibid., p. 13, and *Workers' Weekly*, No. 163, March 19, 1926.

upon working-class men to refuse to join the capitalist army. We further call upon the police to refuse to use their batons on strikers or locked-out workers during industrial disputes."[1]

On April 10, when seven of the twelve were due for release, a still bigger demonstration ("the most tremendous demonstration ever held in any district, the largest district demonstration ever held in London", declared Lansbury)[2] assembled on Clapham Common and marched to Wandsworth Prison to welcome the seven and demand the release of the remaining five. Lansbury and J. R. Campbell, now released, shouted messages through megaphones to those inside. Twenty thousand rallied outside the gaol.[3] There were Labour Party, I.L.P., trade union, C.P.G.B. orators; four of the many platforms on the Common were organised (one each) by the *New Leader*, Lansbury's *Weekly Journal*, the *Sunday Worker* and the *Weekly Worker*.

The campaign of solidarity with the arrested Communist leaders was a genuinely broad movement involving leaders and rank and file workers far from a Communist outlook, and quite a sector of liberal opinion outside the Labour Movement. A resolution demanding the release of the prisoners was adopted at a joint meeting of the General Council of the T.U.C. and the National Executive of the Labour Party at the end of November. More than 100 Labour M.P.s signed a letter calling for the release of the prisoners. At the end of November and the beginning of December the *Daily Herald* printed protests at the trial and the verdict from Walter Citrine, the Acting Secretary of the T.U.C., W. Elger, Secretary of the Scottish T.U.C., Robert Williams, Chairman of the Labour Party, Philip Snowden, M.P., and J. R. Clynes, M.P., as well as many others whose names I have already cited in connection with the solidarity campaign. In the House of Commons even Ramsay MacDonald was pressed into moving a resolution condemning the trial, that was lost by 351 to 127. A really large number of local trade union, Labour Party, I.L.P. and Unemployed Committees adopted some or other type of protest resolution with, as is not surprising, the organisations of the miners, engineers and railwaymen amongst the foremost.

By and large, the trade union leaders who protested at the trial, and in one way or another showed their solidarity, understood that an attack on the Communists was only the herald of an attack on the

[1] *Workers' Weekly*, No. 163, March 19, 1926.   [2] Op. cit., p. 13.
[3] *Workers' Weekly*, No. 167, April 16, 1926.

unions. "The Communist Party," wrote George Hicks, President of the National Union of Building Trades Operatives, "is now in the same position as the trade unions were during the early part of last century."[1] A. J. Cook, just before the arrests, in a message to the *Sunday Worker*, issued yet one more warning to the right wing in the Labour Movement:

> "I warn the right-wing leaders in our movement to cease their attacks upon the left wing. They are encouraging every element of reaction in this country to destroy our militant fighters. If these are beaten, the path lies open for the propertied interests to smash those who call themselves moderate."[2]

Some of the right wing were pushed by the pressure of the movement officially to register a protest at the trial, despite the fact that it was they who had made it inevitable. They were embarrassed by the strength of solidarity let loose by the arrests. MacDonald publicly called it a "disservice" to prosecute the Communist Party at this time and in this way, and said that its "potentialities for sedition" had only been increased. J. R. Clynes complained that the Communist leaders were being "lift(ed) to the level of martyrs".[3]

SIGNIFICANCE OF THE TRIAL

The position was, in fact, abundantly clear. The Brighton Tory Party Conference had given the go-ahead for attacks not only on the Communists but on militant trade unionists. It even threatened the right to strike.[4] The Communist Party was first under attack because it was regarded as the most dangerous and the most consistent enemy of capitalism, which should be knocked out before the general offensive. This was the understanding of the Communist Party itself at the time:

> "From the very outset the Central Committee treated the prosecutions not simply as an attack on our Party, but as an attempt to put out of action the most clear-sighted and resolute section of the working-class in preparation for the resumption of the capitalist offensive in May."[5]

[1] *Sunday Worker*, November 29, 1925, p. 5.   [2] Ibid., October 18, 1925.
[3] Speech at Twickenham, reported in *Daily Herald*, October 17, 1925.
[4] See statement of Colonel F. S. Jackson, Chairman of the Conservative Party, after the Brighton Conference (*The Times*, October 15, 1925).
[5] "Political Report of Central Committee to the 8th Congress" in *Reports, Theses and Resolutions of the 8th Congress of the C.P.G.B.*, p. 2.

That the Communist Party was attacked as the most consistent opponent of capitalism was appreciated by many militants in the Labour Movement. It was, in fact, from the time of the trial that the membership of the Party, which had risen from around 2,000 in the summer of 1922 to around 5,000 in October 1925, began to grow.[1] The Government's acceptance of the Communist Party as its foremost obstacle was no mean compliment.

CHAPTER I—APPENDIX I

INSTRUCTIONS FOR EMBARGO ON COAL MOVEMENTS, ISSUED ON THE EVENING OF JULY 30, 1925

Official Instructions to all Railway and Transport Workers, as agreed unanimously by a Joint Conference of the National Union of Railwaymen, Associated Society of Locomotive Engineers and Firemen, Railway Clerks' Association, and the Transport and General Workers Union Executive, and approved by the General Council of the Trades Union Congress.

RAILWAYS

1. Wagons containing coal must not be attached to any train after midnight on Friday, July 31st, and after this time wagons of coal must not be supplied to any industrial or commercial concerns, or be put on the tip roads at docks for the coaling of ship.
2. All coal en route at midnight on Friday to be worked forward to the next siding suitable for storing it.
3. Any coal, either in wagon or stock at a depot, may be utilised at that depot for the purpose of coaling engines for passenger and goods trains, but must not be moved from that depot to another.

DOCKS, WHARVES, ETC.

Coal Exports—All Tippers and Trimmers will cease work at the end of the second shift on July 31st.

Coal Imports—On no account may import coal be handled from July 31st.

General—A general stoppage of men handling coal on other classes of tonnage on Friday midnight.

---

[1] *Reports, Theses and Resolutions of the 8th Congress of the C.P.G.B.*, p. 2.

WATERWAYS AND LOCKS

All men on canals, waterways, etc., engaged in carrying coal will cease Friday midnight, with the exception of men who have coal en route, who will be allowed to take it to destination and tie up. Safety men for pumping, etc., will be permitted to work for safety purposes only.

ROAD TRANSPORT

All men engaged in delivering coal to commercial and industrial concerns will cease Friday night, July 31st. Men delivering for domestic purposes will cease at 12 noon, Saturday, August 1st.

LOCAL COMMITTEES

For the purpose of carrying out these instructions the members of the organisation herein concerned shall, from each district, establish small sub-committees so as to co-ordinate policy in giving effect to same.

George Hicks (*Chairman, Transport Sub-Committee*)

Associated Society of Locomotive Engineers and Firemen:
  B. M. Jenkins   D. S. Humphreys (President)
  O. W. Skinner   John Bromley (General Secretary)
National Union of Railwaymen:
  F. Fowler   J. H. Thomas (General Secretary)
  Arthur Law   C. T. Cramp (Industrial General Secretary)
  W. Dobbie (President) J. Marchbank (Assistant Secretary)
Railway Clerks' Association:
  George Lathan   T. Gill (President)
                      A. G. Walkden (General Secretary)
Transport and General Workers Union:
  Harry Gosling (President)   Ernest Bevin (General Secretary)
General Council Special Committee:
  A. B. Swales   G. Hicks   B. Tillett
  J. Bromley   J. Marchbank   A. G. Walkden
  A. Hayday   E. L. Poulton   W. M. Citrine (Assistant Secretary)

CHAPTER I—APPENDIX II

COMMUNISTS AND THE LABOUR PARTY

(Statement by the Executive Committee of the C.P.G.B. published in *Workers' Weekly*, October 9, 1925)

The Labour Party Conference was not a defeat for the Communists: it was a blow for the working class. The purely Liberal resolutions adopted, the repudiation of the fight against Imperialism and the Dawes Plan, which are degrading our fellow workers abroad, and thereby striking at British conditions, the failure to face the capitalist attack on wages and hours, were intended to please the capitalists. The T.U.C. has frightened them; the decisions at Liverpool have reassured them.

The T.U.C. issued a magnificent call for unity against the bosses—in the factories, between the unions, internationally. The Labour Party Conference, by repudiating unity and rejecting resolutions based on the class struggle, extended an open invitation to the bosses to attack the workers. That is why the capitalist press is so delighted with the results and is already demanding that the attacks should start by an onslaught on the Communist Party.

The Communist Party was not defeated at Liverpool. In every large trade union delegation, in the I.L.P. delegation itself, there were large minorities on the question of Communist membership of the Labour Party—minorities who felt that the workers want unity, not disruption, and who knew that the workers will continue to send their best fighters, the Communists, as their representatives into the Labour Party, despite the middle-class leaders.

The Communist Party is not daunted by Liverpool. We are not afraid of being a minority for the time being. We know that Liberal resolutions cannot prevent the capitalists from mobilising and oppressing the workers. We know that they cannot hide from the workers the hard facts of the class struggle. We know that the time must come when the workers will discover who it is who really protects their women and children against starvation and murder—those who fight against the capitalists by Liberal resolutions and after-dinner speeches, or those who say there can be no truce, no peace, no friendship with the enemies of our class.

We are not afraid that the press campaign about Communists preaching violence will prevent the workers from realising that it is the capitalists who are preparing to use violence to crush labour. We know that events themselves will win from our Party the support of the overwhelming majority of the working class.

Therefore the Communist Party will go on fighting and growing, unmoved by sham majorities or misrepresentations.

To the workers of Britain we say:

Fellow workers! Don't be lulled into false confidence by pious resolutions. Follow the lead of your T.U.C. The bankers and employers are organising a mass attack on your wage conditions, bigger than their attack of July 31st. Prepare to meet it by closing your ranks.

Form Factory Committees to secure unity at the bottom! Send delegates from the factories to the Trades Councils, and thus consolidate your forces locally! Insist on the formation of the Workers' Alliance under the supreme authority of the General Council! Meet the threat of organised strike-breaking and capitalist violence by insisting on the right to tell your brothers in the Army and Navy that they must not scab on the workers, and by forming your own Defence Corps against the O.M.S. and the Fascisti!

To all active men and women in the Labour movement who want to fight capitalism we say:

Comrades! The Labour Party Conference has shown you how useless it is to rely on those who only utter left-wing phrases and will not organise an opposition to the present Liberal leadership of the Labour Party. If you are sincere in your hatred of capitalism, and your scorn for its agents and puppets in Labour's ranks, you must translate your anger into organised opposition. Otherwise your indignation is a sham and a make-believe, and all your speeches are froth.

Organise yourselves! Make up your minds that the shame of Liverpool shall not be repeated! For our part, we Communists, without forcing our opinions on you, will be willing to fight side by side with you. But no workers will believe that you intend to fight unless you organise.

To our own Party we say:

We shall fight on, comrades! In spite of the capitalists and their friends, the workers are with us. For a time the workers' opinions can still be twisted by propaganda, talked into inaction, bewildered, bullied and misrepresented, but the capitalists themselves are slowly but surely working for us.

Stage-managed Conferences and smooth tongued Liberals cannot prevent our class from learning, step by step, and out of its bitter experience, that our party is its only real champion. We shall continue to struggle against the attempt to isolate us from the working class movement, and in that struggle we will be victorious.

Therefore, strengthen the Party! Continue recruiting! Continue the day to day work in the trade unions, proving to the worker by practical example that our party nuclei are in the vanguard of every struggle against the boss! Resist exclusion from the local Labour Parties! Extend Party influence in all working-class organisations! Build a mass Communist Party!

(Signed)

R. Page Arnot	A. Horner	Beth Turner
T. Bell	W. Joss	N. Watkins
E. H. Brown	A. Inkpin (Sec.)	S. Saklatvala, M.P.
J. R. Campbell	T. A. Jackson	T. Quelch
Helen Crawfurd	A. McManus	G. Hardy
R. Palme Dutt	J. T. Murphy	W. Rust
A. Ferguson	H. Pollitt	E. Woolley
W. Gallacher	C. M. Roebuck[1]	J. R. Wilson
W. Hannington	R. Stewart	

The C.E.C. of the C.P.G.B.

[1] Andrew Rothstein.

CHAPTER II

THE PARTY AND THE GENERAL STRIKE

Preparedness and Unpreparedness—Industrial Alliance—Communist Party Warns—The Royal Commission Reports—N.M.M. Conference of Action—April Deadlock—The Executives Meet—At the Last Minute—The Strike is Solid—The Capitalists and their State—The General Council Prepares to Sell Out—General Council Completes the Sell-out—Revenge is Sweet—Communists and Militants—The Party Line—Three Bulletins, Three Policies—Councils of Action—The Communist Party in the Areas—Elements of Dual Power—Main Targets of Arrest—Y.C.L. and N.M.M.—Lessons of the General Strike—The Nature of the State—Imperialism's Two-fold Strategy—The Nature of Reformism—"Calculated" Unpreparedness—Unwillingly to Strike—Reformist Approaches—Built-in Betrayal—The Mood of the Masses—The Need for a Communist Party—Defeat or Victory?

PREPAREDNESS AND UNPREPAREDNESS

Despite O.M.S. and the arrests of Communists and militant trade unionists, despite the warnings of the Scarborough Congress, in the last months of 1925 and the first months of 1926 preparations for struggle on the part of the General Council of the T.U.C. were conspicuous by their absence.

Instead of preparedness there was more and more public and private reliance on the activities of the Royal Commission on the Coal Industry. The mineowners and the Tory Government, with all its paraphernalia of state, prepared for a decisive struggle. The General Council replied "wait for", "trust in", the Commission Report.

The official Labour leadership made "platonic pledges"[1] of solidarity with the miners, but put all their hopes in a peaceful settlement. MacDonald celebrated Christmas 1925 with a manifesto for "Industrial Peace" printed in Rothermere's *Answers*.

The Miners' Federation stood firm, but its attempt to win the

[1] See R. Palme Dutt, *The Meaning of the General Strike*, C.P.G.B., 1926, p. 11.

backing of the whole official trade union movement met with mixed results.

One of its lines of action, vigorously supported by the Communist Party and the Minority Movement, was work for the formation of an Industrial Alliance.

INDUSTRIAL ALLIANCE

The proposal for an Industrial Alliance had come from the Engineers at their National Committee meeting of May 1924.[1] The idea was actively taken up by the Miners only in mid-1925, at a preliminary meeting which took place in June of that year.

The Miners envisaged a powerful alliance of heavy industry unions, a fighting body, the General Conference of which was seen as a sort of Supreme War Council of the Unions, more militant, more reliable and more mobile than the General Council of the T.U.C.

By the end of September membership included, amongst others, alongside Engineers and Miners, the National Union of Foundry Workers, the Associated Society of Locomotive Engineers and Firemen, and the Electrical Trades Union. Early in November a delegate conference of all the unions concerned met in London and accepted a draft constitution (subject to ballot of members in a number of unions).

But at this same meeting J. H. Thomas for the National Union of Railwaymen proposed as an amendment to the constitution, that a condition of membership of the Alliance should be the preparation of a scheme of fusion for unions catering for the same industry. This, progressive on the surface, was in fact aimed at the A.S.L.E.F., and in essence a blow struck by Thomas and the right wing of the Labour Party and T.U.C. against an alliance which they feared and were determined to destroy.

Though the Alliance eventually and formally included the Transport workers, Locomotive Men, Foundry Workers, Steel Trades, Electricians, Engineers, Workers' Union and Miners, the withdrawal of the N.U.R. and the organising by slow process of balloting, meant that it was in fact still-born—an "addled egg", wrote one historian of the Labour Movement.[2]

[1] For origin of the Industrial Alliance and its constitution, see R. Page Arnot, *The General Strike—May 1926—the Origin and History*, Labour Research Department, 1926, pp. 80–86.

[2] R. Page Arnot, *The Miners—Years of Struggle*, p. 401.

Certainly by May 1926 the Alliance was in no way the strong combative leadership for which the miners had hoped, nor was it in any way an alternative to the General Council of the T.U.C., on which, alas, the miners were dependent.[1]

In January 1926 the General Council met the Miners. Already at this meeting the General Council was working to restrain the Miners' Federation, to preach them patience and faith in the Royal Commission. In the words of Pugh, the General Council's Chairman:

"No special significance need be attached to the Conference. No steps of any kind could be taken until the Report of the Royal Commission had been issued."[2]

At the end of January the General Council appointed its special Industrial Committee to maintain contact with the Miners, a Committee heavily weighted with right wingers,[3] and equally, as *The Times* was not slow to observe, skilled in "unpreparing":

"The Committee can hardly be said at present to have formulated any policy, but it is going on the assumption that the subsidy cannot be suddenly stopped in May."[4]

"Be unprepared" was the pattern from right wing to centre. In February, the Co-operative Wholesale directors officially disclaimed any intention to help the workers in the pending struggles, even to grant them credits.

COMMUNIST PARTY WARNS

Indeed, apart from the miners, and a few militant trade unionists and Labour Party members, the main work of warning, preparing and mobilising for the coming struggle was carried out by the Communist Party and the National Minority Movement.

[1] "Addled egg" though it became, the formation of the Alliance and the Constitution that it adopted reflected very much the mood and desires of the workers. Its aim, the Constitution stated, was:

"to create by means of an alliance of the specified organisation, a means of mutual support, to assist any or all of the allied organisations in defending the hours of labour and wage standards, and securing advancement of the standard of living, or to take action to secure acceptance of, or to defend, any principle of an industrial character which may be deemed vital by the allied organisations."

[2] *Daily Herald*, January 20, 1926.
[3] Thomas, Pugh, Walkden, Citrine, Walker, Hayday, Bromley, Hicks, Tillett.
[4] *The Times*, January 30, 1926.

The arrest of its leaders and the campaign for their release had not weakened the effort of the Party to act as a vanguard in the sense of explaining the coming struggle, and indicating the best way to prepare for it. When the "twelve" were let out on bail, they together with all other members of the Executive Committee played a full part in selecting the acting Political Bureau in the case of their likely enforced absence. And without interruption work continued. In the last months of 1925 hundreds of meetings, rallies, demonstrations were held, particularly in the industrial areas, calling for solidarity with the miners, warning in advance that the Commission's Report would inevitably be a weapon for the mineowners, and urging preparation, organisation of every sort for the inevitable clash in May.

It is indicative, for instance, to compare the front page and leaders of the Communist *Workers' Weekly* at the beginning of 1926 with the *Daily Herald* and other sections of the Labour press.

On January 1, 1926, the main headline on page one of the *Workers' Weekly* was "1926—Great Clash Coming".[1] The article below warned:

> "In May—perhaps sooner—the miners will be called up to defend their hours and wages, and to fight against the system of district agreements, that the Coal Commission will try to impose upon them."

The next issue,[2] under the headline "Don't Wait—Get Busy", printed militant appeals for preparation and action from Richard Coppock, Secretary of the National Federation of Building Trades Operatives, and A. J. Cook, the Secretary of the Miners (who, incidentally, observed that forecasts of the Commission's Report reported in the capitalist press were "a complete justification of the Communist Party's warning that the mineowners mean war").

In big, bold letters the paper put forward the Party's own proposals, in slogan form, for measures of *real precaution* for the struggles ahead:

> "Fight all wage cuts—perfect workers' solidarity—meet attack with attack."

> "Set up Committees in every factory as was decided at Scarborough."

> "Get the General Council to call an All-Executive Conference to prepare plans."

---
[1] *Workers' Weekly*, No. 152, January 1, 1926, p. 1.
[2] Ibid., No. 153, January 8, 1926, p. 1.

"Set up Workers Defence Corps. Release the prisoners."

"Not a penny off the pay: Not a minute on the day."

"All power to the General Council."

The acting leadership of the Party, with Bob Stewart as the Acting General Secretary, called for January 9–10 in London a special meeting of the Executive Committee extended by the invitation of some thirty Party Organisers from the Districts, members from key industries concerned in the coming crisis, members prominent in the trade unions and other Labour organisations.[1]

The sessions were chaired in turn by T. A. Jackson, E. H. Brown and Bob Stewart. Stewart reported on the home and international political situation, Arthur Horner from the South Wales District of the Party and a leading though still young militant of the Welsh miners, opened the second session with a report on preparations for the coming capitalist offensive, R. W. Robson moved a resolution on the organisation of Left Wing Groups,[2] and George Hardy, now, with Wal Hannington in prison, Acting Secretary of the Minority Movement, moved a resolution on international trade union unity.

Following Horner's report a resolution taking the form of a Programme of Action to meet the capitalist offensive was adopted by the meeting.[3]

It warned that the subsidy and the Commission were nothing but a "breathing space", that the capitalists were making open preparations to reverse the victory of Red Friday, were preparing an all-out offensive on the living conditions and the political organisation of the working class.

The need was, the resolution explained, not only working-class unity to *defend* working-class conditions and organisation, but to turn the defensive into offensive struggles against capitalism.

The Party put forward eight main measures needed for the workers to prepare, meet and defeat the coming offensive:

1. That the General Council of the T.U.C., in accordance with Scarborough decisions, should call a Conference of trade union executives, to give wider powers to the General Council to lead the *whole* trade union movement.

[1] See *Workers' Weekly*, No. 154, January 15, 1926, and also "Political Report of Central Committee to 8th Congress of C.P.G.B." in *Reports, Theses, Resolutions of Eighth Congress*.
[2] See page 259.
[3] Full text in Appendix I to this chapter.

2. Completion of the formation of the Industrial Alliance.
3. Working Agreement between the General Council and the Co-operative Wholesale Society (C.W.S.) to ensure the provisioning of the workers during the struggles.
4. Formation of Factory Committees elected by the workers irrespective of craft or sex.
5. Campaign for 100 per cent trade unionism with special attention to recruitment of young workers.
6. Organisation of Workers' Defence Corps, composed of trade unionists and controlled by Trades Councils, to protect working-class meetings from fascists and reactionaries, and effort by the General Council to put the workers' case before the workers in the Army, Navy and Air Forces.
7. Formulation of a Common Programme for the whole Labour Movement (£4 a week for a 44-hour week) supplementary to the special demands of each industry.
8. Strengthening of relations between the General Council and the National Unemployed Workers Committee Movement (N.U.W.C.M.) in order to counter capitalist attempts to use the unemployed as blacklegs.

The Party Executives put these resolutions before a whole series of District Conferences of the Party and Extended District Committees, and the membership did its best to take this line of "preparedness", along with the specific proposals for "preparation", to the different organisations of which they were members and to campaign for them in the Party press and at public meetings.

The fifth Conference of the National Unemployed Workers Committee Movement was held at Stoke-on-Trent at the end of January[1] and endeavoured to prepare the unemployed for the May conflict.

This utter contrast between preparedness and unpreparedness, between the attitude of A. J. Cook and of J. H. Thomas, or between the leadership of the Communist Party and the Labour Party leaders like MacDonald, became even clearer with the publication of the long-heralded Royal Commission Report.

[1] *Report of Fifth National Conference of N.U.W.C.M.*, January 23–25, 1926 (36 pp. 2d.): 93 delegates were present representing 44 committees and 8 District Councils. With Wal Hannington, the National Organiser, in gaol, the main Report was given by Jack Holt, the Secretary.

THE ROYAL COMMISSION REPORTS

July had ended with Red Friday. On September 5, 1925 a Royal Warrant established a Commission on the Coal Industry:

> "to enquire into and report upon the economic position of the coal industry and the conditions affecting it and to make any recommendations for the improvement thereof."

The coalowners and the British capitalists generally were determined on a showdown. Wages must come down, subsidies must be ended, "Red Fridays" made impossible. This was clear.

But British capitalism, as we have seen so often, and shall so often see again, was very experienced, crafty, cunning, twisty, manœuvring, elastic. To prepare the showdown for May 1926 they required not only O.M.S., Emergency Decrees, troops and other state machinery. They needed so far as possible to divide their enemy, the working class and its various organisations, to win over some elements, neutralise others, to isolate the militants which meant, in 1926 terms, above all the miners, Minority Movement and Communist Party. Dividing the workers was not just a crude process of buying over and suitably rewarding some specific "agents", but something much subtler.

British capitalism and imperialism has always alternated the bludgeon and the bribe, ruthless attack and "gentle" corruption, lock-out and arbitration. Most workers influenced by capitalism are blissfully ignorant of the whole process.

The companion of O.M.S., "Fascisti", arrest, was the "sweetly reasonable", "gentlemanly", typically British, Royal Commission on the coal industry. Its aim was to divide the workers, to provide the right-wing Labour leaders with a platform for deserting the miners. Nor was it unsuccessful.

It was announced as neutral, impartial, commissioned by His (neutral) Majesty to make an objective investigation. Unlike the Sankey Commission of 1919, the Buckmaster Court of Enquiry of 1924 or the MacMillan Court of Enquiry of 1925, it contained *no representative of the miners* nor of any other working-class organisation.

Its Chairman was Sir Herbert Samuel (it rapidly became known as the Samuel Commission), a senior Liberal politician with family financial connections, often in Liberal governments serving as both Under-Secretary and Secretary of State for Home Affairs. After 1919 he was British High Commissioner in Palestine.

The three Commissioners who served with Sir Herbert were General Sir Herbert Lawrence, managing partner of Glyn, Mills and Co. banking house, and sitting on the Boards of a number of other important companies, Mr. Kenneth Lee, Chairman of Tootal, Broadhurst, Lee & Co. (a large cotton firm) and also of the District Bank, and Sir William Beveridge, a former leader writer on the *Morning Post* (1906–8), then a leading member of the Board of Trade, who served in the Ministry of Munitions in World War I and, later, resigned from the civil service to take up the Directorship of the London School of Economics.

Sir William was a man who would always do his best to carry out a job of work as efficiently and as honestly as he was able, but though he had plenty of experience in studying affairs of trade, he had no progressive understanding of the class structure and class struggle of the mining industry, and, in the context of this particular Commission, his very sincerity afforded a convenient liberal cover for a body which represented the interests of capitalism.

The Commission took evidence in public from October 15, 1925 to January 14, 1926, held 35 public sittings, heard 76 witnesses; and on March 6, 1926, the Report (300 pages supported by three volumes of evidence) was completed and quickly published.[1]

The essence of the findings, all trappings shorn, was that the mining industry should be reorganised under private ownership at some indefinite *future* date, whilst wages should be reduced *now*.

The proposals for the future were a motley mish-mash combining real measures to make the industry more profitable with vague proposals calculated to conciliate the miners. They included the amalgamation of a number of existing mines where units were considered too small, establishment of co-operative selling agencies especially for exports, retail sale of coal by local authorities, improved research and distribution, better relations of employers and employees through joint Pithead Committees, family allowances, profit-sharing, improved housing, more baths, and annual holidays with pay "when prosperity returns".

Nationalisation was rejected, replaced by the proposal for the nationalisation of Coal Royalties (simply a repetition of the Sankey

---

[1] *Royal Commission on the Coal Industry (1925)* Cmd. 2600, H.M.S.O., 1926. Following are recommended for their summaries and analysis of the Report: *The Coal Crisis: Facts from the Samuel Commission, 1925–1926*, Labour Research Department, 1926 (Foreword by Herbert Smith); R. Page Arnot, *The General Strike—May 1926—the Origin and History*, pp. 87–101; R. Page Arnot, *The Miners—Years of Struggle*, pp. 401–405; Wilfred Harris Crook, *The General Strike*, pp. 315–324, University of North Carolina Press, 1931.

Commission recommendation which had been blissfully ignored). Reorganisation was to take place within *private* enterprise.

Proposals for the present were as emphatic as those for the future were vague. To continue the July subsidies was "indefensible". "The subsidy," stated the Report, "should stop at the end of its authorised term and should never be repeated."

Whatever reorganisation might achieve in the unspecified future, the Report insisted that *for the present* the *miners not the mineowners* should provide the solution. Wages *must* come down, or, in the language of the Commission, "revision of the 'minimum percentage addition to standard rate of wages' is indispensable. A disaster is impending over the industry, and the immediate reduction in working costs that can be effected in this way, and in this way alone, is essential to save it."[1]

This was the Report that was greeted as a victory by the right-wing leaders of the Labour Party and the T.U.C. and used by them to try to divert the miners from the struggle. On March 19 Ramsay MacDonald wrote of the Report in *Forward*:

"It is a conspicuous landmark in the history of political thought and is indeed one of the strongest indictments of private enterprise that has ever been issued as an official paper. The stars in their courses are fighting for us. The miners' leaders have very wisely advised that tongues should be silent for the time being."

A week before, Mr. Cramp, Chairman of the Labour Party and Secretary of the National Union of Railwaymen, had proclaimed that "national problems have to be faced more in the spirit of national efficiency".[2]

The only organisations to expose the Commission Report for what it was and to appeal for its complete rejection were the Communist Party, the Minority Movement and the miners themselves.

Already in January the Communists in the Miners' Minority Movement had put forward a programme for the reorganisation of the industry which stressed the need for nationalisation without compensation and with workers control, and criticised some aspects of the policy put forward by the Miners' Federation to the Commission, proposals which they regarded as too moderate.[3]

[1] *Royal Commission on the Coal Industry*, p. 236.
[2] Quoted by Arthur Horner in *Incorrigible Rebel*, p. 74, McGibbon and Kee, 1960.
[3] See "Political Report of the central committee to 8th Congress of C.P.G.B." in *Reports, Theses and Resolutions of Eighth Congress*, pp. 3–4.

When the *Workers' Weekly* went to press for publication on March 12, the text of the Commission Report was not yet available, so it was in the following issue that the statement of the Party on the Samuel Commission was made public.[1]

The Commission Report, the Party declared, was "a declaration of war against the miners and the whole working-class movement". Its cardinal point was *reduction of wages* and, as the Party had always warned, its method the division of the working class. Two dangers now faced the workers, the statement continued. The first was the *direct offensive* of the mineowners and capitalists whose intentions were not limited to wage cuts but included ending the national minimum and the National Agreements. The second was the hesitation and trepidation of reformist leaders in the Labour Movement who called for reconciliation of classes and preached sweet reason to *the workers*.

What the workers needed was united action under the leadership of the General Council, united action of the type that had brought about the victory of Red Friday. And the Statement concluded with an appeal to the organised workers to exert their strength through such united action and thus to defeat the employers' offensive.

Leading Communists at public meetings and in the Party press tried to combat the effects of the Report and of the support for it by the Labour leadership.[2] Arthur Horner, for instance, repeatedly stressed the divisive, splitting character of the commission and its findings. As he wrote at the time in the *Labour Monthly*:[3]

> "The task of the Commission was first of all to weaken the miners by seeking to alienate the support of the other workers from them. Right through the process of taking evidence, the representatives of other industries have been encouraged to declare that the high production costs of coal, due by implication to the miners' wage rates are mainly responsible for the depression in trade which bears so hardly on the employees, while, on the other hand, the mineowners sought time and again to place the responsibility upon dockers,

---

[1] *Workers' Weekly*, No. 163, March 19, 1926, p. 5.

[2] See, for instance, Emile Burns, *Divide and Conquer*; the Coal Commission's Report Analysed", in *Communist Review*, Vol. 6, No. 12, April 1926, pp. 554–558.

[3] Arthur Horner, "The Coal Report and After", *Labour Monthly*, Vol. 8, No. 5, May 1926, p. 276.

trimmers and railwaymen for their failure to give the miners a decent standard of existence."[1]

The most effective demonstration against the Samuel Report in the weeks that followed its publication was the special National Conference of Action organised by the National Minority Movement with the full support of the Communist Party.

N.M.M. CONFERENCE OF ACTION

This special Conference was held at the Latchmere Baths, Battersea, amidst decorations designed by Rutland Boughton and Christina Walshe,[2] on March 21, 1926, under the Chairmanship of Tom Mann.

It was the biggest conference of the Minority Movement to date, with 883 delegates attending from 547 organisations including some 52 Trades Councils, among them Manchester, Sheffield, Leeds and Coventry. The support of the London Trades Council was only lost by two votes and support from the Glasgow Trades Council was only defeated after a special referendum in which the biggest guns and the dirtiest devices were called into action.[3] In all, around 957,000 workers were represented.

The composition of the delegates provides something of a reflection of the influence of Marxists and militants in the trade union movement of the period. Representation included 153 metal workers' organisations, 121 transport workers' organisations, 103 organisations of general workers, 100 of building workers, 51 of distributive workers, 37 miners' organisations, 33 co-operative, 61 Minority groups and

---

[1] Writing thirty-four years later, after a lifetime of working with and for the miners, Arthur Horner had not changed his view of the Samuel Commission Report or the circumstances that led up to it. See his autobiography, *Incorrigible Rebel*, MacGibbon and Kee, 1960, p. 73:

"The T.U.C. did nothing while the press and right-wing spokesmen wove a mantle of sanctity around the Coal Commission, though it was so clearly composed of capitalists and capitalist economists, who with economic planning and nationalisation ruled out, would inevitably report against the unions and the working class.

"The Report backed the demand of the mineowners for longer hours and reductions in wages. But it was clear that it had been framed with the deliberate purpose of splitting the Labour movement."

[2] See special N.M.M. supplement of *Workers' Weekly*, No. 162, March 12, 1926 (for preparation of Conference) and *Report of Special Conference of Action*, 34 pp. pamphlet, N.M.M., 1926.

[3] *Workers' Weekly*, No. 162, Special Supplement, March 12, 1926.

Shop Stewards Committees and 53 organisations of the unemployed.[1] W. H. Hutchinson attended as a visitor.[2]

Tom Mann, opening the Conference, moved at once into critical analysis of the Samuel Report. Its *real* content, he said, was attack on wages, hours and national agreements. It had done a good job for the capitalist class. It complemented the open attacks on the workers like the O.M.S., and the various fascist and semi-fascist organisations, the arrests of Communists and of anthracite miners, symbolised by the vacant chairs on the Conference platform that should have been occupied by Harry Pollitt the General Secretary of the N.M.M. and Wal Hannington, Secretary of the N.U.W.C.M. and member of the N.M.M. Executive.

The Commission, he continued, on which sat no worker or workers' representative, had hoped that:

> "the reformist elements in the Labour Movement will concur with their recommendations and lose sight of the attacks upon living standards contained in the Report—which the trade unions *must* fight."

In fact the miners' only hope of saving themselves from further and more disastrous attacks was to take the offensive against the measures proposed:

> "*Therefore, prepare at once.* Let us perfect our relations with each other; let us have our industrial machinery ready for *action*. The real central body through which we must function is the *General Council of the Trades Union Congress.* All unions should be affiliated to the Trades Council in the district, and every Trades Council should be genuinely representative of all the working-class organisations in the district, the co-operative guilds as much as the unions. In the shops, factories and mines and on board ship committees should be active in every department; this is where the workers have their chance as against all who do not work. . . ."

Alex Gossip, General Secretary of the National Amalgamated Furnishing Trades Association (N.A.F.T.A.) moved and J. J. Vaughan

---

[1] *Report* p. 34. A written report of the time indicates that in mid-April 1926, 190 trades union branches with 209,207 workers were affiliated to the N.M.M. of which the targets were 13 Trades Councils with 120,700 members. There were 2,755 Associate Members.

[2] W. H. Hutchinson, a leading member of the A.E.U., was for many years a (very independent) member of the Executive of the Labour Party and was the last of them to raise a hand and give his vote in favour of affiliation of the Communist Party to the Labour Party.

of the Bethnal Green Trades and Labour Council (a leading London Communist) seconded a resolution on the Defence and Maintenance of Trade Union Rights which detailed the successive steps taken to strengthen and mobilise the capitalist state for the coming struggles and which put forward five main lines of action:

"(a) To organise the workers on the job into factory and pit committees ... and to set up Trades Councils where none exist.

"(b) To form (through and under the supervision of the Trades Councils) Workers' Defence Corps, in order to protect working-class speakers from bourgeois terrorism, to protect trade union headquarters from Fascist incendiarism, to defend strike pickets against police interference, and, finally, build up a powerful working-class force, capable of defending the political and industrial rights and liberties of the workers.

"(c) To demand the repeal of 'sedition' and anti-Labour laws.

"(d) To resist strenuously any attempts by local authorities either voluntary or at the instigation of the Government to prevent free association and public expression.

"(e) To demand the rights of soldiers and naval ratings to refuse strike services."

A resolution on the Capitalist Offensive was moved by Arthur Horner of the South Wales Miners' Federation and seconded by Peter Kerrigan, member of the A.E.U. and speaking for the Glasgow District Committee of the N.M.M.

The resolution emphasised that the employers had made *separate* attacks upon the seamen, miners, railwaymen, building workers, textile workers, engineers and other sections, with a view to taking them on and defeating them one by one. Now a *general* offensive was being prepared. Against the general offensive:

"it is imperative that all the forces of the working class should be mobilised under one central leadership to repel the attack and to secure the demands of every section of the workers."

There followed an appeal of great importance to the N.M.M. supporters and to the workers generally to develop, through the Trades Councils, all-embracing *Councils of Action* to prepare for the struggles ahead. It should be noted and appreciated that the call for the Councils of Action which were to be the most important organs of struggle during the nine days of the General Strike came first from the

Communist Party and from the Minority Movement. The Conference urged each Trades Council:

> "to constitute itself a Council of Action by mobilising all the forces of the working class in its locality (the trade union branches, the organised unemployed, the co-operative Guilds, and the workers' political organisations). . . ."

Such Councils of Action should work to strengthen the trade unions, to bring in the young workers, to improve workshop organisation, to establish food and supply organisations (commissariats) along with the local co-operatives, to bring the unorganised workers into the struggle.

It urged the General Council of the T.U.C. to convene a National Congress of Action and to take steps to ensure the support of the international trade union movement for the British workers in the struggles ahead.

With a resolution on International Trade Union Unity, moved by George Hardy, Acting Secretary of the N.M.M.,[1] and with an emergency resolution against British measures of repression in China, the special National Conference of Action came to an end. It was probably the highest point in the history of the Minority Movement, did much to heighten the spirit of combativity which was already strong amongst the rank and file, and came like a breath of fresh air in the muggy atmosphere of General Council conciliation and unpreparedness.

A week later a conference of Minority Movement groups from the various coalfields called for the complete rejection of the Royal Commission report,[2] the aim of which, they said, was to divide the miners, and of the subsidy and lower wages and living standards. The miners, they urged, should fight for a guaranteed national minimum wage commensurate with the increased cost of living and recognise that the necessary reorganisation of the coal industry could only take place through nationalisation without compensation and with workers' control.

APRIL DEADLOCK

When reviewing the order of battle as the armies moved into position there is no doubt that the Miners' Federation was well and truly

[1] George Hardy was brought on to the Political Bureau of the C.P.G.B., and became Acting Secretary of the N.M.M. after the arrest of the twelve Communist leaders.
[2] See R. Page Arnot, *The General Strike*, p. 116.

lined up in the militant camp. Here amongst the miners the experience of capitalism was the most bitter, hatred of capitalism the most consistent. Here the Communist Party and the Minority Movement were well supported especially in the Welsh, Scottish and to an extent the Durham coalfields. Here there were young Marxist leaders like Arthur Horner coming to the forefront of the struggle, and here in the months that preceded the General Strike was a militant leader, the Miners' Secretary, A. J. Cook,[1] as eloquent as he was energetic, imbued at this period with deep class feelings, and able to convey them to the miners in words that stirred them, that seemed to bring to the surface their own most profound sentiments and aspirations. Later Horner was to describe Cook at work in these months of preparation:

> "In the months before the 1926 strike, and during the strike, we spoke together at meetings all over the country. We had audiences, mostly of miners, running into thousands. Usually I was put on first. I would make a good, logical speech, and the audience would listen quietly, but without any wild enthusiasm.
>
> "Then Cook would take the platform. Often he was tired, hoarse and sometimes almost inarticulate. But he would electrify the meeting. They would applaud and nod their heads in agreement when he said the most obvious things. For a long time I was puzzled, and then one night I realised why it was. I was speaking *to* the meeting Cook was speaking *for* the meeting. He was expressing the thoughts of his audience, I was trying to persuade them. He was the burning expression of their anger at the iniquities which they were suffering."[2]

The Miners' Federation knew well what lay ahead, constantly called for preparation and mobilisation of the workers, but realised that in the approaching struggles the miners could not stand alone, they would need allies.

With the slow development and then virtual collapse of the Industrial Alliance, the miners were obliged to look more and more to the General Council of the T.U.C., of which, after the Scarborough T.U.C., J. H. Thomas, alas, had become a member; and from the beginning of 1926 joint meetings of the Miners' Executive and the

---
..[1] A. J. Cook had been a member of the Communist Party for a short time in the spring of 1921. He was elected Secretary of the South Wales Miners' Federation with the support of the Communist Party miners.

[2] Arthur Horner, *Incorrigible Rebel*, p. 72.

Industrial Committee were held fairly frequently. As the critical first of May drew nearer and nearer, the right wing within the Industrial Committee became more vocal and the Committee itself became more an obstacle than an impetus to united action.

After a joint meeting held on February 19, i.e. before the publication of the Royal Commission Report, the Industrial Committee issued a firm statement of support for the miners:[1]

> "There was to be no reduction in wages, no increase in working hours, and no interference with the principle of national agreements. This is the position of the trade union movement today."

But with the publication of the Commission Report in the second week of March, and with its respectful reception by the General Council,[2] the line of the Industrial Committee became one of insistence on negotiation, and the pressure they exerted was directed more on the miners than the mineowners.

On the day before the National Delegate Conference of the miners, called for April 9, the miners again approached the Industrial Committee of the General Council for support in any action in defence of wages, hours and national agreements. What they got, instead of the assurances of solidarity of mid-February, was the ominous answer that the Committee reaffirmed

> "its previous declarations in *support of the miners' efforts to obtain an equitable settlement of outstanding difficulties*" (my emphasis, J.K.).

Negotiations, it stated:

> "should be continued without delay, in order to obtain a clear understanding with regard to the Report of the Royal Commission, and to reduce points of difference to the smallest possible dimensions."[3]

By such advice, the miners were undeterred. At their conference on April 9 they categorically rejected the essence of the Royal Commission Report and the proposals of the coalowners and recommended to their District Federations:

---

[1] See Allen Hutt, *Post-War History*, p. 124.
[2] See R. Page Arnot, *The Miners—Years of Struggle*, p. 400.
[3] See Hutt, op. cit., p. 124, which also quotes from the revealing covering letter to the Miners from the Industrial Committee's Secretary, Mr. W. M. Citrine.

"(a) That no assent be given to any proposal for increasing the length of the working day;
"(b) That the principle of a national wage agreement with a national minimum percentage be firmly adhered to;
"(c) That in as much as wages are already too low, we cannot assent to any proposals for reducing wages."[1]

The miners could feel the warm solidarity of workers in pit, rail depot and factory, they had the backing of the Communist Party, the Minority Movement and the militants in Labour Party and I.L.P. and in many thousands of district and local trade union committees. They were in the mood of struggle regardless of the "atmosphere of yielding that was already obvious in the communications from the General Council".[2]

There followed a whole complex sequence of meetings and negotiations which have been described in detail in other works—Miners' Federation and Mineowners' Association, the same with Prime Minister, Miners and Prime Minister, Miners and General Council.[3] All resulted in deadlock.

On April 23 decisions were taken for a Delegate Conference of miners to be held on Wednesday, April 28, to be followed, on April 29, by a Conference of Trade Union Executives, summoned by the General Council.

By the time of this decision the general line-up was becoming clear. The coalowners were demanding not only the wage cuts outlined in the Samuel Report but they were adamant on longer working hours and reverting to *district* agreements. They wanted a show down. They showed not the slightest interest in the condition of the miners and their families. Even so conservative a commentator as J. L. Garvin in the *Observer* admitted that "no responsible body of men has ever seemed more lacking in the human touch".[4] The miners, too, were adamant they were not willing to accept any of the essential demands of the coalowners, and in this they had the backing and sympathy of the mass of British workers, and the active solidarity of the Communists and the Minority Movement.

But the right wing in the Labour Party and the T.U.C. were *already* preaching and practising conciliation. Typical as usual was Thomas.

---

[1] R. Page Arnot, *The General Strike*, p. 112.   [2] Ibid.
[3] These can well be studied in R. Page Arnot, op. cit. and *The Miners—Years of Struggle*; W. H. Crook, *The General Strike*.
[4] *Observer*, April 25, 1926.

"To talk at this stage," he proclaimed at a Monmouthshire meeting, on Sunday April 18,[1]

> "as if in a few days all the workers of the country were to be called out was not only letting loose passions that might be difficult to control, but it was not rendering the best service either to the miners or anyone else . . . instead of organising, mobilising, and encouraging the feeling that war was inevitable, let them concentrate on finding a solution honourable and satisfactory to all sides."

"Disorganising, demobilising, and discouraging" might well sum up the role of J. H. Thomas from the point of view of the miners and militants. In this sad work he was ably assisted by Messrs. Ramsay MacDonald and Arthur Henderson who, on April 23, were appointed by the Industrial Committee to be present at all its negotiations.

"Organising, mobilising and encouraging" the coming struggle could equally well summarise the role the Communist Party carried out to the best of its ability, hampered always by the smallness of its membership, in these critical weeks of April. Every issue of the *Workers' Weekly* called for unity, mobilisation, preparedness and warned against the tendency of the right wing to capitulate.[2] On May 23 the *Workers' Weekly* published a Statement of the Executive Committee of the Party[3] once again analysing the splitting role of the Royal Commission Report, calling for unity around the miners against all wage cuts or increase of working hours, no weakening of national agreements, for the organisation of a supply service (commissariat) jointly by the General Council and the Co-operative Wholesale Society, and for a meeting of Trade Union Executives.

It ended with an appeal for Trades Councils everywhere to prepare for the coming struggles and the formation of all-embracing Councils of Action.

So, as the great conference of Trade Union Executives grew nearer, the political alignment in the country grew more clear. On the one side the coalowners and the Tory Government were united for struggle, a show down, intent on cutting wages, lengthening hours, breaking national agreements, all prepared to take their revenge for the Red Friday of the previous July. On the other side, on the side of the workers, there was no such unity. Miners and militants, involving hundreds

---
[1] *The Times*, April 19, 1926.
[2] See *Workers' Weekly*, No. 166, April 9, editorial, "Every Man Behind the Miners"; Ibid, No. 168, April 23, article by Arthur Horner, "Rally Round the Miners".
[3] See Appendix III to this chapter for full text.

of thousands of trade unionists all over the country, thousands of district and local trade union organisations, very many active and class-conscious members of the Labour Party and the I.L.P. with Communists and the Minority Movement in the vanguard, were all rearing to go, preparing and prepared. But inside the Industrial Committee and General Council of the T.U.C., inside the Labour Party leadership, were those in high places who were counselling and preparing retreat before the battle had even begun.

THE EXECUTIVES MEET

The special Conference of Executive Committees met in the Memorial Hall, Farringdon Street,[1] on Thursday, April 29, and did not disperse until the afternoon of Saturday, May 1. A whole book could well be devoted to the complex negotiations and events which took place between that April 28 and the evening of May 2. The raw material is available for all to study.[2]

On April 28, eve of the meeting, the Communist Party issued a call to the Executive Meeting.[3] It pointed out that the rank and file of British workers were solid in their support for the miners, but warned that:

"Here are official leaders of Labour who are straining every nerve to secure a 'compromise' which will mean for the miners nothing but defeat."

The Party called on the Conference "to bring the whole force of the organised workers into action on the side of the Executives". The *Workers' Weekly* continued to expose various attempts of the Government, with the connivance of right-wing Labour, to reach some sort of compromise "formula", which would, in fact, mean for the miners complete surrender.[4] Very aptly it quoted the previous week's *Economist* to the effect that the Prime Minister, Baldwin, was faced with the task "of finding a formula which will lower wages without appearing to do so". The Party repeated its call for the formation of

---

[1] The Memorial Hall, Farringdon Street, was the same one in which the Democratic Federation became the S.D.F. in 1884, and in which the Labour Party was founded in 1900.
[2] *The Mining Crisis and the National Strike, 1926: Official Report*, T.U.C., 1927 pp. 1A–55A; R. Page Arnot, *The General Strike*, pp. 122–150 and *The Miners—Years of Struggle*, pp. 421–430; W. H. Crook, op. cit., pp. 341–366.
[3] *Workers' Weekly*, No. 169, April 30, 1926, p. 1.
[4] Ibid., No. 169, April 30, 1926, p. 1, "Baldwin Trying To Trick Miners".

Councils of Action,[1] of Workers' Defence Corps, and for national and local agreements between trade unions or Trades Councils and the Co-operatives.

On the morning of April 29, the Conference of Executives was opened by the Chairman, Mr. Arthur Pugh. Already the contradiction was apparent in his speech between a declaration of solidarity with the miners' fight on living standards and an implicit acceptance of the Royal Commission Report as a basis of negotiation. A resolution moved by J. H. Thomas and seconded by Ernest Bevin endorsed "the efforts of the General Council to secure an honourable settlement of the differences in the coal-mining industry", instructed the Industrial Committee of the T.U.C. to continue negotiations "providing the impending lock-out was not enforced", and adjourned the conference until the following day.

On Friday, April 30, Conference resumed in the morning, then continued to adjourn and resume, adjourn and resume, until half an hour before midnight, when Arthur Pugh returned to report on the Negotiating Committee's achievement. This, it soon became clear, was less than nothing. No proposals had been made by coalowners, Cabinet or Prime Minister that meant anything less than the complete surrender of the miners. The attitude of the mineowners was clear. So was that of the miners. Both were ready for the struggle. What was not at all clear was the attitude of the Industrial Committee of the T.U.C. and in particular of its right-wing members.

When, following Mr. Pugh's Report, the press was invited to the Conference Hall, J. H. Thomas described in vivid and revealing terms the ignominious picture of the T.U.C. negotiatiors prostrating low before the Government in the search for a formula of compromise which would have been, in fact, a surrender:

> "My friends, when the verbatim reports are written, I suppose my usual critics will say that Thomas was almost grovelling, and it is true. In all my long experience—and I have conducted many negotiations—I say to you—and my colleagues will bear testimony to it—I never begged or pleaded like I begged and pleaded all today, and I pleaded not alone because I believed in the case of the miners, but because I believed in my bones that my duty to the country involved it."[2]

[1] *Workers' Weekly*, No. 169, April 30, 1926, p. 6, T. H. Wintringham, "Once Again Councils of Action".
[2] T.U.C., *The Mining Crisis and the National Crisis, 1926*, p. 31.

But, as Thomas himself reported, the Cabinet rejected his pleadings and refused even to accede to the suspension of lock-out notices.

With the morning of May 1, the Executives were still formally in session. The Cabinet meanwhile had not only refused all and any action to suspend the lock-out, but had put into motion the Emergency Powers Act (E.P.A.) with all its ramifications. On April 30, the King had signed a Proclamation at Buckingham Palace declaring a State of Emergency. Orders in Council were issued in the form of Emergency Regulations. Local Authorities were reminded by a Ministry of Health Circular of the measures that, as previously arranged, should be taken to cope with a national stoppage. The names of the Civil Commissioners and their staffs were published. An O.M.S. poster calling for recruits was posted throughout the country. It was officially announced that troops had been moved to South Wales, Lancashire and Scotland, and that arrangements had been made to obtain assistance from the Navy.[1] All this before any official call of a General Strike by the General Council.

The giant May Day demonstration went by the Memorial Hall in the course of the Conference's deliberations. The one and only issue of the *Worker's Daily* which appeared on May 3 as the "General Strike edition of the *Worker's Weekly*", reported:

> "It was impossible to count the numbers that took part in the London demonstrations. ... In one procession alone the tail had not reached Hyde Park until the head had been there an hour."

The northern contingent broke into the "Red Flag" as the first section reached the Hall, and an onlooker who had attended many a demonstration has told me that he "had never heard it sung like this before".

At midday the Conference of Executives assembled in the Memorial Hall. A roll-call was held and the representatives of each Executive in turn were asked if they approved of the General Council's "proposals for co-ordinated action". An hour later it was announced that the General Council's proposals had been accepted by the huge majority of 3,653,527 to 49,911 whilst the representatives of 319,000 had not yet been able to give a reply. Even then, it should be noted, the whole wording of the General Council's proposals were extremely "moderate". No mention was made of a General Strike; it was only stated that "trades and undertakings shall cease work as and when required by the

---

[1] See R. Page Arnot, *The General Strike*, pp. 155-159.

General Council", whilst actual instructions to call out the trade unionists on strike were left to the individual unions. Time for the strike to begin was fixed as 11.59 p.m. on Monday May 3.

Even in this solemn session taking one of the most solemn decisions in the history to date of the British working class, the difficulties and dangers were clear to those who could look a little below the surface.

Just before taking the vote on the General Council's Scheme for Action, the Chairman, Arthur Pugh, made the ominous statement:

> "The scheme requires that the Miners' Federation hand over to the General Council the conduct of this dispute".[1]

Herbert Smith, after the voting, thanking the Conference in the name of the Miners' Federation for the decision that they had taken, carefully reserved the right of the miners to state their own case and, in the last analysis, to settle their own affairs. The miners welcomed the support of the General Council, and recognised its right of joint negotiation, so long *as it remained firm*.[2]

Amidst the cheering and stirring statements, like Ernest Bevin's declaration:

> "We look upon your 'yes' as meaning that you have placed your all upon the altar for this great Movement, and having placed it there, even if every penny goes, if every asset goes, history will ultimately write up that it was a magnificent generation that was prepared to do it rather than see the miners driven down like slaves."[3]

came Ramsay MacDonald's adulation of class peace:

> "In the name of everything I hold sacred, in the name of the most conscientious beliefs that I have got, I tell you and I tell the British public, that I have never been associated with a body of men that have striven, that have fought, that have turned phrases and words and facts over more patiently, more religiously, with a more firm desire to make peace and to have peace than the colleagues with whom I have been working during the last two or three days.[4]

And as he closed this last speech in discussion at the meeting that had just decided on the General Strike, he still held out hopes that before the next week came "something will happen . . . which will enable us to go about our work cheerily and heartily and hopefully . . .".

[1] T.U.C., *The Mining Crisis and the National Strike*, 1926, p.33.
[2] Ibid., p. 37.   [3] Ibid., p. 34.   [4] Ibid., p. 38.

AT THE LAST MINUTE

The General Council not only hoped that "something will happen", but did its damnedest to make it happen. As A. J. Cook was later to recount,[1] after the vote of the Executives Meeting most of the delegates returned to their respective homes "with the determination to carry out the policy agreed upon". The miners returned to their respective coal-fields to make preparations now that the men were locked out:

> "They went to this work feeling certain that, as the Government had repeatedly refused to consider any sort of fair terms for the miners after long hours of negotiations, and as the Union E.C.'s had been almost unanimous in their decision to fight and the T.U.C. had undertaken not to negotiate without us, they could leave London safely."[2]

But no sooner had the delegates left for their homes than Walter Citrine despatched a letter to the Prime Minister, in the name of the General Council, advising him that all the unions, including the miners, had decided to hand over the conduct of the dispute to the General Council, and that the General Council was ready for any further discussion with the Government.[3]

Fresh negotiations proceeded, which we shall not examine in detail here, and a "formula" was reached which in A. J. Cook's opinion and that of all militants "meant a reduction of wages and district agreements—conditions against which the T.U.C. had themselves declared".[4]

The General Council was using the powers it alleged it had received to avoid preparing for a General Strike.[5] But whilst it was pressing and pushing the angry miners to accept the new "formula", or at least a version of it, and whilst the most complex negotiations were proceeding between the Industrial Committee, its Sub-Committee, and the miners, it was the Prime Minister himself who abruptly and contemptuously terminated negotiations, in part under the pressure of Churchill and Birkenhead.

---

[1] A. J. Cook, *The Nine Days*.   [2] Ibid., p. 8.
[3] R. Page Arnot, op. cit., p. 143–144.   [4] A. J. Cook, op. cit., p. 10.
[5] There is a good short summary of the last-minute negotiations in Charles Loch Mowat's *Britain between the Wars, 1918–1940*. He writes, p. 305: "There was an interval for further negotiation in which the General Council was determined to use the powers it had just received to avert the strike, not to bring it off."

The *Daily Mail* had prepared a leading article for Monday, May 3 branding the General Strike as:

> "a revolutionary movement intended to inflict suffering upon a great mass of innocent persons in the community. . . . It must be dealt with by every resource at the disposal of the Community."

The leader called on "all law-abiding men and women to hold themselves at the service of King and Country". According to the capitalist and right-wing Labour theory of "neutrality" of the state and "freedom" of the press, workers of the printing trade were supposed to put their skill and craft to the purpose of maligning and defeating their own cause and their own movement.

Instead of this, in a militant and extremely healthy action, the N.A.T.S.O.P.A. Chapel[1] met and, after a brief discussion, informed the management that they would print the paper only if the leader were deleted. They were supported by Chapels in the machine-room, foundry and packing department, and no *Daily Mail* was printed that night.

It was this incident which the Government treated as an "overt act of war", and used as a pretext to break off negotiations despite an ignominious disavowal from the General Council. When the General Council representatives, bearing this shameful letter of disavowal, humbly arrived at Downing Street, they were told that the Prime Minister had gone to bed.

On May 2, when the General Council was making a last desperate effort at a sell-out before the strike had even begun, when the leaders of the miners and hundreds of other militant trade union leaders were out in their areas making preparations for the struggle, the Communist Party issued a final call before the strike commenced.[2]

The supreme need of the moment, the Party affirmed, was "solidarity between all sections of organised Labour". The greatest danger was "that the Government and the Right Wing may succeed in isolating the miners from the rest of the movement. . . ."

What was needed was action. Above all the Party called for the formation of Councils of Action by the Trades Councils, for the organisation of Workers' Defence Corps, for joint committees between the unions and Co-operatives to secure supplies and provisions, and for the organisation of international trade union solidarity to prevent

---

[1] National Society of Operative Printers and Assistants.
[2] For full text see Appendix IV to this chapter.

blacklegging. The call ended with the slogans "A Council of Action in every Town!" and "Every Man behind the Miners!"

The Party's appeal was published in the *Sunday Worker* of May 2. On that evening the headquarters of the National Minority Movement sent out instructions to all its sections and supporters to work for the establishment of Councils of Action.[1] The Councils were to be all-embracing bodies. On them should be represented:

> "every political, industrial, co-operative and unemployed organisation—no organisation should be left outside if we are to defeat the mineowners and the government."

The N.M.M. explained that the Councils of Action should ensure continuous picketing of places of work, establish patrols reporting failures and gaps to the appropriate unions, help to carry out all the decisions for the struggle of the General Council and the Union Executives. They should not, the N.M.M. warned, under any circumstances take over the work of the unions themselves.

Once again, in its circular, the N.M.M. advised Trades Councils to elect press and propaganda bodies to counteract the lies of the capitalist press, and outlined in detail the role of Workers' Defence Corps:

> "They should be trade unionists of good character and under commanders who are trade union officials. Their duty is to protect trade union offices, printing presses, mass meetings, pickets, and trade union officials holding important positions, to maintain peace and order and prevent *agents provocateurs* and spies, whom without a doubt the Government and employers will engage to commit violence."

It proposed, moreover, the formation of a special Committee to work for friendly relations with the armed forces, to explain to them the issues of the struggle, and to show them how it was "the Government which had declared war on the trade unions".

These were the last statements of the Communist Party and the National Minority Movement before the General Strike. They contrast somewhat with the last frantic attempts of the General Council to reach a "formula" and avert the strike.

---

[1] George Hardy, *Those Stormy Years*, Lawrence and Wishart, 1956, p. 185. George Hardy was at that time the Acting Secretary of the N.M.M.

THE STRIKE IS SOLID

Other books and studies provide a detailed record of the nine tremendous days May 4–May 12 of the General Strike.[1] Here we can only look briefly at the events as background to an examination of the role of the militants in general and of the Communists in particular. But these nine glorious, tragic, unprecedented days of struggle laid bare the class and political line-up more clearly than months or years of more "normal" times.

The working class was ready for struggle, rearing to go, responsive to every appeal for action, unhesitant, while their leaders, classic reformists, had been pushed by the pressure of the workers, unwillingly, into a struggle they had tried to avert, and still were desperately hoping to bring to a speedy end. Thus a working class whose official leaders were more fearful of victory than defeat was in conflict with a capitalist class whose leaders were intent on winning a decisive victory and were ready to use every weapon from open force to subtle cunning and manœuvre.

The strike was solid, overwhelmingly solid. At midnight on Monday, May 3 only three unions out of some 1,100 refused to answer the call.[2] The General Council of the T.U.C. in their first communiqué had to admit the splendid solidarity:

> "We have from all over the country reports that have surpassed all our expectations. Not only the railway and transport men, but all other trades came out in a manner we did not expect immediately. The difficulty of the General Council has been to keep men in what we might call the second line of defence rather than call them out".[3]

---

[1] From the very extensive literature we would particularly recommend: R. Page Arnot, *The General Strike, May 1926. Its Origin and History*, Labour Research Department, 1926; Emile Burns, *The General Strike, May 1926: Trades Councils in Action*; Allen Hutt, *The Post-War History of the British Working Class*, Chapter VI, "Nine Days that Shook Britain", Gollancz, 1937; R. Page Arnot, *The Miners—Years of Struggle*, chapter XIII, "The General Strike"; Professor Wilfred Harris Crook, *The General Strike*, chapter XI, 7, XII, Chapel Hill, University of North Carolina Press; R. W. Postgate, Ellen Wilkinson and J. F. Horrabin, *A Worker's History of the Great Strike*, Plebs League, 1927; A. J. Cook, *The Nine Days*, 1926. For political analysis at the time R. Palme Dutt, *The Meaning of the General Strike*, C.P.G.B., 1926, and the review "Our First General Strike" in the *Communist Review* for June 1926.

[2] Postgate, Wilkinson, Horrabin *Workers History of the Great Strike*, Plebs League, p. 19.

[3] Quoted by Allen Hutt, op. cit., p. 136.

The despatch riders sent out by the General Council to take messages and gather information came back with glowing reports:

"On Monday night the first batch of despatch riders set out on their journeys; on Tuesday the reports began to come in. They amazed Eccleston Square. Everywhere a solid enthusiasm. Everywhere a realisation of this simple issue, *we cannot let the miners down this time*. Men with responsible posts and long terms of service had come out as wholeheartedly as any. Villages in which a strike had never been known before were as forward as places believed to be 'centres of disturbance'. As report after report came in, it was clear that what criticism there was was all in one direction. Why were food permits dealt out so freely? Why were the gasworks and the electric power plants running? Why were carters told off to supply 'black' coal to the 'black' gas works, and work alongside blacklegs? Why were not more trades called out? This last criticism, be it noted, came not from the men who were striking but from the men who were left at work. They too wanted to strike their blow in this great adventure. Day and night, at any hour, the despatch riders found the strike committees at work."[1]

The Government-monopolised British Broadcasting Company (B.B.C.), the Government's *British Gazette*, and various capitalist news-sheets tried to give the impression of a constant stream of strikers returning to work, above all in transport.

A serious estimate shows that in London, for example, practically all passenger services ceased on the first day of the strike. There were some 300 "pirate" buses operating, dropping to 40 on the third day due to successful picketing.[2] The largest bus company, the London General Omnibus Company, responsible in normal times for 3,300 of London's 4,400 buses, did not have a single vehicle at work. *The Times*, certainly exaggerating, estimated around 1,000 buses manned by scabs ("volunteers" in *The Times* language) on the last day of the strike, but did not like to dwell on the distances they managed to cover, their average speed, or casualty rate.

Ministry of Transport statistics showed 15 out of 315 trains running on London's underground on the first day, with 99 per cent of Underground personnel solid with the strike, the remaining 1 per cent being supervisory staff or ex-flying corps.[3]

[1] *Lansbury's Labour Weekly*, No. 63, May 22, 1926, "The Secret History of the Great Strike", p. 4.
[2] Professor Crook, op. cit., p. 390.   [3] Ibid.

Despite propaganda to the contrary, and despite the intense dislike of the strike by railway union leaders like J. H. Thomas, the railwaymen, too, were (in the words of Professor Crook, the most serious non-Marxist student of the strike) "surprisingly complete" in their support of it, including the great majority of railway clerks and supervisory staff.

On passenger trains, where scabs were particularly busy, the L.M.S., for instance, started with some 3·8 per cent of normal traffic on May 5, rising to 12·2 per cent on May 11. On the G.W.R. the equivalent figures were from 3·7 per cent to 19·2. On the L.N.E.R. from 3·4 to 12·8.[1] But here again figures tend to exaggerate. For many a blackleg-driven train was never to reach its destination, and with others it was quicker (and safer) to walk. As for freight, traffic on the L.M.S. rose from under 1 per cent of normal on May 5 to 3 per cent on May 11, on the G.W.R. from 5 to 8·4 per cent, on the L.N.E.R. it only reached 2·2 per cent by May 11.[2]

Professor Crook describes as "mythical" the much-proclaimed railwaymen's return to work. Of course this myth, too, was taken up by the right-wing railway and other trade union leaders seeking to justify their call-off of the General Strike, but in fact, as the Professor writes, it was their *failure to return*, their *solidarity*, their increasing militancy, that led to the call-off:

"It seems more likely that the pressing reason for the eagerness with which the railroad leaders accepted the Samuel Memorandum, as a method of ending the strike, was not so much the fear of immediate weakening among the rank and file as a constant fear, with some leaders amounting almost to a nightmare, that, as the strike prolonged its days, the ranks would get out of hand, become disorderly and bring a highly hypothetical civil war into the realm of actuality."[3]

The print workers' support for the strike was exceedingly solid, as the shrunken news-sheets of the capitalist press lords bear witness. It took the loan by Lord Beaverbrook of one of his mechanical superintendents, a former operator, to act as sole typesetter for the early issues to be printed of the Government's own *British Gazette*.[4]

Though the manifold organisations of blacklegs, overwhelmingly

---

[1] Professor Crook, op. cit., pp. 393-399, basing himself on Ministry of Transport reports.
[2] Ibid.   [3] Ibid., p. 398.   [4] See Allen Hutt, op. cit., p. 144.

middle and upper class, did succeed in manning an extremely small number of services, the number of defectors from the ranks of the working class was extraordinarily small. Nor was the absence of strike pay used as a pretext for return to work, nor the frantic appeals of the Government, nor their pledges and promises to blacklegs. Eyewitnesses comment:

> "The first week was passed practically without defection. Unions like the Altogether Builders' Labourers, whose whole funds would barely have sufficed to pay 3s. per head to its members on strike, were holding out as fiercely as unions with full coffers".[1]

In fact, *in the localities, the strike was becoming stronger, better organised, day by day*. By the second week the Councils of Action and various other forms of strike committee (which we shall examine later) were becoming more widespread, more authoritative, more effective. Again eyewitnesses comment:

> "... by the second week of the strike organisation, in nearly all the towns of which we have information, was in full working order, and the workers were reaching out to fresh development. They were, as numerous reports put it, 'just beginning', and the full force of their attack was only commencing to be felt. Mass pickets, defence corps, propaganda, commissariat, federation over wider areas—all these were just coming into play."[2]

By May 10, the *British Worker*, official organ of the T.U.C. (and this was before the call-out of the second line) reported that there were *more* workers out on strike than on the first day. On May 11, the day before the call-off, the Government's *British Gazette* had to admit, thereby contradicting its own propaganda, that there was "as yet little sign of a general collapse of the strike".

In fact when the strike was called off by the General Council on May 12, the number of strikers was at its highest peak, the enthusiasm of the strikers greater and their organisation stronger than at any moment of the Nine Days.

THE CAPITALISTS AND THEIR STATE

The workers were solid for the strike, ready to join it and ready to prolong it. The capitalist class was solidly against it. And, unlike the

[1] *Lansbury's Labour Weekly*, article quoted, p. 5.
[2] Wilkinson, Horrabin, Postgate, op. cit., p. 51.

workers, the capitalists had a leadership, a Government and a State, prepared to make full use of all their resources to break the strike as a prelude to an offensive against the living standards and liberties of the working class.

We have already seen how long and how thoroughly the British ruling class had been preparing for this moment. We have already seen how often and how unavailingly the Communist Party, Minority Movement, Miners' Federation and other militants had warned of the need for their *own* working-class preparation, and how deaf had been the ears of General Council and Labour Party leadership.

Now that the time for which they had been preparing had come, the Government went into action.[1]

On the eve of the General Strike the Government, through the Customs, stopped all export of coal. Ships that had sailed from South Wales with cargoes of coal were ordered back by wireless. Emergency regulations on fuel consumption were issued. An appeal for blacklegs ("volunteers") was broadcast on Sunday night (May 2) by the Government, with no equivalent appeal against blacklegging, be it noted, from the General Council.

With almost mechanical precision the Government proceeded to put into practice Lenin's teaching on the class character of the state.

On Monday night, the Metropolitan Commissioner of Police issued an appeal for citizens below the age of 45 to enroll as Special Constables, pledging them glory and protection, with pensions and allowances for their widows and orphans in case of death in execution of their duty.[2]

In the army all leave was stopped. Troops were moved to important supply and industrial areas like London, South Wales, Scotland. Hyde Park, closed to the public, was prepared as a milk distribution centre. O.M.S., its "day" dawning, put its personnel and organisation at the disposal of the various Volunteer Service Committees in the various localities. All pretence at its *private* capacity was now discarded.

On May 7 the *British Gazette* carried a Government announcement that:

> "All ranks of the Armed Forces of the Crown are hereby notified that any action which they may find it necessary to take in an honest endeavour to aid the Civil Power will receive, both now and afterwards, the full support of His Majesty's Government."

[1] See Professor Crook, op. cit., pp. 386–389.
[2] *The Times*, May 4, 1926, quoted by Professor Crook, op. cit., as above.

The next day two battalions of Guards, with supporting cavalry and armoured cars, occupied London's docks. The navy, as befits its senior status, was given a special position in the strike-breaking task-force, a position, ironically enough, well described by J. R. Clynes, Cabinet Minister in the first Labour Government and a leading exponent of the neutrality of the state. On May 10, he wrote:

". . . the mails to Ireland and elsewhere were being carried on naval destroyers. In the Clyde, where rough mining and other elements [sic!] had caused some trouble, the *Warspite*, the *Comus* and the *Hood* (the world's biggest battleship) towered with their big guns outlined starkly against the sky. Three other warships overawed Liverpool. Destroyers anchored in the harbours of Cardiff, Harwich, Middlesbrough and Portsmouth.

"In London, the power station was manned by naval ratings. Other naval men worked in the docks, where machine guns were held in case of need."[1]

The B.B.C. already on Tuesday May 4, became an open propaganda weapon of the Government, emitting a continuous stream of attacks on the strikers, appeals to blacklegs and distorted rumours of the mythical return to work. Though not yet officially a public corporation, it was put, on a curious "assumption" of John Reith, its General Manager ("assuming the B.B.C. is for the people and that the Government is for the people, it follows that the B.B.C. must be for the Government in this crisis too"), at the service of the Tory Government, denying its use not only to the Archbishop of Canterbury to broadcast a "peace" appeal of a number of Church leaders, but even to Mr. Ramsay MacDonald.[2]

The much-boasted freedom of the press was exemplified not only in the publication of the *British Gazette* issued with the imprint of His Majesty's Stationery Office, printed by blackleg labour on the machines of the *Morning Post*, but by the raid (on May 5) on the *Daily Herald* office delaying the issue of the first number of the General Council's *British Worker*. Later in the week the Government officially took possession of all newsprint, and on Monday, May 10, Churchill announced that supplies would be witheld from any papers that attacked the Government. In fact the preparation and distribution of

---

[1] J. R. Clynes, *Memoirs: 1924–1937*, pp. 86–87.
[2] See J. C. W. Reith (later Lord Reith), *Into the Wind*, pp. 107–113, Hodder and Stoughton, 1949.

Communist Party and militant Strike Committee bulletins became the most frequent basis of arrest and sentence in the course of the General Strike.

Arrests of militant strikers and militant strike supporters, under various clauses of the Emergency Powers Act, began already on the first day of the strike (May 4) with that of Shapurji Saklatvala, the sole Communist M.P., on the pretext of a speech which he had delivered on May 1. Soon arrests and vicious sentences multiplied into hundreds. As we shall see later, these were in the main directed against militants and did not unduly upset the members of the General Council, who allowed the *British Worker* to ignore the question of arrests for several days. But things were happening, too, that the General Council, being what it was, could not ignore.

THE GENERAL COUNCIL PREPARES TO SELL OUT

The Government knew its General Council very well, knew that it had not wanted the strike, that it had been prepared to grovel to prevent it, that it was looking for a pretext to end it, that it feared its development into really militant political struggle, challenging capitalism, far more than the most ignominious defeat.

It proceeded, therefore, in accordance with the traditional tactics of British imperialism, to pursue the General Council along two different but complementary lines. The first was the threat of force, the attack on the General Council as a revolutionary body leading an unconstitutional illegal revolutionary struggle, that would subvert Parliament, democracy, civilisation, that would, inevitably lead to anarchy, that would have to be put down by the most ruthless means including arrest, trial and, if necessary, violence. This line of attack was designed to soften up the General Council members, to instil into them the fear of God (or rather of arrest, massive fines and Red Revolution).

The second, complementary line, the proverbial cunning of British imperialism, was to contrive some form of "negotiation", "compromise", that, though in reality useless, might be construed (by the General Council at any rate) as an "honourable" settlement—to provide a let-out, which disguised as a way out would in fact be a sell-out.

Already on the Monday before the strike, Prime Minister Baldwin began the attack on the "nerves" of the General Council in the House of Commons:

"I do not think all the leaders when they assented to ordering a general strike fully realised that they were threatening the basis of ordered Government, and going nearer proclaiming civil war than we have been for centuries past."[1]

On May 5, under the headline "Hold-up of the Nation", the first issue of the *British Gazette* proclaimed:

"The General Strike is in operation, expressing in no uncertain terms a direct challenge to ordered government."

Day by day the *Gazette* featured blood-curdling speeches and articles by the Prime Minister, by Churchill, Chancellor of the Exchequer, by Lord Oxford and Asquith, Lord Balfour, etc., to the effect that the sacred British Constitution was being undermined.

On May 6, Sir John Simon, Liberal leader, former Attorney-General and Home Secretary, informed the House of Commons in "authoritative" terms that the General Strike was illegal, that every striker who struck in breach of contract could be sued in the County Courts for damages, that:

"Every trade union leader who has advised and promoted this course of action is liable in damages to the uttermost farthing of his personal possessions."[2]

On May 11 Mr. Justice Astbury gave birth to an *obiter dictum* (judgement on a case in which the question was not directly involved) that:

"the so-called General Strike, called by the Trades Union Congress Committee is illegal and contrary to law, and those persons inciting or taking part in it are not protected by the Trades Dispute Act of 1906."[3]

On May 6 the B.B.C. and the official *British Gazette* had refused to let it be known that the Archbishop of Canterbury "after full conference with the leaders of the Christian Church in England" had put forward proposals for a settlement of the strike which included a renewal for a period of Government subsidies and the withdrawal of the mineowners' suggested new wage scales.

---

[1] Hansard, May 3, 1926, col. 71, quoted by Professor Crook, op. cit., pp. 383-384.
[2] Sir John Simon, M.P., *Three Speeches on the General Strike*, p. 5, MacMillan, 1926.
[3] Quoted by Ralph Miliband, *Parliamentary Socialism*, Allen and Unwin, p. 139. Fuller text of the *obiter dictum*, extracted from the *Scotsman* of May 12, 1926, is quoted by R. Page Arnot, *The General Strike*, pp. 209-210.

As counter-blast, the fullest publicity was afforded to Cardinal Bourne's declaration at High Mass in Westminster Cathedral on Sunday, May 9, that the General Strike was:

> "a direct challenge to lawfully constituted authority . . . a sin against the obedience which we owe to God . . ."

and that

> "all are bound to uphold and assist the Government, which is the lawfully constituted authority of the country, and represents, therefore, in its own appointed sphere the authority of God Himself."[1]

An official communiqué dated May 7 declared that:

> "an organised attempt is being made to starve the people and to wreck the state. . . ."[2]

At the week-end (May 8–9) information reached Eccleston Square, the General Council H.Q., that the Government had decided to arrest their members and members of local Strike Committees, to call up the Army Reserve and to repeal the Trades Dispute Act of 1906.[3] On Sunday, May 9, A. A. Purcell, leader of the General Council's Strike Organisation Committee, announced that the Government had issued warrants for the arrest of Ernest Bevin and himself.[4]

Leading a strike that they had not wanted but had not been able to prevent, denounced as revolutionary agitators undermining the Constitution, illegally subverting the state and unlawfully defying the word of God, the right-wing leaders of the General Council, who had all the time been looking for a way out, were by the week-end May 8–9 desperately searching for a pretext to call for a return to work.

For such a pretext they had been looking from the first day of the strike. As Ramsay MacDonald subsequently so well explained, when the strike began:

> "Still, peace efforts went on from the trade union side, every attempt was made to discover contacts that had such influence as to give some promise that their opinion and support would mean something, and at last Sir Herbert Samuel was discovered"[5]

---

[1] Quoted by R. Page Arnot in *The Miners—Years of Struggle*, pp. 433–434.
[2] Quoted by Allen Hutt, op. cit., p. 139.
[3] See *Lansbury's Labour Weekly*, May 22, 1926, p. 5, "Secret History of the Great Strike".
[4] R. Page Arnot, *The General Strike*, p. 201.
[5] Ramsay MacDonald, "The Outlook" in *Socialist Review*, June 1926.

Looking for a let-out the General Council left no stone unturned, and under one of them they found Sir Herbert Samuel. The nature and purpose of Sir Herbert's hurried return from abroad was well described by the Miners' Secretary, A. J. Cook.[1] Sir Herbert:

> "returned post haste to England... as soon as he arrived... he was seen by the Rt. Hon. J. H. Thomas and others, and discussions began in private. Those who had been unwilling and hesitant to go into the strike were continually seeking some way out of it.
>
> "These discussions were held simply with a view to creating some pretext to justify calling off the General Strike...."

The Miners first heard of these negotiations, that were surreptitiously proceeding, at the week-end May 8–9.[2] The Memorandum that was handed to the General Council on May 11, the famous "Samuel Memorandum", contained no concessions, nothing for which the miners were fighting, nothing for which the T.U.C. was supposed to be supporting them, except a vague suggestion of renewal of the subsidy "for such reasonable period as may be required" for negotiation.[3] It definitely envisaged that wages should come down, though after a tenuous reorganisation of the industry. In fact as Herbert Smith, the Miners' President, put it at the time, it was in essence a rehash of the Royal Commission Report, "a new suit of clothes for the same body".

Even had it provided some new basis for negotiation, which it did not, there was *no evidence whatsoever* that the Memorandum had any official status, any Government backing, that there was any guarantee whatsoever that the Government or mineowners would accept it as a basis for renewed negotiation. Indeed, as correspondence between Sir Herbert Samuel and the Minister of Labour, Sir Arthur Steel Maitland, clearly showed (it was only made public *after* the strike) the Government had made clear to Sir Herbert, and Sir Herbert had made clear to the General Council, that he was operating entirely on his own initiative and could give no assurances on behalf of the Government. Indeed, the Government was not even interested in a compromise. Sir Arthur Steel Maitland wrote to Sir Herbert on May 8 (when he was already holding such comradely conversations with J. H. Thomas) that the Government:

---

[1] A. J. Cook, *The Nine Days*, p. 18.
[2] See Miners' Federation Statement of January 12, 1927, p. 10, published in *The Mining Crisis and the National Strike: 1926: Official Reports*, T.U.C., 1927.
[3] Text of Samuel Memorandum is in R. Page Arnot's *The General Strike*, pp. 225–226.

"hold that the General Strike is unconstitutional and illegal. They are bound to take steps to make its repetition impossible. It is, therefore, plain that they cannot enter upon any negotiations unless the strike is so unreservedly concluded that there is not even an implication of such a bargain upon their side as would embarrass them in any legislation which they may conceive to be proper in the light of recent events."[1]

GENERAL COUNCIL COMPLETES THE SELL-OUT

By May 11, eighth day of the strike, the mass of strikers were more solid, united, enthusiastic, militant, confident than ever before. Their organisation in the localities—Strike Committees, Councils of Action—were spreading, becoming more experienced and effective, in a number of cases beginning to develop into alternative centres of power controlling permits, transport, distribution of food. They had no fears of legal action, unconstitutionality, offending the Law or Cardinal Bourne's God. They were becoming *more political*, broader, in outlook. Moreover their reserve forces had yet to be thrown into battle, and at any moment, they thought, large new sections of workers, who were rearing to go, would be called "into the ranks of the strikers". Given the leadership, everything was ready for a new higher stage of mass struggle.

But the leadership was *not* given. The Communist Party, Minority Movement and other militants, who had the line and perspective for the next stage of the struggle, did not yet have sufficient strength and organisation, nor the mass influence, to carry the movement forward *against*—for this is what it meant—the official leadership of the General Council, along with the leaders of the Labour Party and a number of the leaders of the I.L.P.

And for this official leadership the firmness, solidarity and political advance of the strikers became the most potent reason of all for speeding up the call-off of the strike—even more than Government threats of arrests, fines, imprisonment and force. By May 11, the General Council, who had been negotiating for several days with Sir Herbert behind the scenes, had already decided that the strike must end. The point was how to make an abject surrender look like an honourable settlement.[2]

[1] Quoted by Allen Hutt, op. cit., p. 154.
[2] The effect of the Government threats is well illustrated by a recollection of Andrew Rothstein:

"I met Mary Quayle, T.G.W.U., one of the women on the General Council, on the

On the evening of May 11, the miners, unrepresented to date in the "negotiations" with Sir Herbert Samuel, were called in by the General Council.[1] Arthur Pugh, the Chairman, informed them that the Council had *unanimously* endorsed the Samuel Memorandum, that they considered it a reasonable basis for negotiating a settlement, and that they proposed to terminate the General Strike. He implied that the General Council had sufficient guarantees that the Government, too, would accept the Memorandum as a basis of settlement. The miners, unimpressed, asked again and again what and where were these guarantees? A. J. Cook relates:

> "Mr. Pugh was continually pressed and questioned by Mr. Herbert Smith, myself, and my colleagues as to what the guarantees mentioned were, and who had given them. We got no answer. But J. H. Thomas said to me personally, when I asked him whether the Government would accept the Samuel proposals and what were his guarantees: 'You may not trust my word, but will you not accept the word of a British gentleman who has been Governor of Palestine?' "[2]

The miners, still unimpressed, retired for a separate meeting, where they voted a resolution[3] regretting that they had not been invited to the previous discussions, insisting that the General Council's proposals "would even on the best case call for a reduction in the wages of a large number of miners, which is contrary to the repeated declaration of the Miners' Federation", and recalling that "it was exactly on this issue that the General Council helped in their struggle by the declaration of a General Strike". They insisted that if the Samuel Memorandum was used as a basis for calling off the strike, it would be on the authority of the General Council alone.

---

morning of Monday, May 10, after the daily Council meeting. She had a face as long as a fiddle. 'We are beat,' she said. 'Why?' I asked. 'The Government has sent the troops out. Didn't you see about them escorting food from the docks?' I said I had, but didn't the General Council intend to say anything to the troops about strike-breaking? She turned on me like a wild cat: 'What right have you to make such suggestions to me?' —as though I had been saying something improper. 'We are not going to interfere with the forces.' That made everything clear: they wanted an excuse, and this was heaven sent."

[1] There is an excellent short account of the meetings between the Miners and General Council on May 11-12 in Allen Hutt, op. cit., p. 134-155; in A. J. Cook's *Nine Days*; and, more detailed, in R. Page Arnot's *The Miners—Years of Struggle*.
[2] A. J. Cook, op. cit., p. 20.
[3] Full text in R. Page Arnot, *The General Strike*, pp. 208-209.

The rejection by the miners of the Samuel Memorandum as a basis for settlement and for ending the strike prevented the General Council from, as it had hoped, terminating the strike on the evening or night of May 11. On the morning of May 12 the General Council deputation visited the miners who reaffirmed their resolution of the previous day. Hardly had this resolution been received when the General Council proceeded to the Prime Minister at Downing Street where, in the presence of most of the Cabinet, with no guarantees, no terms, no written statement, without even pressing the Samuel Memorandum, they unconditionally surrendered, and called off the General Strike. Ernest Bevin, without success, made some effort to extract a pledge that strikers would be reinstated. But Baldwin promised *nothing* and cursorily dismissed the General Council—"the sooner you get to your work and the sooner I get to mine the better."[1] What work that was we shall see.

Around 1.30 p.m. the bare notice of the call-off, with no explanations, began to flash around the country. At 4 p.m. the B.B.C. announced that the call-off was unconditional and the miners were still out. Capitalist news-sheets began to shout victory.

It is hard to record the complete bewilderment of the great mass of strikers who, just when the strike seemed at its strongest, just when the second line was being called out, just when effective organisation was being established, found the strike called off. Some for a moment thought in terms of victory, but disillusionment was quick to come.

The *British Worker* ran three successive editions on that afternoon[2] and evening of May 12. The first spoke of public assurances by the Prime Minister and gave the impression of a renewed subsidy and withdrawal of lock-out notices. The second, by studied omissions, sought to give the impression that the miners were in agreement with the General Council's decision to call off the strike. The third contained a General Council Manifesto repeating that they had "obtained assurances that a settlement of the mining problem can be secured", explaining that they had decided to end the General Strike in order to resume negotiations for a settlement, and concluding that the unions:

"can be satisfied that an honourable understanding has been reached."

For millions of strikers by nightfall on May 12, the call-off of the General Strike still seemed incomprehensible. The B.B.C. broadcast that "the Cardinal Archbishop of Westminster asks us to announce

[1] Quoted by Allen Hutt, op. cit., p. 157.   [2] See details in Allen Hutt, op. cit., p. 157.

that a *Te Deum* will be sung in Westminster Cathedral after the High Mass at 10.30 tomorrow, Ascension Day".[1]

There was not much doubt, alas, for whose victory Cardinal Bourne would be announcing a song of thanksgiving!

REVENGE IS SWEET

Whilst Baldwin, "sweetly reasonable" in his triumph, was declaiming in the House of Commons on Wednesday afternoon (May 12) that "we should resume our work in a spirit of co-operation", a Government statement, nearer to the real intentions of the capitalist class, was issued and widely distributed:

> "His Majesty's Government have no power to compel employers to take back every man who has been on strike, nor have they entered into any obligation of any kind on this matter."

Revenge is sweet! This was the moment of triumph of the employing class, the moment to hit back, to lower wages, break the trade unions and established factory rights and practices, get rid of "reds" and "agitators". Men returning on Wednesday night and Thursday morning found themselves under open attack.

Some employers were demanding new agreements binding the unions from undertaking strikes except after complex and prolonged notices, conciliation machinery, etc. Some tried to impose on individual trade unionists the signature of "documents" (an old employers' "custom"); some tried to make the tearing up of trade union cards the condition for reinstatement; some forbade the extension of trade unionism to supervisory grades; some insisted on the retention of scabs alongside reinstated strikers. A group of observers, pooling their experiences in a description of the strike, wrote of these days:[2]

> "The bosses in all trades felt, in fact, that now they had the Trade Union movement at their feet, and all they had to do was to stamp on it."

Or again:

> "... employers throughout the country were making a concerted effort to use the strike settlement as a means of reducing wages and breaking Trade Unionism."

[1] Quoted by R. Page Arnot in *The Miners—Years of Struggle*, p. 453.
[2] *Lansbury's Labour Weekly*, May 22, 1926, "The Secret History of the Great Strike", p. 6.

Gradually on that Thursday, May 13, as workers in factory after factory, industry after industry, found not the resumption of negotiations, the peaceful settlement, the guaranteed conditions promised by the General Council, indignation grew and with it action. When the workers realised that the "settlement" was a sell-out, that the lock-out notices had *not* been withdrawn, that the Miners' Federation repudiated the "settlement" and was fighting on, indignation and resistance grew still stronger.

Militants tried to stem the retreat and call for a continuation of the struggle. The Communist Party, in an appeal that we shall analyse later,[1] called on the strikers to refuse to return to work, to reject the Samuel Memorandum, to organise emergency conferences of Strike Committees and Councils of Action, to stand by the miners. A number of union Executive Committees instructed their members not to renew work until previous agreements had been recognised.[2] The Executives of the three railway unions issued joint instructions to members to continue the strike until satisfactory assurances had been received from employers, even the General Council in a statement mildly protested at employers' attempts "to enforce humiliating terms as conditions of the workers resuming their work",[3] and in a message to all unions[4] that had participated in the Strike counselled against signing individual agreements, and promised protection. But the message began with the words that in essence made any real protection impossible: "The General Strike is ended."

Thus on the Thursday (May 13) there was something of a rally which did not go without notice amongst the employers—Baldwin made a more conciliatory speech in the House, "hoping" that employers would behave decently. "Let us get the workers calm as soon as we can," he said. The B.B.C. on Friday (May 14) morning still had to admit that "there is as yet no general resumption of work".

The rally slowed down a little the employers' wholesale and ruthless attack, but it could not do more. Once the General Council had called off the strike unconditionally and ordered the return to work, the left and militants, and this meant above all the Communist Party, were not strong enough to continue the struggle under a new leadership.

[1] *Stand by the Miners: Appeal by the Communist Party of Great Britain*, full text in Appendix VI.
[2] For instance, the National Union of General and Municipal Workers and the Transport Workers.
[3] Text in R. Page Arnot, *The General Strike*, pp. 235-236.
[4] Ibid., p. 237.

There was passionate indignation amongst millions, a feeling of deep bitterness and betrayal, but not yet the political understanding that would have permitted the carrying forward of the strike without and against the General Council.

And so bit by bit the workers had to return. Where they fought harder and the leadership was firmer the losses were somewhat limited, but everywhere the losses were great.

On May 14 a Provisional Agreement was signed between the railway companies and the three railway unions.[1] There were no guarantees of reinstatement save "as soon as work can be found". The trade unions admitted that the calling of the strike was "a wrongful act" and conceded the companies the right to claim damages. They undertook not to strike again except after previous negotiations, to give no support to unofficial strikes, not to call supervisory grades out on strike, and finally agreed that even this settlement should not extend "to persons who have been guilty of violence and intimidation", a convenient cover for sacking militants who had been charged during the strike under E.P.A.

The railway leaders, Thomas, Cramp, Bromley and Walkden declared the settlement "satisfactory". Indeed, it became something of a model for settlements. The railwaymen could not agree.

How "satisfactory" it really was J. H. Thomas himself was to reveal when, speaking at the Labour Party Conference the following October (*against* the proposal for an embargo on coal by the railway unions and *against* a levy on union funds to help the miners who were still fighting on), he admitted that the National Union of Railwaymen:

> "had 45,000 men out who had not gone back to work since May 1st, and 200,000 who were working three days a week."[2]

A similar settlement was signed by the dockers.[3] The print workers were forced to accept a number of "harsh" settlements.[4] Engineering workers, who as part of the General Council's "second line" had only been called out on the last day of the strike, were not spared from wholesale victimisation. Some of the state and Public Authority employers were no less bitter than their "private" colleagues. His Majesty's Stationery Office (H.M.S.O.) posted a notice that it would

---

[1] See Appendix VIII to this chapter.
[2] *The Times*, October 13, 1926, quoted by Professor Crook, op. cit., p. 461.
[3] Text of Dockers Settlement in R. Page Arnot, *The General Strike*, p. 243.
[4] See Professor Crook, op. cit., p. 463.

henceforth employ non-union employees alongside union members.[1] Arthur Henderson informed the House of Commons that the Board of Admiralty was proposing that strikers should forfeit from two to four years' service for calculation of pensions. The Army Victualling Corps had refused to reinstate a number of employees and was replacing them by blacklegs. The London County Council had reduced the wages of a number of strikers by changing their jobs.

When the Prime Minister on May 14 despatched his proposals for settlement to the miners, they were a long way from even the Samuel Memorandum.[2] The offer of a subsidy of around £3 million was conditional on an immediate wage cut of 10 per cent to be followed after three weeks by a further reduction.

The Prime Minister's proposals involved, as well as wage cuts, the abolition of the national minimum, the undermining of the seven-hour day, increased unemployment, the introduction of District Settlements, the replacement of collective bargaining by compulsory arbitration. They meant accepting everything that the General Strike was supposed to have been fought to avoid.

The terms were rejected and the miners, now alone, fought on.

COMMUNISTS AND MILITANTS

In the extensive literature that has developed around the General Strike there is a general consensus of opinion, despite the variety of the different authors' approaches, that the strike was called off by the General Council just when it was at its strongest. It was only the Government, the B.B.C. and news-sheets whistling up their courage and, later, a handful of right-wing Labour leaders seeking to justify their betrayal, who discovered a mythical "weakening" or a mass "return to work".

In fact, day by day as the strike continued, the strikers not only increased their numbers but improved out of all recognition the effectiveness of their organisation—bulletins, communications, pickets, permits, security, etc. and, though less, the clarity of their political understanding of the issues involved.

Day by day, as the strike continued, the organisation of struggle developed more and more *in the localities, around the Trades Councils, strike committees or, as the most militant were usually called, Councils of*

---
[1] Julian Symons, *The General Strike*, p. 214, Cresset Press.
[2] R. Page Arnot, *The Miners—Years of Struggle*, pp. 459–461.

Action. Indeed as the General Council from day to day wobbled and weakened, the local struggles grew stronger, tougher, more united, and the *gap widened* between the effective forces of struggle in the localities and the ineffective General Council. All over Britain tens of thousands of little-known men and women, whose university had been pit or depot or unemployed committee, but who drew their strength from their class, their experience of struggle, in many cases from their Socialist and Communist outlook, and in many cases, too, from their Communist Party, became acknowledged leaders of the General Strike.

It is not easy, within the great mass of courageous militants who became the leaders of the strike to calculate statistically their political affiliation. The miners formed a solid core in the struggle, and there were no few Marxists amongst their leaders, though A. J. Cook was not a member of the Communist Party. There were very many militants in the local Labour Parties and in the Independent Labour Party (I.L.P.). There were very many militants in local and district and national trade union committees of all description. There were a number of militant co-operators who fought against the official Co-operative policy of standing aside from the General Strike. But when you come to examine the most effective strike committees, the best organised Councils of Action, the demonstrations and pickets that caused most anger to the capitalist news-sheets, the men and women that the capitalist State decided to arrest as the most "dangerous" strike leaders, there you will find, among the first, in numbers out of all proportion to the official membership of around 5,000 at the beginning of May 1926, the members of the Communist Party, and with them the members of the National Minority Movement.

The Communist Party, since the victory of Red Friday at the end of July 1925, had been warning, warning, warning of the coming capitalist offensive, and calling and calling again for the working-class movement to prepare. As we have seen, again and again it suggested not only a *political* line of action, but organisational measures for the struggle, including, as the day approached, the formation of Councils of Action. And though it was certainly weakened by the fact that a number of its most experienced leaders were still in gaol, it was ready for the strike when it came, and prepared to the best of its ability to help towards victory.

On the eve of the General Strike a decision was taken to send a number of Executive members out to the Districts, leaving behind in

London a small Working Bureau.[1] The main reasons for this were firstly to see that the Communist Party in each locality could effectively play its part in the coming strike, but also because it was obvious that, under the cover of E.P.A., efforts would be made to arrest the leadership, and that the more that it was distributed the harder this would be.

This Bureau in London met daily in the course of the strike, and with detectives clustered around King Street and other Party premises, the venue was constantly changed. A series of special departments—communications, organisation, publicity—were set up "for the duration" with a Bureau member in charge of each, so that a small, mobile, fairly effective emergency leadership was established, improvising and improving as the strike continued. Despite police raids, the Party Headquarters was left open, as part of a fight against the Government's arbitrary methods and attempts to brand the Party as an illegal organisation.

For the small, financially poor, police-surrounded apparatus of the Party, one of the main problems was communications.[2] A skeleton courier service was set up and a rough plan elaborated for contact with the Districts. Though some Branches of the Party were more or less cut off during the strike, the Districts and most Branches remained in contact with the improvised London centre. The arrest of the London organiser of the Party complicated things for a few days, as on the London District fell the main responsibility for producing the bulletins of the Party and getting the leads and communiqués out to the Districts.

On May 3, eve of the strike, the Party produced a printed *Workers' Daily* in 40,000 copies, containing among other matter the Manifesto of the previous day, first published in the *Sunday Worker*. Already on May 4, first day of the strike, the Party produced in London the first issue of the *Workers' Bulletin*, which continued for ten consecutive days apart from Sunday, May 9, and the main editorials of which were produced collectively by the Political Bureau. The production of the bulletin in London, which started around 5,000 and quickly rose to 20,000, was a quite dramatic episode. Every day paper had to be found, duplicators kept from the police, new places of operation found, copies distributed all over London and all over the country. In many

---

[1] *Workers' Weekly*, No. 170, May 21, 1926, p. 7, and *Political Report to 8th Congress of C.P.G.B.*, pp. 10–11.
[2] *Political Report to 8th Congress of C.P.G.B.*, p. 10–11.

parts of London and in very many parts of the country Party Branches and Districts produced their own Bulletins, reproducing the material of the *Workers' Bulletin* and adding local material, so in effect the bulletin was always circulated in well over 100,000 copies. Police raided office after office trying to locate it, and arrested a number of Party members on suspicion of producing or distributing it, but day after day editing, production and distribution went on.

THE PARTY LINE

The first important contribution of the Communist Party to the militant aspects of the great strike was its *political analysis* of the background of the struggle, the inevitability and nature of the employers' offensive, the dangers of betrayal by the reformist leadership, the general indications of the type of action necessary at each particular stage. The problem was not easy. The Party had at one and the same time to give to the most conscious workers the full socialist analysis of the struggle before them and to put before the mass of workers, who were not yet looking at the struggle in fully political terms, who were not yet socialists, who still saw the central issue as defence of wages and solidarity with the miners, who still in one way or another were under reformist influence and looked for leadership to the General Council, a line of *immediate* action which was comprehensible, acceptable to them and yet would help them to carry the strike forward to victory. The Party knew quite well that at the beginning of the strike the workers were ready for action but not in a revolutionary mood. They were ready to fight on wages, hours, solidarity, but not yet to challenge the social system that gave rise to the problems of wages and hours and solidarity. At the same time, from experience and from Marxist theory, the Party leadership understood that the very participation in so gigantic a struggle as the General Strike could educate workers more in a few hours or days than in months or even years of more "normal" times. The Party, therefore, had to be ready to help the working class *to lift the level of the struggle*, step by step to face its full political implications, in a word, to give political leadership at a time when the reformist leadership would inevitably sell out.

On May 3, eve of the strike, the Party in its Manifesto put forward, as we have seen, solidarity with the miners as the supreme need of the moment, warned against any attempt to isolate the miners and force them to accept lower wages, longer hours or District Agreements, and put forward the slogans of "Not a Penny off the Pay, not a Second on the Day", "Every Man Behind the Miners", and "A Council of Action in every Town".[1] The Manifesto was printed in the *Sunday Worker* the same day and in the sole issue of the *Workers' Daily* on May 3.

On May 5, in the second issue of the *Workers' Bulletin*, the Party published a statement—*The Political Meaning of the General Strike*.[2] In preparing this Manifesto the Party leadership had three considerations in view:

"(1) That the slogan 'Not a Penny off the Pay, Not a Second on the Day', was meeting with the retort of 'economic impossibility', and it was necessary to give the practical alternative to the Coal Commission's Report; (2) That the mere fact of the General Strike had profoundly changed the whole situation so far as the workers were concerned, and they would begin rapidly learning lessons which years of propaganda in 'normal' times would not inculcate . . .; (3) That the fact of police, soldiers, tanks, E.P.A., etc., being paraded before the eyes of the workers was bound to raise before them as a *practical* question the problem of the State, without their necessarily grasping all the *theoretical* implications."[3]

It, therefore, emphasised in the statement that, whilst the miners' demands should remain at the centre of the struggle, the coal problem could only be dealt with satisfactorily by "nationalisation without compensation and under workers' control", and that a victorious advance for the workers demanded the resignation of the Tory government and the formation of a Labour government. The Party continued to put forward its organisational proposals which, at this moment, were already being adopted in many of the most important industrial centres for Councils of Action, Food Commissariats with the aid of the Co-operatives, and Workers' Defence Corps.

On May 5, the Political Bureau considered the economic issues that were facing workers in other industries than mining. It thought that they should be helped to see how much the outcome of the General Strike would affect their *own* as well as the miners' economic position, and how much, therefore, the strike *directly* concerned them all. It was thought that some general slogan that united all the *different* sections of workers, like "wages for time lost" should be put forward,

---

[1] See pp. 114–115 and also text of Manifesto in Appendix IV to this chapter.
[2] Full text in Appendix V to this chapter.
[3] *Political Report to 8th Congress of C.P.G.B.*, pp. 7–8.

and this was discussed and agreed with leading members of the National Minority Movement.[1]

In the following days, in its bulletins and circulars, the Party strongly criticised the General Council's leadership, warned of the danger of capitulation, and warned, too, in a circular of the morning of May 12 that the left wingers in the General Council were shamefully silent about the conduct of the right wing, that the workers must be prepared to take things into their own hands, that emergency meetings should be held of strike committees and Councils of Action. But the surrender of the General Council at midday on Wednesday, May 12, rendered the circular out of date.

The Political Committee met on the Wednesday afternoon and telegraphed early that evening to all Districts an analysis and proposals along the lines that:

"(1) the General Council had surrendered at the very moment when the workers were most enthusiastic;
"(2) the surrender was a betrayal not only of the miners, but of all the workers;
"(3) the left wingers in the General Council, by their policy of cowardly silence, had left the right wing with a free hand to pursue their active policy of treachery;
"(4) the workers must step in where leaders fail;
"(5) the slogans should be 'refuse to resume work', repudiate the Samuel Memorandum, keep the Councils of Action and Strike Committees in being;
"(6) the miners should appeal direct to their fellow workers over the heads of false leaders."[2]

The next day, May 13, the analysis was embodied into a Manifesto—*Stand by the Miners*.[3] It denounced the General Council's decision to call off the strike as "the greatest crime that has ever been permitted, not only against the miners, but against the working class of Great Britain....":

"The British workers had aroused the astonishment and admiration of the world by the enthusiasm with which they had entered upon the fight for the miners' standard of living. But, instead of responding to this magnificent lead by a call to every section of organised labour to join the fight against the capitalists, the General

[1] Ibid., p. 8.   [2] Ibid., p. 9.   [3] Full text in Appendix VI to this chapter.

Council has miserably thrown itself and the miners on the tender mercies of the workers' worst enemies—the Tory Government."

Scores of thousands of copies were distributed in various forms—*Workers' Bulletin*, local bulletins, leaflets; and a special Manifesto, along the same lines, was distributed by the London District of the Party to railwaymen in 10,000 copies.

By May 14 it was clear, with the signing of the shameful Railway Agreement, and of other agreements in important sectors of industry, that there was no hope of keeping the strike going. On May 15 the Party distributed a circular urging the formation of District Conferences of the Councils of Action, raising the issue of their maintenance and the question of changing the leadership of the Labour Movement. The immediate issues were put to the forefront—support for the miners and fight against victimisation.

On May 16, with the employers in full attack, with a feeling of indignation and bewilderment amongst millions of workers, with the danger of a disorganised retreat, the Political Bureau decided to concentrate the efforts of the Party around three key issues[1]—(1) solidarity with the miners (involving the question of embargo on transport of coal, financial support from the unions and credits from the Co-operatives); (2) the fight against victimisation (involving local and district Conferences of the Councils of Action, and pressure on the General Council to call an immediate Conference of the Union Executives; (3) efforts to strengthen the unions and prepare for mass struggles (involving a fight against desertions from the unions, for 100 per cent membership, to replace leaders who had surrendered with those who would fight for the interests of the working class).

In the days before the strike and above all in the nine days of struggle, many workers heard the voice of the Party for the first time; others began to understand its objectives; still others, not yet understanding Marxist approaches, were full of respect for the action of the Party members they had seen in their localities. On May 17 a call went out from the Party for recruitment to its ranks.

THREE BULLETINS, THREE POLICIES

For those who would understand the conflicting policies of the main protagonists in the strike, there can be no better exercise than to study

[1] *Political Report to 8th Congress of C.P.G.B.*, p. 10.

and compare, day by day, three news-sheets or Bulletins—the Government's *British Gazette*,[1] the General Council's *British Worker*,[2] and the Communist Party's *Workers' Bulletin*.[3] They are very different in appearance—the *Gazette* printed, full newspaper format; the *British Worker*, printed half-newspaper size; the *Workers' Bulletin*, a duplicated sheet, roughly prepared, centrally and locally, in a constant chase with the police, on divers types of paper begged, borrowed or purloined, passed from hand to hand, often hidden as its distribution or even possession was, under E.P.A., treated as a crime.

They were very different too, in their content.

It was all honour to the *Workers' Bulletin* that on May 4 it was the first in the field, already pressing that the General Council should produce an official daily Strike Bulletin. It was only as a reply to the Government's *British Gazette*, which came out on May 5 morning, and under heavy pressure from all over the country, that, on the evening of May 5, the first issue of the *British Worker* appeared.

The *Bulletin*'s opening leader congratulated the workers of Britain for the completeness of the response to the call of the General Council. It paid tribute to the print workers whose action on the eve of the strike had "made a splendid prelude to the greatest display of solidarity in British history". It called on all strikers to stand fast, and solemnly warned:

"There is of course a danger—and already the Government's policy makes it clear. They build upon the hope that the T.U.C. will be bamboozled into trying to induce (in the interest of peace!) the miners into retreating behind their minimum demands.

"This the miners cannot and should not do."

From the first issue the *Workers' Bulletin* underlines not only the solidarity of response to the strike but the use of the state against it—in this first issue the movement of troops to the different industrial centres, the arrest of Shapurji Saklatvala, M.P. It printed a soldier's letter, signed *A Worker in Khaki*, asking what should the troops do if the authorities tried to use them as strike breakers.

Why this Bulletin? it asked; and answered, that the Government was

---

[1] *The British Gazette*, published by His Majesty's Stationery Office, May 5–13 (eight issues, no issue on Sunday, May 9).

[2] *The British Worker*, official Strike News Bulletin published by the General Council of the T.U.C. May 5–17 (eleven issues, no issues on Friday, May 14 and Sunday, May 16).

[3] *Workers' Bulletin*, issued by the Communist Party of Great Britain. May 4–14 (ten issues, no issue Sunday, May 9).

trying to obtain a monopoly of news. The B.B.C.'s first act was to call for "volunteer" lino-operators, machine compositors and machine operators. This monopoly must be broken:

> "The Communist Party issues this Bulletin to ensure the circulation of genuine news of the workers' side of the struggle."

On May 5 the first issue of the *British Gazette*, full of the thunder of Churchill its controller, went to its blackleg press on the machines of the *Morning Post*. It warned and stormed:

> "If Parliament were to allow its considered judgement to be overborne under the cruel assault of a general strike, the economic disaster would only be a part of a much greater disaster.... These men [the General Council], would in fact become masters of the country and the power of Government would have passed from Parliament into their hands."

The Government might show a spirit of compromise with the miners ("might" is the operative word, there were no signs of it), but "there can be absolutely none about a general strike". The Government would make use of the B.B.C., edit its own paper, using the "unlimited resources of the state" to raise its circulation day by day.

What had the *British Worker*, which made its début that May 5 evening, to answer to the *Gazette*'s blood-curdling Churchillian rhetoric, its accusations of seizure of power (accompanied by appeals for blacklegs), its list of the Civil Commissioners, its tales of the lack of strikers and cracking of their morale, its reports of "Red Tyranny" in Russia and of a love affair in the Parrot House of the London Zoo?

We have to take care to differentiate between the courage of the print workers and many of the editorial staff who produced this first issue, virtually in a police raid, and kept the paper going often in conditions of extreme difficulty, and the political cowardice of those responsible for its policy. As we have seen, the *British Worker*, that should have been long prepared as one of the most elementary steps for conduct of the strike, only appeared on Wednesday evening in reply to the *British Gazette*. The story of this first issue is told in the second issue.[1] By 8 p.m. that evening it was all ready for printing, copy sub-edited and set, the last stereo plate made and fastened into place. Outside the *Daily Herald* building, where the printing was to be done, large numbers of members of the distributive section of the Paper

---

[1] *British Worker*, No. 2, March 6, pp. 1 and 8, "How the 'B.W.' came out".

Workers' Union were ready with motor cycles and cars. Then came the police raid. Despite the raid 320,000 were printed—more than the first issue of the *British Gazette*.

But what of the content? Here the contradiction is already apparent. The issue abounds with news, irrepressible news, of the magnificent response to the call. The strike, it reports, is *solid*—in London, South Wales, Clydeside, the Midlands—everywhere. Information is already being received of international solidarity. "Wonderful Response to the Call"—"Immediate, Unanimous and Enthusiastic Response to Strike Order"—these are typical headlines.

But when it comes to politics and perspective and advice on *how* to win the strike, the right-wing policy is already apparent. To the *Gazette*'s accusation of revolutionary activity, of undermining the Constitution, to the *open political* use of the state against the strikers, the *British Worker* replies for the General Council:

> "The General Council of the Trades Union Congress wishes to emphasise the fact that this is an industrial dispute. . . ."[1]

When the crying need of the moment is *for every* man and woman to rally to the local strike committee or Council of Action, and to work on supply, information, picketing, food or one or other of the multifold services needed for victory, the *British Worker*, for the General Council, carries perhaps the most classic reformist proposal of all time:

> "The General Council suggests that in all districts where large numbers of workers are idle, sports should be organised and entertainments arranged. This will both keep a number of people busy and provide amusement for many more."[2]

In other words, it was saying to the workers: "For God's sake don't get involved *yourselves* in the strike. Keep quiet, keep out of mischief and leave it to us."

On May 5 the *Workers' Bulletin* brought out its second number. It also carried news of the solidarity of the strikers, and in its four duplicated pages it told of the mass pickets, of attacks by police, of movements of troops, of successful struggles to defeat blacklegs, the stopping of private buses manned by scabs. It carried the news (which was to be used so often for arresting and sentencing distributors of the *Bulletin*) that:

[1] *British Worker*, p. 1, in bold type.
[2] Ibid., No. 1, p. 1, in bold type.

"According to the Government Wireless, a few soldiers, at Aldershot refused to entrain for an industrial centre. From another source, we learn that it was nearly the whole battalion.

"It is reported that the Welsh Guards are confined to their barracks in Chelsea for insubordination."

Above all, it carried the Communist Party Manifesto *The Political Meaning of the General Strike*.[1] Unlike the General Council, there was no timid attempt to justify the strike as a non-political purely industrial conflict, no call to the workers to stay at home and be good and leave it to the General Council, but a call for *militant political* action, for the extension of the struggle, for every man and woman to participate in the Councils of Action and their work. You cannot defeat the political offensive of the Tory Government, said the *Bulletin*, by purely defensive struggle:

"Once the battle has been joined, the only way to victory is to push ahead and hit hard. And the way to hit the Capitalist hard is for the Councils of Action to throw out clear watchwords: Not a Penny off the Pay, Not a Second on the Day; Nationalise the Mines without Compensation under Workers' Control; Formation of a Labour Government."

Three Bulletins—three policies! In the next few days (May 6–9) the main lines of approach became still clearer. The *British Gazette* became more threatening; its accusations against the General Council were more exaggerated (especially in comparison with the latter's true position); its calls to blacklegs, guarantees to troops, reports of state action more blatant.

On May 6 the *Gazette*, big and prominent, quotes the Prime Minister: "*The Constitutional Government is being Attacked!* . . . The *General Strike* is a challenge to Parliament and is the Road to Anarchy and Ruin."[2] On May 7 it menaces: "Everyone must realise that, in so far as the General Strike is concerned, there can be no question of compromise of any kind. Either the country [*sic!*] will break the General Strike, or the General Strike will break the country."[3] On May 9 it prints, in great prominence, the Government's guarantee that all ranks of the Armed Forces who take any action to aid the "Civil Power" in the strike "will receive both now and afterwards, the full

---

[1] See pp. 136–137 and Appendix V to this chapter.
[2] *British Gazette*, No. 2, May 6.   [3] Ibid., No. 3, May 7, p. 3.

support of His Majesty's Government"[1] and appeals to civil servants of every grade, men and women alike, to volunteer for "emergency duties".[2] To underline this lesson in the "neutral state", it splashes with bold headline Sir John Simon's pronouncements on the strike's "illegality".

Against all this, the *British Worker* again and again *ad nauseam* defends itself on its knees. Standing nominally at the head of the biggest contingent of striking workers in world history to date, it pleads for "understanding" from the Tory Government. On May 6, under the headline "No attack on the Constitution":

> "No political issue has ever been mentioned or thought of in connection with it [the strike] . . . at the special T.U.C. it was perfectly clear that nothing was in anybody's mind save the Industrial issue . . . the General Strike is not a 'menace' to Parliament. No attack is being made on the Constitution. We beg Mr. Baldwin to believe that."[3]

Then, in the same issue, as in the first, the famous (infamous!) "Message to Workers":

> "The General Council of the Trade Union Congress wishes to emphasise the fact that this is an industrial dispute. It expects every member taking part to be exemplary in his conduct and not to give any opportunity for police interference. The outbreak of any disturbance would be very damaging to the prospect of a successful termination to the dispute.
>
> "The Council asks pickets especially to avoid obstruction and to confine themselves strictly to their legitimate duties."

On May 7, the *British Worker* prints on top of the front, and thereafter repeats in issue after issue like a ghastly chorus until the sell-out:

> "*The General Council does not challenge the Constitution.* It is not seeking to substitute unconstitutional government. Nor is it desirous of undermining Parliamentary institutions. The sole aim of the Council is to secure for the miners a decent standard of life. The Council is engaged in an industrial dispute. *There is no Constitutional crisis.*"

What is "exemplary conduct" when the *police* interfere? On this the *British Worker* is silent. It is silent on the baton charges. It is silent on

---
[1] Ibid., No. 4, May 8, p. 1. [2] Ibid., p. 3. [3] *British Worker*, No. 2, May 6, p. 4.

the arrests. By the end of the week-end May 9, though the *Gazette* and the Tory news-sheets are full of news of arrests and the B.B.C. is reporting them daily, there is *not an item on the arrest of the strikers*!

What is "examplary conduct" in one of the biggest strikes in history when the Government is using troops and specials and blacklegs, arresting right and left, monopolising the radio and attempting to monopolise the newsprint? On May 9 the *British Worker* tells us.[1] Exemplary behaviour is "special football and cricket matches . . . indoor attractions . . . whist drives". Exemplary behaviour is the Plymouth example, where a strikers' team defeated a police team at football, after the Chief Constable's wife had kicked off.[2] Most "exemplary" was the Cardiff Strike Committee's Appeal approvingly quoted:

> "Keep smiling. . . . Refuse to be provoked. Get into your garden. Look after the wife and kiddies. If you have not got a garden get into the country, the parks and playgrounds. Do not hang around the centre of the city. Get into the country, there is no more heartful occupation than walking."[3]

The *Workers' Bulletin* (May 6 and 7) devoted its space to a different sort of behaviour—the behaviour of the various instruments of state and the behaviour of militant strikers, to arrests and raids, movements of troops, the defeat of blacklegs, the work of Councils of Action. It does not call on the workers to eschew politics, but for militant *political* action.

The Communist Party and the *Workers' Bulletin* could perhaps be criticised that they were slow to answer the Government's specific accusation that the strike was unconstitutional, illegal. In one sense the whole line of the Party's May 5 Manifesto gave the lines of a general reply to this—that the strike was by its very nature *political*, that victory demanded *political* action by the workers. On May 8 the *Workers' Bulletin* turned more in detail to this issue, criticising the defeatist role of the *British Worker*:

> "The anxiety of the *British Worker* to assure everybody that the strike is a 'purely industrial dispute' is almost pathetic . . . the Government every hour makes more of a political issue of it. Their seizure of the stocks of printing paper is not only evidence that they are driven to extremity, but evidence also, that under E.P.A. the 'Constitution' is just what the Government choose to make it."

[1] *British Worker*, No. 5, p. 2, col. 1. [2] Ibid., p. 3, col. 1. [3] Ibid., No. 5, May 8, p. 3.

The raids, the use of troops, the *Workers' Bulletin* continued, are *political*. The whole Government offensive is *political*. Against their *politics* the *workers* need to fight politically for the nationalisation of the pits and for a Labour government.

On the critical days of May 10–12 the *Gazette* continues its blood-curdling denunciations of the "revolutionary" General Council. Lord Balfour declaims that the General Strike is "an attempted revolution" which would mean for Britain "ruin—swift, complete and irresistible".[1] Sir Douglas McGarel Hogg, K.C., Attorney-General, yet once more proclaims "Constitutional Government Challenged".[2] Scabs are promised protection from the state on return to work.[3] Divers reports are produced that the strike is weakening, morale falling, strikers returning to work, traffic returning to normal, only to confess on May 12 that "there is as yet little sign of a general collapse of the strike".[4] In the provinces 200,000 special constables have been recruited and over 40,000 in London, says the *Gazette*.[5] The magistrates have imposed a number of "sharp sentences".[6]

No one could imagine from the *British Worker* that the General Council in these three days was actively contriving a sell-out. "*All's Well*" shouts the headline on May 10,[7] "we are entering upon the second week of the general stoppage. . . . Nothing could be more wonderful than the magnificent response of millions of workers to the call of their leaders", "*Second Week Starts Magnificently*",[8] "So far from 'dribbling back', as Mr. Churchill pretends, the men on strike are standing like a rock, and more are coming out."[9] So that when May 12 came, it was small wonder that, in three successive editions, as we have seen, they tried to conceal the real character of the call-off, to hide the miners' rejection of their act, to disguise the shameful settlement as an honourable settlement.

The *Workers' Bulletin* continued to report the arrests still ignored by the *British Worker*, continued to report the examples of militant Councils of Action, and continued to underline that defeat in the strike would mean an all-out attack on trade unionism.[10] On May 12 it came out, before the news of the call-off but already well aware of what the General Council was preparing and of the dangerous proceedings involving Thomas and Sir Herbert, warning, warning, warning. It

[1] *British Gazette*, No. 5, May 10, p. 1.　[2] Ibid., No. 6, May 11, p. 1.
[3] Ibid., No. 5, May 10, p. 1.　[4] Ibid., No. 7, May 12.
[5] Ibid.　[6] Ibid.
[7] *British Worker*, No. 6, May 10, p. 1.　[8] Ibid., p. 4.　[9] Ibid., No. 7, May 11, p. 1.
[10] *W.B.*, No. 6, May 10, p. 1.

called for emergency meetings of the strike committees and Councils of Action, for strengthening of the strike, for the working class to "stand by the miners".

May 13—the strike was over—three papers with three policies! For the *Gazette* the keynote was triumph; for the *Workers' Bulletin* treachery; for the *British Worker*, let all "forgive and forget".

The *Gazette* in this its last issue[1] printed top centre on the first page the King's Message: "Let us forget whatever elements of bitterness the events of the past few days have created. . . ." But immediately below came the Government's communiqué with big bold headlines: "Reinstatement: No Obligations Incurred", and in a big black box: "Emergency Regulations still in Force".

The *British Worker* lingered on till May 17. On May 13, under mass pressure, it protests somewhat at the failure of employers to receive strikers back with open arms. (Who but the General Council (and perhaps Sir Herbert) had ever said that they would?) "We have trusted you", is the line, don't let us down! Beneath the headline "Peace with Honour" (that was to reappear twelve years later, at a sell-out not so different) the *British Worker* laments:

> "The General Council called off the General Strike in confidence that the Prime Minister meant what he said when he asked for resumption of negotiations towards an honourable peace."

On May 10[2] it reports the shameful railway settlement as "satisfactory". Mr. Thomas hopes "that the men will accept it in the spirit in which the Companies and the leaders signed the agreement". Mr. Walkden of the Railway Clerks was "grateful to the railway managers for the magnanimous spirit in which they had concluded the discussion".

The strike had begun in the first place to defend the miners' wages. The General Council had called it off on the pretext that the Samuel Memorandum gave a basis for negotiation. On May 15 the *British Worker* describes the Prime Minister's proposals to the Miners:[3]

> "Mr. Baldwin's proposals for a Mine Settlement have been presented to the two parties for consideration. They include some but not all the points of the Samuel Memorandum, they suggest reductions of wages."

---

[1] *British Gazette*, No. 8, May 13, 1926.
[2] *British Worker*, No. 10,, p. 1.
[3] Ibid., No. 10, May 15, p. 1.

On May 17 the *British Worker*, on almost the last page of its last issue, discovered that a certain number of strikers had been arrested.

The skill and courage of print, editorial and distribution workers brought its circulation (central and provincial editions together) to over one million by the end of the strike. By that time the circulation of the *Workers' Bulletin* (central and reproduced in the Districts and Branches) was perhaps over 200,000,[1] in comparison small. But relative to the size of the two organisations concerned, not so discreditable.

On May 13, the *Workers' Bulletin* published the Communist Party's appeal *Stand by the Miners*.[2] In face of "the greatest crime that has ever been permitted" against the British working class, it called on the Councils of Action to fight on, and on the workers everywhere to stand by the miners. Unlike the *British Worker* it made clear that the miners had rejected the call-off. The next day it printed a new Communist call—*Reform the Ranks and Fight On*.

It is not by accident that amongst the hundreds of those arrested under one or another section of E.P.A., i.e. for opposing in one form or another the capitalist offensive, a goodly proportion were charged with distributing the *Workers' Bulletin*. Try and find reports of strikers charged with distributing the *British Worker*!

COUNCILS OF ACTION

If the *first* aspect of the role of the Communist Party in the General Strike was what could be called the battle of ideas, the political line, the socialist analysis of the situation at its successive stages and the pointer as to what in this situation would be the most effective course of action, the *second* and, of course, inseparable aspect was the specific leadership of the struggle, the role played by the Communist Party Branches and members in mobilising workers for the strike, in developing unity for and during the strike, in organising every type of activity necessary for the conduct of the strike—above all the help given by the Party in the fight for and organisation of strike committees and Councils of Action.

No one should attempt to paint the tremendous apparatus of strike committees and Councils of Action that grew up throughout Britain

---

[1] This is probably an underestimate. The central edition in London reached a peak of over 20,000 and there were very many copies reproduced in editions of 2,000–20,000 all over the country as well as incorporation of contents into local Party Bulletins.

[2] See pp. 137–138 and Appendix VI to this chapter.

as the monopoly of Communists. Nor is it easy until much more research is done to pin down the specific positions held by Communist Party members or sympathisers in each particular committee. The Party itself and its members put themselves at the service of the manifold strike organisations without demanding a receipt. Thousands and tens of thousands of non-Communist miners and other militant trade unionists, I.L.P.'ers, members of Constituency Labour Parties, helped to form and man the Councils of Action. But certain things should be recognised.

The Communist Party, which was among the first to put forward the idea of Councils of Action in 1920,[1] saw the role that such Councils should play in the General Strike and, long before the beginning of the strike, had been counselling their formation. As the strike drew nearer the Party's proposal grew more specific. Councils of Action were one of the main propositions in the Party's Statement of April 23,[2] in the May 2 Manifesto[3] and in the *Workers' Daily* of May 3.[4]

Officially it might be said that the Councils of Action followed on the "Proposals for Co-ordinated Action" issued by the General Council to trade union Executives on the night of April 30, and accepted by the Conference on May 1:[5]

> "The work of the Trades Councils, in conjunction with the local officers of the trade unions actually participating in the dispute, shall be to assist in carrying out the foregoing provisions (i.e. stoppage of work in various trades and undertakings, and exceptions thereto) and they shall be charged with the responsibility of organising the trade unionists in dispute in the most effective manner for the preservation of peace and order."

But the *effective* Councils of Action and strike committees went *far beyond* the formal co-ordinating committee envisaged by the T.U.C., far beyond the normal functioning of the normal Trades Council or Trades and Labour Council, whose activities in any case had been frowned on by the General Council. With the General Strike and on the initiative of militants, often Communists, moribund Trades Councils were revived, and existing ones were broadened to bring in

---

[1] See Vol. I, pp. 83–87.
[2] See Appendix III to this chapter.
[3] See Appendix IV to this chapter.
[4] See *Political Report of 8th Congress of C.P.G.B.*, p. 7.
[5] Quoted by Emile Burns in *The General Strike May 1926: Trades Councils in Action*, L.R.D., 1926, p. 7.

all types of working-class organisation, including political organisations, until they became real expressions of the *whole* local working class movement.[1]

The Communist Party had pioneered the campaign for many of the forms of action which became essential parts of the activity of the most effective strike committees and Councils of Action—such as the Commissariats (food distribution), the Workers Defence Corps, the local Bulletins.

Though much more research still needs to be carried out, it would seem that in very many of the Councils of Action which were most militant and most effective in their activity, organising mass picketing, issuing widely-circulated bulletins, acting as centre of permits and of transport generally, Communists participated, often in leading positions; where the right wing monopolised the strike organisations, Committees remained formal, often split and unco-ordinated, ineffective.

The Communist Party Districts or Branches often continued to produce their own bulletins (they had a very good base for this in the many factory bulletins which they put out), but in the main they put themselves and their resources unreservedly at the disposal of the Strike Committees. This was true too of the National Minority Movement and of the National Unemployed Workers' Committees, in both of which Communists played a leading part. One of the most impressive aspects of the strike was the degree to which the Government failed to win the unemployed into the various blackleg organisations and, conversely, the degree to which the unemployed rallied to the Councils of Action.

In the examination of Councils of Action made by the Labour Research Department after the strike it was found that the majority of them were composed of (1) Trades Council representatives; (2) strike committee representatives from each of the unions or groups involved; (3) representatives of unions not affiliated to the Trades Council; (4) representatives of political parties and other mass organisations (women, youth, etc.)[2]

Where the right wing dominated, or where there was an excess of craft and local "patriotism" (the two usually went together), the

---

[1] See Emile Burns, op. cit., pp. 11–13. This study is based on reports received from 54 Councils of Action, 45 Strike Committees, 15 Trades Councils, 8 Emergency Committees and 9 Committees otherwise designated in reply to a questionnaire sent out by the Labour Research Department after the General Strike.

[2] Emile Burns, op. cit., pp. 13–14.

genuine unity of the Joint Strike Committee or Council of Action tended to be replaced by a series of *separate* Union Strike Committees, each more intent on vertical contact with its own District or Executive officials than on militant local fighting unity. In such cases picketing was often organised separately, if at all, and was ineffective, mass picketing was frowned on as "contrary to the 1906 Trades Dispute Act", political organisations were not brought in, joint mass meetings discouraged.[1]

One of the main proposals made by the Communist Party in nearly all the "be prepared" statements issued in the months, weeks and days before the General Strike, had been the achievement of national and local co-operation between the trade union and the Co-operative movement, particularly on questions like the Commissariats (food supplies) and credits for strikers and their families in the local Co-operative stores. The lack of such co-operation was one of the weakest aspects of the strike organisations nationally and locally. There was no reference of any kind to the Co-operative Societies in the instructions issued by the General Council. The right wing in both trade union and Co-operative movement seem to have been equally to blame for this separation.

Only in a few localities, nearly always militant localities, was it broken down. There were some examples of local Co-operatives working closely with Councils of Action, usually in relation to credits,[2] sometimes in the form of loans or donations, sometimes by lending halls or premises to the Councils of Action or strike committees. In a few examples the Co-operatives acted as bankers, helping strikers or strike committees to fill in the delay in the arrival of union funds or benefits. Only 5 out of the 140 Councils of Action who answered the Labour Research enquiry reported that local Co-operative organisations were represented on the Councils of Action.

As the strike developed the various strike committees and Councils of Action broadened the scope of their activities. The nature of the situation demanded daily meetings, in a number of the more effective Councils there was an almost continuous session day and night of at least some sub-committee.[3] Bit by bit various special committees or departments were set up such as Finance, Propaganda and Publicity

[1] See C.B. *The Reds and the General Strike*, C.P.G.B., 1926 (2nd edition). This was first published in June 1926.

[2] In the L.R.D. survey, 29 out of the 140 who filled out the questionnaire reported some sort of credit arrangement. See Emile Burns, op. cit., pp. 55–56.

[3] Emile Burns, op. cit., p. 16.

(including Information, Press, Intelligence), Relief and Prisoners' Aid, Pickets, Permits, Transport and Communications, Entertainment, etc.

Picketing was sometimes organised individually by the particular unions concerned with particular enterprises, but where it was most effective, it took the form of mass pickets of a *united* character organised by the Council of Action. Successful mass pickets, as might be expected, were most common in militant industrial areas, particularly in the coalfields and on the railways. Effective mass pickets were organised, amongst many reported, at Stockton, Wakefield, Bolton, Pontypridd, Leyton. In London there was some of the most effective picketing. In West Ham and Poplar the streets were blocked except for transport "By permission of T.U.C.". Clapham tram depot was immobilised by a mass picket. The centralised picket at Bolton organised 2,280 pickets in two days on a duty roster of 4 hours on and 20 hours off.[1] In the Doncaster area, a mass picket of 1,000 repeatedly maintained its organisation despite 80 arrests and repeated police charges.[2]

The Government had prepared its communications ever since the previous August. The General Council improvised at the last moment; despite tremendous efforts by supporters, its transport and communications service was very inadequate. The burden of keeping contact with the centre and with other neighbouring committees, therefore, fell in the main on the local Councils of Action whose resources usually consisted of a few cars reinforced with motor and push bikes. Bolton mobilised 57 motor-bicycles, Coventry 9 cars and 60 motor-bikes, Methil in the Fife coal field—a very strong and militant centre—3 cars and 100 motor-bikes.

On the Councils of Action and the strike committees fell the main responsibility of *information*—meetings, bulletins, etc.—to counteract the Government monopolised B.B.C., the *British Gazette* and multifold reactionary news-sheets. The *British Worker*, as we have seen, reached a circulation of over a million by the end of the strike, but can hardly be said to have contributed much to the organisation and fighting capacity of the strikers. The *Workers' Bulletin* at times may have reached 200,000 or so with its local reproductions. But the gaps were filled by virtually hundreds and hundreds of local Bulletins edited by Councils of Action, Strike Committees, and very often by local

[1] Ibid., p. 25.
[2] Allen Hutt, op. cit., p. 151.

Communist Parties as well.[1] About half of the 140 Councils of Action and strike committees who answered to the Labour Research Department enquiry produced local or area bulletins. A few of these were printed (Gateshead, Preston, Leeds, Croydon for instance), but most were produced on duplicators or typewriters lent by local Labour Parties, I.L.P. and Communist Party Branches, and trade unions. Most of the bulletins appeared daily, in some cases with a circulation of up to 10,000, and everyone reported that demand far exceeded supplies.

Some of the bulletins added to the reports of the struggle and leads for action, poems and paragraphs that, far from the realms of political jargon, roused the people with that deeply-felt humour typical of the British working-class movement.[2] The main and merited target was the scabs. For example:

TO HEAVEN BY L.M.S.
Official Bulletin from 2 Hell-O S.B.

Early in the morning, per broadcast from London, see the little puff-puffs all in a row, D'Arcy on the engine, pulled a little lever. Expansion of the boiler—UP WE GO.[3]

RAILWAY TRIOLET
There's a train comin' in
At the station, my boys;
Tho' there's only the yin
There's a train coming in.
O' the noise and the din
O' the din and the noise;
There's a train comin' in
At the station, my boys.[4]

---

[1] Virtually all rail and motor traffic was stopped (and on the north-east coast, coastal traffic too: here the District Secretary of the Seamen's Union supported the strike despite the official decision of Havelock Wilson and the union.) Thus in most areas outside the Home Counties the initiative lay in the localities. On this R. Page Arnot comments in a note to the author:

"The result was that on the north-east coast and in many other areas north of the Trent or outside the Home Counties it was bound to be like the Battle of Inkerman—'a soldiers' battle'. One of the features was the widespread production by all and sundry among the strikers, naturally with Communists to the forefront wherever there were Communists, of local bulletins wherever there was a stencilling machine available. . . . The historian should fully realise the extent to which it had to be such a 'soldiers' battle', and in this respect it was very fortunate, as it released so much local initiative."

[2] For these and many other examples see Emile Burns, op. cit., pp. 51-54.

[3] *Bristol Central Strike Committee Bulletin*, May 11, 1926, 2LO was the call-sign of the B.B.C.

[4] *Paisley Strike Bulletin*, undated.

"We understand that luncheon cars are to be put on trains running between Westminster and Blackfriars."[1]

"Notices posted on Cemetery Walls at Highgate and Finchley called for Volunteers. We suggest that it should be picketed by Underground men."[2]

Workers Defence Corps or Workers Police was one of the forms of organisation for which the Communist Party had continuously campaigned in the course of the months preceding the strike. Such organisations developed above all around the militant effective Councils of Action in which Communists and other militants were particularly active. The Labour Research survey reports organisations roughly of this character in Aldershot, Chatham, Colchester, Croydon, Denny and Dunipace, Methil, St. Pancras, Selby, Sowerby Bridge, Willesden. The model Defence Corps was, as we shall see, at Methil in the Fife Coalfield, at that time a stronghold of Communist influence.

Relations with the police varied. The Government had done its best to move police from their home areas to "foreign parts" to avoid fraternisation. In some places the police were provocative, looking for trouble, arrest-prone and baton-happy. In others the lower ranks of the police, at least, showed their respect for the strikers. In some places where the strike was strong and well organised the police found it more convenient to keep out of the way. In some the police were virtually besieged in their stations. In others there was a form of fraternisation that was pure class collaboration (the type the *British Worker* liked to report). The specials and various blackleg organisations were pretty vicious, ranging from upper-class warriors openly defending their class interests, through ex-colonial colonels, via Oxford and Cambridge students out for a rag, to members of the British Fascisti. Where there was blatant provocation, more often than not the specials and blacklegs were behind it rather than the regular police force.

THE COMMUNIST PARTY IN THE AREAS

In some cases it is possible to obtain figures of the numbers of Communists serving on the strike committees and Councils of Action; but details are, of necessity, extremely incomplete.

[1] *Westminster Worker*, May 12, 1926.
[2] *St. Pancras Bulletin*, No. 11, May 12.

J. R. Campbell reported immediately following the strike on Communist participation in Councils of Action, etc., in a number of areas of Scotland.[1] In the west of Scotland a joint committee of the Communist Party and Minority Movement remained in more or less permanent session throughout the strike, directing the work in the west of Scotland and keeping contact also with the separate Lanarkshire District Committee. It issued locally the Communist Party Statement of May 2 in some 14,000 copies and a Minority Movement Manifesto to metal workers in 10,000 copies.

During the first week the Committee published emergency editions of the *Worker* and *Workers' Weekly* (4 pages, about 18,000 copies), then the "night shift was picked up by the police". On the second week it published *The Workers' Press* (6,000 edition) with a further issue (10,000) at the end of the strike.

In Glasgow there were five Communist Party members on the Central Strike Committee waging a difficult struggle against a not very active leadership, trying above all to compensate for the inactivity of the Central Strike Committee by the development of local committees. Communist initiative was largely instrumental in the establishment of fifteen local strike committees, which included many Communists elected as trade union representatives. Communists were amongst the most widely demanded speakers sent out by the various committees. There were active Party groups, for instance, in the Councils of Action at Motherwell and Blantyre. At the Andrie and Coatbridge Council of Action there was a strong Party group which included the Chairman. Here a Bulletin was issued (8,000 circulation), a Workers' Defence Corps organised, and mass picketing involving up to 4,000 workers.

In Lanarkshire all the local Councils of Action linked up on a county basis, composing a Committee of 40 delegates of whom eight, including the Chairman, were members of the Communist Party. On the Paisley Committee there were four Communists, on the Kilmarnock Committee two. The Vale of Leven Central Strike Committee of 20 contained nine Communists and was one of the most militant, with functioning sub-committees on organisation, picketing, propaganda, defence and supplies. At Falkirk two Party members were on the Town Strike Committee, and many others were active in outlying towns. In contrast, at Greenock a new Trades Council was formed owing to the positive attitude of the old Trades Council to the Communist

[1] *Workers' Weekly*, No. 170, May 21, 1926.

Party. This new anti-Communist Council, though very "official" and proceeding strictly according to rule, was virtually dead so far as activity was concerned in the General Strike.

In the east of Scotland the Fife coalfield was particularly active during the whole strike. And it is worth while looking more in detail at Methil, where the strength of the Communist Party was particularly high.[1] Here the Trades Council formed a Council of Action, accepting a number of Communist suggestions for organisation, which in its turn set up a Workers' Defence Corps, and sections on Food and Transport, Information, Propaganda, later adding others on Prisoners' Aid and Entertainment. One of the most prominent Communist miners in the area, David Proudfoot, was appointed Convener for all the Sub-Committees. Reporting just after the strike a member of the Council of Action wrote:

> "The organisation worked like clockwork. Everything was stopped—even the railway lines were picketed. The Council had a courier service second to none in Britain with three motor-cars (and a maximum of six available) 100 motor-cycles, and as many push bikes as were necessary. They covered the whole of Fife taking out information and bringing in reports, sending out speakers everywhere, as far north as Perth."[2]

A member of the S.D.F.[3] was convener of the Defence Corps, working closely with Communists. The reporter continues:

> "After police charges on mass pickets, the Defence Corps, which 150 workers had joined at the outset, was reorganised. Its numbers rose to 700, of whom 400, commanded by workers who had been N.C.O.'s during the war, marched in military formation through the town to protect the picket. The police did not interfere again."

A daily bulletin was issued by the Council of Action, which took over the Co-operative Hall as its headquarters. The Communist Party issued its own bulletin and distributed 20,000 of the Party Manifesto. It is not surprising that in this, one of the most militant and best organised areas of the strike, arrests were frequent along with

---

[1] Ibid., Also *Workers' Weekly*, No. 173, June 11, 1926, p. 4.
[2] *Workers' Weekly*, No. 173, June 11, 1926.
[3] A handful of B.S.P. members, associated with Hyndman, after their defeat in the B.S.P. formed their own separate organisation which continued under various names, and eventually adopted anew the old name of S.D.F.

arbitrary prison sentences and few acquittals. Some 7,000 people signed a petition for the removal of one of the police inspectors considered the most hostile.

The Communist miners' leader, Abe Moffat, then a young Communist and militant miner, describes how in parts of the Fife Coalfield control of transport began to pass into the hands of the strikers:[1]

"... Cowdenbeath, Fife ... all motor vehicles had to get permission from the Trades Council before travelling up the Great North Road. We had pickets on in various parts of the road to ensure that no one passed without the permission of the Trades Council. To ensure that no one would pass, miners had a rope across the road. If a motor vehicle had a pass it got through, if it had no pass it had to turn back."

Arrests, as at Methil, were frequent. Abe Moffat, for instance, had a younger brother, David, and a brother-in-law arrested in Cowdenbeath. Another brother, Alex (also a Communist who, much later, succeeded Abe as President of the Scottish Miners' Federation), was imprisoned for two months for a speech made during the strike (Abe himself escaped with a fine).

J. T. Murphy, at that period a member of the Executive Committee of the Communist Party, reported immediately following the strike on events at Middlesbrough and around Sheffield.[2] At Middlesbrough there were four Party members and a number of close associates of the Party on the Central Strike Committee. This was an extremely effective Committee.[3] "It may safely be said that we have never known a strike entered upon with such enthusiasm and determination by the workers before", its Secretary reported afterwards. It met daily, kept an emergency committee on duty at night, organised an efficient despatch riders service. Indeed, Murphy reported that it was so authoritative that it secured the withdrawal of all mounted police and special constables from the streets "in the interests of order".

In Sheffield the Trades Council formed its industrial section into a Central Dispute Committee, which refused an official offer of co-operation from the Communist Party but also sought the support of its individual members, one of whom, George Fletcher, was in fact Vice-Chairman of the Trades Council and a moving spirit of the

---
[1] Abe Moffat, *My Life with the Miners*, p. 45, Lawrence and Wishart, 1965.
[2] *Workers' Weekly*, No. 170, May 21, 1926.
[3] Emile Burns, op. cit., pp. 145–149.

Strike Committee (and of the Communist Party and Minority Movement).[1]

The Communist Party and Minority Movement organised in Sheffield an unofficial strike committee, which produced a daily bulletin of around 10,000 copies (moving heaven and earth and the duplicator to keep out of the hands of the police). After five days the equipment was finally seized, but the No. 6 "Special Strike Bulletin" appeared on May 11, prepared secretly from somewhere in the A.E.U. Institute at Stanley Street, which itself was raided on May 12. Twelve Communists were arrested for their strike activity, including George Fletcher.

In Barrow, there were three Communists on the Council of Action, including its Secretary, and many on the individual union strike committees. The Party published its own daily bulletin, of which around 500 were circulated by the fourth issue.[2]

In what was then the Liverpool District of the Party, the District Party Committee remained in almost constant session throughout the strike.[3] It published a Party bulletin, the *Workers' Gazette* on May 10 and 11, and helped the production of the daily bulletin of the Merseyside Council of Action (3,000–4,000 circulation). There were six Communists on the St. Helens, two on the Garston, one on the Bootle and the Liverpool, two on the Birkenhead, and four on the Wallasey Council of Action.[4]

In and around Manchester there were a number of Strike Committees eventually uniting under the leadership of the North-Western Area Strike Committee, in which Party members actively participated. In the local Communist Party Branches there were a number of Bulletins produced and a system of despatch riders working day and night to maintain contact.

In South Wales, the Party gave all its support to the extremely militant system of strike committees and Councils of Action. A comrade reported after the strike:

"The Party membership rose to the occasion with a vigour and resourcefulness we could not have imagined in our wildest dreams."[5]

---

[1] See Nellie Connole, *Leaven of Life: the Story of George Henry Fletcher*, Chapter 14, "The General Strike", Lawrence and Wishart, 1961.
[2] *Workers' Weekly*, No. 170, May 21, 1926.
[3] Ibid.
[4] Ibid.
[5] Ibid., No. 170, May 21, 1926.

The District Party Committee was in more or less permanent session, and there were Communists on nearly all the Councils of Action. At Blaengarw, for example, there were three Party members on the Council of Action, including its Secretary. This was an effective Council, very comprehensive, with representatives from every eligible union, from the Co-operative, British Legion (and even, it is reported, the Conservative Club). Even in the course of the Strike the Party began winning recruits, 14 in Blaengarw for instance, and 40 in Mardy.

In London, the arrest of the Party District Organiser, R. W. Robson, caused some dislocation which was soon remedied. The leadership met daily in different places and kept contact directly with the majority of branches. The District leadership arranged the regular preparation of the *Workers' Bulletin* and many other bulletins were published by the Branches. It fought not only for the development of comprehensive local Councils of Action, and (meeting strong right-wing resistance, or at best inertia) for some form of all-London Co-ordinating Council.[1]

By May 8, some 15 Councils of Action functioned in London. By the end of the strike there were around 70. When the strike began, the London Trades Council called a meeting of Union District Committees and formed a very formal Central Strike Committee.[2] It was only after the strike was ended that the first real Conference of Councils of Action was held. The London Trades Council Secretary, Duncan Carmichael, did his best, "worked night and day", travelling the London District by motor-cycle and side-car though suffering from an illness which was to cause his death before the year was out.[3] But it was the *local* Councils of Action that saved the honour of the London workers during the General Strike, and on many of the best of these Communist Party members were initiators, organisers, activists.

Poplar Council of Action (with three Communists) edited a regular bulletin, with a 500 circulation. In Stepney there were four Party members on a Council of 15. In Bethnal Green there were four Communists on the Council of Action, in West Ham eight (four on its Executive) and a daily bulletin (300 circulation) edited.

In Battersea, there were ten Communists on a Council of Action of 124, four on the Executive of seven, and a daily bulletin (2,500

[1] *Workers Weekly*, No. 171, May 28, 1926, p. 4.
[2] *London Trades Council, 1860–1950: a History*, pp. 129–130, Lawrence and Wishart, 1950.
[3] Ibid., p. 130.

circulation) edited. In St. Pancras, the Communist Party Branch published its own bulletin (1,000 circulation) daily and two Communists served on the Council of Action and were mainly instrumental in producing the *St. Pancras Bulletin* (4,000–5,000) daily. This was an effective Council of Action, meeting daily, one of those few where the Co-operative had agreed to supply goods on credit for a canteen organised by the Women's Committee, a very united Committee. An agreement was made with the local Labour Party, I.L.P. and Communist Party to run all meetings jointly under the auspices of the Trades Council.[1]

At Islington there were two Communists on an Emergency Strike Committee of five members. A Party bulletin had a circulation of around 1,500 and the Council of Action's *Islington Workers*, something similar.

In many areas the Communist Party produced its *own* bulletins, besides distributing the *Workers' Bulletin* and helping with the production of the publications of Councils of Action or Strike Committees. The South Wales District of the Party, for instance, produced at first the *District Strike Bulletin* and later the *District Strike News*; the Cardiff Party published its *Strike Bulletin*; Rhondda had a *Workers' News Service*, Barrow had a *Workers' Bulletin*, as did the Party in the Merseyside.

ELEMENTS OF DUAL POWER

In a number of areas where Strike Committees or Councils of Action were most effective, where they really embodied the unity of the local working class, really developed efficient organisational methods, carried out mass picketing, issued permits for transport, etc., there began to develop an *embryo* alternative centre of Government, something like a type of "dual power". On a low level this could be seen when the Councils of Action monopolised the granting of local transport permits, its elements were there in the cars and lorries bearing black or yellow labels "*By permission of the T.U.C.*".[2]

An Ashton sheet-metal worker, member of his local Permit Committee, wrote in his union journal:[3]

[1] Emile Burns, op. cit., p. 168.
[2] Andrew Rothstein for instance still holds a permit issued to him by the London Transport Committee as engaged "in legitimate working class activity".
[3] *Sheet Metal Workers' Quarterly*, October 1926, quoted Postgate, Wilkinson and Horrobin, op. cit., pp. 34–35 and Allen Hutt, op. cit., p. 150.

"Employers of labour were coming, cap in hand, begging for permission to do certain things, or, to be more correct, to allow their workers to return to perform certain customary operations. . . . Most of them turned empty away after a most humiliating experience, for one and all were put through a stern questioning, just to make them realise that we and not they were the salt of the earth. I thought of the many occasions when I had been turned empty away from the door of some workshop in a weary struggle to get the means to purchase the essentials of life for self and dependants. . . ."

The Edinburgh *Strike Bulletin* reported the formation[1] of the establishment of a Food Permit system which was working admirably:

"There has been a constant stream of applicants at the Offices and many business firms have been on the doorstep. All kinds of businesses are represented. The Committee insist, however, upon certain conditions which many firms find irksome. Permits are only issued to those men who are members of Transport Unions, and no departure is made from this rule. The Committee believe that in a few days practical control of road traffic will be in their hands, and that the O.M.S. . . . will find their occupation gone."

A later bulletin quoted:

"At Longcroft, the road picket is so effective that the football park is full of vehicles of all descriptions, impounded until a permit and a union driver are produced."[2]

Probably the most effective exercise of power was by the Northumberland and Durham General Council and Joint Strike Committee.[3]

The local Trades and Labour Council called a meeting of its delegates on Sunday evening, May 2, inviting thereto all sections of the working-class movement including members of the Co-operative Board of Management, officers of the Women's Co-operative Guild, Labour councillors and county councillors, representatives of the Plebs League and of the Communist Party. A detailed, comprehensive (and very

[1] Official Strike Bulletin, Edinburgh, May 7, 1926, quoted by Professor Crook, op. cit., p. 411.
[2] Ibid., May 11, 1926.
[3] See Emile Burns, op. cit., pp. 152–154; "Account of the Proceedings of the Northumberland and Durham General Council and Joint Strike Committee" in *Labour Monthly*, June 1926, pp. 359–374; R. Page Arnot, *The Miners—Years of Struggle*, pp. 436–443.

militant) "Plan of Campaign" was put before the meeting, which accepted it and constituted itself into a Council of Action. The plan of action envisaged from the beginning a challenge to the Government distribution of food:

> "*Food and Transport.* The T.U.C. instructions for the general strike, if and when it should come off, include the provision of Food, Transport and Health Services. Whatever the intention of the General Council in laying down this instruction, it is clear that on this point depends the success of the General Strike. Whoever handles and transports food, the same person controls food; whoever controls food will find the 'neutral' part of the population rallying to their side. Who feeds the people wins the Strike. . . ."[1]

On May 4, a meeting of various trade union representatives was held with Will Lawther, a member of the Durham County Miners' Federation Board, and R. Page Arnot, leading Communist and later to become the historian of the Miners' Union, attending in his capacity as Director of the Labour Research Department. Here it was agreed to form a local General Council to cover the whole Northumberland and Durham area and, in addition, a strike committee. R. Page Arnot was co-opted on to both.

Even the Civil Commissioner, Sir Kingsley Wood, had to acknowledge in *fact* if not in theory the authority of the Northumberland and Durham General Council. Arnot writes:

> "After forty hours of the general stoppage [Sir Kingsley] came by night to negotiate personally with the Strike Committee. Sixty hours after the Strike began Sir Kingsley Wood, accompanied by General Sir Kerr Montgomery, were once more at Burt Hall, making a plea for 'dual control' of the transport of food. This proposal was immediately rejected by the Joint Strike Committee ('we cannot agree to our men working under any form of dual control'), which at the same time decided 'that we now use the discretionary powers vested in us by the Trades Union Congress and withdraw all permits today'."[2]

The Minutes of the Strike Committee, after reporting this withdrawal of *all* permits, continue confidently:

---

[1] Quoted in full in R. Page Arnot, op. cit., pp. 436-439.
[2] R. Page Arnot, op. cit., pp. 439-440.

"On Friday [May 7], the success of the general strike appeared completely assured. It was clear to everyone that the O.M.S. organisation was unable to cope with the task imposed upon it. The attitude of the population was favourable to the strikers and unfavourable to the Government. There were no disturbances, the Trade Unionists maintained an almost perfect discipline. There was no change from the ordinary except for the quietness in the streets and the absence of traffic.

"... *The situation as a whole was now well in hand.*" (My emphasis J.K.)

Authority for transport, and for more than this, was beginning to pass into the hands of the organised working class.[1]

---

[1] R. Page Arnot writes to the author concerning the Party position in Tyneside at the time of the General Strike:

"Tyneside, and Durham and Northumberland in general, was in some ways our weakest Party district amongst the great centres of industry in Britain.... At this time Billy Brain had been sent up to organise, and at the same time the magnificent agitator and firebrand speaker Alexander Geddes ... had gone to Tyneside. I had travelled ... straight to Chopwell and it was only after the preliminary decisions had been taken at Chopwell on the Saturday that it was possible to get into touch with Geddes and Brain in the course of the week-end. They learned what I was doing and in conjunction with them an additional series of steps were discussed. The object was as set forth in the plan of campaign reprinted in *Labour Monthly*, 1966. The intention was that the setting up of the Councils of Action would enable the whole theatre of war from Tweed to Tees to be covered with a network of local Councils. From these would arise a more revolutionary leadership, as things developed, than was possible from the ranks of local or district officials of trade unions (who, however, found themselves constituted as the leaders of their members called out on strike). My task was to get them to come together on to a united committee—on which I was the one Communist, unless Jack Little, afterwards A.E.U. President, was a C.P. member at that time. This stage was never reached but this was the aim set for the Party, in discussion with Geddes at any rate, and which was operated in Tyneside and around, where alone it had any members—and these but a few at the time.

"This functioned splendidly. An arrangement was made by which I kept daily in touch with Geddes who was splendid or with Brain. Further, special machinery was created, partly Y.C.L. and partly volunteers, to act as liaison and to supplement what could be done by the ordinary party machinery.

"By this means each day from my 'office' (put at my disposal by N.U.D.A.W.) it was possible to be at once in touch with the party in Newcastle and elsewhere, to receive reports and to have propaganda materials prepared, either (via the young volunteers) for the party or for the various daily meetings of the General Council at Burt Hall, which also had its own 'courier' service: while by day and night the young miners and other motor-bicyclists of Blaydon sped over Durham county or up Northwards with whatever was necessary. The bike-less lads and lasses enrolled themselves in the mass pickets (200-strong at each of the two roads into Chopwell) which beset the Great North Road. Pickets used often to come and see me in Burt Hall with their problems (e.g. apparently unshatterable wind-screens).

"What the C.P. members known to me were doing at the time and in which activity

MAIN TARGETS OF ARREST

"Jix" and his various police and blackleg bands, the Tory news-sheets and Churchill's *British Gazette* directed their main wrath against the militants. Judging by the arrests and sentences, the two main enemies of British capitalism, the two main targets of its "justice", were the miners' organisations and the Communist Party.

Arrests mainly under different sections of E.P.A. started already on the eve of the strike, and quickly began to develop from ones and twos to sixes and sevens to sixties and seventies.[1] How many were arrested in all in connection with the General Strike? Early in June, the Home Secretary Joynson-Hicks informed the House of Commons that there had been 1,760 case of arrest under E.P.A. in England and Wales.[2] Including Scotland, where arrests were often on a bigger scale than Britain (Glasgow, Fife coalfield etc.), and allowing for Jix's omissions, it is usually calculated that the total figure was somewhere around 2,500.[3]

How many of these were Communists? It took several months to compile anything like a list of "casualties". The first Executive meeting following the strike has a list of 100 Communists, nearly all of whom had been arrested for distributing Communist strike bulletins,[4] and of these (at the end of May) 35 were still in prison, 7 on appeal and 30 had been fined. Most of the sentences were 2-6 months. When more each of them was I certainly knew: but I no longer can remember from day to day.

"One feature stands out in my mind: that in action there was intense unity. One communist in Chopwell in the first week of May 1926: three months later there was no hall in Chopwell could hold the Party members: and I had to address the nearly 200 communists of Chopwell in a shallow amphitheatre of a hill-side amid the sunshine and the breeze of an August afternoon. I was never much of an open-air speaker: but verily, in these days the Party was riding the whirlwind and directing the storm.

"There was one little point, as an example of preparedness, that could hardly occur to anybody who had not been both in touch with communists of other countries, and also recently in prison. I had no illusions about the likelihood or otherwise of arrest. For this reason I altered my sleeping quarters every two or three nights in the week, and twice changed my name during the period. By this simple device I was able to avoid the attentions of the Newcastle and County police who were looking for a Mr. Arnot and not for a Mr. Black."

---

[1] See, for instance, the various inserts in the Diary section of R. Page Arnot's *The General Strike*. It starts with the lone arrest of Saklatvala; by May 6, he is reporting 66 arrests in Glasgow, 22 in Edinburgh by May 11, 100 persons sentenced at Glasgow.
[2] *Workers' Weekly*, No. 173, June 11, 1926, p. 2.
[3] *Sunday Worker*, June 6, 1926, p. 2.
[4] *Workers' Weekly*, June 4, 1926.

complete figures were worked out of Communists arrested on all types of charges, the figure exceeded 1,000. In the Political report prepared for the 8th Congress of the C.P.G.B. (October, 1926) it was calculated that not less than 1,200 Party members (between one-fifth and one-quarter of the pre-strike Party membership) had suffered one way or another from Government repression for their support of the miners and of the strike, a proportion to which no other organisation even remotely approached. For Communist Party Branches (Locals) and Districts (D.P.C.'s), police raids, seizure of duplicating apparatus, interception of correspondence, arrests, became a normal part of life during and following the strike. "So did the first training of many hundreds of Party members," the Report adds, "in counter-measures, in the shape of more careful methods." *Lansbury's Labour Weekly* reported, describing the events of the Strike:

> "The 'Special Department' at Scotland Yard was in full cry after Communists in particular. To be in possession of one of their multi-graphed bulletins was as good as a sentence without the option. Almost any news unfavourable to the Government was 'false' now."[1]

The miners had heavy casualties. Will Lawther, then a member of the Durham County Miners' Federation Board, was arrested at Chopwell and sentenced to two months' hard labour. And with him was Harry Bolton, also a miner, Chairman of the Blaydon Urban District Council, and from then on one of the staunchest members of the Communist Party on the north-east coast. Noah Ablett, of the Executive of the South Wales Miners' Federation and of the Miners' Federation nationally, was arrested and ordered to find two sureties of £50 at the South Western Police Court, for a speech "calculated to cause disaffection". In the mining areas of Scotland, South Wales, Yorkshire, the north-east, etc., where miners' mass pickets abounded, miners were arrested by scores. We have described the "medals" received by the Moffatt family in the Fife coalfield. Police raids on Communist, Minority Movement and Council of Action headquarters became commonplace, with seizure of documents, duplicators, paper and anything else that might "cause disaffection" from drain pipes to drawing-pins. The Party headquarters at King Street was under constant siege, and Bob Stewart, Acting General Secretary, was arrested there on

---
[1] *Lansbury's Labour Weekly*, May 22, 1926, p. 5.

Friday May 7. The London District Committee was raided and its organiser, R. W. Robson, arrested (for the heinous crime of carrying a copy of the *Workers' Bulletin*, for which he received six weeks). The *Workers' Weekly* office, the office of the Minority Movement, the Dorritt Press, the Young Communist League office, the St. Pancras C.P. Local, the Bradford District Committee office and many many others were raided, property confiscated, workers arrested.

Bob Stewart's case was typical enough. Police raided King Street looking for him in vain on May 5, confiscated documents (and left a bevy of "splits" outside). On May 7 they found him, arrested him, took him to Scotland Yard for questioning, charged him (on May 8) at Bow Street with:

> "having on premises in his occupation or under his control, documents containing statements, or reports, the publication of which would be an offence under the Emergency Regulations".[1]

Dr. Percival Clarke, on behalf of the Director of Public Prosecutions, explained that the charge was framed under an Emergency Regulation which made it an offence for any person to do any act likely to cause sedition or disaffection among the Forces of the Crown or among the civilian population.[2] Remanded (surety paid by Edgar Lansbury, George Lansbury's son), Bob Stewart came again before the Court on May 14.

The "offending" documents were cited by the prosecution. One was a "Letter to all local Factory Organisations and Groups" of May 3 calling on them to:

> "utilise to the full the machinery of the factory groups. In case of existing papers offer as far as possible to place the paper at the disposal of the local Strike Committee or the Council of Action."

Another was a lock-out bulletin issued by the Bradford District Committee of the Party which included a paragraph to the effect that:

> "Appeals should be made to all forces of the State to realise their class position, and take no action that is calculated in any way to defeat their own class, who are fighting for a decent standard of living."

---

[1] See reports in *Workers' Weekly*, No. 170 of May 21, 1926, p. 2, and *Workers' Weekly*, No. 171 of May 28, p. 4.
[2] Ibid.

Stewart, addressing the court, stated that he had never heard of so flimsy a pretext for prosecution or so preposterous an attempt to interfere with the ordinary and normal business of a political Party. The magistrate, of another mind, declared that without doubt the documents were "calculated to spread disaffection". However, as the strike was ended it would not be necessary to send the accused to prison. He would fine him £100 and costs, or in default, three months' imprisonment.[1]

The most common of the charges were in connection with the production, distribution, or even mere possession, of militant strike bulletins. Marjorie Pollitt, wife of Harry Pollitt, was charged, as publisher of the *Workers' Bulletin*, and fined £50 and costs with an alternative of three months.[2] T. A. Jackson, Acting Editor of the *Workers' Weekly*, was arrested after the strike and sentenced to two months "for having under his control matter likely to cause disaffection", on the evidence of a piece of paper found in his pocket containing notes of a telephone call about opposition to the strike amongst the Welsh Guards.[3] R. Stoker of Manchester was charged and sentenced for having in his car a supply of the *Workers' Daily*, the emergency bulletin produced by the Communist Party on the eve of the strike.[4] On May 8 a Home Office Report stated:

> "The Communist Party continues to circulate false reports with a view to creating alarm. Their Headquarters at Birmingham was raided last night and a number of persons who were printing a paper called the *Birmingham Worker* were arrested."[5]

John Forshaw, following a police raid on the Party office at Salford was sent to prison for one month and fined £100 for being in possession of a leaflet entitled "The Great Betrayal".[6] In South Wales Frank Bright, Communist miner, Emrys Llewelyn, Daniel and Isaac Lewes (the latter 17 years old and Secretary of the Porth Young Communist League) were charged with having committed breaches of E.P.A. "by having in their possession documents which were likely to cause grave disaffection among His Majesty's Forces". The documents, seized at the defendants' homes, included a pit paper and a Y.C.L.

---

[1] See reports in *Workers' Weekly*, No. 170 of May 21, 1926, p. 2. and No. 171 of May 28, p. 4.
[2] Ibid., Nos. 170 and 171, of May 21 and 28, 1926.
[3] Ibid., June 4 and June 11, 1926.   [4] Ibid., May 21, 1926, p. 2.
[5] Quoted by R. Page Arnot, *The General Strike*, p. 193.
[6] *Sunday Worker*, May 23, 1926, p. 2.

Headquarters circular. Bright received two months. The three others were offered opportunities to be bound over for a year during which time they were "to undertake to abstain from circulating Communist literature", which they refused.[1] Twelve Sheffield comrades including Harry Webb, George Fletcher, Ted Lismer, E. V. Smith all received fines of from £5 to £25 for possession of "seditious literature."[2] D. F. Springhall a leader of the Young Communist League, was given two months by a Bow Street magistrate"[3] for possession of the Y.C.L. bulletin *The Young Striker*. George Miles, a publisher of the *Young Striker*, 1,200 copies of which were seized by the police at the St. Pancras Party office, was fined £70 and costs, and Sarah and Bessie Span were bound over for a year in respect of copies of the *Young Striker* found in their flat."[4]

So the story could continue. The second favourite charge was "seditious speech", as with Saklatvala, the Communist M.P., who received two months,[5] and Isobel Brown (wife of the leading Communist E. H. Brown) and already a popular speaker, charged at Pontefract and sentenced to three months[6] for a speech at Castleford where she was alleged to have appealed to the forces not to act against the strikers.

Mass picketers were usually charged with "acts of intimidation", like the 50 Gateshead workers, mostly miners, arrested when holding up blackleg transport. Nothing was too trivial to find a "relevant" clause under E.P.A., as the striker found who was imprisoned for chalking on the pavement, or the young Cardiff girl of 17 who got a month for tripping up a scab.[7] As H. B. Lovell, Acting Secretary of the International Class War Prisoner's Aid (I.C.W.P.A.), put it, based on his experience, "the E.P.A. regulations were as elastic as the police desired to make them".[8]

Many thousands are the names of the "unknown soldiers" of the General Strike and many hundreds could see their names honourably inscribed on rolls of honour if the authorities were as anxious to commemorate the class war as to have remembered their wars of aggression. One day this work of commemoration will be duly performed.

One day, too, historians will compile a Black Book of British class

[1] Ibid., May 23, 1926.
[2] *Workers' Weekly*, No. 172, June 4, 1926, p. 4.
[3] Ibid., No. 170, May 21, 1926, p. 2.
[4] *Sunday Worker*, May 23, 1926.
[5] Ibid., May 16, p. 2.
[6] Ibid.
[7] *Workers' Weekly* No. 170., May 21.
[8] *Sunday Worker*, May 30, p. 2.

justice in which the General Strike trials will well deserve an inglorious page. J. T. Murphy in his study of the General Strike[1] quotes a *Times* report of a dialogue between a magistrate and a striking railwayman (not a Communist) at the Marylebone Police Court of May 27, 1926, summoned for non-payment of £8 to his wife under a maintenance order:

"Did you Strike?" asked the Magistrate (Mr. Halket).

"Yes, Sir."

Magistrate: "Well, it serves you right. I suppose you went off without notice and broke your contract. Have the Railway company proceeded against you for a week's wages?"

"No, Sir."

"Well, they could have done. If you treat your employers like that you cannot expect to be treated very gently yourself. You voluntarily threw up your work, repudiated your contract with the railway company and now you tell this injured woman [his wife] you cannot pay her."

The defendant replied that he was called out by his recognised trade union, the N.U.R.

"You need not have obeyed an order that was obviously illegal."

"We were called out. What could we do?"

"If they asked you to commit a crime you would not do it. Why should you commit this wrong?"

The defendant did not answer the question, but pointed out that he would return to work on Monday at a wage of 31s. which was a reduction of 12s. per week. The order was for 30s. per week.

Mr. Halket made an order for the payment of £8 within 21 days, or 26 days' imprisonment in default, adding the defendant might raise the money from the Union officials who ordered him to go on strike.

About the same time, Murphy points out, summonses against three men for exceeding the speed limit, were withdrawn at the same court (a different magistrate):

"The Commissioner desires", said Police-Sergeant Jones, "that the Magistrate will look upon these cases with favour, as the defendants had been working—one as a volunteer omnibus driver during the strike, and the other two as special constables during the Emergency."

[1] J. T. Murphy, *The Political Meaning of the Great Strike*, C.P.G.B., pp. 120–121, quoting from *The Times*, June 4, 1926.

Said the Magistrate:

"*Very well: withdrawn.*"

At the Gateshead County Police Court on a Thursday, towards the end of May 1926, a miner was summoned for having contravened Regulation 21 of the Emergency Regulations by doing a certain act which was likely to cause disaffection among the civil population by distributing a document known as the "Northern Light".[1]

This journal of the Council of Action at Chopwell, described a demonstration to Gateshead from Spen and Highfield behind the banner of the Garesfield Miners' Lodge. It also contained a passage on the role of the police which the prosecutor proceeded, in tones of indignation, to read:

"The lowest aim in life is to be a policeman. When a policeman dies he goes so low he has to climb up a ladder to get into hell, and even then he is not a welcome guest." (Laughter in Court.)

The prosecution told bloodcurdling stories of how the Chopwell Council of Action was "still carrying on in a terrifying way".

Sir Alfred M. Palmer asked if the accused was a Bolshevist? Defence replied that his client belonged to the Labour Party. The Bench retired and its Chairman sentenced the defendant to three months in prison with hard labour, adding that if he had had *his* way he would also have fined him £100; then continued:

"*Why you and those who are associated with you don't go off to Russia I don't know . . . you are making a mistake living in this country . . . you had far better get away, all of you. We don't want you, or anybody else like you.*"

We don't want you! But "we" did *not* volunteer to replace Edward Wilson, miner, in the pit. Nor did *they*, the miners, nor the Chopwell Council of Action, go to Russia. But there was from the Chopwell miners, following the strike, the greatest local influx of recruits up to that date into the British Communist Party.

Y.C.L. AND N.M.M.

It is hard to separate the role of the Young Communist League during the General Strike from the activities of the Communist Party. In

---

[1] *Blaydon Courier*, May 22, 1926, quoted in "The Police Persecutions: A Document of the General Strike", *Labour Monthly*, June 1926.

most areas young Communists enrolled in the most active sectors of the struggle—pickets, defence corps, communications, the semi-legal work of duplicating and distributing the bulletins of the Party and of the Councils of Action. Many, as we have seen above, suffered arrest, including D. F. Springhall, then the Y.C.L. Acting Secretary.

The Y.C.L. worked under the slogans "United Front of the Young Workers", "All Young Workers into the Strike", "Youth Representatives on the Councils of Action".[1] Centrally, it produced in London, daily in 4,000 copies, a bulletin *The Young Striker*, and extended versions with local news were produced in a number of Districts. When the Party's Executive Committee (May 29–31, 1926) reviewed the work and role of the Party during the General Strike, the Y.C.L. representatives were able to report over 200 new recruits made during the strike, and these figures were far from complete.[2]

In the same way the National Minority Movement which had fought so hard to prepare for the coming strike, once it came put all the strength of its central and local machinery at the disposal of the Councils of Action, though it continued a skeleton organisation of its own. George Hardy, its Acting Secretary, narrowly escaped arrest at the N.M.M. Headquarters[3] and carried on work, the issuing of bulletins, the fight for a militant and organised struggle by the unions, from the shelter of a friendly trade union, whilst police continued to besiege his official office.

LESSONS OF THE GENERAL STRIKE

No event, no struggle of British Labour history has been so much discussed as the General Strike. When it was over each side and each sector of each side proceeded to enquiry and to inquest. The capitalists discussed how to take such measures that a General Strike *could* never recur; right-wing Labour sought to squeeze out from history the conclusion that the General Strike *should* never recur; the militants and left sought out the lessons of the struggle, so that, if and when it recurred, it should do so victoriously.

The Communist Party analysed the lessons of the strike in the meeting of the Executive Committee at the end of May;[4] again and

---

[1] Resolution, "On the Young Communist League" in *Report of the 8th Congress of the C.P.G.B.*, pp. 75–78.
[2] *Workers' Weekly* No. 172, June 4, 1926, p. 2.
[3] George Hardy, *Those Stormy Years*.
[4] See Appendix VII to this chapter, "Why the Strike Failed".

more in detail at the 8th Congress of the Party in mid-October.[1] The Communist International adopted a thesis on "the Lessons of the General Strike" at a session of its Executive on June 8, 1926.[2] The strike was reviewed and discussed in a whole number of articles, pamphlets and books by leading British Communists.[3]

The judgement made by Communists in the months that followed the strike is itself a part of history. Experience and hindsight would perhaps, here and there, demand a modification of the analysis of that time. By and large, however, the essential parts of the Communist Party's assessment would seem to remain correct, incomparably more correct than the analysis offered by any other section of the Labour movement at the time.

Behind the General Strike lay the quickening decline of British capitalism, hastened by World War I. Nor was it accidental that, when it came, the great showdown came on the issue of miners' wages:

"Alike in 1921, in 1925 and in 1926, the issue was the miners' wages. This issue summed up the existing situation. In the first place, it was just such a broad economic issue as wages and the fight against the reduction of wages that could most easily unite the whole body of the working class at the present stage. In the second place, the coal industry was the acutest expression of the whole crisis of British capitalism; the brunt of the decline had fallen hardest on the miners; the inability of capitalism to find any solution, and the naked struggle between profits and the livelihood of the workers was there most clear. Thus the issue of miners' wages summed up the whole issue of capitalism and the working class in Britain, though in a concealed form, and not yet with a conscious and direct expression."[4]

A great confrontation between capital and labour became, in the years that followed the war, more and more inevitable. From July

---

[1] See thesis adapted in *Report of 8th of Congress C.P.G.B.*, pp.. 55–71, the second half of which is published at Appendix IX to this chapter.

[2] "Theses on the Lessons of the British General Strike", adopted unanimously by the Executive Committee of the Communist International (E.C.C.I.), June 8, 1926, reprinted in the *Communist Review*, Vol. 7, No. 3, July 1926, pp. 113–136.

[3] See above all R. Palme Dutt, *The Meaning of the General Strike*, C.P.G.B., 1926 and editorial "Towards a Mass Party" in the October 1926, issue of *Communist Review*.

[4] R. Palme Dutt, *The Meaning of the General Strike* (written June 1926), p. 8. It is interesting to see how closely similar is the analysis of the Miners' Federation in their statement of January 12 on the occasion of the Conference of Trade Union Executives held on January 20, 1927.

1925, the capitalist class, the mineowners, and their Tory Government openly, blatantly, unreservedly prepared for the show-down with every means at their disposal, and set the day for May 1, 1926. O.M.S., the trial of the Twelve, the contemptuous rejection of even the lowest grovel of Thomas and his colleagues, were but links in the chain. The Royal Commission and its Report were not intended as a basis for negotiation, but to obtain a breathing spell, and to confuse and divide the enemy—the working class.

The ruling class went into the battle of the General Strike with clear intentions, and its forces united. It fought with *all* its resources, with *all* its weapons, including, in the first place, the *machinery of State*. Here lies the first lesson.

THE NATURE OF THE STATE

The Tory Government might have set out to prove the truth of Lenin's writings on the State. Where was that mythical reformist dream of a neutral non-partisan State? Baldwin, Churchill and the Government took it for granted that the State was *their* State, the State of British capitalism, and proceeded to mobilise and use it for *their* aims. Army, Air Force, Navy were rushed into service, but never to defend trade unionists. Troops were concentrated in the main industrial areas, armed convoys defended Government supplies and strike breakers. Cruisers were despatched to the north-east when the Strike Committee and Council of Action were beginning to challenge capitalist power in the Northumberland and Durham area. The armed forces were guaranteed State protection. It was a crime to put the workers' point of view to a member of the armed forces. Where was the "neutral" army, the "neutral" navy, the reformist dream?

The class nature of "the Law" was soon revealed. Police courts were filled with strikers, pickets, editors and distributors of bulletins, demonstrators in support of the strike. But where, in what courts, were the strike-breakers, rowdy and drunken "specials", the coal-owners or the capitalists? How many opponents of the General Strike were arrested under the clauses of E.P.A.? Under the Emergency provisions it was a crime even to *possess* a leaflet the reading of which might cause "disaffection". The traditionally slow-moving snail-like process of law suddenly moved with unprecedented speed to secure within a week a High Court decision that the General Strike was "illegal".

The police were directed in one direction only—against the strikers. Police and special police to the number of almost a quarter of a million were spread around the industrial areas to protect strike-breakers and intimidate the strikers. But it was only strikers who were charged with "intimidation".

The Government did their best to monopolise the various organisations and services that in one way or another disseminate "information" or control the minds of the people.

The B.B.C. served one side only. By seizing the newsprint the Government tried to keep control of the press in the hands of the *British Gazette* and the Tory news-sheets. Religious leaders were given open access to B.B.C. and *Gazette* if they attacked the strikers in the name of God. If they called for conciliation or mediation even archbishops were anathema. Lloyd George and other Liberals who wished to express criticism of the Tory Government found the B.B.C. and the *British Gazette* were closed to them. But they were wide open to antistrike Liberals like H. H. Asquith and Lord Grey of Fallodon. Sir John Simon, who discovered the "illegality" of the strike, was *persona* completely *grata* with Government, press and radio. The press and radio were "free" to Lord Grey and Cardinal Bourne, but not to Lloyd George and the Archbishop of Canterbury—let alone to the strikers. Even Ramsay MacDonald and the most defeatist members of the General Council were not permitted to broadcast.

Even *The Times* was indignant when the Government commandeered part of its stock of newsprint along with that of the General Council. Its protest was handed by the Prime Minister to Mr. Churchill, who was no believer in the "neutrality of the State". "I do not at all agree," he replied to the protest, "with your idea that the T.U.C. have as much right as the Government to publish their side of the case and to exhort their followers to combined action." A large number of people were "detached from the conflict", they were waiting "to see whether the Government or the trades union is the stronger".[1]

When the strike was over E.P.A. for a long period remained. Newsprint there was, but what were you allowed to print on it? Of course you were "free" to print that the miners, continuing their struggle, were "reds", "Moscow Agents", ruining the country; but how free were you to call for support of their courageous struggle? Readers of

---

[1] See *Strike Nights in Printing House Square: an Episode in the History of The Times*, printed for private record, 1926, pp. 32-34.

the *Sunday Worker* towards the end of May could see a prominent box on the first page.[1]

> ### E.P.A.
>
> Our readers, in the course of their enjoyment of this weeks' issue of the *Sunday Worker* must bear in mind that the Emergency Powers Act is still in force.
>
> For instance, our printers state that we must not print any direct appeal to railwaymen and other transport workers who may be called upon to handle "black" coal.

The first lesson, therefore, of the General Strike was that the State "above classes", the neutral, unbiased, non-partisan State, is nothing but a reformist myth, the effect of which is to disarm the working class, to doom them to defeat.

If you believed in the "neutral State" then you could claim, perhaps, that the General Strike was a purely economic, a purely industrial struggle. But the General Strike was *political* from the outset, and the capitalists recognised the fact, and from the outset fought it politically, using every political weapon they could command, including every aspect of the capitalist State.

The Communist Party had always challenged the theory of the "neutral" State, and explained that in class society every state is an organ of class power. It fought throughout the strike for open *political* struggle. As soon as the strike was over it did its best to draw the lessons amongst wider sections of the people. The *Workers' Weekly* in its first post-strike issue turned to this question:[2]

> "All the pitiful pleadings of the General Council that the struggle was 'a purely industrial struggle' could not alter or even disguise the plain fact that once the struggle had begun the General Council had to face the stigma of 'illegality' or surrender. They chose to surrender, but the episode has taught us that the capitalist state is to the workers a weapon in the hands of their bitter and ruthless enemies—

[1] *Sunday Worker*, No. 63, May 23, 1926, p. 1.
[2] *Workers' Weekly*, No. 170, May 21, 1926, p. 3, "Gains Wrought from the General Strike".

the British Capitalists. Once the Government put its force behind the coalowners (as it did when it demanded the recall of the General Strike Order and ignored the lock-out to which it was a reply) to defend the miners meant to defy the Government who had taken the coalowners' side."

IMPERIALISM'S TWO-FOLD STRATEGY

If one of the lessons of the General Strike that stood out in relief was the class character of the State, the fact that under British capitalism, the State was so selected and organised that in essence it acted as the defender of British capitalism, the peculiarly cunning strategy of British capitalism also emerged in all its clarity.

British reaction is an old, long-established, capitalism and imperialism, and with its age and its (at least erstwhile) strength, came cunning, elasticity, duplicity, the capacity to manœuvre, divide, disguise, the knowledge of how, when under pressure, to retreat, or at least appear to retreat, in order to advance again with renewed vigour. All these "splendid" qualities were employed in preparing for and carrying out the General Strike.

The O.M.S. District Commissions, E.P.A., blackleg squads, use of armed forces, taking over, though in different ways, of B.B.C. and newsprint, declaration of the "illegality" of the strike, arrests, threats of arrest were the aspects of force; but the temporary subsidy, the playing for time after July 1925, the establishment of the Commission, its composition, its misty unclear Report with vague hints of reforms to come, the popping out of Sir Herbert Samuel from nowhere in the middle of the strike, with his misty unclear Memorandum with its vague hints of reforms to come, were the cunning, crafty, elastic, manœuvring side of British imperialist strategy calculated to confuse, divide and disarm the enemy.

Thus British reaction's two weapons were complementary—club and cunning, prison and division, Jix and Samuel, Churchill and—let us be clear—Thomas and MacDonald. Because—conscious or unconscious, this is not the point—it was the right-wing reformist leaders in the T.U.C. and Labour Party that were British capitalism's most potent force of confusion and division inside the working class. Lenin once called the reformist and revisionist leaders the "Labour lieutenants of the bourgeoisie". Never has this description been more apt than in the British General Strike.

THE NATURE OF REFORMISM

When we examined the outlook, the philosophy of British reformist leaders like MacDonald, Thomas, Snowden and Clynes[1] we saw that the essential lines of their teaching were as follows:

(1) That the path to socialism was one of gradual, inevitable, advance, step by step, by successive reforms, within the framework of capitalism.
(2) That this framework of capitalism, the British State, was something neutral, non-political, above classes, that it would serve equally whichever Party was elected to office.
(3) That the division of society into classes was denied and with it the class struggle.
(4) That advance was seen as an evolutionary not a revolutionary process, and evolution was to be achieved not by continuous mass struggle but by the achievement of a Parliamentary majority and majorities in the local Councils. The role of the masses was to vote for Labour and the role of the activist was to organise this vote at elections.

Unlike their continental colleagues, the British right-wing Labour leaders were not "revisionists" in the true sense of the term, they did not pretend to accept Marxist, revolutionary ideas and then "revise" their content out of existence. They rejected Marxism and the revolutionary change of society openly and unashamedly.

Out of office, in opposition, and particularly in times of relative economic and political "calm", they could speak a militant language, preach "socialism", call on the masses for support. But at times of crisis (in office or in opposition) they would always and inevitably rally to the defence of "the nation", which in real class terms always meant the interests of the dominant section of the nation, the capitalist class.

To paint a picture of proceeding smoothly forward to socialism within the framework of capitalism was, for the reformists, quite in order. But when capitalism itself was in crisis (be it on things political or economic, on Home or Foreign Affairs), then this was the time for all good reformists to rally to the cause of the Nation (capitalism), to "make sacrifices", to "conciliate", to retreat.

[1] See Vol. I, Chapter III.

Thus at times of crisis the reformists inevitably saw the main *threat* from the people threatening capitalism. The militant working class, above all the most militant—the Communists—became the *main* enemy, the struggle against the capitalists was restricted and even forgotten. Betrayal at times of political crisis was not some personal thing, some matter of temperament or character, but a built-in part of the philosophy of reformism. Given the nature of capitalism, and given the outlook of reformism, reformists were bound to betray at critical moments, be they sincere or insincere, honest or rogues. This is not to say by any manner of means that the reformist leaders were all sincere and were all honest. But this understanding of the dynamics of reformism is necessary to understand the attitude of the British reformist leaders, before, during and after the General Strike.

"CALCULATED" UNPREPAREDNESS

How else can we understand the almost incredible seemingly "calculated" unpreparedness of the General Council and Labour Party leaders for a struggle that the capitalists openly prepared and of which miners' leaders and Communists openly and repeatedly warned?

This "unpreparedness" was admitted by all—including leaders of the General Council themselves—*once the strike was over*.

The official Strike Organisation Committee of the General Council admitted:

> "The Strike Organisation Committee desire to emphasise that the organisation was of necessity improvised. The date upon which we were first asked as a 'ways and means' Committee to consider the question in the event of a general dispute, was April 27, and prior to that date, no consideration had been given to the possibility of such an eventuality."[1]

Ernest Bevin confirmed at the Conference of Trade Union Executives in January 1927:

> "With regard to preparations for the Strike, there were no preparations until April 27, and I do not want anyone to go away from this Conference under the impression that the General Council had any particular plan to run this movement. In fact, the General

---

[1] *Report of Strike Organisation Committee*, quoted in A. J. Bennett, *The General Council and the General Strike*, p. 9.

Council did not sit down to draft the plans until they were called together on April 27...."[1]

Describing in his *Nine Days* his own experience in trying to push and press the General Council to prepare the strike, A. J. Cook, the Miners' Secretary, wrote:

> "Time and again we had appealed for that [preparation for the struggle] to be done. But there were certain leaders who were determined that no preparations should be made. Most notable amongst them was J. H. Thomas, arguing that any preparations would only encourage the Government to make ready, and would lead people to believe that we thought a fight inevitable."[2]

Six months later, at the Conference of Executives, J. H. Thomas was still justifying his calculated unpreparedness:

> "Is there anyone in this audience, reviewing the situation calmly today, that would dare say, that if you set out for nine months and deliberately and calculatedly decided that you were going to prepare for a general strike, that anyone in his senses believes you could do it (cries of 'No'). You know perfectly well that two things would follow. First, you could not get into any negotiations that would be likely to bring peace and secondly, the other side could anticipate every move. (A voice 'They did'.)"

The voice was right (a Marxist voice perhaps?). The capitalists did foresee, not every move, but every *lack* of move.

When the strike was over, in the inquests and discussions, *everyone* admitted the lack of preparation on the working-class side—Labour Party, I.L.P., General Council, Trade Union Executives. But before the strike, in the critical months between July 1925 and May 1926, it was only the Miners' Federation and the Communist Party, as we have seen, that *consistently and repeatedly called for preparation*. And it was the Communists who, as Marxists, could look somewhat beneath the surface of things, who could best understand and explain at the time and after why it was that the General Council leaders were *not* preparing, why their unpreparedness was not without calculation, what in their seeming madness was their "method".

---

[1] Ernest Bevin at National Strike Special Conference, January 20-21, 1927, see Report in *The Mining Crisis*, T.U.C., 1927, p. 10.
[2] A. J. Cook, *The Nine Days*, p. 7.

UNWILLINGLY TO STRIKE

They did not prepare for a General Strike because they did not want a General Strike. Once again, *before* the strike it was only the Communist Party that was warning of this. After the strike it was openly and publicly acknowledged. One or two of the right-wing leaders never really concealed it.

J. H. Thomas before the strike began had described it as "the greatest calamity for this country".[1] On May 9, at Hammersmith, he admitted: "I have never disguised that I did not favour the principle of a General Strike."[2]

Ramsay MacDonald, leader of the Labour Party, told the House of Commons on May 3 that "with the discussion of General Strikes and Bolshevism and all that kind of thing, I have nothing to do at all...."[3]

J. R. Clynes, writing about the strike when more than ten years had elapsed, admitted that:

> "No General Strike was ever planned or seriously contemplated as an act of Trade Union policy. I told my own Union in April (1926) that such a Strike would be a national disaster, and a fatal step to Union prestige, and such it eventually proved to be."[4]

C. T. Cramp, with Thomas leader of the National Union of Railwaymen, avowed to the Conference of Trade Union Executives in January 1927:

> "We have not to blame the General Council for taking the action they did in calling off the Strike. The pity of it is that it was ever called on."[5]

The key figures in the General Council and the Labour Party (not forgetting that men like MacDonald were also key figures in the I.L.P.) were always opposed to the strike. Why then did they enter into it?

They entered into it because they could not do otherwise without isolating themselves from the mass of the workers, without being exposed. They entered into it, some consciously, some not so consciously, to *head it off*, to keep it out of the hands of militant leaders,

---

[1] Quoted by Allen Hutt, op. cit., p. 152.
[2] Quoted by R. Page Arnot, *The General Strike*, p. 201.
[3] Quoted by Allen Hutt, op. cit., p. 152.
[4] J. R. Clynes, *Memoirs: 1924–1937*, p. 75.
[5] *The Mining Crisis*, T.U.C., 1927, p. 57.

to keep it "respectable", and to—you can choose your own words—bring it to a rapid end, find a formula, betray.

They entered into it because they knew that if they did not, the strikes of solidarity with the miners would have been pursued under more militant leadership.

Ramsay MacDonald admitted this after the Strike:

> "After the conduct of the Government it was perfectly evident that had no General Strike been declared industry would have been almost as much paralysed by unauthorised strikes."[1]

And so did Ernest Bevin:

> "It must not be forgotten that apart from the rights and wrongs of the calling of a General Strike, there would in any case, with the miners' lock-out, have been widespread unofficial fighting in all parts of the country, which would have produced anarchy in the movement."[2]

As Kingsley Martin wrote when the strike was over, the T.U.C. stood as "a combatant in a war which had been forced upon it, and which it feared to win".[3]

The editorial of the first issue of the *Workers' Weekly* that followed the strike underlined this conclusion:

> "The truth cannot be concealed. We had men at the head of the General Council who were more afraid of winning than losing."[4]

The right-wing reformist leaders of the General Council and of the Labour Party went into the General Strike, hating it, fearing it, and only too anxious to end what they had not been able to avert.

REFORMIST APPROACHES

The reformist approach to the strike is not mirrored only in the calculated unpreparedness for it. When it was eventually, under pressure, organised, the methods of organisation from the centre and the whole General Council approach to the strikers were shot through and through with reformism.

---

[1] Ramsay MacDonald in *Socialist Review*, June 1926.
[2] Ernest Bevin in his trade union journal *The Record*, quoted by Allen Hutt, op. cit., p. 134.
[3] Kingsley Martin, *The British Public and the General Strike*, p. 58, Hogarth Press, 1926.
[4] Editorial "Cashier the Cowards", in *Workers' Weekly*, No. 170, May 21, 1926, p. 4.

The calling of men out by their individual unions (the membership of 82 unions was wholly or partly on strike) reflected a fear of unity. The Union Strike Committees in the localities often overlapped with the local Councils of Action or refused to pool their resources, thus weakening the strike.[1] The cautious and confused method of allotment of permits for food transport reflected a fear of the potential power of the masses. The calling out of the men on strike by stages itself reflected a fear of total involvement, the desire "not to go too far", to be cautious, circumspect, in other words to oppose the full-scale offensive of the employers with a timid tentative action. In fact, as day by day the strikers themselves in the localities began to follow the lead of the more militant sections of the Labour Movement, the Councils of Action began to leave the General Council fumbling in the rear.[2]

The General Council's fear of unity was reflected in its lack of approaches to the Co-operative movement, its inert acceptance of official Co-operative rejection of support for the strike. It was the militants, and the Communist Party was very consistent in this, who called for efforts to be made to draw the trade unions and the Co-operatives closer together and to secure their co-operation in and around the Councils of Action. It was reflected, too, in the almost total lack of effort to mobilise the local Labour Parties and local branches of the I.L.P. In many areas where such branches were militant good co-operation was achieved. But there was no official effort for such co-operation from the General Council, or from the right-wing leaders of Labour Party or I.L.P. An article in George Lansbury's journal (*Lansbury's Labour Weekly*), written just after the strike, underlined the weakness:

> "the General Council decided (in the same spirit) to take no steps to mobilise the local Labour Parties, and, indeed, deliberately decided to request the Party in the House not to raise discussions or take part in debate. Only four selected leaders were to speak."[3]

The fear of unity and of the united action of the labour movement was reflected in the cautious attitude of the General Council to the Trades Councils and to the Councils of Action.

The dialectics of political arithmetic is such that when one

---

[1] See Allen Hutt, op. cit., pp. 141-142.
[2] See criticism of the organisational weakness of the General Council in *Political Report to 8th Congress of the C.P.G.B.*, p. 64.
[3] *Lansbury's Labour Weekly*, Vol. II, No. 63, May 22, 1926.

working-class organisation unites in action with another the result is greater than the sum of the parts. When representatives of fifteen local unions, three local political organisations, and maybe a Co-operative Society, or a women's or youth organisation, knit themselves together in a united Council of Action the resultant strength for struggle was *many times* greater than the strength of the addition of each organisation acting individually, even if the actions were parallel. For the Communist Party this conception was elementary; the need of, and the strength of unity had been central to its whole practice and its whole philosophy. For the General Council, for reformists generally, such unity was almost treason.

Of course this reformist fear of the working class, and above all of the united working class in action, was directed primarily against the militants who most consistently stood for and worked for unity. After the strike, when it was possible freely to discuss such matters, the miners' leaders were to reveal the many ways in which and the many occasions on which the General Council had sought to isolate the Miners' Federation.

Speaking at Porth to a meeting of 5,000 miners, their Secretary, A. J. Cook, declared:

> "We have been fighting . . . not only against the Government and the owners, but against a number of Labour leaders, specially the political leaders, whose position has been compromised. . . ."[1]

In 1921, continued Cook, J. H. Thomas had said to him:

> "You are to blame for this position. You did not allow us to come in before the struggle took place. You refused to consult with us."

Cook made up his mind that in 1926 this excuse should not be used again:

> "This time the T.U.C. went with the miners to negotiate. They appointed a Negotiating Committee and I make this declaration today. I have had experience of being bullied in colliery offices; I had experience in 1920 and 1921 in meeting various Prime Ministers, but never have we been bullied by the employers or the Government to the extent that we were bullied by certain trade union leaders to accept a reduction in wages (Cries of 'shame'). The Government

[1] This speech was made on May 23, 1926. It was not reported in the *Herald*, but the version above was taken by the *Workers' Weekly*, No. 171 of May 28, 1926 from *The Times*.

knew that and the coalowners knew it. One man on the other side said to me 'The T.U.C. will help us', and the Prime Minister on more than one occasion publicly thanked the T.U.C."[1]

As the strike approached, still more after it began, again when the General Council sold out and the miners continued the struggle, the miners began in the eyes of the right-wing reformists to be more of an enemy than the employers themselves.

If this was true of the miners, how much more true of the Communist Party! As the strike approached, as the Communists again and again and again warned of the need to prepare for it and suggested the best way to do so; still more after the Scarborough 1925 T.U.C. had shown that the trade unions were beginning on many issues to heed the Communists, the Communist Party began to become for the right wing the principal enemy. The 1925 Liverpool Labour Party Conference turned its wrath against the Communist Party and opened the gate for the Government to arrest its leaders. It seemed to the reformists of the Thomas and Pugh type that "the enemy" was on the left. The more the workers began to follow the left and to move into action, the more "dangerous" the left became.

And so when Thomas and MacDonald and Cramp found themselves technically leading a strike that they did not want, what they feared most of all was that the workers moving into action should unite, awake, and begin to shed their reformist illusions and to follow the lead of the militants. This was their nightmare. And this is what in fact was beginning to happen in the second week of the strike.

This deep abiding fear was well expressed by Charles Dukes of the General and Municipal Workers, speaking at the January 1927 Conference of Executives:

". . . every day that the strike proceeded the control and authority of that dispute was passing out of the hands of responsible Executives into the hands of men who had no authority, no responsibility. . . .'[2]

Thomas himself, in the House of Commons, made the classic reformist confession on May 13, the day after the call-off:

"What he dreaded about this struggle more than anything else was this: If by any chance it should have got out of the hands of those who would be able to exercise some control, every sane man

[1] Ibid.
[2] "Report of National Strike Special Conference", p. 58 in *The Mining Crisis and the National Strike*, T.U.C., 1927.

knows what would have happened. I thank God it never did. That is why I believe that the decision yesterday was such a big decision, and that is why that danger, that fear, was always in our minds...."[1]

The workers were moving in unity. The Councils of Action were gaining in strength and clarity. Militant influence was growing. The General Council was being left behind by the workers. Reformist logic was inexorable. The strike had to be ended! It *was*; not thanks to God but to Thomas.

The reformist theory of the "neutral State" was another essential component of their inevitable defeat. As we have said, in purely reformist terms it was possible to envisage a purely economic, purely industrial struggle. In that imaginary MacDonald world where the State was unbiased, and where you were to proceed in leisure and pleasure within its benevolent framework forward to the millennium, a non-political General Strike could be envisaged.

But the real world was otherwise and, as we have seen, its State was a political instrument of capitalism. This the reformists refused to face; to do otherwise would have been to admit the falseness of their most essential attitude.

So they repeated and repeated and repeated that this was a purely industrial conflict. To arrests they shut their eyes (*The British Worker*); as for the police, they called for football matches. As for the law, if this neutral unbiased *Law* with a capital L proclaimed the strike illegal, then illegal it must be, and legality with the reformists was a fetish.

The capitalists fought, as we have seen, with a well-organised, when necessary quite ruthless *political, partisan, biased, class* State. The reformist Labour leaders refused to face this, and for this reason also defeat was inevitable. Writing just after the strike R. Palme Dutt explained this:

> "Instead of saying 'we are fighting for decent standards of life, and not against the Government and Constitution', they should have said, 'We are fighting for decent standards of life, and since the Government and the Constitution stand with the employers against this, therefore, we are compelled to fight the Government and Constitution'.
>
> "The General Council was not ready for this. Therefore the General Council could not carry on even the original struggle. The General Council had to abandon the struggle for wages."[2]

---
[1] Quoted by Allen Hutt, op. cit., p. 135.
[2] R. Palme Dutt, *The Meaning of the General Strike*, p. 23.

BUILT-IN BETRAYAL

All the essential reformist approaches—conception of the "neutral" State, respect for bourgeois law, rejection of class struggle, fear of unity, fear of the mass of the workers, fear mounting at times to positive hatred of militants and revolutionaries—made the right-wing Labour leaders oppose a General Strike before it began and, when forced into it by mass pressure, do their damnedest to bring it to the speediest end.

Their betrayal, then, was not just a private individual act of cowardice. (It is true that personal cowardice is often linked with the floating hesitancy, the vacillation, of a reformist position. But reformists can be personally courageous and still sell-out.) The betrayal was, as it were, built-in.

Certainly the Establishment, from the coalowners to the King, counted on it. However much they frothed raucous insults against the "revolutionary" General Council, they knew in their hearts that they could, in the last analysis, rely on it. Arthur Horner, the Miners' and Communist leader, looking back at the time of his retirement, on the stormy days of the General Strike, still felt this as he had felt it nearly forty years earlier:

> "There is not the slightest doubt that Baldwin called the bluff of the General Council, because he knew that the General Council did not believe in the weapon of the General Strike and would not wield that weapon in an effective fashion, and because he knew that the General Council was not wholeheartedly with the miners in their resistance to reductions in wages. He foresaw that the General Council would seize the earliest opportunity to break the Strike, betray the miners, and create the greatest possible demoralisation among the working class."[1]

J. R. Clynes, worthy colleague of MacDonald, Snowden and Thomas, also in his older days looked back on the General Strike. In that reformist classic, his *Memoirs*, he put the whole issue in a (reformist) nutshell:

> "J. H. Thomas, representing the railwaymen found, early in the Strike, that his duties took him to Buckingham Palace. King George asked him a number of questions, and expressed his sympathy for the

---
[1] Arthur Horner, *Incorrigible Rebel*, p. 78.

miners. At the end of the talk, His Majesty, who was gravely disturbed, remarked, it is said: 'Well, Thomas, if the worst happens, I suppose all this—' (with a gesture indicating his surroundings)—'will vanish?'

"Fortunately for Britain and the world, it did not come to the worst. The Trade Unions saw to that."[1]

Not the trade unions, but their right-wing leaders, who in the last analysis were bound to defend the Establishment of which *they* (not the unions) had become a part.

THE MOOD OF THE MASSES

What was the outlook, the degree of real understanding of the strike, amongst the great mass of the workers? How far did that outlook change in the course of the strike? How far did reformist ideas and illusions, at the outset and the end of the strike, dominate the minds of the working class?

All historians of the strike—left-wing, centre and right, from proletarian participants to the most academic and erudite—agree that, at the beginning of May 1926, the workers were ready and eager to strike, that there was no hesitation, that the problem of the General Council was to hold their second-line back, that the unemployed rallied to the strike, that the strike was overwhelmingly solid, that there was a general feeling of confidence. The thesis adopted at the Eighth Congress of the Communist Party summed it up:

"The solidarity of the workers (unionists and non-unionists) was complete. The extent of the Strike gave them a feeling of strength."[2]

As the Party statement said, not only a readiness to strike but a deep feeling of *solidarity* prevailed. It was only the more militant workers who clearly saw that in the struggle it was *their* wages, *their* future, at stake. For millions the essential issue was *solidarity with the miners*. In a sense the limitation of approach to one of solidarity and the failure to see the other issues involved was a weakness, which the Communists tried to remedy; but the fact that it was so brings out in relief the strength of the sentiment of solidarity that prevailed amongst the workers. It was not necessary to be a revolutionary to be imbued with

---

[1] J. R. Clynes, *Memoirs 1924–1937*, pp. 81–82.
[2] Theses adopted at 8th Congress C.P.G.B. See *Report of 8th Congress*, p. 63.

this deep sense of class solidarity, national and international, as Marx found in his contacts with the British workers in the early years of the First International.

The workers fought in the strike with that dogged and determined courage typical of the British proletariat. It was not the courage of the barricades, the defiance of sudden death, but that deep courage that can endure weeks and months of prolonged strike or lock-out, can defy slow starvation.

Again, when the young Engels was describing his admiration of the British proletariat of the 1840's, he wrote:

> "That courage is required for a turnout, often indeed much loftier courage, much bolder, firmer determination than for an insurrection is self-evident. It is in truth, no trifle for a working man who knows want from experience, to face it with wife and children, to endure hunger and wretchedness for months together, and stand firm and unshaken through it all. . . . And precisely in this quiet perseverance, in this lasting determination which undergoes a hundred tests every day, the English working-man develops that side of his character which commands most respect."[1]

This was the type of courage with which the British working class, who in the 1920's certainly still "knew want", went so readily into the General Strike, though the sell-out did not allow them to display it to the full. The miners in the long gruelling starving months that followed epitomised it utterly.

The workers in the General Strike displayed another capacity which serious observers from other countries have always noted—with admiration or fear according to their outlook: the capacity to organise even complex operations in admirable order and discipline. This is a quality that inevitably came in the country of the first industrial revolution—the first great factories, the first great experience of social labour, the first powerful trade unions. It had been displayed in innumerable strikes since the 1760's. It had been displayed by innumerable N.C.O.'s in countless wars even when their officers panicked. In the General Strike the complicated improvised system of communications, preparation and distribution of bulletins, the organisation of mass pickets, the first beginnings that we have seen of an embryo alternative government in certain localities, all bore witness to this

[1] F. Engels, *The Condition of the Working-Class in England in 1844*, chapter VIII, "Labour Movements".

now almost traditional talent. The workers had learned self-reliance in 150 years of capitalist exploitation, and were ready to show it.

It would be wrong to leave without mention that deep humour that is typical of the British working class, and is shown often at the most serious moments. It is something that is hard to put into words, often impossible to translate, and that not infrequently baffles our foreign friends and comrades, and yet is a source of strength and of endurance. Satire of the class enemy, well laced with four-letter invective, one of our longest cultural traditions, was reflected at picket line, in bulletins, in all-night vigils, and made fools of police inspectors and public school blacklegs. A capacity to laugh at oneself, to sort out the humour of the most sacred and solemn occasions, to reject pomposity, to be allergic to adulation of authority including well-loved leaders, has well served the British working class and long may it live!

But readiness to strike, a deep-felt sense of proletarian solidarity, dogged courage, the capacity to organise, self-discipline, humour—these great and admirable qualities were not, by themselves, sufficient.

Drafting the thesis on the strike for the Eighth Congress of the Communist Party, after analysing the militant readiness for struggle, the authors of the statement (the retiring Executive Committee) correctly added these words:

> "Their determination to win was, however, accompanied with a lack of understanding of the full political implications of the General Strike."[1]

The British working class was still in the 1920's paying the price of living in the historic centre of imperialism (even if Britain had already yielded to other imperialist powers its old position). The reformism that goes with imperialism was still exercising a strong influence over the great majority of the British working class, including some of the most militant organised workers. The British working-class movement was still strongly empirical; it fought hard in a class sense and in a class way for its rights and standards within the capitalist system, but still, through the influence of reformism, in the main accepted the existence of the system, or at least, if it wanted to change it, accepted to work from within it, accepted the capitalist State. Many a militant worker who from boyhood had joined the movement, fought for the movement, seen his family starve for the movement,

---

[1] "Theses on General Strike" adopted at Eighth Congress, see *Report of 8th Congress*, p. 63.

and died with the movement uppermost in his heart, yet died not understanding what was imperialism, what was socialism and how to advance from the one to the other. Many a militant worker in Labour Party or I.L.P., in trade union or Co-operative *hated* the old system, longed for a new socialist system, but did not *understand* them. Or, more precisely, they lacked an understanding of the laws of capitalism, of the class struggle, of social development and, therefore, of the political tasks of the struggle for socialism and the need for a political party of the working class. For many of those who were socialists, their socialism was still "sentimental", of the heart and not of the mind, not yet scientific.

When the General Strike commenced, capitalist ideas in many forms, sometimes in Liberal form, sometimes in the guise of non-interest in politics (which meant the acceptance of capitalist politics), but most often in the shape of reformism, still influenced the great majority of the working class.

There were many who on one issue or another were *beginning* to break through, *beginning* to shed their reformist illusions, *beginning* to understand the political nature of the General Strike, beginning through the experience of the capitalist State to understand something of its class character. A typical report from the Dartford Divisional Labour Party[1] recounted that:

"after the third day of the Strike if you spoke about the coalowners the audience would listen with a polite indifference, but if you attacked the Government or even mentioned the word, you had the audience with you, and that with cheers and wild enthusiasm. The issue was the T.U.C. and the Government—the miners and the owners were secondary to this issue."

But this was only a *beginning*. The development of Councils of Action to the point where they were taking over certain of the functions of government was a further advance. But even this was only a *beginning*. The progress of the strike (and the good work done by the relatively small forces of the Communists, helped by a number of militant socialists in local Labour Party and I.L.P. branches) enormously accelerated the process of political awakening. But nine days was not *nearly* enough to transform the hatred of the Tories, employers, coalowners, and the disgust with the General Council, into a positive, scientific, socialist, revolutionary outlook. It is very important for

[1] Quoted by Allen Hutt, op. cit., p. 148.

understanding the next stages of the British working-class movement and of the Communist Party, to appreciate the degree of this political awakening, but *not to exaggerate it* as some British Communists and some sections of the Communist International tended to do at the time. It was a great temptation for those who had fought through the dramatic nine days, understanding their vast significance and potentiality, to imagine that the same level of understanding had been reached by the millions of workers all around them. This was by no means so.

Discussing the lessons and consequences of the Great Strike at the 8th Party Congress the following October, attention was paid to the analysis of the outlook and conduct of the middle strata, the middle sections of the population during the strike—to professional people and students, to shop-keepers, "small" people, etc.[1] Students at the time of the strike were prominent as strike-breakers, though there were a number of student Socialists and Communists who organised to support the strike. The division in the middle sections was seen within the Christian Church where a more progressive wing pleaded for at least mediation and "peace by negotiation". It was seen with the Liberal Party in the attitude of those around Lloyd George. The thesis at the 8th Congress emphasised the need for the Labour Movement to win over or at least to neutralise the salaried workers, professional people, etc. The experience of the decades that followed was to show that, correct though this attitude was, there was not sufficient recognition at the time either of the need for the Labour Movement to win over the middle sections or of its capacity to do so.

THE NEED FOR A COMMUNIST PARTY

The more the achievements of the General Strike are studied, and the more one studies its defeat, the more history shouts aloud, as it were, the need of and the role of a strong Communist Party.

Tens of thousands of men and women and youth of the non-Communist, non-Marxist left played individually within the struggles of the strike a courageous and, sometimes, magnificent part. But only the Communist Party played its role *as a Party, as an organised, coherent, conscious force.*

The tens of thousands of "unknown soldiers" of the class war who, though no great monuments commemorate their courage, manned the pickets, led the Councils of Action, printed and distributed the bulletins,

[1] See thesis adopted at 8th Congress C.P.G.B., *Report*, p. 66–67.

were members of the Labour Party, of the I.L.P., non-party trade unionists, as well as Communists. Many of them had sharp class instincts, hated the guts of the employers, deeply yearned for a new social order, which they called socialism. But most often they lacked any real scientific understanding of capitalism and its methods, or of socialism and its tasks. Most of them lacked any central co-ordinated leadership.

Within the General Council there was (on paper) a strong "left", on paper even a majority. These were men who at one or another time had played a militant role in the trade union movement. But they were far from conscious socialists, their conceptions did not in the main pass beyond the field of trade unionism, they had no science of society, no perspective of transition to socialism, and so they had no power to resist the reformism of MacDonald, and whilst the strike was on ranged from a shameful silence to open support of the Thomas line. At best they were ineffective; at worst they abetted the sell-out.

This wretched role of the "left" group on the General Council showed the lack of consistency and principle of a group of men without clear socialist ideas or co-ordinated leadership. In drawing this lesson at the end of the strike, and in indignation at the pitiful role this group had played, some Communist statements began to exaggerate the "dangers" of such a left, and even to see them as *mainly* responsible for the defeat. This, as we can now see, was wrong and sectarian. The *main* danger came from the capitalists. Within the Labour Movement the *main* danger was the right-wing reformists. However great their failure or complicity, to exaggerate the role of this "left" in the General Council not only concealed the main enemy but tended to offend thousands of genuinely militant workers who were not yet Marxists, and to isolate the Communists from them.[1]

By 1926 it was a complex task to characterise the Independent Labour Party (I.L.P.) with its mixed composition of both leadership and membership. It could be all things to all men (and at the same time). At its base in towns like Glasgow, Manchester, Bradford, Norwich, it had the loyalty of many fine militant industrial workers, more often than not "sentimental" socialists, of passionate anti-capitalist feeling

---

[1] This attack on the "left" in the General Council was most strongly expressed in the Communist International's "Theses on the British General Strike", adopted in June 1926. See *Communist Review*, July 1926 p. 121, and especially section at end (p. 133) on "Our Immediate Tasks" which includes "(6) Exposure of the Left Wing as people who capitulated in spite of their majority and who carried on a Right policy, being thereby mainly responsible for the defeat."

but weak in science. The leadership ranged from a definitely left trend (though sometimes suffering from bitter anti-Communist bias) to the most extreme right-wingers like MacDonald. Thus one cannot speak of an "I.L.P. line" on the General Strike, but only of the line of different I.L.P.'ers or local groups.

Some I.L.P.'ers like H. N. Brailsford and Fenner Brockway saw, to an extent, the dangers of right-wing betrayal before the strike.[1] But it was only *after* the strike that their real offensive against the right wing began.[2] *After* the strike was over the I.L.P. *New Leader* bitterly deplored the sell-out. But what had it done *before*?

On March 12, after the publication of the Royal Commission Report, the *New Leader* waxed enthusiastic:

> "The reading of the Coal Commission's Report has affected us as no printed words have affected us since Sir Edward Grey addressed the House of Commons on that fatal Monday in August 1914. Its tone, like his, is judicial. It holds the balance between the contending sides.
>
> "Our own view is that while it prepares with all its courage and steadfastness for a decisive struggle, the Labour Movement should address itself first of all to the good sense and the corporate conscience of the nation."[3]

What leadership was this? Where was the leadership and the protest of the strong I.L.P. group on the General Council?[4] Two thirds of the Parliamentary Labour Party members at the time of the General Strike were members of the I.L.P.[5] Where was their opposition to the sell-out? The only active I.L.P. leadership in this group during the strike was that of MacDonald's exercised *against* the strike.

Thus whilst many individual I.L.P.'ers and some local I.L.P. Branches did some excellent work during the strike, the position of the I.L.P. *as a Party* was at best negative, confused and confusing.

Yet the deepest lesson of the strike was the need for a clear left leadership.

[1] See Fenner Brockway's article "A Diary of the General Strike" in *Socialist Review*, June 1926.
[2] See H. N. Brailsford in *New Leader*, May 21, 1926.
[3] Quoted by J. T. Murphy in *The Political Meaning of the Great Strike*, C.P.G.B., September 1926, pp. 62–63.
[4] According to J. T. Murphy in "The I.L.P. in the Strike", *Workers' Weekly*, No. 171, May 28, 1926, p. 4, there were at least six members of the I.L.P. on the General Council.
[5] Ibid.

How far was such a leadership provided by the Communist Party?

Of course there were weaknesses in its political appeals and statements, but they were *overwhelmingly correct*. The Party warned of the coming capitalist offensive, exposed the manœuvre of the Royal Commission Report, appealed for unity of the working class, and proposed the main lines of preparation that were necessary—contact with the Co-operatives, strengthening the factory organisation and the trades councils, Councils of Action, Workers Defence Corps. During the strike it revealed the class character of the capitalist offensive, the *political* offensive of the *capitalist* state, and called for a *political* answer by the workers.

Of course there were weaknesses in the activity of this or that Party Branch or Party Committee during the strike; but taken as a whole, for a Party which at the outset of the strike had some 5,000 members, its activity was magnificent. Communists were everywhere in the most active mass pickets, editing and distributing bulletins, manning key positions in the strike committees and Councils of Action.

And this was widely recognised. It was recognised by the capitalist press that pointed its main attacks at the Communist Party, and the capitalist State which made it the main target of arrest.

It was recognised by the international Communist movement. The Communist International, never lavish with its praise, conceded in its theses on the General Strike the correctness of the position taken by the British Party:

"The Communist Party of Great Britain has, on the whole, stood the test of political maturity. The Executive Committee of the Communist International was quite right when it unanimously approved the position taken up by the C.P.G.B."[1]

Miners' leaders like A. J. Cook readily acknowledged the role of the Communist Party and the Communist press in support of the miners:

"I should like to state plainly and emphatically that the splendid solidarity of the miners and the whole working-class movement is due to a large extent to the uncompromising attitude taken by the *Workers' Weekly*. Events since April 30 (1926) have proved conclusively that the *Workers' Weekly* was right."[2]

---

[1] See text of theses in *Communist Review*, Vol. 7, No. 3, pp. 131–132.
[2] A. J. Cook in *Workers' Weekly*, No. 173, June 11, 1926, p. 1.

It was acknowledged again and again by militant trade unionists, miners, transport workers, building workers. Summarising the activities of the Communist Party in the strike those reporting concluded:

> "Mistakes and defects there were, no doubt, but reports from all sides show that many thousands of workers have at last realised that the Communist Party, in the words of some London railwaymen, 'was the only Party that stood by the workers all the time'."[1]

Looking back with the hindsight of forty years, a number of aspects of Party policy before and during the strike warrant thought and discussion.

Considering that some of the most experienced Communist leaders were still in gaol, the organisation of the Party held together remarkably well. Lack of experience of illegal and semi-legal conditions meant that in certain areas too little was done to protect key activists from arrest.

One of the slogans put forward in the period before the General Strike warrants critical re-examination—the call for more powers to the General Council of the T.U.C.

The slogan of "All power to the General Council!" as used in the call printed in the *Workers' Weekly* of January 1, 1926, was certainly incorrect, and the use of the words "all power" liable to lead to confusion between the immediate fight for a more militant trade union leadership and the issue of political power.

But this was not the usual slogan of the Communist Party nor of the Minority Movement. The usual form[2] was a call for "more powers" to the General Council to enable it to become a leading co-ordinating force in the trade union movement. Moreover, the demand was always put alongside the call to develop strong and militant Works Committees and Trades Councils and for a militant line of action for the T.U.C.

But even with this reserve, there is a difference between putting forward a *long-term perspective* of achieving through mass struggle and the pressure of militant trade unionists a militant General Council capable of giving leadership, and the *immediate call* for "more power"

---

[1] *Workers' Weekly*, No. 170, May 21, 1926, p. 7, "The Communist Party Plays its Part".

[2] As at 2nd Conference of N.M.M. (August 29–30, 1925), see pp. 44–46, and in *Statement of Executive Committee of the C.P.G.B.*, January 10, 1926, see Appendix II to this Chapter.

to the General Council at a time when it was under right-wing domination, and much more likely to use those powers against the militant working class.

There are other points too that would warrant re-examination. Were not the political slogans of "Nationalisation of the Mines" and for a "Labour Government" raised too suddenly and too late and without sufficient explanation? Was the Party not slow in the critical early days of the strike to answer the Government's attack that the strike was unconstitutional? It is well that such issues are raised and given proper consideration.

But they should be examined and discussed within the general understanding that the overall Party approach was overwhelmingly correct, and that the Party's practical contribution to the struggle was, in view of its small numbers, quite exceptional. Rarely have so few contributed so much.

The *main* weakness of the Party—and this was something essentially objective, a reflection of the history of the British Labour Movement, of the origins of reformism in imperialism, of the right-wing domination of the trade union movement and Labour Party—was that it was *too small*.

With its 5,000 members, despite rapid recruiting in the latter days of the strike and rapidly increasing support, it had neither the membership nor the influence to take over the leadership of the struggle from the right-wing reformists. Despite the rapid growth of militant ideas in the nine days, reformist influence was still too deep and too widespread for the sell-out to be avoided.

But from what the Party *did* achieve and from what, through insufficient size and influence, it could *not* achieve, two lessons stood out a mile.

The different sections of the left, isolated from one another, lacking common links and a common programme, were weakened, half paralysed. The Left needed unity, but that alone was not enough.

Above all, the British Labour Movement, if it were successfully to defeat capitalism and advance to socialism, needed a Party that would give to the working class and the working people a socialist consciousness, socialist theory, socialist ideas; that would help the workers and the people to fight on all the immediate struggles that confronted them, help to co-ordinate these struggles, to lift their level; that would give at least to the most clear sighted workers a new form of revolutionary organisation.

Many years after the strike, William Gallacher, thinking the problems over, came to the conclusion that:

> "the great lesson of the General Strike is that for the successful carrying through of a class action there must be a reliable, unshakeable class leadership."[1]

Successfully to engage and defeat capitalism, successfully to advance towards socialism, the British working class and the left needed a strong Marxist party.

DEFEAT OR VICTORY?

When the strike was over, amidst discussions, heart-searchings, debates on the nature of the great strike, the issue was raised amongst Marxists as to how far the General Strike presented a revolutionary situation in Britain.[2] It is not to underestimate its extent or deep significance to deny that it did so.

The General Strike took place at a time of, and indeed was a reflection of, a profound crisis of British capitalism, but it cannot be said that the capitalist class was incapable of ruling in the old way; indeed, they went into the General Strike with a marked degree of unity and reactionary purpose. The working class were ready for struggle, certainly—ready for action and sacrifice. But the majority of them still saw that struggle as one for wages, conditions, solidarity, to be waged "within the capitalist system", and were still to one or another degree under the influence of reformist ideology.

The Communist Party played a courageous and conspicuous role, as we have seen, but did not yet exercise sufficient influence to lead a decisive section of the workers to repudiate the sell-out, let alone to repudiate the political system.

Of course the situation was changing, developing fast, it contained within itself revolutionary potentiality. It was for that reason that the reformists so speedily called the strike off. The most advanced Councils of action like that in Northumberland and Durham *began* to represent a step towards dual authority an embryo of "dual power", but this was not by any means so everywhere; and though the parallel with the

---

[1] William Gallacher, Foreword to John Murray's *The General Strike of 1926: a History*, p. 12, Lawrence and Wishart, 1951.
[2] See discussion in R. Page Arnot's "Introduction to the Story of the General Strike", *Labour Monthly*, June 1926, pp. 346–347.

Russian Soviets of 1917 is interesting, it could give rise to illusions about the revolutionary level of the General Strike.[1]

Naturally in all sections of the British Labour Movement one of the subjects for debate was the future of general strikes. Could there, should there be such strikes again? If so under what circumstances?

The right wing used the defeat for which they were above all responsible as a pretext to make their hate and abject fear of general strikes into a theoretical principle. Said J. R. Clynes:

> "We learned that a national strike could not be used as a weapon in a trades dispute."[2]

Said Ramsay MacDonald:

> "The General Strike is a weapon that cannot be wielded for industrial purposes.... If fought to a finish as a strike it would ruin Trade Unionism, and the Government in the meantime could create a revolution...."[3]

A section of the left, particularly within the I.L.P., began to put forward the argument that a general strike is not a tenable weapon of struggle as it can only be part of an armed revolution, and on *this* basis to oppose its use. H. N. Brailsford wrote in the *New Leader*:

> "Much more serious was the failure to think out the question whether the General Strike is an appropriate weapon unless one intends in the event of success to attempt revolutionary action."[4]

The more militant British trade unionists rejected this "never again" approach and rather than rejecting the General Strike as a method of class struggle proceeded to discuss what was needed to make such a weapon successful. "The miners as an organisation believe in the General Strike", declared S. O. Davies, speaking for the South Wales Miners, at the Conference of the Trade Union Executives in January 1927.[5]

---

[1] See "Theses of Communist International of the British General Strike" in *Communist Review*, July 1926, p. 126—"The Councils of Action organised by the trade unions actually developed into District Soviets. The Departments organised by the General Council already resembled in their structure and functions, the departments of the St. Petersburg Soviet in the period of the so-called 'dual power' (February–November 1917)."
[2] J. R. Clynes, *Memoirs: 1924–1927*, p. 95.
[3] Ramsay MacDonald in *Socialist Review*, June 1926, p. 8.
[4] *New Leader*, May 21, 1926, quoted in J. R. Campbell's, "Reflections on the General Strike", *Communist Review*, July 1926.
[5] *The Mining Crisis*, pp. 55–56, T.U.C., 1927.

Within the Communist Party there was at first a certain tendency to say that after the lessons of the General Strike all working-class struggle must henceforth be of a directly political revolutionary character. But after discussion the Eighth Congress of the Party, held in October, far from rejecting national and general strikes, discussed in detail what was necessary in terms of preparation, conduct and leadership, to make them victorious.[1]

Certainly it was true that any general strike must inevitably come up against the *political* action of the capitalists, the resistance of the *capitalist State*, that no general strike could be, in the General Council's language, "purely industrial". But this did not mean and does not mean the only justification of a general strike is at the moment of political struggle for power.

The discussion on the General Strike, on the profound significance of its occurrence, solidity, extension, and also the effect and significance of its defeat, continued in the years that followed. There was, over the next years, much debate on this inside the Communist Party. This belongs to a later period of Party history, and will be treated in its place.

Naturally it must be recognised that the sell-out of the General Strike at its peak period of solidity and struggle was a profound defeat for the Labour Movement, opened the gates wide to ruthless capitalist attack, led to widespread feeling of disillusion. It is not sufficient to say that it was a defeat of the reformist leadership. The *responsibility* for the defeat lay with the reformist leaders, but its bitter consequences fell on the shoulders of the mass of the workers.

The Communist Party was completely correct in laying the blame for the defeat on the right-wing reformist leaders in the General Council and the Labour Party, it was correct to show the need to change the *leadership* of the Labour Movement and change the situation *inside* the Labour Movement. At the Executive meeting which followed the strike and again at the Eighth Congress in October, it correctly fought for 100 per cent trade unionism, stronger Trades Councils and factory committees, solidarity with the miners, resistance to victimisation, better understanding between trade unions and Co-operatives, for the strengthening of the left, and, above all for a stronger Communist Party.

But it is important to note that already in the months that followed the strike the germ can be seen of certain errors.

[1] See especially Thesis on General Strike in *Report of 8th Congress*, p. 68-70.

There was a certain danger of exaggerating the degree to which the mass of the British workers had learned the lessons of the General Strike, had cast off reformist ideas, were ready for a new leadership. There was a danger that ideas that had in truth become obsolete, outdated for the Communists, the vanguard, the militants, should be taken as obsolete for the workers as a whole. In fact the atmosphere of disillusion that spread widely in the difficult days that followed the strike provided a basis for a dangerous spread of right-wing ideas.

There was a danger, too, that the natural and correct and bitter indignation against the official leadership of the Labour Movement should lead to the search for short cuts, to attempt to bypass the traditional mass Labour organisations and the necessary process of helping the mass of the workers to move into struggle and change their outlook.

There was a certain danger that in correctly criticising that group of "lefts" who had abdicated to the right wing in the course of the strike, the "left" should be indiscriminately attacked, its "dangers" exaggerated, and above all contacts cut with the mass of genuine militant workers in Labour Party, I.L.P. and trade unions, who were not yet ready to accept revolutionary ideas.

The Communist approaches before and during the strike bear well the test of history. The lessons that the Communist Party drew from the General Strike stood well the test of time. Certain exaggerations and mistakes that arose in embryo in the weeks and months that followed the strike arose from bitter disgust with the reformists and reformist ideas that betrayed the Labour Movement at one of the greatest moments of its history.

For it was a great moment. There can be deep defeats that yet contain an element of triumph. Such was the Paris Commune. Such was the Russian Revolution of 1905.

At the beginning of May 1926, during those nine glorious days, the wheels of British imperialism stopped. Factories were closed. Traffic was almost at a standstill. The capitalists as they shouted hatred shivered with apprehension. That great giant the British proletariat began to show something of its vast strength. There was a glimpse of the unbounded strength of the British working class once it casts off the fetters of capitalist ideas. There was a glimpse of its unity, organisational capacity, capacity to govern. There was a glimpse of its steadfastness, stout heart, solidarity. Only a glimpse perhaps—but one not to be forgotten.

CHAPTER II—APPENDIX I

STATEMENT OF EXECUTIVE COMMITTEE OF THE C.P.G.B., JANUARY 10, 1926[1]

Vast Struggle Begins—Communist Executive draws up Programme of Action—Whole Class must Unite—A Common Minimum wanted for all Workers

The present industrial situation and the crisis looming ahead fully justifies the Communist Party's warning to the workers that the Capitalist class is determined to return to the offensive, on an even more gigantic scale than last July.

The miners, after the breathing space brought for the owners by the means of a subsidy, and the sham impartiality of the Coal Commission, are now threatened with an open attack on the seven-hour day, on the Miners' Federation and on wages.

The owners have thrown disguise to the winds.

The attack on the miners is the most violent and unashamed; but workers in most of the industries are faced with similar attacks.

The railwaymen are threatened with wage cuts: the engineers, with longer hours: the builders with abolition of craft control won by years of sacrifice.

Coupled with this, nearly two million workers remain unemployed. By artificial brutal administrative restrictions, thousands have been struck off the register, and refused unemployment benefit. They have become completely dependent on the Poor Law authorities, and the crushing burden of maintaining this huge army of reserve workers against possible strikers or lock-outs falls entirely upon local taxation.

These facts, taken together with the steady, if unobtrusive organisation of the O.M.S., point to a definite determination on the part of the British capitalists to prevent a repetition of Red Friday, to challenge the organised Labour Movement and smash it, and to drive the workers down to coolie conditions. By this means they hope to achieve the impossible task of stabilising their system, undermined by war, ruin of foreign markets, chaos in production, and hideous exploitation of colonial workers.

The struggle now opening is of a magnitude hitherto unknown.

[1] *Workers' Weekly*, No. 154, January 15, 1926.

But this enlarged meeting of the Central Committee of the Communist Party believes that the workers can meet the capitalist attack and smash it, as on Red Friday.

More: we believe that the British workers can turn their defensive into an offensive, and present a common demand for better conditions which will be a prelude to a complete victory over the capitalists.

The Central Committee of the Communist Party declares that the following steps are urgently necessary in order to ensure that the workers' forces are properly organised against the capitalist attack, and instructs all Party members to regard a campaign for those measures as their main and immediate tasks in their respective trade unions:

(1) Summoning by the General Council of a *Conference of Trade Union E.C.'s* in accordance with Scarborough decisions, to give wider powers to the G.C. to lead the whole workers' industrial army.

(2) In addition to the campaign for granting full E.C. powers to the G.C., the completion of the *Workers' Industrial Alliance*, to reinforce the workers' defensive preparations against the coming crisis, and in particular the inclusion of the N.U.R., A.E.U., Boilermakers and General Workers, etc.

(3) A working agreement between the *G.C. and the C.W.S.* to ensure provisioning the workers, and a policy of mutual support between the two National centres of the T.U. and Co-operative movements, the T.U.C. and the Co-operative Union.

(4) Formation of *Factory Committees* elected by all workers irrespective of craft or sex, in accordance with the Scarborough Resolution, to ensure unity of the workers from the bottom, and the calling by the Trades and District Committees, of conferences to ensure union support for these committees.

(5) A national campaign for *100 per cent Trade Unionism*, including a National Show Cards Week. Special attention to be paid to bringing all young workers, including apprentices, into the unions.

(6) Organisation of *Workers' Defence Corps*, composed of Trade Unionists and controlled by Trades Councils, to protect Trade Union liberties against the Fascisti, and calling upon the General Council to take steps to place the workers' case before the workers in the Army, Navy and Air Forces.

(7) Formulation of *Common Programme* for the whole movement (£4 a week for 44 hours), supplementary to the special demands of

each industry (Railway All Grades Programme, Miners' Cost-of-Living scale, Engineers 20s. demand, etc.).

(8) The strengthening of the relations between the G.C. and the N.U.W.C.M. in order to secure the realisation of *the Unemployed* demands, as a counter to the capitalist attempt to force the unemployed into blacklegging.

The Central Committee instructs the Political Bureau to pursue this policy, to strengthen its support of the N.U.W.C.M. and the Minority Movement, and to direct the efforts of the Party members throughout the Labour Movement, in such a manner as to ensure the most complete unity of all working-class forces in resisting the latest attack of the employers, and in transforming each resistance into an irresistible advance which shall help completely to shatter the power of capitalism.

In particular this Enlarged Executive declares that the Industrial Crisis emphasises the correctness of the Party Policy, in insisting upon the transformation of the Party on to a Factory group basis, by the formation of militant Party groups in every factory, pit and workshop, and upon greater attention being paid to the functioning and extension of our Party Fractions in Trades Unions and Trades Councils. The Political Bureau should strengthen its work among women.

CHAPTER II—APPENDIX II

Communist Party Statement on the Royal Commission Report on the Mining Industry[1]

The Report of the Coal Commission is a political document of first-class importance. The contentions of the Communist Party have been, once again, vindicated. Their contention that the Commission was only a subterfuge to cloak the preparations for an attack on the wages and conditions of the miners is amply borne out by this report.

RED FRIDAY

Ever since the tremendous and magnificent display of solidarity by the workers on Red Friday, 1925, the employing class have used every device to split the working class into isolated sections. They were particularly successful in creating friction between the engineers and the building trades over the question of steel houses. They attempted

[1] *Workers' Weekly* No. 163, March 19, 1926, p. 5.

the separation of the railwaymen by the Award of the National Wages Board. Their ultimatum to the engineering trades over the question of Hoe's is yet another incident revealing the strategy of the capitalist class.

In each of these political conflicts the workers have lost ground. In the case of steel houses the wage standards of the building trades are threatened. In the case of the railwaymen two grades of workers will be doing equal work for unequal pay. In the case of the engineers, after two years' negotiations for an improved standard, they are threatened with the lock-out and extended hours of labour.

And now the miners are faced definitely with reductions of wage scales which are already much below subsistence level.

WAGES CUT

Reduction of Wages—that is the cardinal point of the Report, which lays bare the full class character of the struggle and demonstrates that there is no alternative which does not involve either an attack on wages and hours or an attack on existing capitalist ownership.

The Commission's Report is a declaration of war against the miners and the whole working-class movement by the capitalist class, with the full power of the State machine, mobilised at their back.

The Commission's proposal to withdraw the subsidy will mean an almost total cessation of the export trade with the closing of pits and unemployment resulting.

PURPOSE OF SUBSIDY

The subsidy has served its purpose well; it not only staved off the clash of forces last July. It was even more useful to the capitalist class in regaining European markets, giving them and their European colleagues a lever by which to drive down still further the conditions of the European workers—who in turn they hope to use as a lever to worsen the conditions of the British workers. Finally, it gave them a breathing space in which to mobilise all their forces for an open struggle against the workers.

To maintain their export trade without the subsidy will entail a far greater reduction of working costs than the proposed reduction from 33 per cent to 20 per cent over basic rates. The proposed reduction of the higher rated men to assist in maintaining the wages of the lower paid workers would result in reducing wages to the pre-war level, or even lower.

FAKE "NATIONALISATION"

The sop of the proposed nationalisation of mining royalties (estimated as it is to cost £100,000,000) will only mean the alteration of rent receivers into interest receivers. It will operate for some time to come only in those areas which are at present underdeveloped. It falls into the same category as the proposed municipal retailing of coal, and pithead baths, etc. All are attempts at bribing various sections who have been advocating these reforms and so detaching them from any united action of the working class against the capitalist offensive.

DANGERS AHEAD

The miners are faced with two dangers today.

In the first place there is the direct offensive of the capitalist class, who mean to abolish the last remnants of the national mininum and national agreements, to set district against district, collier against surface-worker, so that a decadent system of private enterprise may continue to draw life from the living bodies of miners, their wives and children.

The second danger comes from the existence of a number of Labour leaders who are so obsessed with the idea of uniting all classes and speaking of the interests of "the community as a whole" that they fail to defend the workers they represent. Around them will be gathered all the doctrinaire intellectuals, with their utopian theories, who have been attracted to the Labour Movement. With them, too, will be all the weak vacillating elements on the fringe of the working-class movement. All these will make their appeals and address their little questions and votes of censure to the capitalist class and bid the workers be reasonable.

From these elements the working class can expect every hindrance and little or no help.

POWER

The question which has to be faced by the working class can only be answered by the working class. It is the question of power.

That there is power in the hands of the working class if they care to take it was demonstrated last July. Today the need for a united front of the whole working class under the direction of the General Council of the T.U.C. is apparent. For six years the Labour Movement talked about united support of the miners. Only on one day, Red Friday, July 31st, has that unity been translated into unity of action, and then in a few hours it compelled the government to retreat.

ACTION, NOW

Today we need not phrases about unity, but united action. The Communist Party calls on all Organised Workers, miners, engineers, railwaymen, and others to use the weapon of their fighting strength, the General Council of the Trades Union Congress, and through the united front of all workers press forward the minimum claims of all workers as a direct counter challenge to this latest move in the capitalist offensive.

CHAPTER II—APPENDIX III

STATEMENT OF CENTRAL EXECUTIVE COMMITTEE OF COMMUNIST PARTY OF GREAT BRITAIN, APRIL 23, 1926[1]

All Together for the Fight!
C.P. Call to Miners, Engineers & Railwaymen

FORM COUNCILS OF ACTION

Strike Commissariat should be set up by T.U.C.

The Executive Committee of the Communist Party of Great Britain declares that the great industrial struggle which it predicted last August, and for which it has urged the workers to prepare, is now at hand, and only the utmost unity and determination on the part of the whole of [the] Labour movement can avert defeat.

The employing class has utilised the period which has elapsed since last July, to perfect its preparation for the struggle. Through the Coal Commission Report, it hopes to divide the workers both inside and outside the mining industry and secure an easy victory. The Communist Party declares that the proposals for reorganising the mining industry, contained in the report, are inadequate and cannot

[1] *Workers' Weekly.* No. 168, April 23, 1926.

solve its problems. ONLY BY THE NATIONALISATION OF THE INDUSTRY (INCLUDING COKE AND BY-PRODUCT PLANTS) WITHOUT COMPENSATION, WITH WORKERS' CONTROL, CAN THE PROBLEMS OF THE INDUSTRY BE SOLVED.

"TEMPORARY" CUTS

We therefore warn the miners against accepting any "temporary" cuts in wages pending the "reorganisation of the industry". The experience of the workers in the mining industry of other countries has shown that "temporary" sacrifices inevitably became permanent.

The report has also attempted to play off the various grades of workers in the industry against each other. If the miners allow the wages of any section of workers in the industry to be reduced, this will lead to the break-up of the unity of the workers within the industry and the imposition of a general wage reduction. The miners ought to re-affirm their respective declarations that in relation to the cost of living there are no highly paid workers in the mining industry, the wages of all workers in the industry being below pre-war level. The miners, while resisting the wage-cuts being demanded from them at the moment, must not abandon their objective of a living wage equal to 1914 wages, plus an increase commensurate with the increased cost of living.

MINERS, STAND FIRM!

In the meantime, the Communist Party urges the miners to stand by their declaration of April 10, and repulse any settlement which involves any decrease in wages, or any modification of the principle of a national agreement. To abandon the principle of national agreements, would mean the break-up of the Federation. The miners must therefore repudiate any suggestion of district negotiations, as that would be preparing a defeat for the whole working class.

The Communist Party especially warns the miners against the attempt of the mineowners to trick the miners by publishing plausible schedules, and rates of wages based upon a comparison of earnings on an eight-hour day with the seven-hour day. Remember the statement in the report of the Commission that an extension of the working day to eight hours means the displacement of 130,000 miners. A firm and definite fight must be made upon:

NO REDUCTION IN WAGES

NO INCREASE IN HOURS
A REAL NATIONAL AGREEMENT

The Communist Party urges the workers outside the mining industry again to bring pressure upon their officials to support the miners.

GENERAL COMMISSARIAT

At the moment metal and railway workers are demanding an increase in wages. Other workers are preparing to follow. A defeat of the miners means the defeat of this movement for better conditions and the imposition of wage cuts upon the whole working class as the experience of 1921 proved.

We therefore urge the General Council of the Trade Union Congress to call a meeting of all Trade Union Executives with a view to replying to any attempt to reduce miners' wages by a general strike if necessary. Negotiations should be entered into between the General Council and Co-operative Wholesale Societies, with a view to creating a strike commissariat.

We urge the General Council of the T.U.C. to approach the International Federation of Trade Unions, with a view to securing the fullest support of the miners and transport Internationals in the struggle.

All Trades Councils should *immediately*, in the various districts, convene conferences, including all sections of the working-class movement, political, industrial, co-operatives and unemployed, with a view to setting up local Councils of Action, in order to mobilise support for the miners and make the leaders act.

The Miners' Fight is the Workers' Fight!
Break the Capitalist Attack on Wages!
Now for a United Working Class Advance!

CHAPTER II—APPENDIX IV

COMMUNIST PARTY MANIFESTO OF MAY 2, 1926

Published as an advertisement in the Sunday Worker, *May 2, 1926*[1]

For nine months the Communist Party has been warning the workers that the mineowners and their government intended to attack the miners, and through them the whole working class. The Right Wing in the trade unions and the Labour Party has sneered at these warnings,

[1] Printed in full in R. Page Arnot, *The General Strike*, pp. 163–164.

and deliberately neglected to make adequate preparations. The events of the last few days have shown conclusively that the Communist Party was right.

The supreme need of the movement is solidarity between all sections of organised labour. The greatest danger to the workers today is that the Government and the Right Wing may succeed in isolating the miners from the rest of the movement by obscuring the real issues at stake, namely, that whatever reorganisation of the coal industry is needed, the miners shall not be forced to accept lower wages, longer hours or district agreements.

During the negotiations the Government has done its utmost to trap the miners into unreservedly accepting the Commission's Report as a basis for discussion, and abandoning their resistance to its unashamed proposals for lowering their standard of life. This would be fatal, not only for the miners, but for all workers. Therefore, every working-class organisation must tell the capitalists plainly that the miners' declaration on wages, hours and national agreements, repeatedly endorsed by the General Council, are the minimum basis of any agreement whatsoever.

Further, the Communist Party reminds the workers that the Government fears action, not words. The General Council's request for power to call out every industry will not move the Government unless the resolution is accompanied by action. Such action can only be an immediate embargo on transport of coal or blacklegs, and a stoppage of the lying capitalist press.

The Communist Party urges every member of the working class to do his utmost, in the next few days, to mobilise the workers in every locality around the Trades Council, vested with full authority as a Council of Action to press for the creation of a Workers' Defence Corps and a commissariat department jointly with the local Co-operative and to demand that the General Council shall immediately summon an International Conference of all trade union organisations to prevent blacklegging and secure co-ordinated action in defence of the miners.

NOT A PENNY OFF THE PAY, NOT A SECOND ON THE DAY!
A COUNCIL OF ACTION IN EVERY TOWN!
EVERY MAN BEHIND THE MINERS!

The Central Committee,
Communist Party of Great Britain.

CHAPTER II—APPENDIX V

THE POLITICAL MEANING OF THE GENERAL STRIKE

Statement of Executive Committee of the C.P.G.B. issued in the Workers' Bulletin, *No. 2, of May 5th, 1926*

WORKERS OF BRITAIN

You have begun a General Strike of vast extent in defence of the miners' standard of living, knowing full well that further degradation for the miners means immediate attacks on the wages and hours of other workers. The General Strike is not only a magnificent act of brotherly support to the miners, it is an act of self-defence on the part of the working class, who, with their families, constitute the vast majority of the people.

The first watchwords of the General Strike, therefore, have been and remain: "*All Together Behind the Miners. Not a Penny off the Pay. Not a Second on the Day!*"

But now that the struggle has begun, the workers have it in their power to put an end once and for all to this continued menace to their living standards and working conditions. Simply to beat off the employers' present offensive means that they will return to the attack later on, just as they did after Red Friday last year. The only guarantee against the ravenous and soulless greed of the coalowners is to break their economic power.

THEREFORE LET THE WORKERS ANSWER THE BOSSES' CHALLENGE WITH A CHALLENGE OF THEIR OWN: "NATIONALISATION OF THE MINES, WITHOUT COMPENSATION FOR THE COALOWNERS, UNDER WORKERS' CONTROL THROUGH PIT COMMITTEES!"

The Government in this struggle has dropped the pretence of being above all classes. It made no objection to the coalowners' decision to hold the community to ransom by their attack on wages, but it delivered an insolent and provocative ultimatum when the Trade Union Congress decided, in the exercise of its undoubted rights, to defend the miners against starvation wages and slave conditions. Ever since the strike began, the Government has welcomed the aid of the capitalist strike-breaking organisations, the O.M.S. and Fascisti: but it issued an insulting rejection of the trade union offer to maintain essential services without blacklegs. Troops, aeroplanes, and battleships are being used to overcome the workers, if possible, and to crush the General Strike. If the Strike ends, though it be with the defeat of the coalowners, but with the Government's power unshaken, the capitalists will still have hopes of renewing their attack.

Therefore the third essential slogan of the General Strike must be: "RESIGNATION OF THE FORGERY GOVERNMENT! FORMATION OF A LABOUR GOVERNMENT!"

The Communist Party continues to instruct its members and to urge the workers to take every practical step necessary to consolidate our positions against the capitalist attack. Such essential steps are: to form a Council of Action immediately: to organise able bodied Trade Unionists in a Workers' Defence Corps against the O.M.S. and Fascisti; to set up feeding arrangements with the Co-operative Societies; to hold mass meetings and issue strike bulletins, and to make their case known to the soldiers.

But the Communist Party warns the workers against the attempt being made to limit the struggle to its previous character of self-defence against the capitalist offensive. Once the battle has been joined, the only way to victory is to push ahead and hit hard. And the way to hit the capitalist hardest is for the Councils of Action to throw out the clear watchwords:

NOT A PENNY OFF THE PAY: NOT A SECOND ON THE DAY!
NATIONALISE THE MINES WITHOUT COMPENSATION UNDER WORKERS' CONTROL!
FORMATION OF A LABOUR GOVERNMENT!

CHAPTER II—APPENDIX VI

STAND BY THE MINERS!
AN APPEAL BY THE COMMUNIST PARTY OF GREAT BRITAIN

Published in the Workers' Bulletin, No. 9 of May 13th, 1926[1]

The General Council's decision to call off the General Strike is the greatest crime that has ever been permitted, not only against the miners, but against the working class of Great Britain and the whole

---

[1] Also reproduced in R. Page Arnot, *The General Strike*, pp. 233–234, Labour Research Department, 1926.

world. The British workers had aroused the astonishment and admiration of the world by the enthusiasm with which they had entered upon the fight for the miners' standard of living. But, instead of responding to this magnificent lead by a call to every section of organised labour to join the fight against the capitalists, the General Council has miserably thrown itself and the miners on the tender mercies of the workers' worst enemies—the Tory Government.

This was a fight in defence, not only of the miners, but of every worker. Particularly does this apply to the railwaymen and transport workers, whose "high wages" had been menaced by the employers during the Coal Commission. But there is no class of worker that can afford to forget Baldwin's message of July 1925: "Wages in every industry must come down".

The Right Wing in the General Council bears direct responsibility for throwing away the workers' weapons and leaving them almost defenceless against the capitalists. Throughout the General Strike they deliberately avoided any pledge to fight against wage reductions. They gave prominence to appeals by Archbishops and County Councils to call off the General Strike without guarantee as to living standards. They suppressed the news that scores, sometimes hundreds of workers were being arrested or batoned for exercising their right of picketing or propaganda. And most of the so-called Left Wing have been no better than the Right. By a policy of timid silence, by using the false pretext of loyalty to colleagues to cover up breaches of loyalty to workers, they have left a free hand to the Right Wing and thus helped to play the employers' game. Even now they have not the courage to come out openly as a minority in the General Council and join forces with the real majority—the workers—against the united front of Baldwin-Samuel-Thomas.

But the working class is bigger than any leader. If the old leaders turn traitor or coward, the workers are capable of taking charge themselves. They must take charge themselves, if all the effort and courage of this gigantic General Strike are not to be wasted, and if the British capitalists are not to be allowed to smash the trade unions and drive the workers here down to coolie conditions, as they have driven down the German workers. There will be talk of loyalty and discipline. The Communist Party declares that the greatest loyalty is loyalty to the working class. The finest discipline is one that helps the workers to beat the bosses, not the bosses to smash the workers.

Therefore, the Communist Party asks the miners not to despair of their fellow-workers, but to hold on and appeal for support to them.

The Communist Party calls upon all its members, upon those who have realised by experience that the Communists were right and that the Reformists were wrong in their estimation, months ago, of the bosses' intentions, and upon every class-conscious worker, to press for immediate emergency meetings of all Strike Committees and Councils of Action, with a view to continuing the struggle and forcing the leaders to do so. It heartily supports the Minority Movement's campaign for a simultaneous move forward, not only to defend the miners, but also to advance the claims already put forward in a number of the chief industries.

Refuse to Return to Work! Repudiate the Samuel Memorandum! Demand Emergency Conferences of Strike Committees and Councils of Action! Force the Union Leaders to continue the Fight! Put forward your own Programmes! Stand by the Miners! No Reductions—No Longer Hours!

CHAPTER II—APPENDIX VII

WHY THE STRIKE FAILED

C.P.G.B. statement adopted by the Executive Committee at its extended meeting on May 29–31, 1926. Printed in the Workers' Weekly, *No. 172, of June 4, 1926*

The General Strike was the greatest display of solidarity in the history of the British Labour Movement.

The demand for no reductions in wages and no lengthening of hours on which the rank and file workers fought, is one of fundamental importance in the present period of capitalist decline. It is therefore imperative that the lessons of this strike should be speedily assimilated; and the causes for its defeat investigated by the working class. Unless this is done the working class[1].

The Communist Party declares that refusal to discuss the responsibility for the defeat of the strike is simply preparing further defeats.

Since the beginning of 1921, British industry has been torn by gigantic strikes and lock-outs. The mining lock-out of 1921, the engineering and ship-building lock-outs of 1922, the unofficial dock strike of 1923, the locomotive strike of 1924, the mining crisis of 1925

[1] line unfinished in published text.

are steps in the developing struggle which culminated in the General Strike of 1926.

The aim of all these struggles was resistance to attacks on the workers' standard of life.

They record, not the personal failure of any individual capitalist or Trade Union negotiator or politician to arrive at a "reasonable" settlement, but the failure of British capitalism to guarantee to the workers even these miserable standards of life to which they were previously accustomed.

That, and not the blunders of individuals explains the continued capitalist offensive.

A RIGHT WING FAILURE

The General Strike was the high-water mark of British working-class resistance to this continued worsening of their standards. This strike was broken not by the power of the capitalist class, but by the failure of the Right Wing leadership.

The failure of the Right Wing leadership is not a temporary failure of courage or judgement, but a failure of the entire policy which they have pursued. In a period when the alternatives confronting the workers were (1) the complete resistance to all wages cuts and the consequent sharpening of the class struggle up to the point of the workers organising to take power from the capitalists or (2) the adaption of the workers to the conditions of capitalism on the downgrade by the continuous acceptance of wage cuts, the Right Wing has bitterly opposed the first, and cautiously advocated the latter policy. They have been the agents of capitalism in the Labour Movement, telling the workers that their present sacrifices of wages were the way to ultimate prosperity. The working out of this policy is clearly seen in the development of the crisis in the mining industry, the calling of the General Strike and its ultimate betrayal.

NO PREPARATION

In July 1925, the pressure of the workers forced the General Council of the T.U.C. to threaten the Prime Minister with an embargo on coal (which might have developed into a General Strike) if a settlement was not found for the mining dispute. Taken unprepared and afraid of the result of a strike, on Britain's international financial position, the Prime

Minister gave way and granted a subsidy to the mining industry pending the appointment of a Commission of investigation. The threat of the General Council was a political act. The subsidy was a political concession extracted from the Government by threats.

Understanding the realities of the situation, better than the Labour leaders, the capitalists prepared for the struggle when the coal subsidy terminated.

The Government appointed a Coal Commission composed of three capitalists and one capitalist economist, to present a report favourable to wage reductions. It prepared strike-breaking machinery in conjunction with the local authorities. It gave encouragement to the development of the strike-breaking organisations, the O.M.S.

The Right Wing leaders refused to make working-class counter preparations.

They did not carry on a campaign against the packed Coal Commission. They did not set out in the name of the Labour Movement as a whole any proposals in relation to the coal industry, which would obviate any worsening of the workers' conditions. They refused to prepare the Trade Unions for the struggle in front. They turned down the proposals for propaganda among the forces of the capitalist state and for the setting up of Workers' Defence Corps. They spread the illusions throughout the ranks of the working class, that there would be no struggle in May as the Coal Commission would solve the problems of the coal industry. They crowned this policy by attacking the Communist Party, the only workers' party advocating preparation, and endeavoured to expel its individual members from the Labour Party.

RIGHT WING SUPPORTS COMMISSION

When the Coal Commission Report was issued, the Right Wing hailed it with delight.

From the moment when they entered negotiations, the General Council, under the domination of the Right Wing, aimed at avoiding a struggle by inducing the miners to accept lower wages.

The whole attitude of the Right-Wing controlled General Council, in the months between September 1925 and May 1926, was one of preparing working class defeat (1) by refusing to organise the workers for the struggle, and (2) forcing the miners to accept worsening conditions.

THE GENERAL STRIKE

The General Strike was a weapon forced into the hands of the Right Wing against their will. The shortness of time at their disposal towards the end of the negotiations did not allow sufficient time to enable them to induce the miners to accept wage reductions. The pressure of the working class from below rendered it impossible for the General Council to openly desert the miners. Following the formal ending of negotiations by Mr. Baldwin on April 30, the Special Trade Union Conference called by the General Council sanctioned the calling of the General Strike as a weapon to force the opening of negotiations.

On the re-opening of negotiations with Mr. Baldwin, the negotiators on the General Council went back to their old policy of attempting to get the miners to accept wage cuts, and only the abrupt termination of the negotiations by Mr. Baldwin prevented a split in the workers' ranks.

The Government knew that the General Council had not prepared for the struggle, and that it was in favour of wage reductions for miners. Its own strike breaking machinery was in good order, and it had therefore no hesitation in testing the solidarity of the working class and the determination of the General Council itself.

WEAK LEADERSHIP

The response of the workers was beyond all praise. The leadership was beneath contempt.

Once called, the strike should have been readily extended. The General Council hesitated, groping for an excuse to end the strike. The Government, noting the hesitation, were all out to win.

The acceptance of the Samuel Memorandum involving wage reductions followed, and the strike was called off, and the miners were left in the lurch. The Communist Party declares that while it is important to investigate the means by which certain members of the General Council were induced to believe that the Samuel Memorandum had Government backing, that this at best a side issue. The betrayal of the General Council consists in its acceptance of the Samuel Memorandum at all. This acceptance was not forced upon the General Council by the force of circumstances, it was the logical culmination of its whole policy.

A FAILURE OF LEADERSHIP

The Communist Party, therefore, declares that the fundamental failure of the General Strike was a failure of leadership. It asks the working class to repudiate with scorn the suggestion that the strike was weakening, and that it had to be called off in order to prevent collapse.

It warns the workers against the attempt of the Right Wing to pretend that it was the weapon and not those who wielded it who were at fault. The strike was never developed to its fullest capacity. It was controlled by those who did not believe in it.

Nor must the workers accept the argument now being used extensively, that a mass strike of the character which we have recently experienced must end either in Revolution or the complete defeat of the working class. This is a travesty of the facts. The General Strike challenging the capitalist system must either go forward to a revolution or down to defeat, but a General Strike for definite concessions, if led with the necessary courage, still holds possibilities for the working class, and the workers cannot throw aside this weapon meantime, for there is no other that can serve them in the struggle against the capitalist offensive.

The Communist Party draws the attention of the working class in particular to the bare-faced attempt of certain Right-Wing leaders to turn the defeat, which they brought about, into a victory for their own point of view in the Labour Movement, by asserting that while the General Strike failed, parliamentary action will succeed in winning the emancipation of the workers. This is absolutely untrue. A Labour majority in Parliament seriously intent upon challenging capitalism would be up against a greater crisis than that of the General Strike with the present leaders, and failure would be certain. In the mining crisis the Right Wing of the Labour Party not only failed to utilise its opportunities to fight for the miners, but actually joined in the pressure brought upon the miners to accept a shameful settlement. The lesson of the General Strike is not that the strike is a bad weapon and Parliament a good one, but that the Right Wing because of its anti-working class outlook is unable to wield any weapon against capitalism.

The situation resulting from the General Strike, therefore, imposes two tasks upon the working class. (1) The winning of the miners' strike, and (2) the struggle for a new leadership in the Labour Movement.

The miners' strike can still be won on the basis of

No reductions in wages.
No lengthening of hours.
Adequate maintenance of workers displaced by any re-organisation schemes adopted.

Let the workers in the Railway and Transport industries respond to the appeal of the M.F.G.B. not to move coal, and let the workers in other industries give the utmost support not only to the miners, but to those workers who are fighting on their behalf in the railway and transport industries.

FIGHT THE RIGHT WING

At the same time the workers must press forward with the challenge to the Right-Wing leadership to give the fullest support to all those who are prepared to stand for:

NO REDUCTIONS IN WAGES OR LENGTHENING OF HOURS: NO ADAPTATION OF THE WORKING CLASS TO THE NECESSITIES OF CAPITALISM, BUT THE PREPARATION OF THE LABOUR MOVEMENT FOR THE STRUGGLE FOR POWER.

A trade union re-organisation campaign for (1) 100 per cent trade unionism, (2) the granting of greater power to the General Council, (3) the strengthening of local centres of working-class solidarity by the creation of more powerful factory committees and trades· councils.

A systematic campaign in the Co-operative movement in order to break down the bureaucratic opposition which prevented this movement from playing a vigorous working-class role in the strike and to secure the future co-operation of the Co-operative movement with the trade unions in the struggle.

The development of a left-wing policy and leadership in the Labour Party, around a programme of working-class demands which will challenge capitalism in a fundamental fashion and the co-ordination of parliamentary activity with the mass movement outside.

The Right Wing will cling to its position and seek to strengthen itself. The workers will not be able to get the leadership which the struggle demands in time to avoid further defeats unless their opposition to the Right Wing takes an organised form. Only by the development of the Communist Party towards a mass party can the workers be assured that an increasing struggle to fit the Labour Movement for its new tasks.

HELP THE MINERS TO VICTORY!
REPLACE THE RIGHT-WING LEADERSHIP!
BUILD A MASS COMMUNIST PARTY!

CHAPTER II—APPENDIX VIII

THE PRELIMINARY RAILWAY SETTLEMENT OF MAY 14, 1926

Reproduced in R. Page Arnot, The General Strike, p. 239 and in W. H. Crook, The General Strike, pp. 609–610)

(Terms agreed to on Friday May 14):

1. Those employees of the Railway Companies who have gone out on strike to be taken back to work as soon as traffic offers and work can be found for them. The principle to be followed in reinstating to be seniority in each grade at each station, depot or office.
2. The Trade Unions admit that, in calling a strike, they committed a wrongful act against the Companies, and agree that the Companies do not, by reinstatement, surrender their legal rights to claim damages arising out of the strike from strikers and others responsible.
3. The Unions undertake:
    (a) Not again to instruct their members to strike without previous negotiations with the Company.
    (b) To give no support of any kind to their members to take any unauthorised action.
    (c) Not to encourage supervisory employees in the special class to take part in any strike.
4. The Company intimate that, arising out of the strike, it may be necessary to remove certain persons to other positions, but no such persons, salaries or wages will be reduced. Each Company will notify the Union within one week the names of men whom they propose to transfer, and will afford each man an opportunity of having an advocate to present his case to the general manager.
5. The settlement shall not extend to persons who have been guilty of violence or intimidation.

(Signed) On behalf of the General Managers' Conference:

Felix J. C. Pole H. G. Burgess
H. A. Walker R. L. Wedgewood
R. H. Selbie.

On behalf of the Railway Unions:

> J. H. Thomas and C. T. Cramp, National Union of Railwaymen.
> J. Bromley, Associated Society of Locomotive Engineers & Firemen.
> A. G. Walkden, Railway Clerks' Association.

CHAPTER II—APPENDIX IX

COMMUNIST PARTY'S STATEMENT ON THE GENERAL STRIKE, OCTOBER 1926

Extracts from Thesis on the General Strike, Adopted at the Eighth Congress of the C.P.G.B. held at Battersea Town Hall, October 16–17, 1926[1]

THE WORKERS AND THE STRIKE

The solidarity of the workers (unionist and non-unionist) was complete. The extent of the strike gave them a feeling of strength. The impression that all wages were being challenged, and the belief born of experience that the General Strike was the only method of meeting the challenge, made them determined to make the strike as complete as possible. Their determination to win was, however, accompanied with a lack of understanding of the full political implications of the General Strike.

The determination of the workers to win the strike resulted in the workers in many localities where the local organisations were amenable to pressure, going beyond the General Council's instructions. The General Council had given the Trades Councils but vaguely defined powers, and under the necessities of the local situation, these bodies transformed into Councils of Action, and moved beyond the General Council's instructions. The tendency in many localities, was for the local trade union branches to look to their Executives for guidance, and to run the General Strike as a series of parallel sectional strikes. The Councils of Action in the middle of the struggle tried to break down sectional prejudices and secured the unified conduct of the strike from a common local centre.

The General Council's instructions were to keep the workers off the

---

[1] Full text is in *The Eighth Congress of the Communist Party of Great Britain: Reports, Theses and Resolutions*, pp. 55–71. The section reproduced above is the second half of the Resolution.

streets, by arranging concerts, sports, etc. This was inconsistent with the task of carrying out the struggle for the trade union control of road transport, which necessitated a struggle for the control of the streets. The breaking through of the General Council's instructions was necessary before the development of the struggle could proceed.

In practice, the local committees had to exercise a tighter control over food permits than was permitted by the General Council and had to enforce those by more aggressive picketing.

The interference with picketing led in many localities to the organisation of elementary measures of working-class defence, ranging from pickets carrying walking sticks up to Workers' Defence Corps. The development of the strike led to these measures being taken up with increased energy.

The most active struggles in the strike took place around the attempts of the strikers to hold up the Government emergency road transport organisation. The development of the strike revealed the absolute impossibility of replacing the workers in the iron and steel, metal and building industries, which were, however, the industries in which the stoppage was likely to have the least immediate effect. On the other hand, the replacement of the dock and railway workers proved possible on a small scale, proved possible up to a point whose peak was probably reached by the end of the first week. In road transport, on the other hand, the weakness of the General Council's plan and the emergency organisation of the Government provoked the most difficulties to the workers. The road transport pickets set up by the workers in the areas in which the strikers were in the greatest numbers effectively interfered with the Government's organisation, though the purely local form of the workers' organisations, as compared with the regional forms of the Government's transport organisation, co-ordinated in a regional form with the police forces, handicapped the workers severely.

This handicap was just beginning to be overcome by the groupings of the strike organisations on a regional basis, towards the end of the struggle. The presence in most regions of Trades Councils and Strike Committees dominated by Right-Wing elements was, however, a factor militating against the effective extension and defence of the strike and its regional co-ordination.

Thus the experience of the strike weakened trade union sectionalism, undermined the pacifist outlook of certain bodies of workers and exposed the Government as the organ of the capitalist wage cutters.

Under Communist Party and Left Wing influence, the workers in many areas moved beyond the General Council in the development of Councils of Action and General Strike machinery. The activity of the workers' local strike machinery was objectively a challenge to the Government. The issuing and withdrawing of permits, transport picketing with a view to trade union control of transport, replacement of newspapers by Workers' Bulletins, the organisation of elementary measures of defence were attempts to strip the Government of some of its power, and contained the germ of correct tactics that the workers must follow in all mass strikes, which by their nature are a struggle with the Government.

THE GENERAL COUNCIL AND THE STRIKE

The fact that every mass strike is a political strike was clearly revealed in spite of the denials of the General Council. The basic industries were stopped, not to coerce the mineowners, but to coerce the Government. The General Council was objectively decreeing that no newspapers should be printed, that no food should be transported without its permission, or that of its local organisations, that no person could travel to or from work by the recognised public means. To render these prohibitions effective, its local organs had to enter into conflict with the emergency organisations of the Government. It had to call upon the workers to be loyal to their unions, which was in effect to be disloyal to the Government, which was locked in conflict with those unions. The germs of alternative Government were apparent.

The General Council, was, however, acting under pressure. It did not have the will to use the weapon in its hands, but, on the contrary, sought an excuse to capitulate to the Government. Mr. Baldwin's assertion that the General Council was assuming the powers of an alternative Government has to be modified in respect to the General Council's desire to abandon those powers when the excuse for treachery offered.

The General Council's tactics revealed lack of preparation. The partial calling out of workers caused confusion, and the strike was not extended rapidly enough. The refusal to call out workers in the public services and the stoppage of the workers' press along with the capitalist press, weakened the strike.

The technical weakness of the strike plan followed from the General Council's attitude. They believed that the Government in the existing situation was impregnable and sought for an excuse to call off the strike. When the Government raised the cry of "The Constitution in danger", they weakly denied that they were challenging the Government (which, if true, would have made the strike purposeless). The strike was either aiming at coercing the Government, representing the capitalists as a whole, or it was nothing. The Labour Party in the House of Commons stood throughout the strike on the General Council's platform of initiation of re-organisation first, and reduction of wages afterwards. It suppressed its back-benchers, and made humiliating pleas for negotiation. Its cowardly attack strengthened the Government and the capitalist class immensely.

THE GOVERNMENT IN THE STRIKE

The Government acted as an effective capitalist dictatorship. The proclaiming of a state of emergency first and the demand for Parliament to sanction it afterwards was one instance of this. It issued its own paper and stopped supplies for the rival trade union organ, developed strike-breaking machinery, equipped the middle-class Fascists as Special Constables, used the full force of the law against the workers' leaders locally, and commenced through its lawyers and judges an attack on the legal position of the unions on strike.

It gave full powers to the police and the army to suppress any mass movements of the workers, promising to indemnify those in charge of the forces for any action which they took against the workers outside of the ordinary law of the country. The Emergency Powers Act placed the workers absolutely at the mercy of the most vicious class-biassed magistrates. The generalisation of Lenin that dictatorship is an unlimited power resting not on law but on force, was never better exemplified than during the strike.

INTERMEDIATE STRATA

The middle class fluctuated throughout the strike. A section which was actively opposed to the workers was organised by the Government and became an active factor in the struggle. The section sympathetic to "Peace by Negotiation" (Lloyd George, Bishops' proposals, etc.), did not participate actively in the struggle. The sharp division of opinion in the Liberal Party reflected in some measure the fluctuations in the middle-class ranks.

The effect of the Government's attitude on the workers' organisations was to harden the workers and intensify their demands for an extension of the strike. The strong attitude of the workers forced certain elements of the bourgeoisie represented by Lloyd George, etc., to seek a compromise.

At the end of the first week of the strike, both the Government and the rank and file workers were intent on extending the struggle. The workers' leaders, the General Council, feeling power slipping away from their hands into those of the local workers' organisations, were stimulated by growing pressure to seek an excuse for calling the strike off. The General Council seized upon the excuse of the Samuel Memorandum, not because the workers were weakening, but because: (a) this memorandum was in harmony with their own policy previous to the General Strike and (b) they felt the strike could only be won by intensifying the struggle against the capitalist class.[1] This they were afraid to do.

The Government's estimate of the General Council proved correct. The employers moved to cut wages all round. The Government did not reckon, however, with the resistance of the miners, who were not involved in the debacle, and the spirit of the rank and file workers. The result was that the offensive of the capitalists was arrested for a time, though humiliating apologies were made by leaders and individual victimisation was rife. The stand of the miners saved the whole working class from the full consequences of their leaders' betrayal.

Subsequent to the calling off of the strike, the General Council attacked the miners for refusing to accept the Samuel Memorandum, which involved arbitration and veiled District Agreements. They accused the miners of wanting to tie the General Council to a "mere slogan". This expression exposes the treacherous policy of the General Council. The miners were being attacked as a preliminary to attacks being delivered on all other workers, and the leading body of the British trade union movement defines their heroic defence of working-class interests as attachment to "a mere slogan".

The principal lesson of the General Strike was that the class struggle in Britain has entered into a new phase in which the efforts of the

---

[1] The words "power . . . to pressure" are omitted by error in the resolution as given in the *Report of the 8th Congress*. The missing words have been taken from the Draft, "Thesis on General Strike" published as a 12-page pamphlet before the Eighth Congress.

working class to defend itself must bring the working-class movement into ever sharper conflict with the capitalist class, forcing it to realise that the only way to complete victory is the destruction of the capitalist State and its replacement by a workers' State based on the mass organisations of the workers. The necessities of this developing struggle will compel the working class under the leadership of the Communist Party to struggle for the elimination of the present trade union bureaucracy, and the revolutionising of the trade union and Labour Movement in outlook, policy and structure. Without the defeat of the Labour bureaucracy, more and more revealing itself as the agent of capitalism in the Labour Movement, the successful struggle of the workers is impossible.

The Party must explain to the workers on the basis of their experience the impossibility of maintaining even their present conditions without the overthrow of capitalism. It must draw upon the strike experience to expose the real nature of the capitalist dictatorship, and on the basis of this, to dispel all illusions regarding the possibility of realising Socialism through the mechanism of the present State machine.

The political nature of mass strikes was clearly revealed. The workers could not defend themselves without resort to the mass strike. They could not operate the mass strike except by endeavouring to impose regulations upon the country as to the printing of newspapers, the transport of food, amounting to decrees. Against the loyalty to the laws and decrees of the capitalist State, the strike committees demanded a new loyalty to the instructions of the strike organisations.

Even before the war, the State, in face of the growing militancy of the workers was forced to abandon the policy of standing aloof from trade disputes (except in cases of disorder), leaving the parties to the dispute to fight it out themselves. The capitalists were forced to use their State machine to interfere on their behalf during large-scale disputes, on the pretext that the State represented a third party in industry, i.e. the community. The intensification of the struggle has more and more forced the capitalist State to drop this camouflage, and to come out as the open defender of capitalist interests.

The importance of the trade union in mass struggles in Britain was clearly revealed. In many districts, the Strike Committees were the germs of an alternative Government. The great importance of the trade unions in the British Labour Movement makes the creation of a mass Minority Movement imperative.

The strike revealed that the middle class, in view of their numbers, will play a great role in future struggles. The Labour Movement must find ways of winning over or neutralising this class. The Government's policy of forcing the civil service trade unions to disaffiliate from the Labour Party and the T.U.C. demonstrates that the capitalists attach considerable importance to isolating this stratum from the manual workers. The Labour Movement must intensify its efforts to get all the salaried workers brought under its influence.

The failure of the Right-Wing leadership and its class co-operation policy of refusing to struggle against capitalism was revealed as was also that of the Left-Wing phrase-mongers who refused to break with the Right-Wing policy and to lead a struggle against it.

The Communist Party revealed that it was the only organisation with an alternative policy and leadership to that of the Right Wing and their Left-Wing satellites. Its trade union campaigns between Black Friday and Red Friday had popularised the idea of class action. Its campaign of preparation during the truce, for Workers' Defence, "Tell the Forces", "More Power to the General Council", "Alliance with the Co-ops, Councils of Action", etc., showed that it had a constructive policy for the struggle.

The attitude of the Party during the strike, acting as a united body within the local strike committees, made uniformity of action within these committees possible. Its call upon the workers to appreciate the political meaning of the strike, and to struggle for nationalisation without compensation, the resignation of the Government and the setting up of a Labour Government was politically correct.

The attempt by "Left" groups within the Comintern to describe the British Party as a brake upon the British working-class movement is false. Without the Communist Party and the Minority Movement, the pressure of the masses on the General Strike would have been weaker and the General Strike would never have taken place. The endorsement of our Party's policy by the Communist International proves that our policy had the approval of the great majority of revolutionary workers everywhere.

INTERNATIONAL AID

The General Strike revealed the importance of international aid. The General Council struck a blow at international working class solidarity by turning down the Russian workers' gift of money, and refusing to appeal to Amsterdam for international aid, thereby giving the Amsterdam leaders the right to sabotage the strike.

The splendid aid given by the Russian workers has brought the rank and file of the British and Russian unions closer together. The attempt of the "Left" elements in the Comintern to get the Russian unions to withdraw from the Anglo-Russian Committee is absolutely incorrect. The Anglo-Russian Committee is not a union between the leaders, but a union between the millions of trade unionists of Russia and Britain, which the British workers desire now more than ever. The attempts of Right-Wing elements in Britain to dissolve the Committee on account of Russian criticisms with which the British Party agrees and which the General Council's own statement on the Strike justifies, must also be decisively opposed by the workers on the grounds that the Anglo-Russian Committee justified itself in action, and that the general situation in which the workers find themselves make international solidarity in action more necessary than ever.

THE FUTURE OF MASS STRIKES

The impulse behind the capitalist offensive is the fact of capitalist decline, and continues to make itself felt. Future mass strikes are inevitable if the workers desire to defend their standards. The policy of "never again" voiced by the trade union bureaucracy cannot arrest the capitalist offensive, nor prevent the workers from defending themselves. It can, however, hamper the necessary changes in leadership and organisation, and leave the workers unprepared to meet future capitalist onslaughts. If mass strikes are to be successful, the development of mass organs in the factories and the localities is imperative. The building up of all-embracing committees has been of primary importance. Pressure should be brought to bear on the General Council to initiate a campaign for this object. Failing this, the local Trades Councils should initiate the campaign themselves. The factory committees should be affiliated to the local Trades Councils. The local Trades Councils should endeavour to secure greater mass support through these factory committees and through assuming the leadership in all local struggles to a greater extent than before.

In the large cities where the effective control from a single centre proved impossible, the Trades Councils should consider the question of setting up under their control intermediate district machinery more closely in touch with the masses. The campaign for the affiliation of

Trades Councils to the T.U.C. should be taken up with more vigour, and union branches affiliated to Trades Councils should be urged to bring pressure upon trade union Executives to get the proposal carried.

The General Council of the T.U.C. should be forced to undertake a campaign for 100 per cent trade union organisation, which should be conducted through local Trades Councils.

The campaign for "more power to the General Council" must be intensified. The demands of the campaign should be those of the A.E.U. resolution at the Bournemouth Trades Union Congress.

The Industrial Groups of the General Council should meet more frequently in order to arrive at a consistent policy in their respective industries and facilitate amalgamations in them.

The General Council must promote amalgamation conferences in the various industries, all questions that the Conferences are unable to agree upon being submitted to the General Council for arbitration. Rank and file Amalgamation Committees should be formed in order to keep pressure on the officials.

The rank and file of the unions should be urged to demand a revision of rules of the various unions, which will ensure that at least 75 per cent of the delegates to the T.U.C. consist of rank and filers working at their trade and elected by the membership of the union.

An alliance must be created between the Co-operative Union and Wholesale Society and the Trades Union Congress for the purpose of developing a Strike Commissariat, and the question of international Co-op aid for the workers' struggle must be raised at the next Congress of the International Co-op Alliance.

The unprovoked attacks of the police and Fascist Special Constables upon the workers during the General Strike and the miners' struggle justify the Party's demand for the creation of Workers' Defence Corps under the control of the Trades Councils. The Party must carry on an intensive campaign for the creation of such organs of working class defence.

The solidarity of the unemployed workers with the strikers was a marked feature of the struggle. The Party must struggle to create a mass N.U.W.C.M., to secure unemployed affiliation to the Labour Party, and the T.U.C. and to secure a united working class struggle against the Guardian's Default Bill and similar measures, which are designed by the capitalists to lower the standard of life of the unemployed.

A survey of the positions held by Party members during the General Strike reveals that the majority of them owed their positions on the Strike Committees to their membership of the Trades Councils, and not to their position as trade union officials. There is too great an inclination on the part of some comrades to get elected from their branches to the Trades Councils and to overlook the necessity of securing the posts on district committees of their unions.

The capitalist State derives a vast amount of its strength from the fact that the workers who are members of the fighting forces are still loyal to it. It must be part of the functions of the Labour Movement to carry the workers' message to the forces and enlighten them as to their duty to the working class.

The Labour Movement must devote increasing attention to weakening the grip of the capitalist class over the intermediate strata, the Government recruiting ground for Fascists and strike-breakers. This must be done, not by watering down the demands of the workers, in order to appeal to the prejudices implanted in the minds of this class by the capitalists, but by putting their legitimate demands alongside those of the workers, and fighting for both at the expense of the capitalist class.

In this connection, the spread of trade unionism amongst the salaried sections of this class, particularly the commercial employees, and the civil service, must be undertaken.

The carrying out of these tasks must go hand in hand with the replacement of the existing leadership of the Labour Movement, both the Right Wing which dominated the General Council and the sham Left Wing which capitulated to them. A new leadership must break entirely with the Right-Wing policy and stand for a complete Left-Wing policy, rallying the workers to their support on the basis of this policy.

In developing a new leadership on the basis of the above policy, the Party must assist the Minority Movement to organise all the genuine Left Wingers in the trade union movement, whether officials or rank and filers on the basis of the Minority Movement programme.

The trade union movement and the entire working class will find themselves hampered in their endeavours to meet the situation unless the policy and leadership of the Labour Party is completely changed. (The details of this are dealt with in the thesis on the Left Wing). In general, our Party fractions in the unions must ensure that Labour Party business is discussed to a greater extent in the union branches, that the fight against the Liverpool decisions is developed to a greater extent, that the dangers of the present Right-Wing policy are more fully exposed, and a real workers' policy pressed forward.

The General Strike and the mining lock-out have awakened the class consciousness of the rank and file workers who are moving to the Left. These struggles have accelerated the decline of British industry, and the workers will find themselves confronted with new struggles.

Only by the energetic carrying out of the above important tasks can the workers be prepared in time. The Party must at the same time do all in its power to spread its general propaganda, and raise the political level of the workers as a whole.

The new situation will raise in an acute form the question of the struggles of the Labour Movement against the capitalist State for the Socialist Reconstruction of Society.

Only a strong Communist Party will be able to lead the workers to success in this struggle. The victory of the British workers is bound up with the development of a strong Communist Party.

CHAPTER III

THE COMMUNIST PARTY AND THE LABOUR MOVEMENT, MAY–NOVEMBER 1926

When the Strike was Over—Government, Coalowners, Miners, Solidarity—June–July 1926—July–August—September–October–November: Return to Work under Duress—Communist Party and Trade Unions—National Minority Movement—Communist Party and Labour Party—The "Left Wing" Movement—Communist Party and I.L.P.—The Left at the Bournemouth T.U.C.—Margate Labour Party Conference—Differences within Communist Leadership.

WHEN THE STRIKE WAS OVER

So the General Strike was ended, but the miners' lock-out remained. The General Council sold out, and the miners remained in struggle. Inevitably, for every militant worker worth his salt, indeed for every progressive person, the attitude to the miners was the touchstone. By attitude to the striking miners—in deeds as well as words—each person, each organisation has to be judged. It is not by accident, therefore, and, indeed it is something to be proud of, that from the end of the General Strike in mid-May, until its Eighth National Congress in mid-October 1926, and in the month that followed, support for the miners was at the centre of Communist Party discussion and Communist Party activity.

Of course, the problems that faced the British working people, and confronted the Communist Party, in those difficult, shameful days at the end of the great strike, were not easy ones when Churchills and coalowners, gloating with satisfaction, were shouting for their pound of flesh. Now it was clear that the capitalist offensive would hot up against *all* sections of workers, that even those trade union rights that had been won in more than a century of struggle would be called into question, that the right-wing Labour leaders who had sold out the strike would continue their headlong retreat, and that many workers and workers' organisations, that had fought well and truly before and during the strike, would face apathy and even defeatism following the sell out. The workers had to pay for the defeat that their leaders had brought about.

At the meeting of the Executive Committee of the Communist Party which discussed the lessons of the General Strike during the last week-end of May 1926,[1] six main lines of action were envisaged.

In the first place the Party put solidarity with the miners, which meant in *real*, *in practical* terms, the struggle for a *levy* on wages to provide financial support for the miners and for an *embargo* on the external and internal transport of coal.

Secondly, the need arose to defend and strengthen the unions, to fight against apathy, to work for 100 per cent trade unionism, to combat attempts at wage cuts and lengthening of hours, to face up to the question of the powers of the General Council, to work for some sort of working agreement between the co-operative and trade union movements, to strengthen the Trades Councils and factory committees, and to defeat every type of repressive attack on trade unionism from the side of the Government and employers.

Thirdly, it seemed that both Tory Government and right-wing Labour leadership were preparing some sort of ideological offensive. They had *practised* class-collaboration. Now, in a typically British way, it was necessary for them to advance some ideological grounds for the class collaboration that had already been put into practice. Though it could not yet be clear exactly what form this would take, the Communist Executive statement of end-May already issued a warning against the "adaptation" of the working class to the necessities of capitalism.

Fourthly, the Party saw the need to work for a *new leadership* in the Labour Movement. The old leadership of both T.U.C. and Labour Party had miserably failed. How could the left and militant forces—Communists, militant trade unionists, Minority Movement, left wing in I.L.P. and Labour Party, join together, and through some form of left unity work for a new militant leadership for Labour, exposing at the same time the "sham left", those who talked left but in practice supported Thomas and MacDonald, as the "left" of the General Council had done during the strike?

Fifthly, and clearly enough, it was necessary to rally the movement to fight for the defeat of the Tory Government, and its replacement by a new Labour Government. The campaign for the dissolution of the Baldwin Government had began during the General Strike. It was continued now that the strike was over.

Lastly, but by no means least, the Party sought to build and strengthen

[1] See *Why the Strike Failed*, Executive Committee statement printed in Appendix VII to Chapter II.

its own organisation. Its courageous record during the strike, and the realisation of the correctness of its successive pre-strike warnings, was turning many workers, particularly miners, towards the Party. Now was the time to work towards a mass Communist Party.

At the centre of all these lines of action was the compelling task of *solidarity with the miners*.

GOVERNMENT, COALOWNERS, MINERS, SOLIDARITY

The General Strike was over, the miners' lock-out remained. For six long months the miners fought on in conditions that, more and more, verged on starvation.

Many were the brave words and moving appeals. George Lansbury wrote, at the end of May, that:

". . . one cold, brutal, inexorable fact stands out clear and distinct. Over one million mine workers together with their womenfolk and children at this moment are starving—yes, comrades, starving in the midst of plenty, starving in a land at the centre of which, here in this great Metropolis, wealth produced by the toilers of Britain is being poured out like water in an unparalleled orgy of wanton extravagance and luxurious pleasure."[1]

But whilst many militants and humanitarians wrote of the miners' hunger, the coalowners used it, the Government abused it, the leaders of T.U.C. and Labour Party shut their eyes and ears to it, and even some of those who lamented it did but little in practice to assuage it, and still less to end the conditions from which it arose.

The coalowners moved in for the kill, remorseless and bloody-minded to a degree which shocked even some of their hard-baked colleagues. The Government, with its repeal of the Seven Hours Act of 1919, its monthly renewal of E.P.A., and with pressure even on the local authorities to withold relief from and suspend services (like free milk for babies or free meals for children in need) for the locked-out miners and their families, showed itself a government of and worthy of the coalowners.

The right-wing Labour leaders—General Council or Labour Party Executive—shouting "Never Again" to the General Strike, did their best to see that it never *could* happen again. A Communist miner, then a

[1] *Lansbury's Labour Weekly*, Vol. II, No. 64, May 29, 1926.

young militant leader in the South Wales coalfield, Arthur Horner wrote at the time:[1]

> "When the General Council betrayed the miners, its members had perforce to prevent the miners from winning in order to secure justification in the eyes of their own men. There being no neutrality in the class struggle, the traitors were bound to turn assassins of their previous allies, in their own defence. Having made prophecies of a miners' defeat, they must now assist events to prove that they were right."

It was left to the militants—militant trade unionists, much of whose effort was channelled through the Minority Movement, militant members of the Labour Party (and the Womens' Committee for the Relief of Miners' Wives and Children, led by Dr. Marion Phillips, then Chief Woman officer of the Labour Party, deserves special mention), militant I.L.P.ers (usually in their individual or local capacity) and, above all, the Communist Party to carry on consistent work of support for the miners.

In the key political aspects of the struggle—the fight for the levy and the embargo—the Communist Party and the Minority Movement took the lead from the start.

Those who believe or who purport to believe that callous capitalists and the betrayals of reformists are so many empty communist invectives would do well to study the story of those six months of the miners' agony, those six months of weary and bitter struggle. It forms the essential background for any understanding of the politics of the period. The activities of the Miners' Federation, its negotiations with coal-owners (Mining Association), Cabinet, and General Council, have been brilliantly described in R. Page Arnot's *History of the Miners*,[2] from which I have in this section gratefully and unashamedly drawn.

The May 14 Government proposals to the miners meant, as we have seen,[3] in addition to wage cuts, the abolition of the national minimum, the undermining of the 7-hour day, the substitution of compulsory arbitration for collective bargaining and the weakening of the Miners' Federation by the introduction of District Settlements.[4] It was small wonder that on May 20 they were rejected by the reassembled Miners'

---

[1] Quoted by Allen Hutt, *Post-War History*, p. 166.
[2] R. Page Arnot, *The Miners. Years of Struggle*, Chapter XIV "The Great Lock-Out of 1926".
[3] See p. 132.   [4] R. Page Arnot, op. cit., p. 461.

Conference. What was less, perhaps, to be expected, was that these terms, which meant almost total surrender by the miners, should also be rejected as insufficient by the coalowners, who wanted an 8-hour day and what they called "freedom from political interference", in other words, no binding conditions whatever—for themselves. It was clear at this stage that there could be no quick or easy end to the lock-out.

It was on May 19 that the Miners' Federation first raised the question of embargo, at this stage only in connection with the transport of coal already stacked in sidings or at the docks. A. J. Cook for the Miners wrote to the Amalgamated Society of Locomotive Engineers and Fireman (with a similar letter to the National Union of Railwaymen):

"We feel sure that your members will not do anything detrimental to our interests and will still assist us as far as possible in the struggle which we are engaged in. I am sure you will realise that by handling coal it would affect us in our struggle."[1]

By return post came a joint reply, signed C. T. Cramp for the N.U.R. and J. Bromley for the A.S.L.E.F., that:

"in view of the fact that the Railway Unions took common action on the instructions of the General Council of the T.U.C., along with other Unions, and declared the strike off on the instructions of that body, we consider that we have carried out our obligations in conjunction with the other Unions."[2]

The key unions concerned in the embargo thus rejected it completely without even the grace of discussing it with their membership.

The first number of the *Workers' Weekly* following the General Strike was issued on May 21, too late for comment on the Miners' correspondence with the Railway unions. But the first Editorial of this first post-strike issue, was entitled "Stand by the Miners". The General Council, it stated, "have broken this pledge; have covered themselves with ignominy; have made their various excuses—and *left the miners to battle alone.*" The only course for the miners was to stand firm by their demands, and now that the right-wing leaders had failed the miners, it was up to the rank and file to show their solidarity.[3]

At the end of May, the Miners' Federation produced a public appeal "To the Organised Workers of Great Britain and Every Country", the first *public* appeal since the call-off of the General Strike. In big

---

[1] R. Page Arnot, op. cit., p. 466.   [2] Ibid., p. 466.
[3] *Workers' Weekly*, No. 170, May 21, 1926, p. 4.

bold letters the *Workers' Weekly* published this appeal on the first page of the May 28 issue.[1] The Miners' explained the Governments' proposals, why they had rejected them, and, over the signatures of A. J. Cook and Herbert Smith, called for solidarity:

> "We earnestly ask the workers of Great Britain in the first place [and] of the whole world, to continue to help us by refusing to handle black coal, by refusing to produce extra coal for Great Britain, and by continuing and increasing their generous financial assistance.
> "Every ton of coal shipped to Great Britain by continental or American dockers, unloaded by British transport workers, or carried by British railwaymen means a miner's child robbed of its crust of bread. Every shilling contributed from working-class pockets helps us a step forward towards winning decent conditions for our people."

Above this Appeal of the Miners' was printed the Communist Party's response:

> "All coal is black! All who handle it willingly or unwillingly, are damaging the miners' cause.
> "The Communist Party asks every union branch affected, every Strike Committee, and every Trades Council, to consider this at once and to decide not to handle coal in their areas."

It called on Co-operatives to give generous credits to the locked-out miners, on other unions to give loans and to guarantee credits made available by the Co-operatives. It continued:

> "A five per cent levy on all wages ought to be agreed to by the Unions *at once*. . . .
>
> "No Blacklegging on the Miners!
> "Five per cent Levy on Wages!
> "Trade Unions to Guarantee Co-op Credits!
> "The Miners Must Win!"[2]

By this time—the end of May—the Government was preparing for siege. Steps were taken to ensure the import of coal; coal for domestic purposes was rationed to 1 cwt. a fortnight (partly to turn public opinion against the miners); and on May 31, the Emergency Powers Act was renewed for yet another month.[3]

[1] *Workers' Weekly*, No. 171, May 28, 1926, p. 1.   [2] Ibid.
[3] R. Page Arnot, op. cit., p. 463.

JUNE–JULY 1926

Early in June the Baldwin Government, spurred on by its most right-wing elements, tried to divert attention from the miners' struggle by a campaign of hostile protests and accusations against the Soviet Union, ostensibly for transmitting financial aid to the British miners and their families.[1] On June 11 the Government delivered an official protest. The money, collected by Russian trade unionists in answer to the miners' appeals, became "Russian Gold" in the mouths of Government spokesmen. At the end of June the House of Commons debated the question.[2] The Speakers' eye did not catch a single one of the nearly 50 miners in the House. But George Lansbury, after reading a letter from his daughter Violet, then resident in the Soviet Union, turned the Tory attacks on Russia back where they belonged:

> "I do believe in the class war. I believe the class war is responsible for the starvation of my kith and kin, people who are bone of my bone and flesh of my flesh, down in the coalfields of Britain. The only thing that is being asked today by the Government and the capitalists is that the workers should sacrifice. I hope to God that the workers will be able to stand out and with their women defeat the most nefarious campaign that has ever been waged against them. . . ."[3]

The Government, at this time, was still claiming to be a "neutral" arbitrator between the coalowners and the miners, a convenient myth which no one at all believed, least of all themselves. At a meeting of the Tory leaders on June 22, Lord Chancellor Birkenhead revealed the nature of this impartiality and the long-term Tory intentions in a plan for restricting trade union rights, for the amendment of the 1906 Trades Disputes Act, the compulsory auditing of trade union accounts, balloting and "proper legal notice" before all strikes.

In mid-June, the Miners' Federation sent out a circular letter to the secretaries of all trade unions,[4] reporting the results of negotiations since the end of the General Strike, the mineowners' terms, their rejection by the miners, and calling again for support.

They made no nice distinctions between the attitudes of the coalowners and the Tory Government:

---

[1] Soviet aid to the British miners is treated more in detail on pp. 318–321 of this chapter.
[2] R. Page Arnot, op. cit., p. 464–465. [3] R. Page Arnot, op. cit., p. 465.
[4] Given in full in the *Workers' Weekly*, No. 174, June 18, 1926, p. 1.

"The mineowners and the Government are now merely waiting until the sufferings of our people become unendurable, and they are forced by sheer starvation to submit."

Again they specified that "support" meant not merely resolutions but financial aid and the embargo on the transport of coal.

The letter was published in full in the *Workers' Weekly*. Indeed, the Communist press, limited in scope though it was, was by this time one of the few places where the struggles of the miners, their statements, sufferings, and appeals were faithfully and sympathetically reported. From June 11 onwards a special two-page supplement was added to the *Workers' Weekly* devoted entirely to support for the miners, and this was continued until the end of 1926.[1]

All this time the General Council was conspicuous by its organised inactivity in support of the miners and in answer to their appeals for aid. Weeks went by and the General Council remained silent, though it was, in theory, under an obligation to report back to a new Conference of Trade Union Executives. The pretext given out for the delay was that the Council was unwilling to prejudice the settlement of the dispute. At last, under pressure, the Conference of Executives was announced for June 25. The Executive Committee of the Communist Party drafted a statement to be put before the Conference of Executives, demanding a strong vote of censure on the General Council for selling out the General Strike and calling for a series of actions which included an embargo on the transport of coal, support for railway and transport workers who might come under attack for carrying out the embargo, the election of a special Emergency Committee to lead the struggle in support of the miners, and the calling of an international trade union conference including both the Amsterdam Federation and the Russian unions, and also a meeting of the Anglo-Russian Trade Union Committee to discuss practical help for the miners.[2]

In fact, the statement was outdated by the time it appeared. The General Council was playing for time and there was nothing they wanted less than a public inquest on their conduct during the General Strike. They proceeded to "work on" the Miners' Federation, to trade on their difficulties and the danger of their isolation, and, suddenly, a couple of days before the Conference was due to meet, on June 23, it

---

[1] The special Supplement started in *Workers' Weekly*, No. 173, June 11, pp. 7–8 under the title *Fight Like Hell: Miners' Supplement to the Workers' Weekly*. It carried, next to the title, two slogans "Every man behind the miners" and "A five per cent levy on all wages".

[2] *Workers' Weekly*, No. 175, June 25, 1926, p. 1.

was announced jointly by the General Council and Miners' Federation that the Conference was to be postponed until *after* the settlement of the mining dispute, that mutual criticism was to cease and that A. J. Cook's pamphlet *Nine Days* was to be withdrawn from circulation.[1] In fact the cessation of criticism was hardly mutual, for, whilst the miners' kept their part of the bargain, John Bromley, Secretary of the A.S.L.E.F. and member of the General Council, "leaked" in the July issue of his union journal to the public a large part of the Report which the General Council had prepared for the Conference. Needless to say the General Council's Report was full of attacks on the miners and their leaders.

It was at this point that the Communist Party began to criticise certain aspects of the tactics of the Miners' Federation. The miners they felt were being ensnared by the General Council and their compromise was an error that would weaken their struggle.

The Executive Committee of the Party issued a statement on the postponement of the Executives' Conference.[2] It considered "that the miners' leaders have made a serious mistake in subscribing to the General Council's decision not to call the Conference". A particular mistake was the agreement to avoid statements which might cause friction:

"By accepting the postponement of the Conference, without any guarantees, they have enabled the Right-Wing leaders to hide their real face from the workers for a little longer, they have enabled the 'Left Wing' leaders to go a little longer without declaring once and for all where they stand, they have won no permanent advantage either for the miners or for the workers generally, and they have placed themselves at the mercy of the General Council in any manœuvre it may now undertake in pursuance of its settled policy of forcing wage reductions on the workers."

JULY—AUGUST

As usual the General Council's lack of support for the miners was accompanied by the Government's active support for the coalowners. In the last week of June the Coal Mines Bill of 1926 was passed through the House of Commons and became the Coal Mines Act with the Royal Assent on July 8.[3]

[1] See R. Page Arnot, op. cit., p. 467, and Allen Hutt, op. cit., p. 169.
[2] *Workers' Weekly*, No. 176, July 2, 1926—on p. 2 of the *Miners' Supplement*—"Why was the Conference Called off?"
[3] R. Page Arnot, op. cit., p. 468.

By this Act the 7-hour day, that had been secured by the miners in July 1919, was suspended for five years. The lengthening of the working day to 8 hours became legally permissible (and the 8-hour day would mean in fact an average time spent underground of around 8½ hours, as the 8 hours only covered the time from the *last* man down to the *first* man up).[1]

Thus the "impartial" Government once more met the demands of the coalowners and once more jettisoned the proposals of the inglorious Samuel Commission.

The General Council, on July 2, issued a statement to its affected organisations denouncing the 8-hours Bill and calling, in general terms, for financial aid for the miners, but the miners' appeal for a levy on the wages of all trade unionists and an embargo on the handling of coal were both rejected.[2] Encouraged, the Government developed its plans for the purchase of coal abroad, and on July 7 permission was voted in the House of Commons to purchase further coal to the value of £3,000,000. Meanwhile, in the mining districts, contented coalowners posted new notices based on the 8-hour day.

On the credit side, an Anglo-Russian Miners' Committee was set up on July 10 after a visit to the Soviet Union of A. J. Cook and the Miners' Treasurer, W. P. Richardson; and the volume of aid was increasing from the Labour Women's Fund.

In mid-July the Executive of the Miners' Federation had to consider the mediation proposal of a number of leaders of the Christian Church. Their proposal was that the miners should resume work immediately on the conditions that pertained prior to April 30, 1926, and that the Government should grant temporary assistance pending a national settlement to be reached within four months. Referred to the districts, the miners voted fairly evenly, with 367,650 *against* and 333,036 *for*.[3] But in any case the Government had no intention of granting a subsidy, no matter how little or how briefly, and Baldwin was uninterested in the bishops' approaches, except in so far as they might be used to confuse or divide the miners.

The Communist Party was suspicious of the mediation, however well meaning its initiators might have been. It saw the bishops' proposals being used, like the Samuel Commission Report, to divert the miners from the struggle, warned against them, and criticised the

---

[1] Ibid.   [2] Ibid., p. 467.
[3] Ibid., p. 471. No vote was taken in Scotland or in Cleveland.

miners' leaders for the degree to which they had entertained them.[1] Instead of diverting the energy of the movement into discussion of the pros and cons of the bishops' proposals, the Party considered that the need of the moment was to stiffen the campaign for the embargo, and appealed to all trade union branches to press their leaderships to this effect.[2]

By the beginning of August, the fourth month of lock-out, slow starvation was creeping through the coalfields, taking its toll of miners and their families, and celebrated by the peculiarly vicious message to America by Mr. Baldwin, declaring that there was no hardship or destitution amongst the British miners—a classic example of mine-owning and capitalist morality.

But the hunger *was* there, and money *was* short, and the right-wing Labour leaders *were* doing everything to isolate the miners and to secure their return to work at any price. It was not surprising, therefore, that difficult problems faced the Special Conference of the Miners' Federation which met at the Kingsway Hall on August 16–17, that a trend towards surrender should develop, that divisions amongst the miners should begin to arise.

The Conference had to decide, should the Federation stand by its original principles—no change in wages or hours, no District Agreements—or should it begin to negotiate for something less. After two days of debate the Conference decided by 428 to 360 to empower the Executive to open fresh negotiations with the Government and coal-owners for a settlement of the dispute.[3]

But when miners and mineowners met on August 19 the employers wanted, not fresh negotiations, but *total surrender*—wage cuts, longer hours and District Agreements. The issue was simple—submit and surrender or continue the fight. To Evan Williams of the Mining Association the Miners' President, Herbert Smith, with dignity replied:

> "If your answer from your people is that, first, we have got to work an eight-hour day, and second, we have got to have district agreements, and third, without any enquiry at all, we have to have a reduction in wages—I will say to you this afternoon 'Good afternoon, we have met you. We are parting again until you people think otherwise'."[4]

---

[1] See *Workers' Weekly*, No. 184, July 23, 1926, p. 1. Statement on the Church Memorandum, and p. 2 editorial, "The Bishops' Offer".
[2] Ibid.   [3] R. Page Arnot, op. cit., p. 473.
[4] Quoted by R. Page Arnot, op. cit., p. 474.

When, a week later, the miners' delegation met His Majesty's Ministers, led, in Baldwin's absence, by Winston Churchill, there was nothing to distinguish the Cabinet's approach from that of the coalowners. Again Herbert Smith spoke for the miners—"We are forced to fight on."[1]

When the mining dispute was debated in the House of Commons at the end of August, Churchill made it clear that the Government would leave the way clear for the coalowners, and the coalowners' spokesman made it equally clear that, so far as they were concerned, National Agreements were dead. Indeed, they were quick to compliment George Spencer, M.P., the miner from Nottingham (Member for Broxtowe) who was to lead the breakaway from the Miners' Federation. R. Page Arnot quotes the speech of the old militant miner Robert Smillie, bringing to the debate the deep feelings of the miners and their families, the breath of the coalfields:[2]

> "In this fight we have everything against us. The fight is absolutely unequal . . . there will be no hunger in the homes of the colliery owners, their children will be fed and clothed, housed and educated just as usual, no matter how long the stoppage continues. On our side, there is privation, there is hunger and there is untimely death caused by the dispute. Therefore we are not on equal terms.
>
> "I want . . . to say that there is another force against us besides the employers. The Government of the country is on the side of the mineowners and against the miners in this dispute. . . ."

Government and coalowners were united against the miners. They were helped, directly or indirectly, by the General Council. For there was only one language that the coalowners could understand, and that was struggle. The only hope for the miners lay in keeping their unity, maintaining their struggle, and securing the backing of at least the militant sections of the British working class.

This was the content of the Communist Party resolution at the end of August,[3] which congratulated the miners for the courage of their stand, warned that every concession encouraged the owners to demand surrender, and pledged its efforts to fight for support—above all for the embargo:

> "Baldwin and the coalowners cannot be placated . . . but they may be moved by an extension of the fight, which would effect their economic interests. That involves the embargo."

[1] Ibid., pp. 475-476.   [2] Ibid., pp. 478-479.
[3] *Workers' Weekly*, No. 184, August 27, 1926.

SEPTEMBER–OCTOBER

When the Miner's Conference reassembled on September 2, 125th day of the lock-out, things seemed very grim.[1] Money was running out. Cash still in hand amounted to 1s. 8d. per head. Contributions received stood well to the credit of the Soviet workers and the British Labour Women, but the contribution of the General Council was pitifully, disgracefully small. Of the £889,500 received to date, £517,000 had come from the Russian trade unionists, £112,000 from the Labour Women's Committee, £25,000 from the International Miners' Federation, £16,000 from the Amalgamated Society of Woodworkers, £15,000 from the Amalgamated Weavers' Association, but only £38,000 from the T.U.C.

The drift back to work had begun, but was not yet grave. Some 31,785, or less than 5 per cent of the total (mainly in the Midlands), had returned to the pits.

A majority of 557,000 to 225,000 (South Wales and Lancashire) authorised the Executive "to take the necessary steps to submit proposals for the setting up of a National Agreement for the Mining Industry". The next day the Miners' Federation wrote to Churchill asking him to convene and attend a Conference of Miners' Federation and Mining Association, stating by way of concession: "We are prepared to enter into negotiations for a new national agreement with a view to a reduction in labour costs to meet the immediate necessities of the industry."

Contacted by the Government, the coalowners refused even to consider a *national* agreement. Any suggestions, they declared, should be made by District Federations to District Associations.

In mid-September when the Bournemouth T.U.C., despite a courageous stand by a group of Communist and Minority Movement delegates,[2] was giving little help or hope to the miners, the mineowners publicly declared to Churchill that, "except for one small inland pit", the 24 District Associations declined to give the Mining Association any power or authority to negotiate nationally on their behalf. The Government purported to be indignant, even spoke of stubborn coalowners, "discourteous and stupid", but passed on to the miners' the mineowners' proposals for District Agreements.

[1] R. Page Arnot, op. cit., pp. 479–481.
[2] See pp. 271–277 of this chapter.

The Communist Party statement of September 22,[1] drew the lesson. The Government was "a coal-owners' Government". Its pressure was not on the coalowners but on the miners. The defeat of the miners would be the prelude to a general attack on workers' conditions. The only defence lay in struggle—a 5 per cent levy on wages (the low-paid Party functionaries had levied their own wages) and the embargo. The I.L.P. was talking of the defeat of the Tory Government, but to talk of dissolution without fighting for the levy and embargo was "mere froth".[2]

At the end of September, the Special Conference of the Miners' Federation assembled yet once more. Now some 80,000 miners had returned to work (Midlands 34,000; Nottingham 16,000; Derbyshire 10,000). And once again it adjourned to consult the Districts on the Government proposals.[3]

On October 6 the Miners' Delegate Conference reassembled to consider the Districts' vote on the Government proposals. The extreme conditions of the Government, their demand for a virtual surrender on the owners' terms with wage cuts, lengthened hours and the ending of national agreements, had rallied the spirit of resistance. The District vote gave the huge majority of 737,000 to 42,000 against acceptance of the Government's proposals.[4]

The South Wales Miners' Federation was one of the most consistently militant. It was the Federation of A. J. Cook, the Federation where Communist miners like Arthur Horner enjoyed a mass support, the Federation of the "Red Rhondda", of long revolutionary tradition. The South Wales Federation proposed to the Conference a stronger line of attack. It put forward a resolution calling for the withdrawal of safety men from every colliery, for a fresh campaign for the embargo, for the stopping of work on outcrop coal, and for the convening of a special meeting of the T.U.C. to discuss the position of the miners and how to extend support for them.[5]

Seconding the resolution, Arthur Horner put the issue. Sops, he saids meant surrender, the only way was struggle:

"I believe we are definitely at the parting of the ways in policy. We have had two months' experience ever since the Bishops' proposals came into being. Sweet reasonableness. Attempts by every means that we know to appeal to these people on the grounds that we were

[1] C.P. Records.   [2] See pp. 262-271 of this chapter.
[3] R. Page Arnot, op. cit., p. 492.   [4] R. Page Arnot, op. cit., p. 493.
[5] Arthur Horner, *Incorrigible Rebel*, p. 82.

desirous of bringing this thing to a termination. We have thrown sop after sop. None of these things has met these people's demands."[1]

And he concluded:

"Our proposals mean this: let us drop making our men's hearts sick by continually arousing hope in them that must be deferred to the following week and till the next move comes. Let us face the position. Take back our proposals and decide how we are going to wage the struggle from tonight. Let us see if we can get some restriction on the transit of foreign coal. Let us start a new campaign with a new spirit, a new faith, with a belief in our strength to carry on."

The South Wales resolution was carried by 589 to 199 (Derbyshire, Nottingham and Scotland opposing). But to an extent this militant vote covered up the growing difficulties. The Nottingham breakaway was becoming dangerous. G. H. Spencer, M.P., an official of the Notts Miner's Association, had been negotiating the return to work of one of the pits in his area. He was summoned to the Conference, accused of blacklegging, and ordered to leave the Conference by a vote of 759 to 4, whilst his expulsion from the union and suspension as Miners' M.P. was referred to the Notts Federation.[2]

But there were other difficulties as well. Reports on the embargo campaign from the International Miners' Federation were not too favourable; moreover Frank Hodges, secretary of the Miners' International, was actively sabotaging (in Horner's words) the miners' cause. Finances showed a tiny balance of some £12,500. Once again the South Wales resolution was referred to the districts. Nor was it a walkover. The district vote now showed 460,150 votes for the South Wales militant position and 284,336 against. It was clear that the conflict between resistance and surrender was extending *inside* the Miners' Federation.

The Margate Labour Party Conference (October 11-15), which we examine later, was marked by bitter attacks on the miners by the Labour Party leadership. And the courageous defence of the miners by the militant minority, led by men like Harry Pollitt and David Kirkwood, could not bring much hope to those who were watching their families starve in the coalfields, deep though the appreciation was for

[1] Arthur Horner, *Incorrigible Rebel*, pp. 82-83.
[2] R. Page Arnot, op. cit., p. 494; Arthur Horner, op. cit., p. 83.

their political stand. A ballot vote had been taken, meanwhile, in the Notts coalfield on the burning question—"Are you in favour of ceasing work and standing by the Federation's policy or are you in favour of seeking district agreements which may mean severance from the Federation?", and support for the Federation's policy was carried by 14,331 to 2,875. But up and down the coalfields miners were still trickling back to work.

The Eighth Congress of the Communist Party, meeting on October 16–17, did its best to express solidarity with the miners and to put forward a policy of struggle.[1] It attacked the right-wing miners' leaders like Spencer, Varley and Hodges. In a sympathetic way, the resolution adopted "On the Miners' Struggle" criticised aspects of the conduct of A. J. Cook. It praised his "intense devotion . . . to the the cause of the miners and the working class . . . his personal courage and tireless energy", but criticised his share of responsibility in calling off the June 25 Conference of Executives, support for the bishops' proposals, and wavering on the call-out of the safety men.

The Party resolution warmly supported the South Wales resolution condemning the attitude of the Margate Labour Party Conference, which could only help the Government; it called for a renewed and strengthened campaign for levy and embargo, for support for the Miners' Federation in their efforts to maintain complete stoppage in the wavering districts, and a general campaign for the dissolution of the Tory Government.

On October 22 the Executive of the Miners' Federation met with the General Council of the T.U.C. and urged once again the need for a levy on the membership affiliated to the T.U.C. By this time, of the £1,600,000 received, £986,000 had come from the Soviet trade unions, £249,000 through the Women's Committee Fund, and only £68,000 through the T.U.C.[2]

The government was doing all it could to further the breakaway. Towards the end of October it started to prohibit public meetings at which miners' leaders like Cook and Herbert Smith were billed to speak. When the General Council representatives met the Miners' Executive on October 29, they admitted that they had signed a statement expressing the view that, given certain measures of Government review and co-ordination, the Miners would be prepared to negotiate an immediate end of the dispute by *district settlements*. Even words like

---
[1] Resolution on "The Miners' Struggle", *Report of 8th Congress of C.P.G.B.*, pp. 72–74.
[2] R. Page Arnot, op. cit., pp. 497–498.

betrayal seem to whitewash such an act. November opened for the miners with nothing but the gloomiest prospects.

NOVEMBER: RETURN UNDER DURESS

November opened ill. On its first day came news that G. A. Spencer with other suspended Miners' officials were meeting local owners to negotiate a district settlement in Nottingham. The next day, the leaders of the British railway and transport unions again rejected the embargo, despite the fact that the import of coal had risen from 600,000 tons in June to 4,000,000 tons in October.[1] On November 3 a levy (of 1*d.* a day) was at last agreed by a Conference of Executives, but it was too late and too little to be effective.

When the Miners' Delegate Conference met on November 4, it was clear that the end was near, in Horner's words that "there had been a swing over of opinion and that most of the delegates were in favour of finding ways of calling off the strike, rather than intensifying the struggle."[2]

Militants amongst the miners and in the general movement still tried to stiffen resistance. Horner himself tried to at the Conference, but found himself isolated. On November 6, and again on November 15 Communist Party statements[3] warned that this was the moment of danger, that the General Council, the right-wing group in the Miners' leadership, along with the Government, were all trying to force the miners to surrender to the coalowners, that there should be *no surrender, that new efforts should be made for trade union solidarity*. But it was too late. The odds against the miners—coalowners, Government, reformist leaders of Labour Party and T.U.C., breakaways within—and starvation—were too great.

Difficult negotiations developed on a district basis from positions of retreat; unauthorised return to work accelerated, until by Monday, November 29, work had resumed in all important coalfields except South Wales, Yorkshire and Durham. The next day South Wales and Yorkshire returned, and on the last day of the month—grudgingly, angrily—the Durham miners resumed work.

[1] R. Page Arnot, pp. 499–500.
[2] Arthur Horner, op. cit., p. 86.
[3] C.P.G.B. statements, *The Government and the Miners*, November 6, 1926, and *Reject the Slave Terms*, November 15, 1926. See also statements of November 26, *The Communist Party and the Miners*; "The Communist Party and the Miners" in *Workers' Weekly* No. 199, December 10, 1926, p. 1–2.

The miners had been defeated on all counts. They returned with lower wages, longer hours, district agreements. The Government had been a *coalowners'* Government, and the right-wing leaders of the Labour Party and T.U.C.—men like Thomas, Clynes, Hodges, Spencer, MacDonald—had, consciously or unconsciously, directly or indirectly, defended within the labour movement the interests of capitalism.

Some of the worst suffering came, ironically enough, when the miners returned to the pits. They returned mostly to an 8-hour day and to a pitifully low wage, which provided little to sustain the laborious work in the mines. Looking back after almost forty years Arthur Horner bitterly commented:

> "The sufferings of the aftermath of the strike were greater than the strike itself. It's a thought that probably did not occur to anyone outside the coalfields, that hundreds of thousands of miners spent their first summer in sunshine.
>
> "At that time we were losing twelve hundred men a year killed in the coalfields, so one could calculate that seven hundred men were alive at the end of the strike who would have been dead had it not been called, and tens of thousands escaped injury."[1]

Should they have returned earlier? Should they have acknowledged defeat and surrendered to the coalowners? Were the Communists wrong who, within the Miners' Federation or in the labour movement generally, called to the bitter end for struggle and resistance? Certainly the miners respected the Communist Party for its line of maximum resistance and for its consistent solidarity. Through those bitter six months of struggle, miners were turning to the Party, and thousands were joining it.[2] It was the coalfields where the Party was strongest that resisted hardest, like South Wales and Durham. Many miners, like Arthur Horner, saw from their experience the need for a new militant leadership in the labour movement of which the Communist Party would form an essential component:

> "The fact that the men who betrayed the miners were the most venomous in their attack on the Communists and their allies, while the Communists fought with the miners, reinforced my belief that the first stage in the battle must be to secure a militant leadership

---

[1] Arthur Horner, p. cit., p. 90.
[2] See section on recruiting on pp. 345-346.

in the Trade Unions and the Labour Party. I regarded that as a task in which the Communists had a vital part to play. Our purpose was not to act as a separate organisation, but despite the bans put on us, to play our part as an integral part of the Labour Movement."[1]

The miners were defeated. But there are defeats which at first bring sorry hardships and yet, in the long term, contain the seeds of future advance. Throughout the history of the working-class movement there have been struggles that have ended in defeat, but the very fighting of which has allowed those who fought to keep their pride in their class, to look their comrades—and posterity—in the eyes.

Horner concluded:

"Of one thing I am certain as I look back on that struggle, we had to fight, and in the end the victory of the coalowners was a Pyrrhic victory. The very severity of the settlement which they imposed upon us, the exposure of the inability of privately owned industry to maintain any standards for the workers employed, made our claim for nationalisation inevitable.

"If there had been no '26, there would not have been such a tremendous feeling for nationalisation after the Second World War."[2]

COMMUNIST PARTY AND TRADE UNIONS

The miners' dispute was the background to the struggles and conflicts within every type of labour organisation from the end of the General Strike till the end of November 1926. Locally and nationally, within every trade union, trades council, Labour Party Branch, and often within the Co-operative organisations, the issue was debated—for or against the call-off of the General Strike, for or against the continued miners' struggle, for or against the levy and the embargo.

Where the right wing dominated, their struggle to justify their own misconduct was often accompanied by an all-out attack on Communists and supporters of the Minority Movement who headed the condemnation of the General Council and the call for solidarity with the miners.

At the First Biennial Congress, since amalgamation, of the National Union of General and Municipal Workers (N.U.G.M.W.), held at the end of May 1926, J. R. Clynes, in his Presidential Address, made a

[1] Arthur Horner, op. cit., p. 93.   [2] Ibid., p. 90.

The Party and the Labour Movement, May–November 1926

heavy and hardly-veiled attack on the Minority Movement and the Communists. Congress turned down the proposal of a levy on all members to support the miners and an embargo on handling coal, but insisted on an embargo on its branches joining Trades Councils affiliated to the National Minority Movement. Despite the well organised right-wing leadership around Clynes, a considerable opposition, led by a Communist, C. J. Moody, fought against the bans and prohibitions and for support for the miners. A resolution to make elected officials permanent was carried only by 62 to 23, and C. J. Moody himself, standing for the post of Union President, won 23,000 votes against Clynes.[1]

The Amalgamated Society of Woodworkers (A.S.W.) was one of the unions in which there was a strong Communist and Minority Movement influence. A ballot vote showed a majority in favour of the levy and embargo. The Executive of the A.S.W. was strongly critical of the General Council's conduct of the General Strike.[2]

In the National Union of Railwaymen (N.U.R.), the leading group around Thomas was particularly active in the attempt to justify the General Council's conduct in the General Strike, for which Thomas himself bore so great a responsibility. And it was particularly active in rejecting the embargo. Their policy was challenged by an actsve Minority Movement group which included J. B. Figgins (a future General Secretary of the N.U.R.), F. Wadge and W. C. Loeber (a well-known Communist). The struggle came to a head at the Weymouth Annual General Meeting of July 6. And despite the "dramatic" reading by Thomas of some private correspondence between militant N.U.R. members, obtained by dubious means, the platform only succeeded in securing support for Thomas's policy by 52 votes to 25. The left-wing opposition had the support of around a third of the delegates.[3]

In the local trade union organisations, Communist and Minority Movement policy often prevailed over that of the right wing, particularly in the Trades Councils. The Lancashire Conference of Trades Councils, for instance, on the eve of the Bournemouth (1926) T.U.C., unanimously supported both levy and embargo.[4] The Conference of London Trades Councils (July 10, 1926), with 74 representatives from 24 District Committees in the London area and from 30 Trades

[1] *Workers' Weekly*, No. 172, June 4, 1926, p. 5.
[2] S. Higenbottam, *Our Society's History*, pp. 266–267.
[3] Philip S. Bagwell, *The Railwaymen: the History of the National Union of Railwaymen*, pp. 494–495.
[4] Allen Hutt, op. cit., p. 167.

Councils, supported a 5 per cent levy on wages, a complete embargo on the handling of coal, and urged that engineering workers should refuse to instal alternative fuel plant during the dispute.[1]

NATIONAL MINORITY MOVEMENT

Following the General Strike, the National Minority Movement remained one of the principal centres of militant trade union activity. It turned at once to furthering aid for the miners, campaigning, wherever it was of influence, for a 5 per cent levy on wages and an embargo on the handling of coal.[2] In particular it endeavoured to rally support for the embargo inside the railway and transport unions, thus earning the special hostility of J. H. Thomas. Another form of action in the mining areas was the organisation of demonstrations of miners and their wives demanding adequate relief from the Boards of Guardians.[3]

At the end of August, the Third Annual Conference of the National Minority Movement was held in the Battersea Town Hall.[4]

The very act of coming to a National Conference was a problem of no mean order for those delegates who were locked out or unemployed. Miners from South Wales or Lancashire started out ten days in advance and walked to the Conference, spending nights in casual wards and days on the road.[5] Some came by bicycle, and a few by train.

In all 802 delegates attended, representing around 956,000 workers, an increase on the Second (1925) Conference but a little less than the attendance and representation at the March 1926 Conference of Action.[6] Only two trade union executives were represented—the National Amalgamated Furnishing Trades Association (N.A.F.T.A.) and the United Ladies Tailors Union, but some 200 area organisations sent delegates and some 50 Trades Councils sent 90 delegates. The best represented trades were (in that order) engineering, building, transport, general workers, miners, distributive, and clothing. The National

[1] *Workers' Weekly*, No. 178, July 16, 1926, p. 1.
[2] See interview with George Hardy, Acting Secretary of N.M.M. in *Workers' Weekly*, No. 172, June 4, 1926, p. 5.
[3] *Workers' Weekly*, No. 173, June 11, 1926, p. 8.
[4] See *Final Agenda of Third Annual Conference of N.M.M.* (46 pp.) and *Report of Third Annual Conference of N.M.M.* (74 pp.)
[5] *Workers' Weekly*, No. 185, September 3, 1926, p. 1.
[6] Ibid., and Introduction to *Report of Third Conference*. Attendance at Second Conference was 683 delegates representing 750,000 workers. Attendance at March 1926 Conference of Action was 883 delegates representing 957,000 workers.

Unemployed Workers' Committee Movement and its Committees were also well represented.[1]

Solidarity with the miners came first. It was the keynote to Tom Mann's Presidential Address. It was the heart of the *Open Letter to the T.U.C.*, moved by Arthur Horner as a member of the South Wales Miners' Executive. The Government and coalowners, said Horner, were counting on two weapons to defeat the miners—the unimpeded import of foreign coal and its transport over British railways, along with the stocks accumulated before the lock-out, and starvation. The *Letter* appealed to delegates to the forthcoming Bournemouth T.U.C. to:

> "insist on the miners' fight being discussed. Suspend Standing Orders and discuss ways and means of helping them. Send out a call to the workers of Britain and the world for an embargo on coal, and a levy on wages. STAND BY THE MINERS!"

Solidarity with the miners was the theme of the emergency resolution on "The Labour Party and the Miners" moved by George Fletcher of the Operative Bakers' Union, a prominent Sheffield Communist. A. J. Cook sent a moving message to the Conference—above all a call for unity:

> "It is not our fault victory has not been secured. What a different story could be told today if May 12 had not marred victory by calling off the General Strike. Even now with a United Front, with an embargo on coal, with a levy to help feed our wives and children, we could secure victory. If only the Trades Union Congress would realise the position. We have had a terrific struggle. I say again the whole trade union movement has upon its shoulders the responsibility of victory or defeat. . . .
>
> ". . . Poverty was an unwelcome guest before the lock-out. I dread to think of the future if we are beaten. I appeal to all comrades to make one final effort to back the miners, the greatest fighters for justice in the world. The three issues that are in the balance are: National Agreements; hours; standard of living. Don't let the miners be beaten by starvation. . . ."[2]

---

[1] *Report*, p. 73. Metal workers had 143 delegates; building workers, 103 (including 34 from N.A.F.T.A.); transport workers, 96; general workers, 80; miners, 49; Co-operative organisations, 30; distributive workers, 26; clothing workers, 10; Minority Movement groups, 68; N.U.W.C.M. committees, 41.
[2] *Report of 3rd Conference of N.M.M.*, pp. 16–17.

Apart from the central issue of solidarity with the miners, the N.M.M. Conference concentrated its discussions around the issue of trade union defence—defence of the trade unions from Government attack, defence from the attacks of the right-wing leaders, defence of long established trade union principles. A resolution was adopted (moved by Sam Elsbury, a National Executive member of the Tailors and Garment Workers Union) and seconded by Jack Tanner (a National Committee member of the A.E.U.) warning against anti-trade union legislation,[1] including Government proposals for compulsory arbitration in the civil service, and for the disaffiliation of civil service trade unions from the Labour Party and T.U.C. Tom Mann had noted in his Presidential Address that the Government's aim was on the one hand repressive measures against *militant* trade unionism, but on the other the fostering of a tame establishment trade unionism that would take its obedient place within the capitalist system.[2] The Conference warned, too, that the attacks on the unions came not only from Government and employers but from the right wing *within* the unions. Attention was directed especially against the attacks on the Minority Movement that had been organised by J. R. Clynes and other leaders of the General Workers Union. The N.U.G.M.W. Executive had, in November 1925, instructed its Districts to withdraw branches from any Trades Councils that affiliated to the N.M.M. It had not found it so easy to secure obedience to this command. A vote to continue the affiliation of the London Trades Council to the N.M.M. was lost, for example, by only two votes, and it was perhaps significant that 50 delegates from the N.U.G.M.W. attended this Third N.M.M. Conference despite prohibitions.

In a resolution on "The Future of the Trade Union Movement"[3] the N.M.M. put forward its conception of the type of trade unionism needed at that time by British labour. The issues that it stressed were along the following lines:

(1) The development of all-embracing factory committees, affiliated to local Trades Councils.
(2) The affiliation of Trades Councils to the T.U.C.
(3) The granting of more powers to the General Council, along with an effort to change its composition in a progressive direction.

[1] *Report of 3rd Conference of N.M.M.*, pp. 65-66.
[2] Ibid., p. 12.
[3] Ibid., pp. 55-56.

(4) The election of the General Council by the rank and file of the unions in place of the Industrial Groups of the Council electing by ballot their representative on the Council.
(5) Promotion of amalgamation between the unions in the various industries.
(6) Revision of the rules of the various unions to ensure that 75 per cent of the delegates to the T.U.C. were rank and file workers at their trades.
(7) The development of co-operative–trade union collaboration.

Organisational discussions at the Third Congress revealed an affiliated membership of just over 200,000.[1] Naturally enough it was the Miners' Section which had seen most growth in recent months. A new leadership, with Tom Mann as Chairman and Harry Pollitt as Secretary, was elected, along with a National Executive Committee of 24 members and a National Advisory Council.[2] It was decided that the national journal of the N.M.M.—*The Worker*—should be published from London, instead as previously—from Glasgow.

That the Minority Movement was correct to campaign for a new leadership in the trade union movement can hardly be doubted after the experiences of the General Strike. But the wisdom of the organisational proposals for the structure of the N.M.M., adopted at this Third Congress, can well be queried. The gist of the proposals was that the N.M.M., instead of a broad, loose, militant movement campaigning for a progressive line of trade union policy and action within the official trade union structure, should itself become a more tight co-ordinated organisation, and fight for the control of trade union machinery. The *Organisational Statement* adopted at Conference argued that to bring about a change in trade union leadership:

"it is necessary that the forces producing the leadership shall express themselves in organisational form and defeat the organised forces of the old leadership in the process of the merciless organisational struggle. The ideological leadership of the Minority Movement over masses of workers must be transformed into a stubborn contest for control of the organisational machinery of the Trade Unions".[3]

[1] *Report of 3rd Conference of N.M.M.*, p. 21.
[2] Ibid., pp. 70–71.
[3] Ibid., p. 57.

The slogan must be:

> "A complete united front of all those ready to fight against the offensive of capital", and "An alternative leader against every union official who has failed the workers in their struggle."[1]

With this end in view, it was envisaged that the N.M.M. should form a definite organisation of its forces in every Union District Committee, in every local Branch, in every Trades Council, in every delegate body and executive from top to bottom of the trade union structure, that each unit of N.M.M. should be led by a small selected committee, connected with and responsible to the higher committee next above it. It was envisaged, too, that a special leading N.M.M. Committee should be established in each industry, and attached to it a committee for each separate union, charged with the special responsibility for organising and directing forces of the N.M.M. in that union and conducting the struggle for the control of that union.

Finally it was envisaged that the existing loose affiliations of local union branches, district committees and Trades Councils should be tightened up, and that the existing individual membership should be extended a hundredfold:

> "we are organising the shock troops for the struggle to conquer the unions for the class war.
>
> "it is absolutely essential that the new leadership produced by the Minority Movement comes to the control of the existing unions, to transform them into real class war organisations."[2]

The conception developing was one of a complete *organisation* within the official trade union structure, a *minority* organisation that would challenge the official organisation and eventually, as a *majority* organisation, come to replace it. It was a very different conception from that on which the Minority Movement had been founded—i.e. a loose body fighting for a militant policy and militant action within the official trade union bodies. Events were to show that this was not to be a step forward.

The official leadership of the T.U.C., the General Council, had shamelessly sold out the General Strike and shamelessly deserted the miners. Leaders of the type of Thomas and Clynes were continuing these policies within their own unions. There was a general right-wing

---

[1] *Report of 3rd Conference of N.M.M.*, p. 57.   [2] Ibid., p. 59.

trend towards *organised class conciliation*, the development of an "official", "accepted", "tamed" trade unionism with a comfortable niche within the system of capitalism.

It was a hundred times correct and necessary to challenge the policy and action of this leadership. It had to be challenged! And their actions against militants, the beginning of bans, proscriptions, even expulsions, had to be challenged too. On this background, a combative response to the betrayal of the General Strike by the right-wing leadership was understandable enough.

But *organisational* steps were *not* the best method. The scheme for a counter-organisation, organised from top to bottom *within* the official structure, was impractical and unhelpful, could invite repression, would not be understood by many workers, and above all could divert from the necessary struggle on the plane of trade union policy and trade union action.

In fact after its Third Conference, the N.M.M. began to lose some of the strength which it had shown in preparation for the General Strike. This retrogression was already visible by the end of the year.[1]

COMMUNIST PARTY AND LABOUR PARTY

If within the trade union movement, the Minority Movement and other groups of trade union militants in individual unions, in general terms under Communist Party leadership, were preparing to challenge the General Council in the September T.U.C. at Bournemouth, a similar mobilisation was taking place inside the Labour Party in preparation for the October Margate Conference, and also, to an extent, inside the Independent Labour Party.

The Labour Party leadership continued to justify the "Liverpool line" of total exclusion of Communists from the Labour Party, and indeed, after the General Strike, if anything, sharpened its anti-Communist attitudes.

In June 1926 the Tory Government had published, as we have seen, a Blue Book—*Communist Papers*—an odd selection of diverse papers it had amassed in the raid on the King Street Party Headquarters and on the Minority Movement office in October 1925, and on which it had based, in part, the case for the prosecution against the Communist

---

[1] It was discussed at a joint meeting of the Political Bureau of the C.P.G.B. and leaders of the N.M.M. on October 7, 1926. There was no advance in the N.M.M. and a setback n all sections except the miners.

leaders.[1] On July 2, 1926, the Labour Party leadership saw fit to issue a circular to affiliated organisations based on extracts from these papers, in particular documents dealing with Communist "fractions and nuclei" in organisations of the Labour Movement, and on a bulletin of the London District of the Communist Party concerned with preparations for a Labour Youth Conference, for a Conference of the London Trades Council, for the support of "Left Wing" groups and other similar problems.[2] The Communist Party had not hidden the fact that it organised at that time its members in other mass organisations into fractions and nuclei, so that they could discuss the policy of these organisations, formulate if they wished their own policy, and work to win support for it. Right-wingers, Fabians, I.L.P., and religious groupings had done so ever since the mass organisations of labour existed, and long before the formation of the Communist Party was ever considered. The Labour Party in particular had been founded as a grouping of *all* trends of the Labour Movement, within which its founders had taken for granted that different groups and tendencies would contest. But the issue here is not so much how far the Communists were correct or incorrect in the organisation of fractions, which is a fair question, but why this fact, which had been known for years, should *just at this moment* have been used as a basis for an anti-Communist attack.

Another considered attack on the Communist Party was the adoption at the end of July of an official Labour candidate, Mr. O. G. Willey, to stand against a Communist, Dr. Robert Dunstan, who had the respect and support of a very large number of Birmingham Labour Party members with whom he had long worked and served inside the Labour Party.

At the elections of October, 1924, Dr. Dunstan, standing as a Communist, had received over 7,000 votes in Birmingham West in a straight fight with the Conservative, the Rt. Hon. Arthur Chamberlain, who only beat him by a 4,000 majority.[3] A few months later the Labour Party adopted an "official" candidate to stand against Dr. Dunstan, but

---

[1] See Chapter I, pp. 72–73. *Communist Papers* was distributed by His Majesty's Stationery Office as Cmd. 2682.

[2] This circular, signed Arthur Henderson, is reproduced as Appendix VIII to the *Report of the 26th Annual Conference of the Labour Party*, Margate, 1926, pp. 319–320. See also Communist answer to this circular in *Workers' Weekly*, No. 178, July 16, 1926, p. 1. Of interest in this connection is the article by William Gallacher, "Fractions—Vulgar and Otherwise" in the *Sunday Worker*, No. 84, October 17, 1926. p. 4.

[3] See Appendix VI to Chapter III, Vol. 1, p. 368

in June 1925 this candidate left the Division, and the field was once again free for a "united" candidate. Dr. Dunstan enjoyed very great popularity for his work in the constituency and on the editorial board of the *Sunday Worker* and there was a strong feeling that he should be adopted by the Labour Party. The doctor himself proposed that the issue should be decided by the aggregate vote of four open conferences to be held within the Division. But this was rejected and the "official" Labour candidate adopted.[1] Perhaps the main reason for the timing of the anti-Communist measures was the growth of an organised opposition inside the Labour Party to the Liverpool exclusion of Communists.

In fact, ever since the Liverpool Labour Party Conference of October 1925, resistance to the anti-Communist measures adopted had been developing inside the Labour Party, and a "left-wing movement" emerging in opposition to the right-wing leadership.

THE "LEFT-WING" MOVEMENT

Discussion of the nature, significance and role of the "left wing" in the Labour Party and the possible emergence of a "left-wing movement" in the Labour and trade union organisations took place at several meetings of the Communist Party leadership starting from the end of 1924.[2]

The movement itself was mixed, amorphous in development, and did not lend itself to easy characterisation. By the end of 1924 there was a "trade union left" with men like Purcell, Bromley and Hicks, a "Parliamentary left" including such diverse types as James Maxton, George Lansbury and E. D. Morel, and something like an "intellectual left" again, with such diverse elements as G. D. H. Cole and former Communists like Walter Newbold, Phillips Price, R. W. Postgate who had joined the Labour Party, and who for a period at the end of 1924 ran a journal called *The Left Wing*. At this period of end-1924 and for the greater part of 1925 the "left wing" was much more a diversity of trends than in any sense a "movement". At its Seventh Congress (May–June 1925), the Communist Party was sceptical about the importance of these trends at this stage:

[1] See *Workers' Weekly*, No. 178, July 16, 1926, p. 4; "The Truth about Birmingham: an open letter from Dr. Dunstan" in *Workers' Weekly* No. 181, August 6, 1926, p. 4; "Birmingham Tale of Treachery", *Workers' Weekly*, No. 186, September 10, p. 2.

[2] Report by Albert Inkpin at end of 1924 (Party Records); discussion at Seventh Congress of C.P.G.B., May–June 1925; discussion at Executive Committee meetings in October and December 1925.

"As yet the 'left wing' groups are confused and without any definite programme beyond resentment at the policy of the right wing. Its unorganised, unformed character leaves the leading spokesmen of the left in the power of the right wing, who advance them or push them into the background according to the exigencies of the situation, while maintaining control of the whole apparatus of the Labour Party. The fears and political confusion of the left wing is seen in the futile attempts to create a grouping of left forces which will provide a centre functioning as a barrier between the Labour Party and the Communist Party."[1]

The emergence of a more coherent "left wing" movement within the Labour Party dates from the Liverpool Conference of October 1925.[2]

Bitterly opposed to the right-wing attack at Liverpool, not just on Communists and the Communist Party, but on what seemed to them to be accepted socialist principles, ten local Labour Parties in the London area, at the invitation of the South-West Bethnal Green Labour Party, held a delegate Conference on November 21, 1925, to discuss how to bring the Labour Party back, in their own words, "to the idealism and fighting spirit of Keir Hardie" and the pioneers. A representative Provisional Committee was elected to prepare a draft "left wing policy" which would form the basis of discussion at a further Conference of Labour Parties in and around London.[3]

The Communist Party was, in general, sympathetic to this movement, which included a number of Communists who had always been Labour Party members and who had not been expelled by their local Labour Parties. At an Executive Committee discussion opened by J. R. Campbell and Harry Pollitt in October 1925, which reviewed the Liverpool Conference, it was agreed:

"to reaffirm the Party's previous policy in regard to the Labour Party; to continue to press for affiliation and for membership.

"To help and strengthen the Left Wing within the Labour Party in opposition to the right-wing policy of MacDonaldism,"[4]

[1] From "Thesis on the International and National Battlefront" adopted at Seventh Congress of C.P.G.B., *Report of 7th Congress*, p. 185.
[2] A short history of the early period of the "Left Wing Movement" is given in the pamphlet *The Left Wing—its Programme and Activities* issued around November 1926 by the National Left Wing Provisional Committee (20 pp.). An earlier pamphlet *The Left Wing and its Programme* was published by the Greater London Left Wing Committee.
[3] *The Left Wing—its Programme and Activities*, pp. 3-4.
[4] See *Workers' Weekly*, No. 140, October 9, 1925.

Discussions were continued in the December Executive, and there were different views on the role of a "Left Wing Movement".[1] In January 1926, there was a more detailed discussion at the extended meeting of the Executive, when R. W. Robson moved a resolution on the formation of left-wing groups and a resolution was unanimously adopted[2].

The Executive welcomed the development and first co-ordination of the left-wing groups, renewed its offer for a joint campaign with the Independent Labour Party, congratulated the *Sunday Worker* for its success in providing a "militant platform" on which all left-wingers could unite, and instructed all its members:

> "to redouble their efforts (while retaining their Party identity, and the right of frank and loyal criticism) to join with all non-Communist workers in the Labour Party in building up a great Left Wing Movement to fight for a policy of:
>
> (1) Mobilising the workers around a Socialist programme to overthrow the capitalist class.
> (2) Making the Labour Party safe for Socialism instead of Liberalism."

On January 23, 1926, a second Left-Wing Conference met in the Library Hall at Bethnal Green, with some 50 local Labour Parties officially represented and with delegates from left-wing groups in other local Parties where the right wing still held sway. Again a draft programme was discussed and adopted and a committee elected to serve as a co-ordinating centre for left-wing Labour Party Branches and left-wing groups within Labour Parties in the Greater London area. The general mandate given by the Conference to the Committee was to win the support of Labour M.P.'s and Parliamentary candidates, to organise aid for minorities or individuals within the movement, whether Communist or non-Communist, whose positions might be threatened by the right wing, and, above all, to consolidate left-wing influence within the Labour Party. The Committee began, from time to time, to call meetings and to issue circulars.[3] It also served as a co-ordinating centre for those London Labour Parties and other Labour organisations that had been disaffiliated by the Labour Party on the pretext of the

---

[1] E. H. Brown favoured, for instance, the development of a single left-wing Labour membership organisation (Party records).
[2] See *Workers' Weekly*, No. 154, January 15, p. 5 (1926).
[3] *The Left Wing—its Programme and Activities*, p. 6.

Liverpool decisions.[1] It was in the London and Glasgow areas that such disaffiliation had been most widespread.

Following the General Strike there was a certain acceleration in the left-wing movement developments, but though some local and area committees were formed outside London (in mid-June there was a Conference in Burnley, for instance) the main centre remained the Greater London area, and on June 19 the Third Greater London Conference was held.[2] This was attended by representatives of some 40 Labour Parties of the Greater London area, 23 left-wing groups, and four Women's Sections, and a few delegates from other parts of the country (Portsmouth, Bristol, Barnsley, Hull, Sheffield). It was opened by Joe Vaughan, a member of the Bethnal Green Labour Party, one of those disaffiliated after Liverpool, the Chairman of the Greater London Left-Wing Committee, greeted by prominent left-wingers like A. J. Cook, William Paul (now of the *Sunday Worker*), Alex Gossip of N.A.F.T.A., George Lansbury and Tom Mann, and addressed by its Secretary, W. T. Colyer.

The main concern of the discussions and resolutions was aid for the miners (especially a 5 per cent levy), a working agreement with the trade unions and co-operatives to form a Workers' Commissariat (supply base) for use in need, demands for a £4 minimum wage, a 40-hour week, holidays with pay, nationalisation without compensation, and above all measures to secure the withdrawal of the restrictive measures against Communists and militants adopted at Liverpool. Resolutions were discussed that could be submitted to the coming Margate Labour Conference.[3]

The movement began to spread. In July the London Trades Council, defying prohibitions, elected J. J. Vaughan, Chairman of the Left-Wing Committee and well-known member of the Electrical Trades Union, as its delegate to the Margate Labour Party Conference.[4] Committees were formed in Manchester, Yorkshire, South Wales, Southampton, Portsmouth, though London remained by far the strongest sector. And on September 18–19, 1926, to mobilise left-wing forces in preparation

---

[1] See report of Executive Committee of the Labour Party, 1925–1926, printed in *Report of 26th Annual Conference*, Margate, p. 19, for list of disaffiliations.

[2] *The Left Wing—its Programme and Activities*, pp. 5–6; *Workers' Weekly*, No. 175, June 25, 1926, p. 5; *Sunday Worker*, No. 68, June 27, 1926, p. 6. Minutes of Political Committee of C.P.G.B., June 22, 1926.

[3] Amongst the borough Labour Parties and Trades Councils represented were Bethnal Green, Finsbury, Hackney, Holborn, Lewisham, Poplar, St. Pancras.

[4] *Sunday Worker*, No. 70, July 11, 1926, p. 3.

for the October (Margate) Labour Party Conference, the First National Conference of the Left-Wing Movement was held in the Poplar Town Hall,[1] with 150 representatives from 73 London Labour Parties and left-wing groups and 25 Labour Parties and left-wing groups in the provinces.[2]

The Conference discussed and approved with some amendment the political programme adopted at previous Greater London Conferences.[3] It considered methods of co-ordinating the work of the Labour Party Branches and the Trades and Labour Councils disaffiliated by the Labour Party Executive. It discussed preparations and co-ordination of the left-wing forces at the coming Margate Conference, and finally elected a Provisional National Committee[4] (to work alongside the Greater London Committee) and a National Advisory Council.

In the Left-Wing Movement were Communist and non-Communists (the majority), but both agreed on the need for unity. The non-Communist left respected the position of the Communists even if they disagreed with aspects of Communist policy, and the Communists saw the importance of a left in the Labour Party fighting to repeal policies of exclusion against the left and to bring the Labour Party back to genuine socialist principles.

Throughout the successive episodes of the Left-Wing Movement there were different approaches inside the Communist Party. In general two main trends can be discerned.

On the one hand there were those who thought that the movement should develop *on the basis of the existing organisations* of the labour movement; on the other, some thought that there was a place for some separate national organisation which should neither be part of the recognised organisations of the trade union and labour movement nor part of the Communist Party. Naturally enough, this latter trend was strengthened when a number of Labour Parties containing members not ready to join the Communist Party were disaffiliated from the

---

[1] *The Left Wing—its Programme and Activities*, pp. 6–7, 16–20; *Workers' Weekly*, Nos. 187, 188 and 189, September 17, 24 and October 1, 1926.

[2] 52 of the organisations represented were Borough and Local Labour Parties or Trades and Labour Councils.

[3] The programme covered foreign policy ("break with the past, no 'continuity' "), a socialist programme for the abolition of the British Empire, a socialist policy for industry (nationalisation), a policy for land and agriculture, for unemployment, for national and local finance, for health and housing, local government and constitutional reform.

[4] The Provisional Committee consisted of J. D. Mack (Leeds), G. A. O'Dell (Southampton), E. G. Llewelyn (Rhondda), Mrs. M. Allerdyce (Wallsend) and W. Crick Manchester).

Labour Party. It was the first conception that dominated at the Eighth Congress of the Communist Party (October 16–17, 1926) which instructed its Central Committee:

> "to continue and extend its efforts for the building up of a broad left-wing opposition in the Labour Party, based on the widest possible militant programme and including all elements genuinely desirous of fighting for the overthrow of the capitalists and the establishment of the rule of the working class."[1]

But at the same time it drew a distinction between what it considered to be a *genuine* left, like the Left-Wing Movement in the Labour Party, and the Minority Movement in the trade unions, and what it considered a "sham left", of left-wing phrases and right-wing action. This Communist Party conception of a "sham left" to a large extent included, by mid-1926, the Independent Labour Party. This needs examination.

COMMUNIST PARTY AND I.L.P.

After the fall of the Labour Government at the end of 1924 the position of the Independent Labour Party became more and more confused and contradictory.

To meet criticisms from its more left-wing members, the I.L.P. began to discuss aspects of a socialist policy, to campaign for "Socialism in our Time", to which the Labour Party was, supposedly, to be converted. The I.L.P. Conference of April 1925 demanded the establishment of a "Living Wage Commission" which would nationalise all industries that could not pay a "living wage". But the same I.L.P. still had Ramsay MacDonald as a leading member, and the same 1925 Conference, by a vote of 398 to 139, congratulated the Labour Government for its conduct of affairs. "Facing all ways", commented the *Workers' Weekly* at the time.[2]

The I.L.P. still had at this time considerable support from workers in a number of areas, with Glasgow, Bradford and Norwich amongst the most important. It still had amongst its supporters many genuine and militant socialists who, though they might not be *scientific* socialists, strongly and genuinely wanted to advance to socialism. On the other hand they had in the leadership some of the outstanding right-wingers

---

[1] Resolution, "On the Left Wing". *Report of 8th Congress of C.P.G.B.*, pp. 78–79.
[2] See Ralph Miliband, *Parliamentary Socialism*, pp. 152–153; *Workers' Weekly*, No. 115, April 17, 1925.

of the day, and others of the left who were not prepared to break with the right wing, and who were wont to cover with left-wing phrases and generalisations a policy of virtual inaction. Different members and different branches went different ways.

In October 1925, when the capitalist offensive was in full swing and the need of the hour was preparation for the struggles ahead, the Communist Party wrote to the I.L.P. (letter of October 17) proposing that the two parties:

> "should co-operate in a campaign of agitation throughout the length and breadth of the country".

and suggesting that the issues for co-operation should include 100 per cent trade unionism, nationalisation of the mines, a living wage, and workers' self-defence against the O.M.S.[1]

The I.L.P. replied on November 6, 1925, that they appreciated the gravity of the industrial position and were *themselves* conducting a campaign for the nationalisation of the mines and the living wage, but that:

> "in view, however, of the differences of method of your Party and ours, we think more good will be done in the long run by each Party developing its own campaign on its own lines. Under these circumstances we regret that we are not able to accept your suggestion that we should appoint representatives upon a joint Committee."[2]

A number of I.L.P. Branches were indignant at this rejection,[3] and in January 1926, the Communist Party Executive repeated its offer for a joint campaign with the I.L.P.[4]

In March, with the General Strike approaching, the Communist Party again appealed to the I.L.P. for a joint campaign:

> "whatever obstacles there may have been, in the view of your N.A.C. to such a joint campaign when we first proposed it last October (1925), we feel that the industrial situation today is of such a character as to justify reconsideration of the question."[5]

---

[1] *Workers' Weekly*, No. 146, November 20, 1925, p. 2.
[2] Ibid.
[3] See report of E. H. Brown at the Executive Committee of the Communist International, in *Orders from Moscow*, p. 15.
[4] See Executive Committee resolution on "The Left Wing" in *Workers' Weekly*, No. 154, January 15, 1926, p. 5.
[5] *Workers' Weekly*, No. 165, April 2, 1926, p. 2.

There had been useful experiences in many areas of joint activity in the "Release the Prisoners" campaign, and the Communist Party appealed for a joint discussion between deputations of the C.P. Executive and the I.L.P. Administrative Council.

In a letter of March 18, Fenner Brockway, writing for the N.A.C. of the I.L.P., rejected the proposal for joint activity:

> "so long as your Party is committed to the present thesis of the Third International, insisting that an armed revolution is the only means of establishing socialism, and that it is the duty of your Party to prepare the workers for this armed conflict, it is difficult to see how there can be co-operation between our two national organisations.
>
> "The point of view from which you approach socialism is that of the inevitability of armed conflict followed by dictatorship. The point of view from which we approach socialism is the bold utilisation of developing political and industrial opportunities to establish socialism by the consent of the majority of the people.
>
> "So long as we are divided so fundamentally in method, co-operation would be unreal and of little value...."[1]

The I.L.P., the letter continued, was suggesting to the Second International that it should approach the Communist International to explore the possibilities of unity, but in the meantime it "seems best that we should each carry on our work on separate lines".

It was difficult to see how a genuine desire for *international* unity could be combined with the rejection of *immediate* united action on urgent practical ussues at home. And this was the essential content of the Communist Party's reply of March 26. The I.L.P., the Communist letter stated, was *ignoring the practical proposals;* it was putting forward differences of *doctrine* not method, which would be legitimate if the discussion was an amalgamation of the two Parties rather than joint action between them. So far as theory was concerned, the I.L.P. had been informed in 1920 already that:

> "The Communists do not exclude the possibility of the workers gaining power without bloodshed, as in Hungary, or by a parliamentary majority."

But an honest socialist must *warn* the workers to be prepared for the capitalists to launch a civil war. Whatever the opinion on these matters and whoever was correct, this should not prevent practical

[1] *Workers' Weekly.*

co-operation on the issues suggested—100 per cent trade unionism, a living wage for the miners, workers self-defence against O.M.S. and nationalisation of the mines.[1]

The General Strike came, and whatever else it did or did not do, it underscored the need for united action. And when the strike was called off, and the miners fought on alone, one thing seemed to stand out in relief above all others—the need of the miners for aid.

Again the I.L.P. was in a contradictory position. Some of those most responsible for the great sell-out were among the most well-known members of the I.L.P. And yet most of the membership of the I.L.P. and some of its leaders were bitterly indignant and calling for action to aid the miners. Unity was needed, and the moment seemed most ripe—all the more as the N.A.C. of the I.L.P. had adopted a resolution advocating, in general terms, a policy of embargo on the handling of blackleg coal.

On June 15 Bob Stewart, as Acting Secretary of the Communist Party, wrote to the I.L.P.[2] Referring to the past, he regretted that the previous proposals for a joint campaign had been turned down. A joint campaign would have helped to avert the collapse on May 12, more especially as so considerable a number of members of the General Council were members also of the I.L.P. But important, above all, he wrote, was what next:

"We believe that, at such a moment as this, when the fate of the whole movement is trembling in the balance, differences of doctrine cannot be allowed any longer to stand in the way.

"A vigorous joint campaign (a) for the embargo, (b) for credits from co-operatives, (c) for a declaration of full official support for the embargo from the Conference of Trade Union Executives [not yet adjourned, J.K.] on June 25th, would go far towards undoing the evil work done on May 12th.

"And, in view of your declarations and of the statements made in the *New Leader*, we propose to you that we should together conduct such a united campaign on behalf of the fighting miners and the larger unity of the working class in face of the capitalist offensive."

The I.L.P. replied on June 24 acknowledging the Communist proposals, and stating that any change to the previous I.L.P. attitude towards joint work with the Communist Party would have to be

[1] Ibid.
[2] See text in *Workers' Weekly*, No. 174, June 18, 1926, p. 2.

discussed by the National Council which did not meet until July 24.[1]

But there was a quick response from a number of I.L.P. Branches and from some of its prominent left-wing leaders. A joint campaign on the embargo began at Derby and at Leith.

Fred Longden, a member of the N.A.C. of the I.L.P., declared in the *Sunday Worker* at the beginning of July that:

"every branch of the I.L.P. should unite locally in order to demonstrate that the resolution [on the embargo, J.K.] was not one of mere words, but a lead for action."[2]

Walter Scobell, another prominent I.L.P. member, publicly pronounced that unity should include the I.L.P., C.P. and the left wing of the T.U.C., that:

"the immediate issue is the lock-out. United action (not talk) can win now. The embargo is the test of united action."[3]

Dan Griffiths, another prominent I.L.P.'er, Labour candidate for Stroud, supported a joint C.P.G.B.–I.L.P. campaign for the embargo.[4] Joseph Southall of Birmingham, a stalwart of the left wing, member of the I.L.P., declared:

"there seems to me no reason at all why the C.P. and the I.L.P. should not act jointly on this [embargo] and, indeed, on many other issues."[5]

The call for a joint I.L.P.–C.P.G.B. campaign on the embargo won the support of W. Crick, an I.L.P.'er, member of the Manchester Borough Labour Party, and of Will Lawther, a militant Durham miner, member of the I.L.P. and of the Labour Party Executive[6]. Many more Branches in different areas began in practice to carry out a united campaign.

But officially having adopted the resolution "urging I.L.P. members to support the policy of the refusal to transport black coal", the I.L.P. and its organ the *New Leader* grew more and more silent on the issue of the embargo. When, on June 18, the Miners' Federation publicly appealed to all unions to support the embargo, the *New Leader* permitted itself a short paragraph only.

[1] *Workers' Weekly*, No. 178, July 16, 1926.
[2] *Sunday Worker*, No. 69, July 4, 1926, p. 3.　[3] Ibid.
[4] Ibid., No. 70, July 11, 1926, p. 3.　[5] Ibid.
[6] Ibid., No. 72, July 25, 1926, p. 3.

At the end of July the N.A.C. finally met. The I.L.P. issued a manifesto, very solemn and radically phrased, calling on its branches throughout the country:

"to initiate a determined campaign to demand the dissolution of Parliament so that the electorate may have an opportunity of replacing a Government which has revealed itself as hopelessly bankrupt in policy, by a Labour administration prepared to solve the mining problem by nationalisation of the industry and its scientific reorganisation so that justice can be done to the miners, who perform an essential and dangerous service to the public, and the industry to be placed on a sound social basis."[1]

Dissolution of Parliament! But not any single mention of the embargo, despite the resolution of two months earlier, and despite the fact that a victory of the miners demanded an embargo, and the miners' defeat would make the dissolution of Parliament an empty slogan.

From the same National Council meeting came the I.L.P.'s reply to the Communist unity call,[2] and this was a flat rejection. The main reason given was that the I.L.P. could not campaign for measures that had been turned down by the unions concerned:

"As you know, the Council has urged members of the I.L.P. to support the *policy* of the embargo, and we shall continue to do so; but we must face the fact that it has been turned down by the Unions concerned. Under such circumstances, the effect of the kind of campaign which your Party is conducting would be, if successful, to induce individuals to take isolated action without the endorsement of their organisations, which we believe would be both ineffective, would tend to disrupt trade union organisation, and would expose them to loss of livelihood without Union support."

A second reason given was the oft-repeated argument of fundamental difference of approach between the two organisations:

"The Executive Committee of the Communist International understands this so well that in its official instructions to you, it demands that your Party conduct 'active agitation against the I.L.P'."

---

[1] See *Workers' Weekly*, No. 180, July 30, 1926, p. 1.
[2] See Text in *Workers' Weekly*, No. 181, August 6, 1926, p. 2—"The I.L.P. against the Miners". The I.L.P. reply was dated July 26.

In this circumstance, the I.L.P. letter concluded, it was difficult to believe in the sincerity of the repeated Communist proposal for association between the two organisations.

The Communist reply was strong.[1] There had been two resolutions from the I.L.P. since the General Strike supporting "the policy of the embargo", it said, but the N.A.C. had done nothing to make them a reality. The *New Leader* had made only passing references. There were no instructions from N.A.C. to I.L.P. branches to fight for the embargo, nor appeals from the editors of the I.L.P. press. "Support" without action was hypocrisy.

It was shameful, it continued, to use as a pretext for inaction on the embargo "the fact that it had been turned down by the unions concerned". It was true that the embargo had been rejected by the Railway Unions at the beginning of July, but what was the I.L.P. doing to prevent this in May and June? The C.P., much smaller in membership than the I.L.P., had mustered 20 supporters for its policy at the N.U.R. Conference against 50 supporters of Thomas. How much larger would this support have been if the I.L.P. had joined with the Communist Party! And how influential such a *joint* campaign could have been, in Trades Councils and in other unions!

The failure of the I.L.P. leadership to take effective action to support the miners, its acceptance of the embargo in words but rejection in action, its refusal of joint action with the Communists at a time when so desperately needed, all contributed to a growth of bitterness within the Communist Party, and the conviction that the I.L.P. leaders were using left words to divert left-moving workers *away* from the Communist Party and back (in practice) to support of the official Labour Party leadership. There was, too, by the end of 1926, a strong feeling within the Communist International that the British Communists were pulling their punches with regard to what in the International they considered a sham-left reformist left.

Something of this feeling was expressed in the Resolutions of the Eighth Congress of the C.P.G.B. (October 1926). The Communist International's *Thesis On the International Situation* stated, for instance, that:

> "The I.L.P. has, during the last 18 months, shown itself to be the most dangerous, because the best organised weapon of reformism within the Labour movement."[2]

[1] *Workers' Weekly*, No. 181, August 6, 1926, p. 2.
[2] *Report of 8th Congress of C.P.G.B.*, pp. 32–33.

It campaigned against MacDonald in words, the thesis continued, whilst it supported him in practice. It passed resolutions at Conferences (Gloucester and Whitley Bay, 1925 and 1926) about "Socialism in our Time", nationalisation, etc., whilst in practice, even before the General Strike, it advocated reformist schemes like municipal trading agencies for coal, and capitulated on the essential issues. It spoke in favour of the miners, but turned down the campaign for the embargo. It advocated on paper unity between the Second and Third Internationals, yet rejected united action with the Communist Party in Britain:

> "Although action by many local Branches of the I.L.P. (in defiance of their leaders) have shown that there are many honest working class and other elements in that Party, who are genuinely desirous of fighting for socialism, this Congress warns them that, by remaining in the I.L.P. without fighting for a revolutionary policy, they are playing into the hands of the sham 'Left' leaders, and, therefore of the reformists and capitalists."[1]

By this time the same type of criticism was being applied to *Lansbury's Labour Weekly*. The C.I. thesis continued:

> "The same applies with even greater force to the followers of *Lansbury's Labour Weekly* which has been proved in practice to be uttering semi-Communist phrases while pursuing a practical policy closely akin to that of the I.L.P. leaders."[2]

And it warned

> "the left-wing comrades in the local groups and committees that the example of the "Left wing" on the General Council, the "Left" leadership of the I.L.P. and the "Left" group round *Lansbury's Labour Weekly* is a proof that there is no half way house between working shoulder to shoulder with the Communist Party, and working shoulder to shoulder with Ramsay MacDonald and J. H. Thomas. Those who genuinely stand for a fight of the masses against the capitalists cannot follow the lead of those who always defend the capitalists against the masses, without assisting the capitalists in their work."[3]

---

[1] Ibid.
[2] See also *Workers' Weekly*, No. 182, August 13, 1926, p. 2—"Lansbury's Weekly in Role of Betrayer".
[3] *Report of 8th Congress of C.P.G.B.*, p. 34.

To understand the bitterness of this criticism it is necessary to remember the context in which it was being made. The greatest strike in British Labour history had been sold out, and one of the greatest fighting forces of the British workers—the organised miners—were being betrayed and left to starve. In October, when this resolution was passed, hunger, internal breakaways, the pressure of the General Council, were gradually, inexorably, pushing the miners to retreat and defeat.

And to the militants and Communists who were giving everything they had to help the miners, those who *claimed* to be socialist, militant and yet did little or nothing to help seemed to be the greatest traitors of all.[1]

Yet experience, hindsight, reconsideration of this and similar problems would, I think, make us today pass judgement on some aspects of the British Communist attitude at this time to the I.L.P. In the letters and appeals for unity there was too much criticism and harping on the past, too much "I told you so", "we have been proved correct," "history will judge you". There was insufficient differentiation between the many militant members and the role of the leaders, and criticism of the leaders was itself too indiscriminate. The criticisms advanced were sometimes of such a type that far from winning I.L.P. members towards communism, they tended to repel them; there was a tendency to cram men like George Lansbury, genuine advocates of unity whatever their weaknesses, into a category of "sham lefts" and to write them off from the ranks of progress. Lastly, and this was an error for which the Communist International must share largely in the blame, there was a beginning of the development of the very wrong conception that the "left" critics of the Communist Party, like the I.L.P. leaders, for instance, were the *greatest danger* to the advance to socialism. This was itself a very dangerous outlook, for the main enemy was capitalism, and the main force of capitalism within the British Labour Movement was in this period, overwhelmingly, the right-wing reformism of the MacDonald and Thomas type. All this does not mean that it

---

[1] It should be noted that the I.L.P. attitude at this period was not just right-wing activity concealed under left-wing words. The words were often right-wing too. For instance, soon after the General Strike, the I.L.P. offered to publish for the miners a special supplement—*The Miners*. A. J. Cook, in the difficult, almost desperate, position of the miners, accepted. The paper, edited by John Strachey, continued with its line of "formation of selling agencies", etc., along with a general non-militant, defeatist line.

In the bitter struggle *within the miners' unions* between continued resistance and retreat, the I.L.P. preached defeat whilst the Communists fought for resistance. It is not surprising that the Communist Party made harsh judgements of the I.L.P.

was incorrect to criticise and criticise severely the leadership of the I.L.P. which did indeed "face two ways" and which was definitely defeatist at the critical period of the miners' struggle which followed the General Strike. But despite all this the character of the criticism which began to be put forward towards the end of 1926 helped to hold back the unity of the left and contributed to the isolation of the Communist Party.

Whatever the strength and weakness of the critique of the I.L.P., the Communist Party did make a continuous effort to unite with non-Communists in the trade unions and Labour Party, to fight the right-wing leadership, to try to change the policy of the Labour Party and the T.U.C., to try to help the miners, to defend the trade unions, to work for international trade union unity against colonialism and war. The degree of success achieved was put to the test at the Bournemouth T.U.C. and the Margate Labour Party Conference.

THE LEFT AT THE BOURNEMOUTH T.U.C.

The Fifty-eighth Annual Trades Union Congress was held at Bournemouth from September 6–11, 1926. Left-wing delegates attending could not but feel from the outset how little had been fulfilled of the militant resolutions adopted at the Scarborough Congress of the previous year—the magnificent resolution against imperialism, the decision on international trade union unity, the resolution demanding examination of the powers of the General Council, the call for well-organised factory committees. Scarborough had taken very good decisions but elected a very bad General Council, and the Council, not surprisingly, had ignored the decisions.[1] This more than anything underlined the crying need for a new progressive leadership in the trade union movement.

But much had changed since Scarborough. Scarborough looked forward to a great mass struggle against the employers, to the General Strike; Bournemouth took place after the General Strike had been sold out. The group of left trade union leaders—Purcell, Hicks, etc., who had played a positive role at the Scarborough Congress, had sometimes watched the sell-out in silence and sometimes contributed to it, had accepted the policies of Thomas and Clynes and MacDonald. At Bournemouth they no longer stood with the left, and it was the

---

[1] See R. P. Dutt, "From Scarborough to Bournemouth", in *Workers' Weekly*, No. 185, September 3, 1926, p. 6.

Communists and Minority Movement members, supported on occasions by individuals like Ellen Wilkinson, M.P., and J. Hallsworth (Distributive and Allied Workers), who represented the left and struggled for militant policy. The left was there, and fought hard, though in minority.[1] It was men and women like Arthur Horner of the South Wales Miners' Federation, Jack Tanner of the A.E.U., Sam Elsbury of the Tailor and Garment Workers, J. Strain of the Amalgamated Society of Woodworkers, G. W. Chandler of the A.S.L.E.F., W. C. Loeber of the N.U.R., A. G. Tomkins of the Furnishing Trades Association, J. McLaughlin of the General Iron Fitters and Mrs. Norah Bradshaw of the Weavers' Association—some Communists and all associated with the N.M.M.—who, at Bournemouth, kept flying the flag of militant trade unionism. The absence of Harry Pollitt, still in prison, was deeply felt. The issues of conflict between left and right were many.

The new conception of tamed trade unions, trade unions as part of the Establishment, accepted by the employers, was clearly put in Arthur Pugh's presidential address, which contrasted sadly with the forceful address of A. B. Swales the previous year.[2] The trade unions had become, he said, "as much a part of the life of the community as the Law Courts or Parliament itself". He launched the conception of a "wages policy", accepted by capital and labour alike, and by which class struggle for the division of the product would be replaced by an amicable agreement, an illusion which was to haunt the right wing of the Labour Party and the T.U.C. for many years to come.

> "A scientific wage policy for the unions requires to be thought out in relation to some generally acceptable set of principles for determining the division of the product of industry among those who have a rightful claim to it."

The left-wing critique of the platform began with an amendment from A. G. Tomkins regretting:

> "the little advance made in the direction of industrial unionism."

and instructing the General Council:

---

[1] See L.V.B., "The Bournemouth Congress", in *Labour Monthly*, Vol. 8, No. 10, October 1926, p. 595. "L.V.B." was Andrew Rothstein.

[2] See Report of Fifty-eighth Bournemouth T.U.C., pp. 68–78. See also Allen Hutt, op. cit., p. 172.

"to call Conferences of the trade groups of the Congress in order to arrange for the merging of the separate unions within these groups into industrial unions."[1]

He was supported by A. J. Cook of the Miners who, speaking from bitter experience, declared that:

"In an industrial struggle we have more to fear from the sectional unions than from the employers."[2]

And, despite delaying tactics from the platform, the amendment was carried by 2,172,000 to 1,480,000.

Sam Elsbury then challenged the General Council's Report on the paragraph (57) dealing with furtherance of the Trades Councils[3]. This, he said, was inadequate. He was supported by Jack Tanner of the A.E.U. In the General Council's report a ruling had been reported "that affiliation to the National Minority Movement, in the opinion of the Council, was not consistent with the policy of the Congress and the General Council, and that the Council could not, therefore, approve of affiliation with the National Minority Movement."[4] This ruling, said Tanner, was not accepted by or acceptable to the Amalgamated Engineering Union. It should be left to the unions themselves to decide their affiliations. McLaughlin of the Iron Fitters moved the reference back of this paragraph, supported by Ellen Wilkinson[5] ("surely it is not inconsistent that the minority should hope by affiliation it will become the majority, and that the resolutions it puts forward will in time become the declared policy of the Congress"). But the reference back was lost by 2,710,000 to 738,000.

The militant group criticised the General Council for insufficient protest and action against the Emergency Powers Act (Ellen Wilkinson, Sam Elsbury),[6] and then attacked again, more forcibly, on the issue of the powers and duties of the General Council. To a resolution calling simply for further investigation of General Council powers, A. G. Tomkins moved an amendment, that the time had now come for *definite* powers to be given to the General Council:

"(a) to assist unions or alliances of unions contemplating entering upon a struggle for the improvement of, or in defence of, conditions of labour of their members, by taking over the direction and control of the struggle.

[1] *Report of 58th T.U.C.*, p. 329. [2] Ibid., pp. 331–333. [3] Ibid., p. 340.
[4] Ibid., p. 165. [5] Ibid., p. 342. [6] Ibid., pp. 345–349.

"(b) to have power to levy all or part of the affiliated organisations.
"(c) to have power to call for a gradual, partial, or complete stoppage of work by all or any part of the affiliated organisations.
"(d) To make arrangements with the C.W.S. for provisions of food, etc., when necessary.
"(e) To render all possible assistance to Trades Councils, in order that they may efficiently function as the local organs of the General Council, and so take such other steps as may be necessary...."[1]

He was supported by J. McLaughlin of the Iron Fitters and P. Lee of the Miners' Federation, but Ernest Bevin, of the Transport and General Workers, and C. T. Cramp, of the National Union of Railwaymen, opposed *both* the amendment and the original resolution. The amendment was lost by 3,202,000 to 848,000 and the original motion was also defeated.

Congress then moved over to the issue which all were awaiting—to discuss or not to discuss the General Strike and the issue of aid for the miners.

Jack Tanner, of the A.E.U. moved the reference back of paragraph 13 of the General Council's Report dealing with the mining situation and the General Strike.[2] He opposed the decision to adjourn the discussions of the General Strike until a Conference of Executives, to be held *after* the termination of the mining dispute:

"We feel that an attempt is being made to prevent the workers and the delegates here particularly from knowing the whole truth in regard to the national strike....

"The rank and file are accusing the General Council of being cowards for calling off the national strike, and they are accusing them of being weak fools for accepting the Samuel Memorandum and failing to get the necessary guarantees before calling off the National Strike."

Supported by W. C. Loeber of the N.U.R., but opposed by A. J. Cook who appealed for suspension of the debate till after the settlement of the dispute, the reference back was lost by 3,098,000 to 775,000. Cook was beginning to break under the strain of a struggle which, apart from Communist support, he was forced to bear

[1] *Report of 58th T.U.C.*, see debate on General Council powers, pp. 376–387.
[2] Ibid., pp. 388–392.

almost single-handed, in public and within the Miners' Federation.[1]

Bob Smillie of the Miners, sadly enough, moved for the platform a routine emergency resolution, recording, "high appreciation of the generous financial assistance both national and international... afforded to the miners during the protracted lock-out in the mining industry", and calling for continued financial aid.[2] The contrast was great between the moving words of this veteran of many miners' struggles, describing the hunger and distress in the mining villages and the courage of the miners and their wives, and the cold hypocritical words put in his mouth in this resolution framed by the General Council. Appreciation of "generous financial aid", when the T.U.C. contribution had been pitifully inadequate, when there was no mention of levy, still less of embargo!

It was not only the militant minority at Congress who felt bitter. When J. Bromley rose to second this resolution for the General Council, he was, in the gentle words of the official report, "recipient of a hostile demonstration". The delegates demanded that someone more suitable should replace him, and Congress had to be adjourned. Militants like Elsbury and Strain were prevented from amending the resolution.

The embargo was excluded from discussion. The following dialogue is symbolic:

> A. G. Tomkins (Furnishing Trades)
> "What steps has the General Council taken to get the International Federation of Trade Unions to hold an enquiry into the possibility of preventing black coal coming to Britain?"
> Pugh (Chairman)
> "That does not arise in this part of the Report."
> Tomkins
> "On what part does it arise?"
> Pugh
> "I am afraid I cannot tell you."[3]

In April 1925 British and Soviet trade unions had agreed to press the International Federation of Trade Unions to meet the Russian trade unions, and that, if the I.F.T.U. should refuse to call such a meeting and

---

[1] See L.V.B., "The Bournemouth Congress", in *Labour Monthly*, Vol. 8, No. 10, October 1926, pp. 598–600, 604.
[2] *Report of 58th T.U.C.*, 420.
[3] Quoted by Allen Hutt, op. cit., p. 167.

enter preliminary discussions on world trade union unity, then the General Council of the T.U.C. should *itself* convene such a meeting. This approach was endorsed at the Scarborough T.U.C. As was indeed expected, the I.F.T.U. flatly declined such a meeting. Then the General Council, refusing to fulfil its obligations, declined to do so in its turn.

This position was questioned by the left at the Bournemouth T.U.C. in part in the form of challenges to particular paragraphs in the General Council Report (paragraphs 161, 163, 165) made by Arthur Horner, Sam Elsbury and Jack Tanner, and in part in discussion on a resolution moved by Elsbury calling for the General Council to work for the formation of a single trade union international, and on an amendment moved by Tanner instructing the General Council:

> "to insist upon the I.F.T.U. summoning a Conference free from all restrictions between the I.F.T.U. and the R.I.L.U. as representative of the two big world groups among the Trade Unions, in order to endeavour to lay the basis for International Trade Union Unity."[1]

The resolution was carried, but Tanner's amendment was lost. The General Council, once strong advocates of international trade union unity, had moved over almost to the position of Oudegeest, and Sassenbach, the Dutch and German right-wing leaders of the I.F.T.U. whom they had once not so long ago so strongly attacked.

The judgement of the Communist Party at the time was that, compared with Scarborough, the Bournemouth T.U.C. was a big step back.[2] Later this judgement was to come under discussion.[3] The Party summarised its view of the Bournemouth Congress in a mid-September statement "T.U.C. Leaders' United Front against the Workers".[4] It considered that the whole official leadership of the T.U.C. had turned against the interests of the working class, that the former "Left" on the General Council, had "completed their abject and shameful surrender to the right". It criticised A. J. Cook for supporting the General Council in postponing discussion of the General Strike.

---

[1] For discussion on international unity, see *Report of 58th T.U.C.*, pp. 435–446. See also Political Report of C.C. in report of Eighth Congress of C.P.G.B., p. 17 and J. T. Murphy and R. Page Arnot, "The British T.U.C. at Bournemouth", *Communist International*, Vol. III, No. 1 of October 15, 1926.

[2] Compare *Workers' Weekly*, No. 186, September 10, 1926. Editorial "Running Away" on p. 2.

[3] See article by J. T. Murphy and R. Page Arnot in *Communist International*, Vol. III, No. 1 of October 15, 1926. See also pp. 287–288 of this chapter.

[4] *Workers' Weekly*, No. 187, September 17, 1926, p. 1.

But it stressed that even such a Congress, "composed . . . of more than one half of officials", showed considerable support for the left, and that the elements of the new leadership which the movement so badly needed were revealed in the principled fight for progressive policy put up by the group of Communists and Minority Movement members, assisted on different issues by other individual delegates. It was this group, the statement stressed, that was the genuine left at the Congress.

Considering the right-wing line-up which at Bournemouth seemed to stretch from Cramp to Clynes and from Purcell to Pugh, the Communist and Minority Movement group had not done badly in carrying some of its motions and in raising a 20 per cent minority vote even when most heavily under attack.

MARGATE LABOUR PARTY CONFERENCE

If at the Bournemouth T.U.C. the Communist Party and Minority Movement together constituted a militant opposition defending the miners and trade union principles, at the Margate Labour Party Conference the following month a similar role was played by the delegates who were members of the Communist Party or connected with the left-wing movement.

The Margate Conference was held from October 11 to 15, 1926. To the delegates as they assembled was distributed an *Open Letter* from the Communist Party.[1]

For the Party, the attitude to the miners' struggle was the touchstone of socialist sincerity. The *Open Letter* started with a "text" from A. J. Cook:

> "There is no use in advocating socialism in the sweet by and by unless you are going to give the miners a living wage now. If this was to be obtained, the Movement must not only give applause. It must be prepared to take a levy as had been done in Russia, and organise an official boycott of black coal on the railways."

The Party called on the delegates in the first place to rally to support the miners, as Cook had called for, by adopting a levy and support for the embargo.

It appealed for a reversal of the anti-Communist measures adopted at the Liverpool Conference:

[1] *Workers' Weekly*, No. 190, October 8, 1926, p. 2, "An Open Letter to the Delegates at Margate".

"Condemn the policy of the Labour Party Executive in expelling Divisional Labour Parties for no other crime than refusing to split the movement.

"Accept duly elected Communist delegates and reverse the Liverpool decisions in relation to the Communists."

It called for a policy of nationalisation, for a struggle for defeat of the Tory Government and for a defeat of the right-wingers in the election of the new Executive. What was needed, the *Open Letter* stated, was a new leadership, a leadership of militants.

It was clear enough long before the Margate Conference opened that the Labour Party leadership had no intention of repealing the Liverpool decisions, that, on the contrary, their objective was to carry the Labour Party still further to the right, to isolate and crush what remained of the left.

This was not to prove so simple. Despite the various measures of "purge" that had followed Liverpool, despite disaffiliation of recalcitrant branches and militant Trades Councils, there were 23 resolutions received from 28 organisations calling for the admission of Communists to membership of the Labour Party and affiliation of the Communist Party to the Labour Party.[1] And within the Conference, from the beginning, there was a united stand of the left-wing delegates ranging from Communists like Harry Pollitt, Arthur Horner and Frank Jackson, and militant trade unionists like Alex Gossip, to members of the left-wing movement like W. Crick, H. S. Redgrave and Joseph Southall of Birmingham (a pacifist Tolstoyan member of the I.L.P.)[2], joined, on certain issues, by Labour Party leaders or I.L.P.'ers like David Kirkwood and George Lansbury. But the I.L.P.'ers joined the left as individuals rather than as members of their Party, for in the different contests and struggles at Margate there were members of the I.L.P. on the left, the right and in the centre, ranging from Joseph Southall to Ramsay MacDonald.

As at Bournemouth, the turn to the right of the leadership was revealed at once in the Presidential Address, delivered by Robert Williams who had travelled very far, alas, from his erstwhile Communist affiliations.[3]

---

[1] *Workers' Weekly*, No. 186, September 10, 1926, p. 2.
[2] See Joseph Southall, "Margate and the Left Wing", in *Labour Monthly*, Vol. 8, No. 10, October 1926.
[3] See *Report of 26th Conference of Labour Party*, pp. 167–172.

Williams attacked the miners and their struggle:

> "The Miners' decision to continue the dispute is heroic. They may be likened to the sightless Samson feeling for a grip of the pillar of the Temple, the crashing of which may engulf this thing we call British Civilisation."

What was needed was not struggle, not conflict, but publicity and persuasion:

> "I venture to opine that had one-tenth of the money which was spent on the conflict of May last been spent on obtaining publicity for Labour's plans ... a settlement of the mining dispute ... would have given justice to the mine workers and a lasting benefit to the Community."

He attacked the conception that real change in society will come through struggle and strike and contest. What was needed, he explained, was not conflict but conciliation within the framework of capitalism:

> "Sight is lost of the fact that the majority of our Trade Unionists are served by one or another form of conciliation machinery between Union and employers.
> '... it should not be forgotten that conciliation has played, is playing, and must continue to play, an important part in trade union work. If peace should be sought for internationally, I say, let us seek industrial peace through methods of conciliation.
> "In a resourceful, resilient, industrial community like our own, we cannot subvert or overthrow, we must supersede capitalism."

The miners, said Williams, called for an embargo: "this despairing policy may be magnificent, but it is not war". The Communists and Minority Movement, he taunted, "still believe in the General Strike". His *own* view of the General Strike he had given a little earlier in Lord Rothermere's journal *Answers*.[1] The General Strike had failed "because the resources of the country were—and are—stronger than the resources of the trade unions". The unions could do good work, he added, by discrediting the theory that every employer "is an enemy of the working class". Within Williams' speech at Margate—his condemnations of class struggle and of strikes, call for class conciliation and

---

[1] Quoted by Allen Hutt, op. cit., p. 172.

industrial peace—were the rudiments of the whole policy that in the next period was to go under the name of Mondism.

The first contest, a skirmish, took place on the question of the youth. During the 1925–1926 period some 200 of the Young People's Sections of the Labour Party had been established. Reviewing the position of this youth organisation the National Executive had decided that the name should be changed to the Labour Party League of Youth, that the age of members should be from 14–21, whilst those from 21–25 could retain membership provided they became individual members of the Labour Party, that the Annual Conference of the League of Youth should be held at the same time and place as that of the Party, starting in 1927.[1] Joseph Southall moved that the branches of the Young Socialist League should be allowed to affiliate to local Labour Parties:

> "They must not endeavour to put the youth of the Movement in a strait-jacket . . . the older ones should not try to tyrannise over them and say, 'You must conform to our rules and organisation!' "

But, opposed by the National Executive, his resolution was lost.[2] Alex Gossip of the Furnishing Trades' Association, demanded to know why no reference had been made to the Youth Delegation to Russia on which Young Socialists and Young Communists were both participating,[3] but was told that they had gone without official sanction and did not, therefore, enjoy "official" existence.

Joseph Southall protested strongly against the nomination in Birmingham West by the Labour Party of an "official" candidate in opposition to the Communist Dr. Dunstan, who enjoyed such wide Labour support.[4]

> "He had tested the feeling of the rank and file, and he was prepared to testify that they were not behind the attack upon this man to whom they owed so much and for whom they had so much regard."

George Lansbury vigorously supported him:

> "He felt that the Movement in doing what it was doing was going towards disaster. He came from East London, and if all the implications of the Party policy with regard to the Communists was carried out there, when the next election took place they would be divided and smashed into smithereens."

[1] *Report of 26th Conference of Labour Party*, p. 10.   [2] Ibid., p. 178.
[3] See p. 357.
[4] *Report of 26th Annual Report of Labour Party*, pp. 181–184.

The reference back of the relevant section of the report was lost by a show of hands, but Lansbury's personal tribute to Communists and their role in the Labour Party was very courageous and very telling (all the more so because the Communist Party at this time had not been over-moderate in its attacks on Lansbury). In the Labour Party, he declared:

> "they had men and women who avowed Communist principles, who were members of the Communist Party, and who had been with them for thirty or thirty-five years. When they were told to turn such men out, the Party would do no such thing. . . .
> ". . . he did not take the view that the Communists were their enemies; he did not take the view that in regard to social and political affairs the Class War did not matter, that it did not exist. To him it did exist, and to him the philosophy of the Communist Party was sound—(applause)—but their methods he happened to disagree with."

From the West Birmingham candidate the debate passed over to the general ground of Communist Party–Labour Party relations. At the Liverpool Conference in 1925 the National Executive had demanded that the anti-Communist measures adopted "be consistently administered by constituency and local Labour Parties in the appointment of their officials".[1] From the Scottish Council of the Labour Party, following Liverpool, had come a request that the Executive should define "officials". Definitions are never easy, and after due pondering, legal consultation, and scholastic hair-splitting, the wise men of the Executive ruled:

> "that the terms 'officials' when used to designate the appointments for which members of the Communist Party are not eligible be interpreted as meaning 'officers', the Executive Committee and delegates".[2]

Regardless of definitions, the Executive had proceeded to operate, particularly in London and Glasgow, a process of disaffiliation of Labour Parties and Trades and Labour Councils accused of harbouring

[1] Report of National Executive in *Report of 26th Annual Conference of Labour Party*, pp. 17–19.
[2] Ibid.

prohibited persons.[1] It had also, as we have seen, sent out the July circular denouncing various Communist misdeeds (fractions, nuclei, etc.) within the Labour Party.[2] This was the background of the Margate debate.

When Frank Jackson, delegate from the St. Pancras Borough Labour Party and Trades Council, moved a resolution protesting against the disaffiliation of Bethnal Green and Battersea Local Labour Parties, he was interrupted with the question as to whether he was himself a Communist. "Yes, Sir", man of few words, he replied, and was told that in that case neither himself as a delegate nor his resolution could rightly be said to exist.[3] Harry Pollitt, who, as delegate from the Boilermakers' Trade Union, could not so easily be ruled out of order or existence, moved the reference back of the sections of the General Council's Report dealing with Labour–Communist relations.[4]

The National Executive, he said, was interpreting the Liverpool resolutions to the local Labour Parties and Trades Councils in a way that they dared not interpret them to the trade unions. A study of the organisations disaffiliated by the Executive would show that they were in centres of appalling poverty, "they stood for a real unity where the job of this Party had to be carried out". With regard to the attack on Communist fractions and nuclei, he reminded the delegates of the history of the I.L.P., which had always organised *within the Labour Party* to win it for certain positions, and which had certainly done so on the issue of "the living wage" in preparation for this present Margate Conference. The policy of disaffiliation "was the first step towards the wholesale disunity of the British working-class movement". Opposed by Herbert Morrison for the Executive Committee, the reference back was defeated by 3,414,000 to 209,000.

The bitterest debate at the Margate Conference took place on the mining crisis.[5] The resolution moved for the Executive by Rhys J.

---

[1] By the time of the Margate Conference these included Battersea Trades Council and Labour Party, Bethnal Green Trades Council and Borough Labour Party, South-West Bethnal Green Divisional Labour Party, Greenwich Trades and Labour Council, Stratford (West Ham) Divisional Labour Party, East Lewisham Divisional Labour Party, Westminster Labour Party, Chelsea Trades Council and Labour Party, Holborn Trades Council and Labour Party, Bridgeton (Glasgow) Divisional Labour Party, Gorbals (Glasgow) Divisional Labour Party, Kelvingrove (Glasgow) Divisional Labour Party, Springburn Divisional Trades and Labour Council, and others.

[2] Printed in full in *Report of 26th Conference of the Labour Party*, pp. 319–320.

[3] *Report of 26th Annual Conference of the Labour Party*, pp. 185–186.

[4] Ibid., pp. 186–188.   [5] Ibid., pp. 192–202.

Davies, M.P., epitomised the sell-out. It greeted the "magnificent resistance of the miners" as if it was a thing of the past, condemned the Government for "mishandling of the crisis" and declared that solution could only come by the adoption of the scheme of nationalisation and development submitted by the Miners' Federation, General Council and Labour Party Executive to the Royal Commission. "One would never have known," wrote Harry Pollitt at the time, "that a mining lock-out involving a million men and their families was in progress."[1]

Pollitt rose at once to oppose the resolution, but the chairman first called David Kirkwood, of the I.L.P., who moved the reference back supported by Pollitt. The miners needed, said Kirkwood, not comfortable statements, but *money*, a *levy*. The I.L.P. resolution which had been replaced by that of the Executive had called for a levy. "There was no goodwill in capitalism, and therefore it was no good coming forward with a pious resolution such as this."

Pollitt brought the delegates straight to the point. It was true that the Conference could not itself impose a levy or embargo but he was confident:

> "that if the Executive could bring back a resolution in favour of the embargo and in favour of a levy, and concentrate the whole of the Movement in popularising these things, the dissolution of the Conservative Government would be the result of that campaign. . . ."

The reference back was supported by R. C. Wallhead, M.P., of the I.L.P., by a certain Oswald Mosley of the I.L.P., by W. J. Brown of the Civil Service Clerical Association, by W. P. Richardson of the Miners, by Arthur Horner who told the Conference in no uncertain terms what the miners were asking from the delegates:

> "Let the Labour Movement of the country give the Miners such a vote as he thought they were entitled to expect from it, and such help as the Coal Owners were getting from their clients, the Government. Let them have the money and let them have an embargo. If the Miners won, they would win a victory not only for themselves but for the whole working-class movement. If they lost in this struggle through the cowardice of the working-class movement, then God help the miners and God help the other workers afterwards."

[1] Harry Pollitt, *What Margate Means*, C.P.G.B. pamphlet, 14 pp., 1d., p. 5, reprinted in *Selected Articles and Speeches*, Vol. I, p. 27.

But it was not to be. All the big guns of the right wing were brought out to shoot down support for the miners, to reject the embargo and levy. J. H. Thomas, once so satisfied with the call-off of the General Strike and the railway settlement that followed it,[1] declared that in addition to 200,000 railwaymen on a three-day week, 45,000 had never gone back to work since May 1. How could they, he asked, provide a levy?

> "He would say to the Conference, 'Do not deceive the Miners; do not lead poor men and women to believe you are going to do something you cannot do.'"

Ben Tillett spoke of the Transport Workers' Unions deeply in debt, with 80,000 unemployed and 100,000 under-employed. How could *they* provide a levy?

And Ramsay MacDonald himself, with tearful eloquence, came to the platform to call for trust "in the people who were working their way through all difficulties behind the scenes", trust in your leaders, trust in the future Labour Government, trust in its future policy of nationalisation—but *no* embargo and *no* levy now!

The Chairman's decision to take the vote and terminate the debate was only carried by 2,037,000 to 1,276,000 and the reference back was defeated by 2,159,000 to 1,368,000—in the context of Margate an important vote of opposition to Executive policy.

Thus with pious expression of admiration for the miners' past struggles, and pious hope in some future nationalisation, the reformist leaders satisfied their elusive consciences. For the present they gave *nothing* except the charity of a round-with-the-hat collection. While the Chairman was preparing to take the vote to reject the levy, Mrs. Ayrton Gould of the Norwich Labour Party was speaking of the experiences of the Womens' Relief Committee:

> "The work of every Relief Committee was made a hundred times more difficult by the fact that they had to turn their backs on three-quarters of the distress for lack of means. Every week the need for funds became a hundred times more urgent. Every week some new Board of Guardians stopped giving relief altogether. Every week some new Education Authority stopped feeding the school children."[2]

---

[1] See p. 131.
[2] *Report of 26th Annual Conference of the Labour Party*, p. 201.

No levy, no embargo! And as the shillings and pennies tinkled in the Executive hats, Mrs. Gould continued:

> "A few days ago she saw a little grey-faced baby die in a home denuded of every comfort, with its mother half starved, sobbing her heart out because she had not the means to give it the necessary nourishment to save its life.... It would be a lasting disgrace to the Labour Movement if the Miners were beaten to their knees and defeated by the hideous and intolerable suffering which was being inflicted on their helpless wives and children."[1]

The Chairman said the collection had been taken. The reference back was defeated. The resolution was then carried by a large majority and miners continued to starve. If there were dockers, railwaymen and others who were hungry too, it was not the result of the General Strike, but the result of calling it off, the result of the betrayal of the General Council, wrote Pollitt, following Margate.[2]

The Communist Party did its best to sum up the lessons of Margate, and to rally the left for the policy which Margate had rejected. It called more than ever for action for levy and embargo. It warned of the need to defend the trade unions from Government action. Only a week before Margate the Tory Party Conference had called for "reform" of existing trade union law:

> "To make illegal any strike called without a secret ballot of the members of the trade union affected.
>
> "To increase the security of the individual worker against victimisation and intimidation on account of his political beliefs.
>
> "To make mass picketing and the picketing of a man's private residence illegal.
>
> "To require the national accounts of trade unions to be audited by chartered accountants."[3]

and already at the time of Margate, the Government was preparing the repressive Trade Union Act for the following year.

The Communist Party called on all sections of the left to work for a new leadership in the Labour Movement. Discussing the lessons of Margate, Harry Pollitt wrote:

[1] Ibid.
[2] Harry Pollitt, *What Margate Means*, pp. 6–7 (in edition of *Selected Articles and Speeches*, pp. 28–29).
[3] Quoted by Harry Pollitt in "The Margate Conference", *Communist Review*, Vol. 7, No. 7, November 1926, pp. 307–313.

"the working class can never win their struggle under the leadership of middle-class liberals and the old school of Trade Union leaders who use the whole power of the machinery of the working class movement to stifle the rising tide of the workers demands. . . .

"This leadership cannot be achieved by more agitation and propaganda; much more is necessary. It will take years of steady, persistent organisation to replace the present leadership, locally, in the districts and nationally, by new, genuine and honest working-class fighters."[1]

To replace the old leadership by a new and militant leadership the Party called for a united left—for a stronger Minority Movement, for a stronger left-wing movement, for greater collaboration between trade unions and co-operatives. The role of the left-wing movement delegates had been one of the main features of the Margate Conference.[2] In Pollitt's words "there were no 'big names' or 'star turns' among them, but by good team work, they created the impression that here was the first open organised opposition at a Labour Party Conference."[3]

The need was to develop the movement further, in the trade unions, in the Labour Party, in the co-operatives, to develop the Minority Movement and left-wing movement, a movement of left-wing unity in which the Communist Party would play an open, integral and leading part.

Embargo and levy; the fight for a new leadership in the Labour Movement; the fight for the defeat of the Tory Government and its replacement by a militant Labour Government; the fight for a mass Communist Party; the fight against war and imperialism—this was the line for which Communists fought at the Bournemouth T.U.C. and the Margate Labour Party Conference. This was the line along which Gallacher, Hannington, Inkpin, Pollitt and Rust issued their appeal when released from gaol at the end of September 1926.[4] This was the line as we have seen of the Eighth Congress of the Communist Party, meeting at the Battersea Town Hall on October 16–17, 1926.

[1] *What Margate Means*, pp. 12–13 in pamphlet; pp. 34–35 in *Selected Articles and Speeches*
[2] See editorial "Margate", in *Workers' Weekly*, No. 192, October 22, 1926, p. 2; Harry Pollitt, *What Margate Means*, p. 13 (or p. 35 in *Selected Articles and Speeches*; Harry Pollitt, "The Margate Conference", in *Communist Review*, Vol. 7, No. 7, November 1926, p. 312.
[3] Pollitt, *Communist Review*, op. cit., p. 312.
[4] *Message to the British Workers*, in *Workers' Weekly*, No. 188, September 24, 1926, pp. 1–2.

DIFFERENCES WITHIN COMMUNIST LEADERSHIP

Already by October 1926, with the new problems arising, there were some differences of approach beginning to show themselves within the leadership of the British Communist Party. They were reflected most clearly in the article by J. T. Murphy and R. Page Arnot on "The British Trade Union Congress at Bournemouth" published in the *Communist International*[1] (October 15) and in the reply from the Executive Committee of the British Party (October 30).[2]

The nature of the charges of Murphy and Page Arnot (and there was a note that they were supported by the Executive Committee of the Communist International and by the Editorial Board of the *Communist International* journal) was that, after the General Strike, there were "vacillations to the right in the ranks of the British Communist Party of rather in its leadership". This right-wing trend, the authors of the article claimed, was first revealed by the opposition of a section of the leadership to the criticisms of the General Council made by the Soviet Trade Unions from within the Anglo-Russian Trade Union Committee. It was shown by the failure properly to criticise the sham left like Purcell, and the lack of criticism of the errors of A. J. Cook. It was shown at the Third Conference of the Minority Movement where the N.M.M. Executive agreed "to restrict themselves to a mild criticism of the General Council" instead of "concentrating during the Congress all the force of their blows on the treacherous position of the General Council". It was shown in the assessment of the Bournemouth T.U.C. as a "step backward on Scarborough" when, in reality at Bournemouth "a tremendous step forward has been made by the working masses". The militant character of Scarborough had been exaggerated.

Replying, the Executive Committee deplored that such criticisms had been made without consultation by two of its members who shared in the responsibility for any errors.[3] They argued that the Communist and Minority Movement delegates had carried out sharp criticism of General Council policy at the Bournemouth T.U.C. A mistake was

---

[1] J. T. Murphy and R. Page Arnot, "The British Trade Union Congress at Bournemouth", *Communist International*, Vol. III, No. 1, October 15, 1926.
[2] "Our Party and the T.U.C.", by Executive Committee of C.P.G.B., *Communist International*, Vol. III, No. 2, October 30, 1926.
[3] J. T. Murphy had sent a telegram acknowledging his share in the errors; this had been published in the English but not in the Russian, French or German editions of the *Communist International*.

acknowledged on the Russian Trade Union Manifesto on the General Strike, but it was strongly denied that this was part of any general right-wing trend within the leadership of the C.P.G.B. There had been consistent criticism of the General Council's betrayal, of the attitude of the sham left in the T.U.C., and of the errors of A. J. Cook. The Bournemouth T.U.C. could not be neatly summarised in some phrase like "a step forward" or "a step back". The "crystallisation under the leadership of the Party and Minority Movement at Bournemouth is a step forward". But, at the same time, Bournemouth showed also "a tremendous consolidated bureaucracy ... a rapid differentiation is taking place in the working-class movement, and the bureaucracy is rapidly consolidating itself against the mass of the workers".

This was the beginning only of what was to be a prolonged political debate and struggle within the British Communist Party over the next two years, and which was to lead to considerable changes in the composition of the leadership. But consideration of this discussion, of the attitudes of the different groupings within the leadership, and of the Communist International, belongs to the next volume of this history.

CHAPTER IV

AGAINST IMPERIALISM AND WAR, 1925-1926

Analysing Imperialism—A Common Struggle—The 7th and 8th Congresses of the Party—Fulfilling the Resolutions—Solidarity around the World—"Hands Off China"—Aid to Victims of Reaction—Relations with The Soviet Union and the Soviet Trade Unions—Anglo-Soviet Trade Union Relations—C.P.G.B. and Communist International.

With the return of a Tory Government at the end of 1924, a major offensive was prepared and carried out against the working-class and trade union movement at home.

It is natural enough that this period from the end of 1924 to the end of 1926 should be for the Communist Party one in which the main emphasis of work lay with things at home, with combating the employers' offensive. It was the period of Red Friday, the General Strike, the miners' lock-out, the arrest of the Party leaders, the struggle against reformism. But the reactionary offensive conducted by British imperialism against the British workers in 1925-1926 was accompanied by a parallel offensive on a world scale. This living connection between home and international struggles was understood by the Party. So 1924-1925 was the period not only of Red Friday and the General Strike but of struggle against imperialism, closer links with the national movements in the countries of the British Empire, the campaign on "Hands off China", a period of international working-class solidarity with the British miners, and of solidarity of the British workers with the victims of imperialism or white terror in many parts of the world. The Seventh Congress of the C.P.G.B. (May-June 1925) and the Eighth Congress (October 1926) reflected equally the home and international aspects of Party policy and action.[1]

ANALYSING IMPERIALISM

In the Communist Party press, at public and private meetings, at educational classes, much time was devoted to analysis of the nature of

[1] See "Thesis on the Colonial Question and the British Empire" and "Resolution on Imperialism" (with the relevant discussions) of Seventh Congress of C.P.G.B. (*Report of 7th Congress*, pp. 194-197) and "Resolution on Imperialism" at Eighth Congress C.P.G.B. (*Report of 8th Congress*, pp. 80-81).

imperialism in general and British imperialism in particular. Lenin's *Imperialism* was republished and widely distributed, and there was much discussion on the declining position of Britain and the rising role of the United States within the imperialist world, and of the contradiction between them.[1] It can be said that the Party pioneered the understanding in Britain of the rise of United States imperialism to a dominating position in the capitalist world. The connection of imperialism and war was widely analysed and discussed, and the methods of imperialism in the colonial and semi-colonial lands.

Reformism had done much to break down the international traditions of the British Labour Movement. The Communist Party, in this period, considered it a special responsibility to put the British working-class struggle in its international setting, to make known to the British workers the struggles of the working class and colonial peoples in all parts of the world, to give the workers the sense that they were an integral part of an international movement.

In particular, the Party stressed the growth and the importance of the anti-imperialist struggles of the working peoples of the countries of the British Empire.

In this the Communists, small in numbers, played a role of particular importance. By and large the reformists taught the acceptance of Empire, at best with certain moderate reforms *within* it. In the I.L.P. there were a number of leading figures who did good work exposing the suffering, hardship, privations, of the colonial people, but for the most part without linking this with the role of imperialism and, still more, without seeing the tremendous significance of the anti-imperialist struggles of the colonial peoples.

The Communist Party made it quite clear that it *welcomed and supported* the struggle of the colonial peoples against British imperialism, that it would do all that it could to support these struggles, and that, in fact, the struggle of the British working class and the working people of the colonial countries of the British Empire *was a common struggle against a common enemy*.

A COMMON STRUGGLE

Delivering the opening Chairman's Address at the Seventh Congress of the Party, Harry Pollitt declared, speaking of the people combating

[1] See for instance the thesis on "The International and National Battlefield" at the Seventh Congress of C.P.G.B. and relevant discussion there, *Report of 7th Congress*, pp. 180–182. See also R. P. Dutt, "Notes of the Month", *passim*, in *Labour Monthly* of this period.

imperialism in Africa and Asia, in Egypt, China, Iraq, Kenya, Palestine, India, Ireland:

> "To these millions this Congress sends fraternal greetings and says: 'Your enemies are our enemies; we are of one class. We all fight against the British ruling class. We in our sphere will fight against them here at home, and do our utmost to help you in your revolutionary struggle against them. . . .
>
> "The struggle of the colonial peoples all over the world against British imperialism is also our struggle, and we shall help the colonial workers to the very best of our ability and power."[1]

It is difficult to emphasise sufficiently the fundamental significance of this conception of a *common struggle* of the British working class and the anti-imperialist movement in the colonies and semi-colonies of the British Empire put forward so consistently by the British Communist Party and, at that time, by no other British organisation. It was put forward again and again, sometimes in general terms, and sometimes in relation to some particular struggle in Egypt, or India or China. It was incorporated in the resolutions of the Seventh and Eighth Congress of the Party. It was taken by the Communists into the National Minority Movement, and by members of the Communist Party and the N.M.M. into the trade unions and the Labour Party. One of the main supporters of this conception was R. Palme Dutt who, in the *Labour Monthly* of which he was editor and in his other writings, continuously underlined it. "On the day", he wrote,

> "when the British workers realise their common interests with the working masses of the subject countries, and not with the common exploiters, on that day the basis of power over the Empire, and, therefore, the basis of power of the British bourgeoisie is ended."[2]

As part of this conception of the *common struggle* against British imperialism, the British Party took steps, sometimes at this period steps of an illegal or semi-legal character, to make direct contact with the anti-imperialist movements, trade unions and, in certain cases where they existed, Communist Parties, of the colonial countries of the Empire. Tom Bell, introducing the Thesis on Imperialism at the Seventh Congress of the Party, could say:

[1] *Report of the 7th Congress of C.P.G.B.*, p. 10.
[2] R. P. Dutt, *Empire "Socialism"*, C.P.G.B., 20 pp., 2d., February 1925, p. 5.

"Our Party has now commenced to take very definite steps to establish close relations with the Communist Parties of the colonies of the British Empire. In all of these countries we have established for the first time a definite personal contact between our brother parties, and very definite progress has been made."[1]

Contact was made, for instance, with the Communists in Egypt, with Marxist circles in India, with the beginnings of a Communist Party in Palestine, with the Chinese Communists and with the Kuomintang, with various revolutionary and trade union groups in Ireland. The Communist International was able to give great assistance in the establishment of such contacts.

The fiery anti-imperialist speeches of Saklatvala, the Communist M.P., denouncing in the House of Commons the role of British imperialism in Egypt, India, Palestine, etc., did much to encourage these early struggles and these early contacts. It is hard to overestimate the significance of the election by the *English* workers of Battersea of an "Indian immigrant" (as he would be called today) as *their* Communist representative in Parliament. From their most difficult conditions of struggle against British imperialism in all its ruthlessness, Marxist, trade union and anti-imperialist groups in the colonies and semi-colonies began to see that they had a *real ally* within the fortress of British imperialism, waging a common struggle, transcending colour and transcending race.

Naturally the critique of imperialism and support for the anti-imperialist struggles of the colonial peoples brought the Communist Party head on against the conception of Empire held by the right-wing Labour leaders, and their direct or indirect support for it.

Traditional British reformism of the MacDonald–Thomas type accepted Empire and openly defended it. At best it demanded certain moderate reforms—economic or social—within the imperial framework; at worst it openly condemned the anti-imperialist struggles of the colonial peoples and condoned their oppression and repression, accepting, defending and even, when in government, operating the use of British troops and gunboat diplomacy.

For the right wing, who always preferred the expression "British Commonwealth" to "British Empire", the *effective* commonwealth was the handful of white dominions. They were largely disinterested in the fate of the black, brown and yellow millions who formed seven-

[1] Report of 7th Congress of C.P.G.B., p. 76.

eighths of the Empire's population.[1] The Commonwealth Labour Conferences which they organised omitted representation of the main anti-imperialist organisations of the greater part of the colonial Empire. They even in 1925 supported Baldwin's scheme for "Imperial Unity" or "Imperial Federation" and presented it as a conversion of the Tories to socialism.[2]

Inside the left wing of the Labour Party and the I.L.P. were some who genuinely felt for the *sufferings* of the colonial people, who condemned their oppression, poverty, ill-health, morally and sentimentally, but without condemning the imperialist system that was responsible, who put forward, philanthropically, schemes for repairing the injustices and privations, whilst accepting or repairing or reforming the system of colonialism.

This, too, the Communist Party of these days severely criticised, at times perhaps too severely, not seeing sufficiently that for many workers the demand for this or that improvement in the condition of the colonial people *could* be a step towards support for the anti-imperialist struggle. But in its essence the Party criticism was a necessary and a correct one. It was necessary to show the nature of imperialism, to win *support* for the colonial peoples' struggles, to see that this was a *common* struggle that *equally* concerned British workers and colonial peoples, to end the condescending patronage of charitable appeal and to call for an *equal fraternal* struggle of comrades facing a common enemy and to give, where possible, *direct* support to the struggles of the colonial people, including organisational assistance.[3]

It was necessary, too, as the Communists did, to show that the advanced section of British workers stood not for some new "Constitution" or "self-development" or "gradual enlargement of rights" within an enforced Empire but *the complete right of self-determination, the right of complete independence.*

It was along these lines that the Party sought to show the connection of the fight against imperialism with the daily struggle of the British workers. In an article on "Labour Imperialism",[4] Arthur MacManus wrote in this period:

[1] See R. P. Dutt, *Empire* "Socialism".
[2] Ibid. The *Daily Herald* wrote "Tories dress up in socialist clothes". The *New Leader* (of the I.L.P.) claimed "Mr. Baldwin borrows from the I.L.P."
[3] Already at this time a number of Communists had undertaken missions to help colonial trade unionists to organise. Ben Bradley was shortly to be sent on such a mission.
[4] *Communist Review*, Vol. 7, No. 3, July 1926, p. 142.

"The general impression has been created in the minds of the workers, that the wages struggle in Britain is purely a trade union affair between the British trade unions and the British employers, and that the general conflict against capitalism is purely a parliamentary struggle confined within the walls of Great Britain. Reports of uprisings, rebellions, mutinies, etc., in Egypt, India, Africa or in some other remote part of the Empire are viewed with an attitude of superb aloofness. Such things are viewed as being no direct concern of ours. When we do betray an interest it is generally based upon a sort of sentimental concern in 'the welfare of suffering peoples'."

But the Labour Movement, he continued:

"has never attempted either to understand or to explain to the workers that talk of 'international brotherhood' is sheer empty nonsense unless steps are taken to destroy the forces which are setting race against race, and class against class throughout the domains of the British Empire."

AT THE SEVENTH AND EIGHTH CONGRESS OF THE PARTY

These approaches, so fundamentally different from the approaches of any other progressive or working-class organisation, to the role of imperialism and the struggles of the colonial peoples, were outlined in detail at the Seventh Congress of the C.P.G.B. (May–June 1925) in the Thesis on the Colonial Question and the British Empire[1] and the Resolution on Imperialism.[2]

The last two sections of the Thesis underlined the need for a complete break with imperialism and the Empire, and the readiness to support any national liberation or nationalist organisation, whatever its class leadership, providing it was genuinely fighting against imperialism. It warned, however, that:

"'independence' will have no real meaning until it is achieved through the overthrow of Imperialism by a united working-class movement embracing the peasantry, and all the exploited peoples of the Empire."

Experience was to prove that when at a later period of history the socialist system had grown strong in the world and there was a new relation of international class forces more could be achieved under

---

[1] *Report of 7th Congress of C.P.G.B.*, pp. 194–196.   [2] Ibid., pp. 196–197.

bourgeois-led national movements. But experience was to show, too, that *political* independence once won, there were still many struggles to wage before full economic all-round independence could be achieved. The warning, therefore, was not without significance.

The Resolution dealt with the more practical side of the fight against imperialism. It expressed determination to end the shame of a Labour Movement in the metropolitan country "sharing the prejudices and ideology of the British bourgeoisie on colonial exploitation and rule". The Communist Party, it declared:

"is determined to reverse this role of the British Labour movement."

It called on all members of the Party to:

"take up the fight against the imperialist prejudices still existing amongst large sections of the working class in Great Britain."

It appealed to the Party to do everything possible to raise inside the Labour Party and the T.U.C. the issues of imperialism and solidarity with the colonial peoples.

At the Eighth Congress of the Party (October 1926) the Seventh Congress Resolution on Imperialism was reaffirmed.[1] Some successes in the struggle (in particular the fight at the 1925 Scarborough T.U.C.) were listed, and once again it was underlined:

"It is more than ever the attitude of the Communist Party to continue the work against imperialism and it must be one of its more important tasks to mobilise the support of the working class of this country for the workers and peasants of the oppressed countries in their struggle for independence."[2]

FULFILLING THE RESOLUTIONS

One of the ways of fulfilling these resolutions was the constant treatment of imperialism, the continuous publication of news of the national liberation struggle in the Party press and in publications or journals that the Party could influence. A study of the *Workers' Weekly*, of the *Communist Review* and *Labour Monthly*, of the pamphlets and leaflets of the 1925–1926 period, speak well for the sincerity of the effort to bring this question sharply and continually before the British Movement.[3]

During this period there were a number of specific campaigns or

---
[1] *Report of 8th Congress of C.P.G.B.*, pp. 80–81.   [2] Ibid., p. 80.
[3] See Appendix I to this chapter on *Party Press and Publications on Imperialism, 1925–1926*.

Campaign Weeks organised by the Party on issues relating to imperialism and war.

In February 1925 a week's campaign was organised (February 8–15) "Against Imperialism and White Terror" jointly with the British section of the International Class War Prisoner's Aid (I.C.W.P.A.).[1] Meetings were held in London, Manchester, Birmingham, Glasgow, Edinburgh, Plymouth, South Wales, etc. Particular stress was given to the conditions in the Indian prisons, the treatment of political prisoners in India, and famine relief in Ireland. Indian speakers and Jim Larkin, the Irish working-class leader, spoke along with Saklatvala and leaders of the British Party.

Anti-War Weeks were organised by the Party in both 1925 and 1926,[2] maintaining a tradition started in August 1924. In the 1925 campaign Open Letters were sent by the Party to the General Council of the T.U.C. and the Labour Party Executive asking that they should take steps to bring to the members of the British armed forces some understanding of the pending capitalist offensive.

In the 1926 campaign an issue of the *Workers' Weekly* was devoted entirely to the question of imperialism and war. Very incomplete reports reveal the holding of some 95 meetings, the distribution of 100,000 leaflets,[3] but the campaign was somewhat pushed into the background by activity around the miners' lock-out.

It should be added that throughout the period there was a constant effort by the Party itself to find ways of speaking to the soldiers and sailors, to explain to them the political background of capitalist Britain, and to help them to understand their links with their fellow workers in industry and the dangers of being used by the Government as instruments to repress progressive industrial and political action. This was not easy work. And it was apt to meet with arrest and repression. But the Party, in this period of capitalist offensive at home and abroad, felt that it was a duty. As Tom Bell put it at the Seventh Congress:

> "We are taking on definite work among the forces of the British military machine. We must ever keep before the army and navy, the class solidarity and identity of interests between the workers in the armed forces of the State and the workers in the workshops, and try to secure a greater bond of solidarity between all these."

[1] See *Workers' Weekly*, Nos. 104 and 105, January 30 and February 6, 1925, also *Report of 7th Congress of C.P.G.B.*, p. 154.
[2] Political Report of C.C. to Eighth Congress in *Report of 8th Congress of C.P.G.B.*, p. 15.
[3] Organising Report of C.C. to Eighth Congress in *Report of 8th Congress*, p. 48.

But perhaps the most important aspect in this period of the Party's struggle against imperialism was its initiative in bringing the issue before the national congresses of the Labour Party and the T.U.C., not only on particular issues like Egypt and China (which we examine separately) but the general issue of the nature of imperialism and the fight against it.

The 1925 Scarborough Congress of the T.U.C. was, as we have seen, a militant congress, in which the left was united, in which Communist and non-Communist militants worked together and isolated the right wing, not only on questions of the coming offensive at home, but on questions of foreign policy and international affairs. It was a time of close collaboration of Communist leaders in the trade unions like Harry Pollitt with many of the left trade union leaders and this collaboration was seen in presenting to the Scarborough T.U.C. the Resolution on Imperialism.[1]

A. A. Purcell, speaking for the Furnishing Trades' Association, moved that:

"This Trades Union Congress believes that the domination of non-British peoples by the British Government is a form of capitalist exploitation having for its object the securing for British capitalists (1) of cheap sources of raw materials; (2) the right to exploit cheap and unorganised labour and to use the competition of that labour to degrade the workers' standards in Great Britain.

"It declares its complete opposition to Imperialism, and resolves: (1) to support the workers in all parts of the British Empire to organise the Trade Unions and political parties in order to further their interests, and (2) to support the right of all peoples in the British Empire to self-determination including the right to choose complete separation from the Empire."

This was a resolution of the greatest significance and which, ever since, the right wing in the Labour Movement has done its best to revise or to forget. Naturally enough it was opposed by J. H. Thomas, who tried to imply that it was "ridiculous". But Thomas was followed by Harry Pollitt who, whenever he could, liked to follow Thomas in trade union debates,[2] and who used the short three minutes at his disposal with great effect. "This resolution", he said,

[1] See *Report of 57th Annual T.U.C.*, Scarborough, pp. 553–555. The "Resolution on Imperialism" had been put forward under Communist initiative within a branch of the Furnishing Trades' Association, and then upwards through the union machinery.

[2] See Harry Pollitt, *Serving My Time*, p. 206.

"was simply a clear definition of what the policy of the working-class movement should be towards the subject peoples of the Empire. British Imperialism meant the appalling conditions they saw today amongst the textile workers of Bombay and Calcutta, it meant women going down the mines and doing 36 hours work at a stretch, and it meant that the people had no right of combination and no legal redress. Imperialism meant the slavery which existed in Kenya at the present time. It meant that the principles they went into war for should be preserved. Empire to the whole of the exploited races of the world simply meant that they were being exploited by a set of capitalists. The Indian workers could not hold a strike meeting without being shot. The Egyptians could not go on strike without being shot. China was being held down by Britain and America.

"If they passed this Resolution they would give a message of encouragement and hope to their fellow workers all over the world who did not look upon the Union Jack as the last word in economic equity and political freedom. . . . It was an Empire in which every single yard of territory was drenched with the blood of British soldiers and of native soldiers who tried to keep British soldiers out of their country. Empire was simply tyranny and exploitation. . . ."

Thomas might think the resolution "ridiculous". The Congress, however, adopted it by 3,082,000 votes to 79,000. This was a signal victory for the Marxist approach to imperialism.

The Liverpool Labour Party Conference of 1925 was a big step backwards from the Scarborough T.U.C. And this was so not only on home affairs, but on world issues too. A vague and wordy resolution was moved by the Rt. Hon. J. R. Clynes (on behalf of the Executive of the Labour Party) on "A Labour Policy for the British Commonwealth of Nations".[1] It represented a complete retreat from the Scarborough resolution of the T.U.C. Instead of the outright condemnation of imperialism there was a call for closer political relations between the States of the British Commonwealth and for a "scientific redistribution" of population within the Commonwealth. Whilst it politely criticised the "evils of capitalist exploitation of the tropical and sub-tropical regions of the British Commonwealth of Nations", as a remedy it called for the "safeguard of the natives' right to the land", the supervision of recruitment of labour, the control of the use of

---

[1] See resolution and debate on it in *Report of 25th Annual Conference of the Labour Party*, Liverpool, 1925, pp. 228–236.

capital—all within the Empire—and asked the League of Nations (at that time completely dominated by imperialist powers) to elaborate a code for the protection of native rights.

An amendment was moved and seconded by militants, C. J. Moody of the Richmond Labour Party and Trades Council (then a Communist), and W. T. Colyer of the Holborn Labour Party, which in fact was an *entirely new resolution*, analysing and condemning British imperialism and ending with a call for "the speediest possible realisation of the principle of self-government and complete independence".

Just before a resolution on "putting the vote", Gallacher, on a point of order, enquired "whether in the event of the Resolution being carried, the Labour Party was pledged to fight to defend the Empire in the process of developing it into a 'socialist Empire'". But nobody cared (or dared) to answer him. The amendment was lost and the resolution carried. It was significant that this resolution, a classic of reformism, of reform *within the framework of the British Empire*, was seconded by Roden Buxton of the I.L.P.

A resolution on *Foreign Policy*[1] which *inter alia* recorded with "pride and appreciation" the nine months' foreign policy of the Labour Government, was also seconded by a representative (E. E. Hunter) of the I.L.P., who declared that he had been

"proud to see one of the members of the I.L.P., Mr. Ramsay MacDonald, taking a leading part in the work of stabilising the international situation throughout the length and the breadth of the world."

Again a militant amendment, moved and seconded by M. Jacobs of the Bethnal Green Labour Party and C. J. Moody, supported by Harry Pollitt (who analysed and criticised the Dawes Plan, supported in the same debate by Ramsay MacDonald) and by W. Gallacher, was defeated, and the resolution adopted.

Liverpool was a big step back, but at least the anti-imperialist positions of Scarborough were strongly defended by a group of Communist and left Labour delegates, including Pollitt and Gallacher.

The Margate Conference of the Labour Party (October 1926) was held in still more difficult conditions for the militants.

A very dilute, milk-and-water resolution on *Imperialism* was moved, calling for reforms *within* an accepted Empire, asking that "in all

---

[1] For resolution and debate on it see *Report of 25th Annual Conference of the Labour Party*, Liverpool, 1925, pp. 252–260.

non-self-governing parts of the Empire" we should restore "the natives'" right to the land, see that they were educated for self-government, and fight against industrial conscription.[1]

When this was carried a further much more militant resolution, well in the Scarborough tradition, was moved by John Gibbons for the Wimbledon, Morden and Merton Labour Party:

> "That the Labour Party Conference believes that it is only possible to maintain the British Empire by the forcible domination and exploitation of hundreds of millions of coloured workers. It therefore sends greetings to our coloured brothers struggling to be free, and declares it is with them in their opposition to Imperialism, and supports their demands for self-determination, even to the point of seceding from the Empire."

It was opposed by the Rt. Hon. J. R. Clynes, whose statements should be recorded for some future textbook of reformism. "In his judgement":

> "it *was* possible to maintain the British Empire—or, he would prefer to call it, the British Commonwealth, without forcible domination and without the exploitation of hundreds of millions of workers. The job of their Party for the moment was to watch over the interests of their fellow subjects in all parts of the Empire. . . ."

To pass Mr. Gibbon's resolution, he continued:

> "would be one more act of denouncing their own country, whether right or wrong, and they could not afford to throw away such popularity as they now had by such an unnecessarily provocative resolution."

Who could have put it better? The reformist position was defence of Empire; at best reforms *within it*, at worst the condoning of armed repressive imperialist action to *preserve the Empire* (in order to reform it?). To support the anti-imperialist struggle meant the loss of popularity (with whom?) and provocation (who would be provoked, not 95 per cent of the population of the colonial countries?).

Against this line, the Communists, with their colleagues and allies in the left of the Labour Party and trade union movement, fought to condemn imperialism and with it the British Empire, and for active

[1] For resolution, amendment and debate see *Report of 26th Annual Conference of the Labour Party*, Margate, 1926, pp. 252-253.

solidarity with all anti-imperialist forces, for the complete right of self-determination, *without reserve and without delay.*

SOLIDARITY AROUND THE WORLD

Solidarity was shown in many forms and on many diverse issues. On Communist initiative the more militant workers came to know the nefarious activities of their rulers in many parts of the "far-flung Empire", and of the national liberation efforts of the colonial and semi-colonial peoples.

On several occasions in the 1925-1926 period the Party raised the issues of Egypt and the Sudan.

At the beginning of November 1924 six Egyptian Communists were arrested (including Hosny El Oraby, who was the Secretary of the small Egyptian Communist Party) and given three-year sentences. The British Communist Party called for solidarity and at the same time began to campaign for the withdrawal of British troops from Egypt.[1]

A little later, on November 19, 1924, Sir Lee Stack, the British Governor-General of the Sudan, was assassinated and this became a pretext for the British Tory Government to tighten its hold on the Sudan, to insist on the evacuation of Egyptian troops from that land, and to launch a general attack on the nationalist Egyptian Government headed by Zaghoul Pasha. The Egyptian Parliament was closed down, an ultimatum delivered to the theoretically "independent" (imperialist style independence "with reserves") Egyptian Government, the Custom House at Alexandria occupied by British troops.

The Communist Party Executive issued a manifesto denouncing the British ultimatum,[2] explaining that the British Government was using the murder of Sir Lee Stack as a pretext for taking control of the Sudan into its own hands and thus obtaining a stranglehold on Egypt by control of the upper reaches of the Nile, that the British Government was afraid of the Egyptian nationalist Government and therefore was putting a puppet in its place.

The Party, through the *Workers' Weekly*, effectively revealed the reasons for Britain's "sensitivity" to the slightest democratic developments in Egypt or the Sudan. *It is Loot that They are After* was the title of an explanatory article by Gallacher.[3] Another was entitled "History"[4]

[1] *Workers' Weekly*, No. 93, November 14, 1924, p. 3.
[2] Ibid., No. 95, November 28, 1924, pp. 1 and 4.
[3] Ibid., p. 4.   [4] Ibid.

It quoted Mr. Gladstone *in 1882* that "it is our object to take the greatest care that the occupation of Egypt does not take a permanent character" or, four months later (December 1882), Lord Granville, the Foreign Minister, who wrote to the Egyptian Government to intimate "that it is the desire of Her Majesty's Government to withdraw the troops from Egypt as soon as circumstances permit". They were still there in 1922 when Egypt's "independence" was formally proclaimed. And "History", showed that, in November 1924, they were *still* there.

When the British Party Council met on November 30, 1924[1], it discussed the position in Egypt and again demanded the *complete* withdrawal of British troops and *complete* self-determination for the Egyptian and Sudanese peoples.[2] At the same time it issued an appeal to all Labour M.P.'s to support the national striving in these countries.[3]

The Party also, and very aptly, reproduced in the *Workers' Weekly* the magnificent anti-imperialist poem of Francis Adams—"England in Egypt".[4]

---

[1] See Chapter V, p. 336.   [2] *Workers' Weekly*, No. 96, December 5, 1924, p. 4.   [3] Ibid.
[4] Ibid. Francis Adams's book of revolutionary poetry, *Songs of the Army of the Night*, was first published in Australia in 1887, and reproduced in London in 1890. When Adams died he left two revised copies of the *Songs* into which he had written "England in Egypt" and a few other poems, and from one of these the posthumous edition of 1894 was printed. Perhaps a couple of verses at least belong to this History, as it was the Party who fought to bring them back to the British Labour Movement.

> And the silent Arabs crowded, half-defiant, half dismayed.
> And the jaunty fifers flung their challenge to the breeze,
> And the drummers kneed their drums up as the reckless drumsticks played,
> And the Tommies all came trooping, tripping, slouching at their ease.
> Ah! Christ, the love I bore them for their brave hearts and strong hands,
> Ah! Christ, the hate that smote me for their stupid dull conceits—
> I know not which was greater, as I watched their conquering bands,
> In the dusty jaded sunlight of the sullen Cairo streets.

> And my dream of love and hate
> Surged, and broke, and gathered there,
> As I heard the fifes and drums,
> The fifes and drums of England,
> Thrilling all the alien air!—
> And "Tommy, Tommy, Tommy,"—
> I heard the wild fifes cry,
> "Will you never know the England
> For which men, not fools, should die?"
> And "Tommy, Tommy, Tommy,"
> I heard the fierce drums roar
> "Will you always be a cut-throat
> And a slave for evermore?"

During that December 1924, the Party maintained its pressure on the Egyptian question, and at the same time attacked the approach of the right-wing Labour leaders.[1] When in that month C. P. Trevelyan for the Labour Party raised the issue of Egypt in Parliament, Chamberlain was able to reply for the Tories that the Conservative Government was simply continuing the policy of MacDonald during the first Labour Government, and to read out a despatch from MacDonald on which that policy was based:

> "I found that despatch when I entered office. The first telegram of consequence that I sent to Lord Allenby was founded upon that despatch and the policy that His Majesty's Government have pursued throughout the crisis is the policy for which that despatch was prepared."

The Seventh Congress of the C.P.G.B. (May–June 1925) reported on the Party's activity around the Egyptian question[2] and action was continued into 1926.[3] It was also developed by Communists and left-wing Labour Party members inside the Labour Party and the trade unions. At the Liverpool Labour Party Conference (September–October 1925) Herbert Morrison, supported by C. P. Trevelyan for the I.L.P., moved an evasive resolution on Egypt proposing to hand over to the League of Nations the problems of Suez, the control of the Nile water, and the Sudan (which in the context of that date meant to take them away from imperialism and hand them back to imperialism). An amendment was moved by W. T. Colyer for the Holborn Labour Party proposing that the issue of the Nile should be solved between Egypt and the Sudan. The important thing, he said, was to take control of the Nile and of the Sudan out of the hands of imperialism.

From the end of 1924 to the end of 1926 there were repeated activities by the Communist Party in defence of Communists and anti-imperialists suffering political persecution in India, like the four Communist leaders (including Dange, Das Gupta, Shaukat Usmani and Muzaffar Ahmed) condemned to four years' imprisonment for the co-called "Cawnpore Conspiracy"[4] In the summer of 1925 the Party organised a campaign of support for the Indian textile workers who had been locked out to secure a 11 per cent wage cut, and succeeded in securing

---

[1] *Workers' Weekly*, Nos. 97 and 98, December 12 and 19, 1924.
[2] *Report of 7th Congress of C.P.G.B.*, p. 137 and p. 153.
[3] *Workers' Weekly*, Nos. 171–173, May 28, June 4 and June 11, 192'.
[4] Ibid., No. 93, November 14, 1924, p. 3.

the opening of a Lock-out Fund which realised over £1,000.[1] Saklatvala repeatedly raised in Parliament the issue of Indian independence and the conditions of the Indian workers, just as he had raised the issue of Egypt. He strongly opposed in Parliament, in February 1926, the British Government's decision to prolong the British "mandate" in Iraq, but the Government was once again able to put forward the defence that it was but "continuing" the policy of the previous Labour Government.[2]

Contact with and support for the struggle in Ireland was raised by W. Gallacher at the Seventh Congress of the C.P.G.B.[3] At the same Congress a resolution, moved by Tom Bell, was adopted on the situation in Morocco, pledging support for "the Moroccans and the other African peoples in their struggle against both French and British imperialism".[4]

One of the issues raised by Saklatvala in the House of Commons on behalf of the Party was the British base at Singapore, so often justified by the imperialists as the gateway to the East:

> "The world is round and every spot of surface on the world can be described as the gate to somewhere and to somebody's country. The Straits of Gibraltar is a gateway because it is a narrow neck of water. The Cape of Good Hope is a gateway because it is at the head of a vast expanse of ocean. Colombo is a gateway because it is in the middle of the Indian Ocean and Singapore is in the middle of the Pacific Ocean."[5]

The Party began in this period to campaign against the colour bar in South Africa, particularly in relation to the passing of a new Colour Bar Bill in mid-1925. It attacked General Hertzog's statement that "we are determined to make South Africa a White Man's Country", and strongly criticised the South African Labour Party for its support for the Bill. The British Labour Party, wrote the *Workers' Weekly* in June 1926, should denounce this Bill and ally itself with the coloured people, "otherwise all talk of equality of peoples, etc., is empty, futile talk".[6]

---

[1] Political Report of C.C. to Eighth Congress C.P.G.B., *Report of 8th Congress*, p.15.
[2] *Workers' Weekly*, No. 160, February 26, 1926.
[3] *Report of 7th Congress of C.P.G.B.*, p. 90.
[4] Ibid., p. 99.
[5] *Workers' Weekly*, No. 112, March 27, 1925, p. 2.
[6] Ibid., No. 175, June 25, 1926, p. 1.

"HANDS OFF CHINA"

The most important anti-imperialist campaign carried on by the Party over these two years was for solidarity with the national-liberation forces in China, the campaign for "Hands off China".

Solidarity with the Chinese workers and people developed in two main streams which eventually merged into one. In mid-1925 it took the form of support for the great strikes, particularly the strikes of the Shanghai textile workers, and protest against foreign participation in their suppression. But very soon the support for the Chinese strikers became part of a wider movement of solidarity with the national liberation movement fighting for independence from foreign, including British, imperialism.

The British Communist Party at the time described the Chinese struggles in many articles in the *Workers' Weekly* and Party press. The two particular Party publications dealing with China—*Murder—An Indictment of British Imperialism in China*,[1] and *The War in China*[2]—stand up remarkably well when checked against modern Chinese accounts of the struggles of those days.[3]

By 1925 foreign capitalism dominated every field of Chinese industry and finance and the greater part of the Chinese working class worked for foreign rather than for Chinese masters. It is easy, therefore, to see why a movement of economic struggle on wages and hours and conditions should become so speedily part of a general movement against foreign imperialism. Both the Hong Kong seamen's strike of 1922 and the Shanghai textile workers' strike of the following year were directed in the main against *foreign* capital.

In 1925 a big strike movement began in the textile mills of Shanghai, at first in those that were Japanese-owned, where exploitation and oppression were particularly ruthless.[4] Strikes began in February 1925, affecting at first some 40,000 workers. Police in the International Settlement of Shanghai began to attempt the suppression of the strikers, killing and wounding many.

[1] Pamphlet, 20 pp., published by C.P.G.B. mid 1925.
[2] Pamphlet, 24 pp., *id.*, C.P.G.B. early 1927.
[3] For instance Hu Sheng, *Imperialism and Chinese Politics*, Foreign Languages Press, Peking, 1955, and Ho Kan-chih, *A History of the Modern Chinese Revolution*, Foreign Language Press, Peking, 1959.
[4] Between 1913–1925 the proportion of spindles in the Japanese-owned factories in China out of the total number in China rose from 13·6 to 45·3 per cent. See Ho Kan-chih, op. cit., p. 89.

The strikes spread. Strikers gave their support to the great anti-imperialist struggles and the national movement added support to the strikes. On May 28 the Central Committee of the Communist Party of China discussed the need of linking still more closely the economic struggle of the workers with the anti-imperialist struggle.[1] Communist initiative played a great role in the vast demonstrations of May 30 in Shanghai—demonstrations of students and workers. The movement (later known as the May 30 movement) spread all over the country, joined by workers, students and merchants. And the more it met foreign repression—British, American, Japanese warships and troops—the more it extended. The biggest of the ensuing struggles was the great Canton-Hong Kong Strike, which lasted 16 months from June 1925 to October 1926.

By 1925 too, the Nationalist or Republican Government was firmly established at Canton and taking measures to extend its power all over China. To accomplish this meant defeating the old warlords, like Chang Tso-lin in the north or Wu Pei-fu in Honan, who were backed and aided by the arms and the navies of Britain, U.S.A., Japan and the other foreign would-be owners of China.

In mid-1926, from its base in Canton, the Revolutionary Army started its great Northern Expedition, which Sun Yat-sen had planned before his untimely death in 1925. "The purpose of the expedition," Sun Yat-sen had written:

"is not only to overthrow the warlords but also to drive out imperialism upon which the warlords in China depend for their existence."[2]

As the Revolutionary Army moved north, winning victory after victory, defeating Wu Pei-fu and the other warlords, enthusiastically supported by the working class, peasants and other sections of the working people, imperialist intervention became more and more dangerous. The British capitalist press was calling for large-scale war "to defend British interests" and "protect British lives". Gunboat diplomacy was the order of the day. Rumours were spread that the Soviet Union was "behind" the Chinese Revolutionary Army, and intervention against China was seen in some circles as a prelude to a new anti-Soviet war.

It was only towards the end of 1926, when the victories of the Revolutionary Army had become so extensive, when Hankow had

[1] Ibid., p. 92.
[2] *Complete Works of Sun Yat-sen*, Vol. I, pp. 65-66.

fallen, when their victory seemed inevitable, that British imperialism, with its characteristic cunning, began to change its tactics and plot to turn the right wing of the victorious Kuomintang (the wing of the big comprador bourgoisie) against the Communists and the militants.

Shanghai strikes had started again in February 1925. By May there was a mass strike movement. By June a quarter of a million workers up and down the country were on strike, whilst hundreds of workers and students had been killed or wounded by the foreign police of the foreign "concessions". British, French, Japanese warships and gunboats were "merrily" shooting off their guns.

The *Workers' Weekly* wrote:

"The British Labour Movement must demand not only the withdrawal of British troops, but also the abolition of all special privileges for foreigners, of all foreign control over the Chinese railways and revenues, no interference with the internal affairs of China in any shape or form whatsoever."[1]

The Party appealed to the Executive of the Labour Party to convene a conference of all sections of the Labour Movement to consider steps to help the Chinese people in their struggles for independence.[2]

The General Council of the T.U.C., which in this period was responsive to the feelings of its left and militant wing, telegraphed in mid-June:

"The General Council is confident that the united stand the Chinese workers are making will result in the firm establishment of militant industrial organisation in China, and will do much to build up a powerful bond of unity between Eastern and Western Trade Unionism."[3]

The Communist Party welcomed this statement, but asked that it be followed by *practical* measures, by the formation of a representative "Hands off China" Committee, by efforts to stop imperialist intervention in China, by the sending of leaflets to soldiers who were being used to break the strike, by the prevention of the transport of munitions for China, by demands for the abolition of all special privileges for foreigners.

On June 19 the Political Bureau of the Party discussed the Chinese question. On June 23 it took further steps for the organisation of

[1] *Workers' Weekly*, No. 123, June 12, 1925, p. 1.
[2] Ibid., No. 124, June 19, 1925, p. 1.   [3] Quoted ibid., p. 3.

meetings.[1] By July resolutions of solidarity with the Chinese workers were coming in from trade union branches and branches of the Labour Party. A thousand people attended a "Hands Off China" meeting at Bethnal Green, organised by the Communist Party and Young Communist League.[2] The Minority Movement began to mobilise its supporters, and in August the Second Annual Conference of the N.M.M. launched an appeal for financial aid for the Chinese workers.[3]

The Party stressed at its "Hands Off China" meetings and in its writings that the Chinese workers and people were fighting *a common struggle against a common enemy*. R. Palme Dutt wrote at this time:

"The struggle in China is important to the British workers not because we take a liberal paternal philanthropic interest, from our superior height, in improving the 'conditions' of the Chinese factory workers, but because the Chinese masses are our brothers in arms, fighting our common fight, the fight of all humanity against the imperialist exploiters.

"We do not share the hypocritical attitude of the Labour representatives in Parliament, who speak of a 'common purpose' with Baldwin and the first necessity of 'protecting British lives' which means in fact using guns and bayonets to maintain the stranglehold of the British opium lords and sweaters in China. . . .

"What matters is that the present grip in China is being maintained by British soldiers, marines, guns and bayonets. To get these off China is our first duty . . . the complete withdrawal of all British forces and garrisons from China—this is the only possible position for the British working class."[4]

The Hull Trades Union Congress, in September 1924, had instructed the General Council to arrange an examination of conditions of the workers of the East. By mid-1925 the General Council was not only receiving reports of the great Shanghai strikes, but details of the appalling situation in the Shanghai mills where conditions prevailed reminiscent of the earliest days of the British industrial revolution, above all in *the foreign-owned mills*. Reports showed adult factory workers on a 14–16-hour day, young children in the mills at the age of

---

[1] *Minutes*, Party Records.   [2] *Workers' Weekly*, No. 126, July 3, 1925.
[3] Executive Report to Second Conference. See also George Hardy speaking at the Extended Meeting of the Executive Committee of the Communist International in February–March 1926, *Orders from Moscow*, pp. 41–42.
[4] R. Palme Dutt, "Notes of the Month", *Labour Monthly*, Vol. 7, No. 8, August 1925, pp. 454–455.

five, babies and infants sleeping on filthy mill floors whilst their mothers worked, complete lack of safety precautions, starvation wages.

The appeals of the Communists, Minority Movement and militants fell on fertile soil, therefore, at the Scarborough T.U.C., where a Communist, A. G. Tomkins of the Furnishing Trades' Association, (a union where the Communists and militants were strong) moved a resolution (which was accepted) instructing the General Council to get in touch with the organised workers:

> "with a view to doing everything possible to put a stop to the murderous crimes being perpetrated against our working class Chinese comrades who are struggling to improve their horrible working conditions."

And condemning:

> "in the strongest possible language the use of British armed forces as strikebreakers in the interests of the gang of unscrupulous capitalists and imperialists who are exploiting the lives of men, women and even children of tender age in China at the present time, and insists on their immediate withdrawal."[2]

Seconding, V. Beacham of the House Painters and Decorators, and a member of the Communist Party, ended his speech by declaring that the atrocities in China surely:

> "justified even modest trade unionists in taking up propaganda or publicity amongst their comrades, the soldiers and sailors, who were called upon to do that dirty work."

Under the impulse of the "Hands off China" campaign in Britain even the Liverpool Conference of the Labour Party (September–October 1925), reaction-dominated as it was, adopted a resolution, moved by Ben Tillett of the Transport and General Workers, recording its indignation:

> "at the recent murdering of Chinese workers and students"

protesting at:

> "the conditions endured by the Chinese workers as a result of their exploitation not only in the Chinese mills, but also by British and Japanese capital . . ."

[1] See *Report of 1925 Scarborough T.U.C.*, pp. 314–315.   [2] Ibid., pp. 487–488.

and calling upon the Government:

> "to treat the Chinese people as a Sovereign state responsible for their own Government: to enter freely into negotiations with that Government for the revision of all the Treaties imposed upon them...."[1]

1926 was the year of the great "expeditions" of the Chinese Republican (Canton) Government and its revolutionary armies against the warlords. As we have seen, "against the warlords" meant, inevitably, "against the imperialists". In March 1926, the Kuomintang telegraphed to the T.U.C., Labour Party, I.L.P. and "Hands off China" Society, calling for action to restrain the British Government from intervention in China.[2]

No sooner was the General Strike concluded, than, despite the mass of "home" problems that assailed it, the Communist Party turned again to "Hands Off China", by now a very urgent issue.[3]

The *Workers' Weekly* campaigned against British intervention in China and the threats of full-scale war:

> "Only the efforts of the organised movement can prevent war. It is a foul lie to state that the intervention is to protect British lives...."[4]

It was apt and fitting that it was Arthur Horner—Communist and miner—who moved (and got carried) an emergency resolution of solidarity with the Chinese people at the Bournemouth T.U.C. (September 6-11, 1926), stressing the danger of intervention not only against China, but the Soviet Union:

> "Seeing that the war clouds are gathering in the East, and that we understand that Chang So Ling,[5] the War Lord, has already seized ships which belong to the Chinese Eastern Railway owned by the U.S.S.R., and it is clear that this action would not have been undertaken without the promised help and support of the Conservative Governments of Great Britain and Japan, this Congress protests against any action of the imperialist governments which might lead to a new war either in the Far East or in the West...."[6]

---

[1] *Report of 25th Annual Conference of Labour Party*, Liverpool, 1925, pp. 260-261.
[2] *Workers' Weekly*, No. 164, March 26, 1926, p. 3.
[3] See, for instance, *Workers' Weekly*, No. 170, May 21, 1926, p. 3—the first issue after the General Strike.
[4] *Workers' Weekly*, No. 186, September 10, 1926.
[5] We have used the spelling Chang Tso-lin above.
[6] *Report of Bournemouth 1926 T.U.C.*, pp. 488-489.

Throughout September 1926, the C.P.G.B. extended the campaign for "Hands Off China" in leaflets, meetings, contributions at trade union gatherings. It worked to persuade Trades Councils to organise special delegate conferences, it called for support for the Kuomintang's overseas fund, it appealed for the formation of local "Hands Off China" committees.[1]

Early in October the Executive Committee of the Party adopted a clear and moving resolution on the Chinese question, giving the history of British intervention in China and of the Chinese workers and anti-imperialist struggles, and again calling for "Hands Off China", for recognition of the Chinese National Republican Government and for the immediate evacuation of "all armed forces, naval and military, from Chinese waters and territories". The resolution remains to this day an excellent summary of the whole question.[2] At its Eighth Congress (October 1926,) the Party discussed the development of the campaign,[3] and accorded an enthusiastic reception to the fraternal delegate of the Kuomintang (introduced by Gallacher), who spoke of the support in China for the British General Strike and the British miners' struggle. Congress adopted a resolution, moved by Arthur MacManus, greeting the struggle of the Chinese national movement, and again demanding the withdrawal of all British army and naval forces from Chinese territory.

The feeling in British Labour circles was growing strong. The Trades Councils, and the London Trades Council especially, were active by this time in the "Hands Off China" campaign, and this itself reflected Communist and militant influence.[4] So strong was the feeling that, once again, a reaction-dominated Labour Party Conference—the Margate Conference (October 11-15, 1926)—"welcomed the national and democratic tendencies among the Chinese People", protested at the bombardment of Wanshien by British naval forces, but omitted the demand for the withdrawal of British warships from Chinese territorial waters.[5]

---

[1] See *Workers' Weekly*, Nos. 188 and 189, September 24 and October 1, 1926.
[2] Full text of this resolution in Appendix II to this chapter.
[3] *Report of 8th Congress of C.P.G.B.*, pp. 13-14.
[4] The London Trades Council had taken an active interest in the Chinese revolutionary movement already in mid-1925 demanding the withdrawal of British armed forces from Shanghai, and condemning the activities of British-controlled Sikh police in firing on unarmed strikers there (June 11, 1925). Support for the "Hands off China" Committee was continuous (Decisions of September 9, October 28, and November 11, 1926). See *London Trades Council, 1860-1950*, p. 126.
[5] *Report of 26th Annual Conference of the Labour Party* pp. 255-256. The I.L.P. delegate, Mr. Scurr, who seconded the resolution, protested at this omission.

By the end of the year, the sweeping victories of the Chinese Revolutionary Army, the successive defeats of various warlords, caused the British Government to think again.

If the nationalist forces were bound to win, how could they be diverted? How could they be split? How could the defeat of Britain's interventionary plans and of her warlord allies be turned into a victory?

How? To find out how was the task given to the new Minister to China, Miles Lampson. Very creditably, the British Communist Party, who knew something of the wiles of its rulers, perceived and warned of this new danger.

The British capitalists, wrote the *Workers' Weekly*, early in November 1926:

> "have recognised the inevitable in the victory of the Kuomintang ... their policy is subtly changing from that of the brute force to the wooing over into the imperialist camp of the 'Right' or anti-Communist wing of the Kuomintang Party."

And it warned:

> "If the British imperialists are successful through their new representative in Pekin, Miles Lampson, in splitting the united national front, then the day of the interventionist will come again."[1]

At the end of December it warned again in a statement of the Central Committee:

> "... the Central Committee declares that the danger of military action against the Chinese Revolution is increased rather than diminished by the latest manœuvres of the British Government. It condemns all attempts to show that policy in a specific light and calls upon the whole Labour movement to form active 'Hands Off China' Committees to work for ever closer relations with the Chinese workers. ...
>
> "For the unconditional recognition of the Chinese Republic!
>
> "For the cancelling of unequal treaties, concessions!
>
> "For the complete withdrawal of foreign armed forces from China!"[2]

These warnings, alas, were all too prophetic.

[1] *Workers' Weekly*, No. 195, November 12, 1926, p. 1.
[2] Executive Committee of C.P.G.B., "Statement on 'Events in China'", December 23, 1926.

AID TO VICTIMS OF REACTION

During this period, from the end of 1924 to the end of 1926, there was a continuous effort by the Party, in association with such organisations as the Workers International Relief (W.I.R.) and the International Class War Prisoners Aid (I.C.W.P.A.), to express solidarity with the struggles and aid for the sufferings of the working people all over the world. In this there was a marked degree of unity at least within the left of the Labour Movement, and men like George Lansbury of the Labour Party and Alex Gossip of the Furnishing Trades' Association played an outstanding part in all these efforts. It was, however, in this same period that organisations of this kind, which had a specific aim that should have been common to all sections of the Labour and socialist movement, and which had indeed been founded in unity, began to come under fire from right-wing officialdom, and the notorious bans and proscriptions, already extended to the Communist Party, began to be extended into further fields.

In January 1925 a delegation from the W.I.R.[1] met the Joint International Section of the Labour Party and the T.U.C. which demanded that all W.I.R. activity should be clearly disassociated from political propaganda and all funds that it collected devoted to specific works of relief. The Annual Conference of the W.I.R. was held in the Battersea Town Hall in April 1925, with George Lansbury in the chair and with Jim Larkin and Mrs. Despard amongst the speakers.[2] The 264 delegates who attended the conference devoted a great part of their time to the question of Irish famine relief. They also decided to accept the demands of the Labour Party and T.U.C. But the T.U.C. and Labour Party were still unsatisfied. At the Liverpool Labour Party Conference, Alex Gossip moved the reference back of the relevant section of the Annual Report, but this was defeated.[3]

The British Section of the I.C.W.P.A. had been established in December 1924, with the aim of organising aid for political prisoners in all parts of the world.[4] We have already seen something of its work for

---

[1] Mrs. Helen Crawfurd, G. C. T. Giles and Alex Gossip, the first two Communists, the third a Labour Party trade union leader. See *Report of Liverpool 1925 Labour Party Conference*, p. 62.

[2] Ibid., see also *Workers' Weekly*, No. 116, April 24, 1925.

[3] Ibid., pp. 200–201.

[4] Ibid., No. 101, January 1925, article by Wal Hannington "What is the International Class War Prisoners Aid?"

British political prisoners. The Communist Party gave full support to it, again in association with numerous militant Labour Party and trade union leaders. A resolution was moved at the Seventh Congress of the Communist Party (May–June 1925) on *White Terror*, expressing support for the I.C.W.P.A. and calling for aid for the political prisoners in Bulgaria, Esthonia, Germany, Hungary, Ireland, Poland and Rumania.[1] A special message of support was sent at the same Congress to the workers suffering under the Bulgarian White Terror.[2] Said Harry Pollitt in the Chairman's opening address:

"Everywhere the working-class movement is persecuted. In Esthonia, Poland, Bulgaria, and Rumania, thousands of the very best have been taken from us, and every conceivable method of torture is inflicted upon prisoners in the jails of Esthonia and Poland in particular. Everywhere terror is perpetrated against members of the Communist International. But those who have gone, have gone with the satisfaction of knowing that this great movement of which they were part, will surely have its vengeance. They know that our enemies will never sweep back the rising tide of Communism. They know that those now dealing out justice will one day themselves be dealt with by the working class."[3]

And so almost every week Communist Party and I.C.W.P.A., nearly always with the support of militants from the Labour Party, I.L.P. and trade unions, campaigned for the victims of political persecution in different parts of the world—Bulgaria, Esthonia, for the Hungarian Communist Rakosi (who was condemned after a prolonged trial to eight and a half years imprisonment in August 1926). Money was collected, delegations sent to embassies, lawyers despatched for the defence, publicity organised, relief given to the families of the arrested and imprisoned.

One of the most active campaigns was that in defence of Sacco and Vanzetti, the American anarchists unjustly arrested (and eventually killed). By August 1926 scores of trade union branches, branches of the Labour Party, I.L.P. and Communist Party, together with more than 50 Labour M.P.'s, had in one way or another called for their release. Solidarity with the German workers was continued throughout the whole period, ranging from particular campaigns for the aid of arrested

[1] *Report of 7th Congress*, pp. 18–20.
[2] Ibid., p. 4–5.
[3] Ibid., p. 9.

workers to a general campaign against the Dawes Plan and, later, the Locarno Pact.[1]

Communists and militants opposed the right-wing Labour leaders who supported the Dawes Plan. At the Scarborough T.U.C. (September 1925) a resolution condemning the Dawes Plan was moved by J. Strain of the Amalgamated Society of Woodworkers, then a Communist, supported by A. J. Cook and Harry Pollitt, and, despite opposition, carried by a large majority.[2]

RELATIONS WITH THE SOVIET UNION AND THE SOVIET TRADE UNIONS

The issue of relations with the Soviet Union remained, of course, contentious during the whole of these two years, but was not under such strain as in the immediate years before or the immediate years to come. The Party continued to campaign for decent trade, diplomatic and cultural relations with the U.S.S.R., raising the issue in trade union and Labour Party fields, at public meetings and in the press.

There were one or two moments when anti-Soviet attacks by the Government and its press were especially violent[3]—in connection with Chinese affairs in the summer of 1925 and again towards the end of 1926, also in the period immediately following the General Strike—and at these moments the Party raised the level of its activity. From the autumn of 1925 it began to explain the nature of the Locarno Pact not only as a continuation of the Dawes Plan but as a pact directed in the first instance against the Soviet Union.[4]

Ever since its foundation the Communist Party had been trying to combat the continuous, fantastic propaganda barrage of British capitalism—newspapers, journals, radio, books—and at times of British reformism, against the Soviet Union, a barrage of slander which in these early years ranged from "indiscriminate assassination" to the "nationalisation of women."

The Party tried to reproduce the documents of the Soviet Government, Party, trade unions, to publish reports of honest visitors even

[1] See "A Student of the Revolution"—"The Pact of Locarno", *Communist Review*, Vol. 6, No. 8, December 1925, pp. 350-362.
[2] *Report of Scarborough 1925 T.U.C.*, pp. 542-546.
[3] See Political Report of Central Committee to Eighth Congress, *Report of 8th Congress of C.P.G.B.*, pp. 14-15.
[4] Ibid., p. 15.

when they were critical, to organise different forms of contact between workers in the Soviet Union and Britain.

Of extreme importance, therefore, was the publication of the report of the official British Trade Union Delegation which visited the U.S.S.R. in November and December 1924,[1] because when this 250-page report was published by the T.U.C. in 1925, it was seen to confirm, not the Red-baiting ravings of the Tory press or of right-wing reformism, but the main contentions of the Communist Party. It was hard to accuse this representative delegation, which consisted of six respected members of the General Council and the Secretary of the T.U.C.,[2] of secret Communist affiliations, the more so as it was assisted by "advisory delegates" who knew the Russian language.

It was this delegation which summing up its findings declared:

"(1) *On Politics*

". . . this Delegation is of opinion that the Soviet system of representation and its scheme of constitutional and civil rights, so far from being undemocratic in the widest sense of the word, gives in many respects a more real and reasonable opportunity of participation in public affairs than does parliamentary and party government. . . .[3]

"(2) *On Industry*

". . . the present Delegation has come to the conclusion that the existing economic system is not only viable, but has real vitality; that it does not stunt but can even stimulate the economic recovery that peace has now made possible. . . .[4]

"(3) *Red Army*

". . . It is evident to the delegation that in the Red Army a soldier is not only a citizen, but that his soldiering is utilised to instruct him in citizenship, and that discipline does not seem to suffer thereby.[5]

---

[1] *Russia: The Official Report of the British Trade Union Delegation to Russia and Caucasia, November and December 1924*, 250 pp., T.U.C., 1925.

[2] It consisted of Herbert Smith of the Miners' Federation, Ben Tillett of the Transport and General Workers, John Turner, long time leader of the Shop Assistants' Union, John Bromley, M.P., of the Society of Locomotive Engineers and Firemen, Alan A. H. Findlay, of the United Patternmakers' Association, A. A. Purcell of the Furnishing Trades' Association and Fred Bramley, Secretary of the T.U.C.—all members of the General Council.

[3] *Report*, p. 17.
[4] Ibid., p. 59.
[5] Ibid., p. 88.

"*(4) On the Judiciary*

"The conclusion reached by the Delegation in the matter of law and order is that public order is now on a footing well above that in most Continental countries; that justice is equitably enforced in the new courts, and under new Codes that constitute a judicial system still in its youth, but adequate for its present purpose. . . .[1]

"*(5) Social and Religious Conditions*

"The Delegation is . . . strongly of the opinion that, as a result of the new social system, the Russian nation is acquiring great social benefits in culture, recreation and freedom of self-expression; and that the moral tone is likely to be greatly improved by the new status acquired by women.[2]

"*(6) Education, Press, Art, etc.*

". . . it will be realised that every opportunity and encouragement is given to the worker, no matter what may be his or her calling, to obtain the best instruction in any branch of art, industry, science or literature for which he may feel he has an aptitude. The results which were seen by the Delegation in all the districts visited were certainly astounding, especially when it is considered that the whole system has not yet been in operation for three years. . . . The pathetic feature in our own civilisation of wasted and dormant talent the slave of circumstance, owing to the absence of all possibility of outlet or instruction through lack of means, seems likely to become very rare among the workers of Russia."[3]

And so it continued. Perhaps it is hardly necessary to note that the report was received with fury and indignation by the British capitalist press and conspicuous lack of enthusiasm by MacDonald and his companions. On the shoulders of the Communist Party, indeed, fell a large degree of the responsibility for making it known in the Labour Movement.

It is hard to imagine MacDonald, Thomas and those in the leadership who had from the first maligned the Soviet Revolution, welcoming the delegation's statement in the chapter on trade unions that "in Russia the workers are the ruling class",[4] or their "final conclusions" that:

". . . the Delegation has come to the following conclusions: that the U.S.S.R. is a strong and stable State; that its Government is based

[1] Ibid., p. 98.   [2] Ibid., p. 108.   [3] Ibid., p. 121.   [4] Ibid., p. 136.

firstly on a system of state Socialism that has the active support of a large majority of the workers and the acceptance of an equally large majority of the peasants, and, secondly, on a federal structure that gives very full cultural and very fair political liberties to racial and regional minorities, together with full religious toleration: that the machinery of Government though fundamentally different from that of other States seems to work well, and that the government it gives is not only in every way better than anything that Russia has ever yet had, but that it has done and is doing work in which other older State systems have failed and are still failing. . . .[1]

Equally, it is not difficult to understand that the Communist Party welcomed the report, which, though perhaps it did not with full clarity explain the *reasons* for the successes there in reporting the role of the Communist Party, of Marxist ideas, of the socialist revolution—faithfully reported what the delegates' eyes had seen and what their ears had heard. After all, it was such things that—against the stream—the Communist Party had been trying to make known since it was first founded.

ANGLO-SOVIET TRADE UNION RELATIONS

The period of growing militancy and left unity in 1925 had also been reflected in closer relations between the British and Soviet trade unions, and we have seen[2] how in 1925 the Anglo-Soviet Trade Union Committee was established, and how the two trade union movements took the lead in working for international trade union unity.

A testing moment came during the General Strike. Financial and political help for the British strikers came from the working class of many countries—Belgium, Canada, China, Czechoslovakia, Denmark, France, Germany, Holland, India, Japan, New Zealand, Norway, Poland, Sweden, United States, several countries of Latin America, and other lands as well.[3] The Communist International and the Red International of Labour Unions (R.I.L.U.) were active in the campaign for both financial aid and for an embargo on transport of "black" cargoes to Britain. Many of the sections of the Second International and of the International Federation of Trade Unions were also active but

[1] *Report*, p. 171.   [2] *Chapter I*, pp. 13–21.
[3] See *Sunday Worker*, May 16, 1926, pp. 4 and 5; Hutt, op. cit., p. 145; T.U.C., *The Mining Crisis*, p. 57, etc.

their International leaderships refused all proposals for a united campaign and remained relatively passive.

As soon as the General Strike began, the All-Russian Council of Trade Unions (A.R.C.T.U.) moved into action.

On May 5 a special session of the A.R.C.T.U. was convened in conjunction with the Central Committees of the different Russian unions. The Chairman, Tomsky, declared:

"such a strike as this is a new phenomenon in history. Thanks to the collective participation of the British workers, the miners' lock-out has developed into a gigantic general strike . . . help must be given without delay, for the matter is urgent. Our business is promptly to organise a campaign in support of the British workers."[1]

It was agreed that all organised workers in the U.S.S.R. should at once contribute one quarter of a day's wages to support the British strikers and that 250,000 roubles from A.R.C.T.U. funds and the funds of the individual unions should be despatched at once to Britain as an earnest of what was to come. This was despatched on May 6 to the General Council. On May 7 a further 2 million roubles was despatched.

Apart from financial aid, the Central Committees of the Russian Water Transport Workers and of the Local Transport Workers Union issued an instruction to dockers in all Soviet ports to prevent the loading of ships bound for British ports and the supply of such ships with fuel. The Local Transport Workers Union telegraphed to all concerned:

"Take measures to prevent the shipping of such [bound for Britain] freight from all ports, and also of any freight which you have reason to believe may be transhipped to Britain from other countries. The loading of ships from England is only permissible upon instruction from the British General Council."[2]

The General Council, however, was not grateful. They were yielding already to capitalist pressure and when the British capitalists shouted aloud "Red Gold", the General Council bowed to the blackmail. A laconic statement in the *British Worker* of May 8 declared:

"The Council has informed the Russian Trade Unions, in a courteous communication, that they are unable to accept the offer and the cheque has been returned."

[1] *Red Money*, prepared by the All-Russian Council of Trade Unions, published by Labour Research Department, October 1926, p. 16.
[2] Ibid., p. 23.

It was not much consolation to the British strikers to be thus so courteously betrayed nor to the Russian workers that their aid should be so courteously repudiated.

The Soviet trade unions, however, at this stage, kept their tempers, and decided that the money collected and rejected should be given to the British miners, and that collections, to be put at the disposal of the Miners' Federation of Great Britain, should be continued. When the General Strike had ended, the money was handed over to the Soviet miners for transmission to their comrades in Britain, and when A. J. Cook was asked whether and where it should be sent, he wired back: "The British miners are in desperate need of it."[1] Some £270,000 was at once transmitted.[2] The Soviet trade unions' embargo on transport of all cargoes to Great Britain was continued until May 19, and then lifted *except for oil and coal*.[3]

Collection continued despite, following the General Strike, a rabid anti-Soviet campaign by Tory spokesmen who accused the Soviet Government of fomenting strife in Britain with Moscow Gold. All the hoary old slanders were revived. The *Morning Post* reports, for instance, a typical gathering of anti-Soviet incitement:

> "The General Strike, Sir Henry Page-Croft[4] continued, was announced by Zinoviev in Moscow six weeks before it took place as due for the first week in May. I want to warn you, he added, most seriously, that the Government of Russia is making war on our country day by day. Mr. Cook ('Shoot him! Lynch him') has declared that he is a Bolshevik and is proud to be a humble disciple of Lenin. He is treating the miners of this country whom we all respect and honour—(cheers)—as 'cannon fodder' in order to achieve his vainglorious ambitions. . . . We are met here tonight to tell the Government that we support them in any step that they think necessary at the present time. Give the Arcos[5] and all those others who have come to make trouble in our midst 48 hours' notice. (Loud and prolonged cheers.)"[6]

---

[1] *Red Money*, p. 26–27.
[2] *Workers' Weekly*, No. 171, May 28, 1926, p. 3.
[3] Ibid., No. 173, June 11, 1926, p. 1.
[4] A Tory M.P., subsequently Lord Croft.
[5] Arcos was a joint stock company registered in Great Britain in accordance with British law. It was housed in the same building as the Trade Delegation of the U.S.S.R. in Britain. See W. P. and Zelda Coates—*History of Anglo-Relations*, Vol. I, pp. 266 ff. It was later to be raided by the British police.
[6] *Morning Post*, July 16, 1926.

Reporting the same meeting the *Daily News* revealed:

> "The speakers vied with one another in coining choice epithets to apply to Soviet agents and supporters. These were samples: Hired vilifiers; purveyors of sedition; scum of our gutters; outpourings of foreign sinks; mercenaries of Moscow; mad Mullahs of socialism; swindling syndicate; aliens and animals; microbes of Bolshevism."[1]

Collections continued. By the beginning of October 1926, Soviet trade unionists had contributed £832,000 for relief of the British miners,[2] and the final total was to be around £1,250,000.[3] This was no small effort. The total received in the General Council's 'National Strike Fund' (May 4–December 31, 1926) was £137,000 and in its 'Special Miners Appeal Fund' (August 21–December 31, 1926) £94,000 of which the I.F.T.U. contributed £35,000 and £80,000 respectively.[4]

But now relations between the British and Soviet trade unions began to deteriorate. The General Council had sold out, and knew it. The Soviet trade unions knew it too, and were no longer content to be silent. The majority of Soviet trade union leaders were *for* the continuation of the Anglo-Soviet Trade Union Committee, though they came under fire from Trotsky and a minority group of leftists in the Communist Party of the Soviet Union and in the Communist International who took a completely negative view of the role of the British workers in the General Strike and wanted the dissolution of the Anglo-Soviet Committee.

The All-Russian Council of Trade Unions wanted the Anglo-Soviet Committee to continue, but to continue *actively*, and, in the first place *to organise aid for the British miners*. Moreover they felt, rightly or wrongly, that they had the duty of expressing publicly their criticism of the conduct of the General Council, the right-wing reformist and the silent "left" within the General Council during the General Strike.

Early in July the All-Russian Council of Trade Unions despatched an urgent telegram to the General Council asking for an immediate

---

[1] *Daily News*, July 16, 1926. The meeting, held in the Albert Hall, London, on July 5, was reported by *The Times* to have been attended by 7,000 people and to have been addressed amongst others by Colonel John Gretton, M.P. (who presided), Commander Locker-Lampson, M.P., Sir Hamar Greenwood, M.P., and Mr. Mitchel Banks, M.P.

[2] *Red Money*, Introductory Note.

[3] W. P. and Z. Coates, op. cit., p. 228.

[4] *Mining Dispute National Strike*, report of General Council to Conference of Affiliated Unions, pp. 53 and 57.

meeting of the Anglo-Russian Committee with the object of organising further aid for the British miners.[1]

A little later the All-Russian Council published a *Manifesto on the General Strike*.[2] Why was the General Strike defeated, the manifesto began, despite the magnificent showing of the British workers? It outlined a number of reasons. Defeat was due in the first place to the right-wing leaders of the General Council and the Labour Party—men like MacDonald and Thomas. It was due to the capitulation of the "Left"—Hicks, Purcell, etc. It was due to "the incapacity of the present leaders of the British workers . . . to lead the great struggle of the workers against the capitalist class with all the necessary consistency and resolution". It was not the strike weapon that was bankrupt but the General Council that was supposed to lead the strike.

The Russian manifesto criticised the General Council for refusal to accept the money collected by the Russian workers. There was still, it declared, "necessity of a firm union between the workers of Britain and the U.S.S.R." "That is why", it continued:

"in spite of the fact that the Trade Union leaders have inflicted a heavy blow upon the British working class, upon the cause of international unity and upon the Anglo-Russian Committee we not only do not propose the abolition of the Anglo-Russian Committee, but call for its whole-hearted revival, strengthening and intensification of its activity."

The General Strike, the manifesto concluded, had shown the "incapacity and futility of the International Federation of Trades Unions", by its passivity and indifference towards "the greatest strike in the world". It had revealed the need for "a single class-conscious effective international of trade unions".

No militant in Britain, no Communist or active miner, could have found fault with the criticisms outlined. Indeed, similar criticisms had been made *much earlier* by the British Communists, by miners' leaders like A. J. Cook and others. The contentious issue was should the Russian trade unions have taken it on themselves to raise publicly their views concerning the *British* working-class movement as part of its correspondence and contact with the British trade unions? A majority of the Political Bureau of the British Communist Party was at the time critical of the Russian manifesto precisely on these grounds, considering that it

---

[1] *Workers' Weekly*, No. 177, July 9, 1926, p. 1.
[2] Ibid., No. 178, July 16, 1926, p. 4.

could lend itself to the accusation of interference in British affairs, and be used against Anglo-Russian trade union unity,[1] and a protest was made to the Executive Committee of the Communist International.[2]

A meeting of the Anglo-Russian Committee held in Paris at the end of July could reach no agreement, and decisions were postponed till a later meeting. The Russian delegates wanted the Committee to campaign in support of the miners and to this the General Council would not agree.[3] The next meeting was held in Berlin in the following August.

Immediately disagreement arose around the agenda, on which the Soviet delegates wanted the first point to be aid for the British miners, whilst the General Council representatives considered that this was not strictly within the competence of the Committee, but, in the end, agreed to the Soviet request.

The Soviet delegation, then, put forward a 14-point set of proposals in connection with the British miners' struggle. It welcomed this continued struggle, declared that the most urgent need was an embargo on the transport of coal and other fuel to Britain and within Britain. It criticised the I.F.T.U.'s lack of solidarity. It called on the General Council to be more energetic in the organisation of financial aid for the miners. It wanted both the Russian and British trade unions to call on the unions for a 1 per cent levy on wages in aid of the miners, and it wanted the General Council to press the Labour Party into greater and more effective action on behalf of the miners.[4]

The British delegation would not accept these proposals. All this, it said, had already been considered and carried out inside Britain, and action by the Anglo-Russian Committee on such issues would do more harm than good.

The Soviet delegation, in its turn, strongly criticised the General Council's position. How could it say that "all had been done"? The Miners' Federation had to date received £740,000 of which around £500,000 had been collected by Russian trade unionists. Was that adequate? What had been "done", it asked about the embargo, when Churchill could claim that one million tons of coal was being imported

---

[1] This was reported at the Executive Meeting of July 7, 1926 (Party Records).
[2] This protest was also voiced by J. T. Murphy, on behalf of the C.P.G.B. at the meeting of the Presidium of the Executive Committee of the Communist International on August 7, 1926. Stalin spoke at this meeting against the protest. See J. V. Stalin, *Works*, Vol. 8, p. 204–214
[3] *Workers' Weekly*, No. 186, September 10, 1926, p. 5.
[4] Ibid.

weekly into Britain? How could it be said that the Anglo-Russian Committee was "incompetent" to aid the British miners?

Thus, once again, the meeting ended without agreement, and with a further deterioration of relations. This deterioration continued further at the time of the Bournemouth T.U.C. at the beginning of September 1926.[1]

The British Government had refused to grant visas for the Soviet delegation, no doubt aided in this decision by the fact that the General Council was by no means eager at this time to receive their Russian colleagues. The General Council had indeed protested, but an Emergency Resolution put to the Congress by the miners was not taken, and when Arthur Horner, on the miners' behalf, moved the reference back of the relevant section of the Report, this was rejected by Congress.

A telegram from the All-Russian Council of Trade Unions to the Congress was circulated, again raising criticisms of the General Council's conduct in the General Strike and lack of support for the miners since the end of the strike. Support for the miners, it said, was the central question of the whole international trade union movement. Despite these criticisms, it called for the continuation and strengthening of the Anglo-Russian Committee.

The General Council had circulated this message, but felt it necessary:

"to register the strongest possible protest at what can only be regarded as a most regrettable abuse of the ordinary courtesies expected of fraternal delegates."

Towards the end of October the All-Russian Council of Trade Unions issued a fresh appeal for continued support for the British miners. By September 28, it stated, of the £1,261,326 which had been received by the miners around £823,000 or 66 per cent had been collected by Soviet workers. Aid should be increased.

The British Communist Party was strongly opposed to those leftist groups in the Communist Party of the Soviet Union and in the Communist International who wanted to bring to an end the Anglo-Russian Trade Union Committee. They were themselves doing everything they could to win support for the British miners—whether by finance or embargo. Naturally enough, they welcomed the aid given the Soviet workers. There was some difference of opinion, as we have seen, not on the Soviet trade unionists' critique of the General Council,

[1] See *Report of 58th T.U.C.*, pp. 463-464, and 509-511.

but on the method and place of expressing it. Amongst the miners there was strong support for the Soviet effort, and no feeling whatsoever that the aid given was being used for political interference. Arthur Horner, looking back to those days, after many years, has written:

"I must say that in the discussions which Cook and I had with the Soviet trade union leaders, they made no attempt at all to influence the policy of the M.F.G.B. in return for the assistance they had given us. They acted in the real spirit of working-class solidarity and, despite their own poverty, they gave us more than one million pounds."[1]

C.P.G.B. AND COMMUNIST INTERNATIONAL

The Fifth Congress of the Communist International was held in Moscow, June 17-July 8, 1924, i.e. in the period of the first Labour Government in Britain.[2] During the period between the end of 1924 and the Eighth Congress of the C.P.G.B. (October 1926) there were no further congresses of the International, but two Extended Plenums of its Executive Committee, the Fifth in March-April 1925[3] and the Sixth in February-March 1926.[4] A report on the Fifth Plenum was given by W. Gallacher at the Seventh Congress of the C.P.G.B. and the discussions at the Sixth Plenum were reported to the Party in pamphlet form.[5]

A special Organising Conference preceeded the Fifth Plenum, and at this "satisfaction was expressed" with the progress made by the British Party.[6] At the same time the need was stressed for a greater organisational unity in the central leadership of the Party, and the importance stressed of building factory groups.[7] The Executive of the C.P.G.B. reported to the Seventh Congress that:

"the relations of the Party with the Communist International have been cordial. There has been no difference of opinion regarding the

---

[1] Arthur Horner, *Incorrigible Rebel*, p. 94, MacGibbon & Kee, 1960.
[2] The British delegation to the Fifth Congress was E. H. Brown, E. Douglas, Bert Joy, A. MacManus, J. T. Murphy, Mrs. Robinson, Bob Stewart and J. R. Wilson, with W. Rust and D. F. Springhall from the Y.C.L. See *Report of 7th Congress of C.P.G.B.*, p. 142.
[3] Attended by George Allison, Thomas Bell, E. H. Brown, W. Gallacher, A. Geddes and W. Rust.
[4] See Appendix III to this chapter.
[5] *Orders From Moscow*, C.P.G.B., 61 pp., August 1926.
[6] Gallacher's report to Seventh Congress C.P.G.B., *Report of 7th Congress of C.P.G.B.*, pp. 89-90.
[7] Ibid., p. 90.

nature of the situation in Great Britain, nor of the tasks which the Party should pursue in this situation."[1]

At the Sixth Plenum of E.C.C.I.[2] (February–March 1926) there was a special discussion on the situation in Britain, and a resolution was prepared with the help of the C.P.G.B.[3] In general, the resolution warmly approved the work of the British Party:

> "The Communist Party has played an important and leading role in developing the revolutionising of the working class struggle of Great Britain. Its successes in this field have been achieved thanks to its quick response to the day-to-day struggles of the workers and its correct application of the united front."

Amongst the aspects of British Party activity singled out for praise were the unity of the leadership, the lack of factionalism, experience of trade union struggle, struggle for affiliation to the Labour Party, the combination of the fight of the unemployed with that of the employed workers, the campaigning for international trade union unity, the consistent support for the miners, the struggles for solidarity with the colonial workers, and the attention drawn in the mass movement to the importance of winning the armed forces to the side of the labour movement.

It was recommended that all this should be continued, and attention was drawn above all to strengthening the Party membership and the Young Communist League, winnning women into working-class struggle, elaborating a policy for agriculture and, above all, preparing to meet the capitalist offensive.

In June 1926 the Executive of the Communist International discussed the British General Strike and adopted the thesis which we have already discussed. Again there was substantial agreement with the C.P.G.B. and general approval for the attitude of British Communists during the strike. The criticisms made by a leftist group in the International were overwhelmingly rejected.

In general there were no special problems during this period between the British Party and the Communist International. It was after the Eighth Congress of the C.P.G.B. (October 1926) that problems began to arise, and these belong to the next volume.

---

[1] Ibid., pp. 139–140.
[2] Attended by E. H. Brown, Aitken Ferguson, George Hardy, R. W. Robson with D. F. Springhall and W. Rust from Y.C.L.
[3] *Orders from Moscow*, pp. 55–61.

The discussions at the Fifth Congress of the Communist International on the attitude of Trotsky within the Russian Communist Party and within the International, and the condemnation of his attitude, were brought to the attention of the British Party.

At the Party Council meeting of November 30, 1924, the matter was discussed and a resolution adopted approving the position taken up by the Soviet Party and by the International.[1]

Disagreement with this resolution was expressed at a London aggregate of the Party on January 17, 1925, when Arthur E. E. Reade moved an amendment regretting "the hasty vote" of the Party Council. The amendment was rejected by a big majority.[2]

At the Seventh Congress of the C.P.G.B. (May–June 1925) a resolution on Trotskyism was moved by Thomas Bell[3] reaffirming the decision of the Party Council and declaring:

"complete agreement with the Central Committee of the Russian Communist Party in its estimation of the principles of Trotskyism and the measures taken to combat them."

The criticism levelled against Trotsky at this time was not one of conspiracy or counter-revolution. His considerable services to the revolution were recognised,[4] but his theories and attitudes within the Russian Communist Party and within the International were considered harmful, and a rallying point for opposition to the building of socialism in the U.S.S.R.

The question of Trotskyism was raised anew in the British Party in the summer of 1926 in connection with Trotsky's attitude to the role of the British Communists in the General Strike[5] and to his demand for the disbandment of the Anglo-Soviet Trade Union "Joint Advisory Council".[6]

---

[1] *Workers' Weekly*, No. 96, December 5, 1924, p. 2. *The Truth about Trotsky* by T. Bell. See also "Trotskyism—a Peril to the Party", by C. M. Roebuck in *Workers' Weekly*, No. 103, January 23, 1925.

[2] The *Workers' Weekly* at the time reported that the amendment received 10 votes out of 300 present. A. Reade in a letter stated that it was 15 votes out of 200. Arthur Reade was later suspended by the Political Bureau from the London District Party Committee. His appeal against this decision was rejected by the Executive Committee on April 26, 1925 (Minutes).

[3] *Report of 7th Congress of C.P.G.B.*, pp. 116–118.

[4] See Gallacher at *7th Congress of C.P.G.B.*, p. 85.

[5] Trotsky's article (or rather collection of fragments) published in the *Communist International*, No. 22, of 1926, present a picture of a helpless Communist Party. It also contains an acutely sectarian approach to the left in the Labour Movement.

[6] See resolution of the Political Bureau on "Discussion in the C.P.S.U.", adopted August 9, 1926, in *Workers' Weekly*, No. 182, August 13, 1926.

CHAPTER IV—APPENDIX I
PARTY PRESS AND PUBLICATIONS ON IMPERIALISM, 1925–1926

A full list of Party writings on imperialism would need a chapter in itself. Here are a few incomplete indications to bear witness to its activity in this respect during the 1925–1926 period:

(a) From *Communist Review*, Volumes 6 and 7 (May 1925–January 1927)

Author	Article	Issue
M.H.D.	Blood or Cotton (on East Africa)	July 1925
H. P. Rathbone	Should the Empire be Broken Up?	Aug. 1925
A. MacManus	The British Commonwealth Conference	Sept. 1925
—	Our Empire (on Palestine)	Sept. 1925
A. MacManus	Mosul and Irak	Oct. 1925
"A Student of The Revolution"	The Pact of Locarno	Dec. 1925
H. P. Rathbone	The Reality behind the Freedom of the Dominions	Jan. 1926
J. Crossley	The Rising Tide in Syria and the Near East	Jan. 1926
J. D. McDougall	The Struggle for Supremacy in the Pacific	Feb. 1926
J. D. McDougall	The Political Groupings in the Pacific	March 1926
D. Ramsay	The Negro Arrives (on Africa)	April 1926
J. Crossley	Britain Annexes the Sudan	April 1926
A. MacManus	Labour Imperialism (on Reformism and Empire)	July 1926
Agit-Prop Dept.	The Fight against War	Aug. 1926
J. McDougall	The Anglo-French Conflict in the Near East	Sept. 1926
E. N. Armitage	Indian Currency	Nov. 1926
M. N. Roy	The British Imperial Conference	Dec. 1926
C. P. Dutt	Results of the Imperial Conference	Jan. 1927

(b) *Labour Monthly,* 1925–1926

Author	Article	Issue
U.D.C.	*The Diplomacy of Mr. Ramsay MacDonald,* I	Jan. 1925
M. N. Roy	*The Empire and the Proletariat*	Jan. 1925
U.D.C.	*The Diplomacy of Mr. Ramsay MacDonald,* II	Feb. 1925
J. T. Walton Newbold	*Diddling Them with Dawes* (on the Dawes Plan)	Feb. 1925
Evelyn Roy	*Indian Political Exiles in France*	April 1925
M. Abdullah	*The Trust of Empire and Mr. MacDonald a Trustee*	April 1925
Tang Chin Che	*Sun Yat Sen's Life and Work*	May 1925
Scott Nearing	*The Labour Situation in West Canada*	May 1925
Henri Barbusse	*The Roy Case: a Protest*	May 1925
Jacques Doriot	*The New War in Morocco*	June 1925
Clemens Dutt	*Indian Politics: an Analysis*	July 1925
W. N. Ewer	*The Writing on the Chinese Wall*	July 1925
Tien Sen Shiao	*"Face Pidgin"—The Chinese Struggle*	Aug. 1925
Allen Hutt	*The Riff War of Independence*	Aug. 1925
W. N. Ewer	*Hatching a War with Russia*	Sept. 1925
Maurice Spector	*The Empire Labour Conference*	Sept. 1925
R. Page Arnot	*The Far Eastern Tangle*	Oct. 1925
W. N. Ewer	*Getting Mosul into Perspective*	Nov. 1925
Karl Marx	*India under British Rule*	Dec. 1925
J. Crossley	*Egypt at the Crossroads*	Jan. 1926
D. Riazanov	*Karl Marx on China*	Feb. 1926
M. G. Desai	*Colour versus Class in South Africa*	March 1926
Karl Marx	*The Revolution in China and in Europe*	March 1926
W. N. Ewer	*The Mosul Victory*	Aug. 1926
Col. C. L. Malone	*Canton*	Aug. 1926
Clemens Dutt	*British Labour and India*	Sept. 1926

Author	Article	Issue
Ralph Fox	*Fascist Imperialism*	Sept. 1926
P.R.S.	*Empire and Socialism in Australia*	Oct. 1926
Maurice Spector	*Where is Canada Heading For?*	Oct. 1926
Eugen Varga	*Mexico Today*	Nov. 1926
Stewart Smith	*The Results of the Canadian Elections*	Nov. 1926

and in nearly every issue of *Labour Monthly* during this issue the question of imperialism is treated in R. P. Dutt's "Notes of the Month".

(c) Publications and Leaflets between Sixth and Seventh Congress of the Party, treating of imperialism (12 months May 1924–May 1925)

V. I. Lenin, *Imperialism* (a new edition was prepared).
R. P. Dutt, *Empire "Socialism"* (5,000 copies), 2d. pamphlet.

Leaflets[1]

Persecution of Indian Workers (50,000)
Hands off the Soviets (25,000)
Imperialist Terrorism in India (20,000)
The War on the German Workers (25,000)
War What For? (Cartoon) (50,000)
War What for? (100,000)
Women Workers against War (15,000)
Lenin's Lash for Pacifist Hypocrites (50,000)
British Workers and Colonial Workers (50,000)
Back the Russian Treaties (75,000)

CHAPTER IV—APPENDIX II

RESOLUTION ON CHINA

Adopted by meeting of Executive Committee of C.P.G.B. early October 1926[2]

The revolutionary struggle which is taking place in China is of the utmost importance for the British working-class.

It is the struggle of the Chinese against enslavement by foreign imperialism using as its tool the decaying feudal class.

The chief of the imperialist powers engaged in the exploitation of

---

[1] *Report of 7th Congress of C.P.G.B.*, p. 152.
[2] *Workers' Weekly*, No. 190, October 8, 1926, p. 4.

China is Great Britain which has for nearly a century been the leader of the international brigands who have used naval and military force to extort from the Chinese people territorial and financial concessions.

By means of unequal treaties foreign powers are enabled to maintain armed forces, special police, and their own law courts in China. They have monopolised the customs and salt tax and taken away from China the use of her chief sea ports.

British Capitalism, by using to the full these privileges, has built up in China an unheard of system of exploitation of the peasantry and working class.

BELOW SLAVERY

The Chinese coolie employed in the textile factories of Shanghai and the coal mines of Central China has been degraded below the level of slavery.

This degradation of the Chinese workers will be used by the British capitalists for the further degradation of the British workers.

The aim of British diplomacy in China has been and still is to support anarchic semi-feudal generals like Wu-Pei-Fu in order to prevent the Chinese people from obtaining the national unity which should have come as a natural result of the Republican Revolution in 1911.

In May 1925, the workers of Shanghai struck against the shameful and unbearable exploitation imposed on them by their British masters. The reply of the imperialists was to massacre the strikers.

When the democratic republic of Canton demonstrated against the Shanghai massacre British troops shot down the peaceful demonstrators from ambush in the Island of Shameen.

Finally, only last month British gunboats bombarded the open city of Wanhsien, killing and wounding many thousands of innocent men, women and children.

Incidents like these demonstrate the brutality and "frightfulness" of British capitalism; they also explain the intense anti-British sentiment that is so evident in China.

The Democratic Republic of Canton, founded in 1924 by Sun Yat Sen on the three principles of national freedom, democracy, and socialism, has led the fight for liberation. Today the armies of the Canton Republic, which are controlled by the Kuomintang (People's Party), have united China up to the Yang-tse River and are marching on Shanghai, hailed by the whole population as deliverers.

DESPERATION

British capitalism sees a fruitful field of profit disappearing and is making a desperate effort to reconcile the rival powers interested in the exploitation of China with a view to intervention.

Wild stories are being spread in the press to the effect that behind the Chinese Revolution stands the Union of Socialist Soviet Republics. While it is true that the U.S.S.R. has alone treated the Chinese as equals and has recognised the National Government, it is ridiculous to try and make them responsible for the fruits of generations of atrocities and oppression by Great Britain and other powers.

Intervention in China is only the prelude to intervention against Soviet Russia and the final crushing of the militant working class movement throughout the world. It is the prelude to fresh imperialist wars in the Pacific arising out of the mutual rivalries of Great Britain, Japan and the United States.

WHOLE MOVEMENT

The Central Committee of the Communist Party of Great Britain calls upon the organised working class in Great Britain to support the Chinese struggle for national freedom, to demand that the Government immediately recognises the Chinese National Republican Government at Canton and evacuates immediately all armed forces, naval and military, from Chinese waters and territories.

The Central Committee of the C.P.G.B. further calls upon the Labour Party and the T.U.C. to cooperate with it in fighting the danger of intervention and in putting forward the demand for summoning immediately a conference of the Powers concerned to abolish the unequal treaties and effect the complete recognition of the Chinese National Republic.

CHAPTER IV—APPENDIX III

CONGRESSES AND EXTENDED PLENUMS OF THE COMMUNIST INTERNATIONAL, 1919-1926[1]

Congress	Extended Plenum of E.C.C.I.	Date
First		March 2-6, 1919
Second		July 19-August 7, 1920
Third		June 22-July 12, 1921
	First	February 21-March 4, 1922
	Second	June 7-11, 1922
Fourth		November 5-December 5, 1922
	Third	June 12-23, 1923
	Fourth	June 12-13, 1924
Fifth		June 17-July 8, 1924
	Fifth	March 21-April 6, 1925[2]
	Sixth	February 17-March 15, 1926
	Seventh	November 22-December 16, 1926

[1] *Kommunisticheskii Internatsional v. Dokumentakh, 1919-1932*, Moscow 1933.

[2] In December 1924 there was an important discussion on the British question at a meeting of the Presidium of E.C.C.I.

CHAPTER V

COMMUNIST PARTY—LIFE AND ORGANISATION
1925–1926

For a Mass Party—Forms of Leadership—Factory Groups—Factory Papers—Building the Party—The Districts—Party Press—Party Training—The Y.C.L., 1925–1926

FOR A MASS PARTY

The discussions amongst Communists that followed the fiasco of the first Labour Government turned, naturally enough, in part around the nature and role of the Communist Party. The more life showed the total incapacity of the Labour Party, with its reformist leadership and reformist ideas, to lead the way to socialism, the more responsibility seemed to fall on the shoulders of the Communist Party.

The whole period 1925–1926 was again and again to force this issue to the fore. The employers' offensive, the refusal of the right-wing leaders of T.U.C. and Labour Party to prepare, the sell-out of the General Strike, the renewed and still more ruthless employers' offensive, the exposure of reformism, and the ineptitude of the I.L.P. and "left" trade union group, kept leading back to the same question—what was the alternative?

And if it was the Communist Party, how could the Party be extended and improved? The "mass Party" became a central slogan, and, in the words current in the Communist International at the time, "the Bolshevisation of the Communist Party". It was the discussion of how to "Bolshevise" the Party that dominated the organisational side of the discussion at the Seventh Congress of the C.P.G.B., held at Glasgow from May 30–June 1, 1925,[1] where theses on the Mass Party and on Bolshevisation were discussed and adopted.

"Bolshevisation of the Party" was defined as:

"its transformation into a mass organisation, saturated with the ideas of Marxism and Leninism, and capable of utilising them in the most varying circumstances and in most varied ways, according

[1] See "Thesis on the Mass Party", *Report of 7th Congress C.P.G.B.*, pp. 165–168, and "Thesis on Bolshevisation", ibid., pp. 198–202.

to the concrete circumstances of the moment, and always for the preparation of the proletarian revolution."[1]

For many British militant workers there was something "alien", "foreign-sounding", about words and slogans like "Bolshevisation". And experience shows that it would have been better that the ideas contained in the slogans had been presented in terms more proper and comprehensible to the British working-class movement, for there was nothing alien in the ideas.[2]

For the Party at the time, "Bolshevisation" meant a large party, a "mass Party", a party with roots in, close contact with, the mass of the workers, a party with scientific socialist, Marxist-Leninist principles, a party that could apply the general principles of socialism to the particular problems of Britain in the mid-twenties, a party so organised that it could effectively lead the workers in the struggles that confronted them. In 1925-1926, and most specifically at the Seventh Congress at Glasgow, the three main tasks put to the Party in this connection were to increase the membership, raise the level of Party training in socialist principles, and the reorganisation of the Party so far as possible on the basis of factory groups.

FORMS OF LEADERSHIP

There were no great changes in the forms of Party leadership between the Sixth (May 1924) and Seventh (May-June 1925) Congress of the Party, nor between the Seventh and the Eighth (October 1926) Congresses.

Between the Sixth and the Seventh Congress a number of Open Sessions of the Executive Committee were held in different parts of the country—Manchester, London, Birmingham—to which comrades were invited from the area of venue.[3] This was an experiment aimed at a closer relationship between the leadership and the membership and at drawing on the experience of the most active members in the areas.

In view of these open sessions only one meeting of the Party Council

[1] Ibid., p. 198.
[2] The use of "alien", "foreign sounding" words and slogans should, however, be understood in its context of history. Part of the origin was enthusiasm for the Russian Revolution and the achievements of the Soviet Communist Party. Perhaps a still greater factor was the desire to make a clean break with old discredited reformist forms of organisation. *Tout comprendre*, however, cannot be, for a Marxist, *tout pardonner*.
[3] *Organising Report of C.E.C. to 7th Congress*. Report of Seventh Congress, pp. 141-143. Three were held—Manchester, September 28, 1924; London, October 11, 1924; Birmingham, January 9, 1925.

was held between the Sixth and Seventh Congresses,[1] and in January 1926 an extended meeting of the Executive was held on a still wider basis than envisaged for the Council.[2] In general the Party Council, *as a statutory body*, was not proving particularly helpful; rather experience seemed to point to the need for holding extended Executive meetings as and when the situation demanded and adapting the form to the circumstances.

A new definition of the purpose of the Party's Control Commission was adopted at the Seventh Congress and incorporated in the Rules, in which it was accepted that the Commission should investigate complaints against departments of the Party and suggest to the Executive how to remove the causes of such complaints, that it should investigate the complaints of individual Party members, of Party Locals and Districts against any disciplinary measures and report its opinions to the Executive, and that it should audit all Party financial accounts. Its members were not to be members of the Executive or District Committees, but to have been active in the revolutionary movement for at least seven years.[3]

A certain change in the method of electing the Executive Committee was adopted at the Seventh Congress.[4] The Executive, elected by Congress, was henceforth to consist of 20 members. The new Executive would then elect a Political Bureau and an Organising Bureau, and would appoint the Party Secretary from amongst its members. It would also appoint a Secretariat of four, one of whom would be the Party Secretary, the other three chosen from the Organising Bureau.[5] It was considered more correct, and likely to contribute to the strength of the Executive and to the unity of the leadership, that this method should replace the previous custom of election of the Party Secretary by Congress as a whole. Membership of the Control Commission was reduced from four to three.

The first meeting of the Executive elected at the Seventh Congress met on June 13, 1925, elected in its turn the various departments and

[1] London, November 30, 1924. See Organising Report of C.E.C. to Seventh Congress, *Report of 7th Congress*, p. 143.

[2] Organising Report of C.E.C. to Eighth Congress, *Report of 8th Congress*, p. 39.

[3] *Report of 7th Congress*, pp. 164–165, 168–179.

[4] Ibid., pp. 79–83.

[5] At the Executive Committee meeting of June 13–14, 1925 the function of the Secretariat was defined: "(a) to examine the decisions of the two Bureaux and see that they are carried into effect; (b) to attend to technical matters, correspondence, etc., in order to save the time of the two Bureaux; (c) to act in emergencies when neither Bureau is available". C.E.C. *Minutes*.

bureaux,[1] and appointed Albert Inkpin as General Secretary. The Executive functioned until the Eighth Congress in October 1926, though the arrest of the twelve Communist leaders at the end of 1925 necessitated some emergency changes.[2]

FACTORY GROUPS

The most important organisational change in the Communist Party in the 1925-1926 period was the attempt to put the Party, so far as possible, on a factory group basis in the localities. This was a question of principle.

For a reformist party whose essential perspective was the gradual transformation of society by victory at parliamentary and local government elections within the framework of the capitalist State, the main demand on the member is punctilious voting at election time. The local agent or leadership are essentially canvassers for and recorders of votes. The most important aspect of leadership is the Parliamentary Group which, against all democratic principle, is usually above the Party Conference or Congress. The local party organisation has as its main purpose to mobilise its members for the vote.

Though a revolutionary organisation can participate in national and local elections and may attribute great importance to such participation, mobilisation for the vote *is only one part of the purpose of local organisation*. The local party units have to take socialist ideas to the working class and working people, have to help to lead the working class and people in all the immediate industrial, social, political struggles that confront them, have in revolutionary moments to lead them in revolutionary struggle. They must seek the best forms of organisation to mobilise and unite the workers, and where can this be done more effectively than in factory, pit and rail depot?

It is in factory, pit and depot that workers of every type—young and old, men and women, skilled and unskilled, workers of different trades and different trade unions—can best be united. It is in the factory that the working class can best be mobilised to struggle for their daily interests. It is the key factories, pits and depots and offices that give political leadership to whole industrial areas. It is in the factories, at the point of production, that the workers can best come to understand the nature of exploitation, the nature of capitalism, that they can

[1] For composition of Executive and Bureau and emergency changes after the arrests see Appendix II to this chapter.
[2] Ibid.

experience the discipline of social labour, learn the discipline of social struggle and, with the help of socialist ideas, come to see the need for the socialist transformation of society.

For all these reasons, at the end of 1924 the Party began to develop the work started in September 1923 for the formation of Party groups within the factories, to make such groups basic units of the Party, and to put forward the aim of replacing the local groups, so far as possible, by factory groups of the Party, i.e. to organise all those Party members who worked in factories, pits, railway depots, etc., into factory groups of the Party.

By March 1925, incomplete reports showed that some 50 factory groups had so far been established,[1] of which some 22 were in Scotland and 16 in London. In view of the fundamental importance given to the aim of putting the Party on a factory group basis, Ernie Woolley of Manchester was appointed in this month to supervise the work. On March 15, 1926, a special discussion on the problem of factory group development was opened by Tom Quelch at the Executive.[2] At the end of the month a circular was distributed to all Districts and Locals insisting on attention being given to this transformation of approach and attitude:

> "The factory groups will be the basic units of the Party. Above all our work must be directed towards the factory."[3]

The turn to the factory and to the factory group was, perhaps, the most essential point in the theses on "Bolshevisation" and on "The Mass Party" adopted at the Seventh Congress of the Party (May–June 1925).

It was admitted that there was still resistance, that members in the areas still held on to old organisational forms:

> "Many of the old traditions of socialist propaganda and party organisation still cling to the Party membership. There is still considerable hesitation in wholeheartedly adopting the factory form of organisation."[4]

But it was strongly argued that this should change:

> "The chief road towards becoming a real mass party for us lies through the factory, the workshop, the mill, the mine. . . ."[5]

[1] *Workers' Weekly*, No. 109, March 6, 1925, p. 4.
[2] Ibid., No. 111, March 20, 1925, p. 6.
[3] C.P. circular of March 26, 1926, Party Records.
[4] "Thesis on the Mass Party", *Report of 7th Congress C.P.G.B.*, p. 166. [5] Ibid.

At the Congress Arthur MacManus reported that there were now approximately 100 factory groups in the Party embracing 10 per cent of the membership, and that these groups between them published 40–50 factory papers, some of which had a circulation of 800–900.[1]

E. W. Cant, the London District Organiser, at the same discussion, reported 32 factory groups in London, involving around one-fifth of the membership, with 22 factory papers and a fortnightly circulation of around 5,500.[2]

By the end of July 1925, the number of factory groups had risen to 120 with some 500 members and 60 papers,[3] the greatest progress in the London, Scottish (Glasgow, Fife) and South Wales Districts, the least at Bradford and Liverpool.[4]

Further progress continued to be reported in the last months of 1925 and the first months of 1926,[5] especially in London and South Wales.

On the eve of the General Strike, on paper at least, some 240 factory groups had been registered,[6] but during the strike the groups as such played little direct role. Their members were involved up to the hilt in all the manifold activities of the strike. As far as the Party's own

---

[1] Report of 7th Congress C.P.G.B., pp. 36–37.
[2] Ibid., pp. 40–41.
[3] Workers' Weekly, No. 130, July 31, 1925, p. 2, "Our Factory Groups".
[4] The breakdown by District and area reported at this time was:

	Factory Groups	Factory Papers
London District	34	34
South Wales	34	4
Glasgow	23	12
Fife	5	1
Dundee	3	1
Manchester	8	4
Liverpool	1	1
Sheffield	6	1
Bradford	4	1
Barrow	1	1
Devonport	1	—
	120	60

[5] Workers' Weekly, July 10, 1925. At the London District Conference July 4–5, 1925, it was reported that there were 200 Party members in factory groups and that the factory papers had a circulation of over 7,000 fortnightly. Workers' Weekly No. 137, September 18, 1925, p. 4, reports 18 pit groups, 12 colliery groups, 1 steel group in South Wales.

[6] Report of E. H. Brown to the Organising Conference of the Communist Party held at Bethnal Green Public Library on October 18, 1926, the day following the Eighth Congress of the C.P.G.B., Party Records.

organisations were concerned it was the local rather than the factory groups that maintained independent activity.[1]

After the strike came the mass influx of new recruits, mainly miners, to the Party. The fact that the pits were closed, that the new recruits were mainly *locked-out* miners won to the Party at great public local meetings, but not at the pits, made it more difficult to strengthen specific factory and pit organisation, though it gave a fine basis for this to be done in the future. In London there was good progress, particularly in transport,[2] but by and large whilst 1925 had been a year of advance in factory group organisation, the period between the General Strike and the Eighth Congress in October 1926 did not show the same concentration on factory organisation.

THE FACTORY PAPERS

The factory papers produced by the factory groups bear living witness to the vitality of the best of them, to their contact with the workers, knowledge of their problems, combativity, and capacity to write (and illustrate) in a way and a language that the workers would appreciate.

At times official statements of the Party were, in these early days, couched in so specialised a language that they could be fully understood only by those who had mastered the technical words, phrases, and categories of Marxism-Leninism and also the style current in the international Communist movement. This was a weakness because, whilst technical language is fully justified for speed and precision in all scientific writing, including that of the social sciences, it is meant for those who are conversant with it, and for those who are not it becomes an awkward and alien jargon.

The factory papers showed that the members of the Party in the localities were able to assimilate the ideas of Marxism and put the

---

[1] The Executive Committee of the Communist International (E.C.C.I.) resolution on the organisational activity of the C.P.G.B. at the end of 1926 commented that one of the main organisational weaknesses of the British Party was that the factory groups did *not* play, as such, a prominent part during the General Strike. See resolution in *Communist Review*, Vol. 7, No. 6, October 1926, pp. 256-262.

[2] The London District Party Committee reported to the London District Congress of June 26, 1926, that there was Party organisation in 27 railway depots and stations, with 12 papers with a fortnightly circulation around 4,000. Party membership on the tramways had trebled. Here *Live Rail*, in charge of Emile Burns, was now a printed paper with a circulation of 1,500, and there were three groups in tram depots. There was a paper produced for the all-London bus fleet, and two dock papers with a circulation of around 1,000.

policy of the Party into the idiom of their workmates. No one can accuse them of "Party jargon", though you can find there the jargon of the pits, of the rail depot, of the bus garage, with those short Anglo-Saxon monosyllables so admirably suited to apt characterisation of the ruling class.

At a peak period there were over 100 of them ranging from two sides of a duplicated sheet to a 6-page printed magazine. Most of them appeared fortnightly. Some carried caricatures. The contents ranged from bonuses to Bolshevism, from philosophy to football. There were no holds barred. Picture and satire described the greedy employer, the domineering foreman, the workshop creeper. Time has, alas, destroyed many of these papers,[1] and only a few have been found still available

[1] We list below those factory papers we have been able to locate and study. We would be grateful for information about others, and, of course, the Communist Party Librarian would be grateful for the gift of them.

(a) Published by Communist Party Groups

Bystander—the Battersea Loco—a railway shed paper published in Clapham.
The Black Squad—organ of the Gowan Communist Group, edited by "Zinoviev".
The Cambrian Xray—issued by the Cambrian Group of the Communist Party.
Courage—organ of the Idris workers.
The Cymmer Searchlight—issued by the Cymmer Group of the Communist Party.
The Dawn—issued by the Parkhead Group of the C.P.
The Forge—issued by the Communist Group of Pearson and Knowles Ltd.
The Feltham Tatler—issued by the Communist Group of the Feltham Repair Depot.
The Mardy Leader—organ of the Mardy Communist Colliery Groups.
The Piano Worker—issued by Communist Group.
Red Dawn—organ of the Ferndale Communist Pit Group.
The Red Observer—issued by Tylorstown Communist Colliery Group.
The Searchlight—organ of the Imperial Tube Works Communist Group.
The Spark—organ of the Methil C.P. Pit Group.
Steam—issued by Railway Communist Group, Cardiff.

(b) Issued by militant but not specifically C.P. Groups

The Idris Ginger—organ of the Idris Workers.
The Live Rail—paper of the Holloway Road Tram Depot Workers.
Napier Searchlight—issued by the "Reds" of Napiers.
The Punch—organ of the Southern Railway Workers.
The Ranelagh Worker.
The Rawlings Truth—issued by "Comrade Trotsky".
The Nine Elms Spark—paper of the Nine Elms railwaymen.
The Star—paper of King's Cross Depot railwaymen.
The Hornsey Star—issued by Hornsey, Wood Green and Finsbury Park Railwaymen—all grades.
The Sugar Factory Workers' Guide—issued in North Woolwich.

(c) Issued by Y.C.L. or Youth Groups

"Anti-Jelco"—Manchester young workers.
The Young Rebel—published by young workers at the General Gas Appliances Company.
The Young Woodworker—Y.C.L.—"Lusty" newsheet.

but their very titles savour of the workshop—*The Cambrian Xray* (published by the Cambrian C.P. Group), *The Feltham Tatler* (published by the Communist Group of the Feltham Repair Depot), *The Mardy Leader* (organ of the Mardy Communist Colliery Groups), *The Red Dawn* (fortnightly organ of the Ferndale Communist Pit Group), *The Spark* (published by the Methil Communist Pit Group), *Steam* (issued by the Railway Communist Group, Cardiff). Some were not specifically Communist papers but issued by left groups of workers, working fraternally with the Communist groups, like *The Live Rail* (paper of the Holloway Road Tram Depot), *Napier Searchlight* (published by "the Reds of Napiers"), or *The Idris Ginger* (organ of the militant Idris workers). One or two were issued by the Young Communist League or groups of young workers, for instance *Anti-Jelco* in Manchester, or *The Young Rebel* (published by young workers in the General Gas Appliances Company).

Circulation ranged from a hundred or so to around a thousand. Workers' letters were encouraged, though fear of victimisation meant that signatures were pseudonyms.

Humour and satire were an essential feature of the factory papers, and often effective weapons of socialist education. Here is an all-too brief sample:

Ode to a Wizard[1]

Lloyd George no doubt, when his life ebbs out
Will ride in a flaming chariot,
Seated in State on a red hot plate
Between Satan and Judas Iscariot.

Ananias that day to the devil will say
My right to first place surely fails
So raise me up higher away from the fire
To make room for that blighter from Wales.

Notice in the Ranelagh Worker[2]

"A few of the older and loyal workers object to this paper because they say it is 'causing trouble', interfering with the m.m and upsetting our 'peaceful' relations with the firm. That is just the point, we *do* want to

---

[1] From the *Cambrian Xray*, No. 5, of December 4, 1925—a 2-sheet, 4-sided duplicated, 1d. paper of the Cambrian Group of the C.P.

[2] *The Ranelagh Worker*, No. 4, June 18, 1925.

upset this so-called 'peace' and also to show the Boss Class waging definite war against the workers."

Notice in the Red Observer[1]

"Lady so-and-so and Lord Whats-is-name left on the *Aquitania* today for America where they will be met by Lord and Lady Dolittle, who have prepared to welcome them.

"Dai Down and Out will leave on Wednesday, on his feet, for the Labour Exchange, where he will meet the Rotary Committee who will endeavour to stop his dole."

"Notice"[2]

"On and after March 22/25 all workers will work as hard as they possibly can to produce enough sugar to fill the new warehouse as soon as possible in order that they can be put on short time as soon as it is done."

By Order of the Management.

Manager or Policeman?[3]

"The way Allan the Manager creeps round corners, darts in doorways and peeps through windows in the hope of catching someone, makes one wonder if he is employed as a policeman, or if he likes playing Red Indians.

"*He can terrorise you—in so far as you have not a Workers' Committee backed up by Mass Support.*"

Special Thomas Issue[4]

The front page carries a picture of J. H. Thomas saying to a group of lads:

"Work hard, honour the King, be humble to your employers, and you too may become a successful capitalist. It may be necessary for me some day to accept your invitation to dinner in the interests of industrial peace."

[1] *The Red Observer*, organ of the Tylorstown Communist Colliery Group, No. 4, October 9, 1925—a printed 4-page paper.
[2] From the *Sugar Factory Workers' Guide*, special edition, edited in North Woolwich.
[3] *Napier Searchlight* issued by the "Reds of Napiers," No. 1, April 8, 1925. The aim of the journal was "greater unity in the shop".
[4] *The Nine Elms Spark*, No. 3, April 3, 1925, special J. H. Thomas issue.

BUILDING THE PARTY

A "mass Party" meant not only a party in close contact with the mass of the workers, but a *larger* party. In 1925 and 1926 recruiting was under constant attention and, in this respect, the period following the General Strike was one of considerable success.

At the Sixth Party Congress in mid-May 1924, Party membership was around 3,900. Some progress was made in recruiting at the end of 1924 and in the first months of 1925. A special Recruiting Department was established at the Party Centre. The Extended Executive Committee meeting at Birmingham in January 1925 adopted a statement entitled *Towards a Mass Party*.[1]

Speaking at the Seventh Congress of the C.P.G.B. (May 30–June 1, 1925) Arthur MacManus could announce that Party membership had reached 5,000, an increase of 1,100 or around 25 per cent, over the figure at the previous Congress. The best results had been achieved in the London, South Wales, Glasgow and Birmingham Districts, whilst Manchester, Liverpool and Sheffield were less satisfactory, and the position on Tyneside was bad.[2] But the Party, despite the increase, was still "lamentably small".[3] Why should it be, asked MacManus, that if the *Workers' Weekly* had a circulation of around 50,000, of which half were regular readers, *membership* of the Party should remain so small?[4]

Despite the importance given to recruiting at the Seventh Congress, results were sparse in the months that followed. The efforts of the Party were turned outwards, first to prepare for "Red Friday", then for the General Strike.[5] A special recruiting week was held in September 1925 ("Red Week") when some 750 new members were made, but this was barely enough to offset normal flux. The arrests of the Communist leaders did not lead to any resignations, indeed some signified their indignation by joining the Party—the composer Rutland Boughton, for instance.

---

[1] The statement or thesis ends: "Let our slogan for 1925 be: A MASS COMMUNIST PARTY." See also *Workers' Weekly*, No. 101, January 9, 1925, p. 2, and No. 107, February 20, 1925, p. 6. Article by George Deacon, "A Mass Party".

[2] *Report of 7th Congress C.P.G.B.*, p. 35.

[3] Words of Executive Committee Report to Seventh Congress, *Report*, p. 148.

[4] *Report of 7th Congress C.P.G.B.*, p. 37.

[5] At the Party Executive of October 3–4, 1925, Inkpin, the General Secretary, stated that there had been no change in membership over the previous six months. *Minutes of E.C.*, Party Records.

But the real influx into the Communist Party began in the last days of and immediately following the General Strike. The Methil Branch (Fife) reported:

> "Then [immediately after the strike] the workers began to flock into the Party. The group increased in little more than a week from six to 150 members, including 40 to 50 women—an entirely new phenomenon—and, in addition, 45 young workers joined the Y.C.L."[1]

This was something new in the history of the Party, and very exhilarating it was. The General Council had sold out the strike. The miners fought on. In all the coalfields great mass meetings were held at which workers, above all miners, turned to the Communist Party in scores, and even in hundreds.

The July 14, 1926, Executive could report 3,000 new members since the General Strike and *Workers' Weekly* sales up to 70,000.[2]

A letter from the Tyneside reported:

> "At a public meeting held at Chopwell [which earned itself the title 'Little Moscow'. J.K.] addressed by comrade Brain, we received 125 applications for membership on July 4th and at an aggregate meeting of these comrades we had an additional 25 applications making a total of 150...."[3]

District Congress after District Congress reported recruiting successes. The London Congress (July 17) announced 350 new members since the General Strike, Communists elected to 82 Trades Councils, 50 Left-Wing Groups.[4]

The Fife District Congress (July 18), with David Proudfoot in the chair, announced 253 new men and 142 women members. In that same week the *Workers' Weekly* sold 75,000 copies.[5]

In July and August miners came flocking into the Party in Scotland, South Wales, Lancashire, Yorkshire and above all the Durham coalfield. A meeting in County Durham, organised by the Tatfield local of the Party, made 230 new members.[6] Albert Inkpin, the Party's Secretary reported to the Executive on August 20:

---

[1] *Workers' Weekly* No. 173, June 11, 1926, p. 4. [2] Ibid., No. 178, July 16, 1926.
[3] Ibid., No. 179, July 23, p. 4. [4] Ibid.
[5] Ibid., No. 180, July 30, 1926, p. 4.
[6] Ibid., No. 182 August 13, p. 4.

"In the whole of the Durham coalfield recruits are rolling in at a rate which creates an acute problem for the Party."[1]

There are "acute problems" that are sweet! Tyneside membership now was 1,900 with a long waiting list (waiting whilst new locals should be formed). The very phrases used, however, reveal a certain persistence of what might be called a "small-Party outlook", and habits of work which made it difficult to respond to new requirements and possibilities.

Right up to the Eighth Congress of the Party the "rolling-in" continued. Women came along with men. Alec Geddes, speaking at the Sheffield Conference on work amongst women, reported that his meetings were "packed with women".[2] The Methil Branch now had 134 women members. Isobel Brown in a short campaign on the Tyneside had made 200 women recruits. A special Congress of the Manchester District on September 19 reported 400 new members since the General Strike.[3]

By the Eighth Congress of the Party, October 16–17, 1926, the membership of the previous Congress had been doubled and there were *over 10,000 members* of the Communist Party.[4]

With this new influx a tremendous task and responsibility opened out for the Communist Party. It was a very excellent thing, to win to the Communist Party so many militant workers, mainly from the pits. But these were for the most part men and women who had come to hate the guts of the right-wing leaders, to see them as traitors, to feel hatred and disgust for the system of capitalism. They wanted a new, better, juster system of society, they desired a radical change. They admired the Communist Party for its principles, for the stand that it had taken during the General Strike, for the solidarity it had shown to the locked-out miners, for its complete rejection of reformism, for the hatred that the capitalists and the coalowners had for it. But they were not yet Marxists in their theoretical outlook, and they were not yet organised into functioning units of the Communist Party. The problem of retention of members, educating members in socialist ideas, organising members in an effective manner, *still had to be faced.*[5]

---

[1] *Minutes of Executive.*
[2] *Workers' Weekly*, No. 186, September 10, 1926.
[3] Ibid., No. 189, October 1, 1926, p. 4.
[4] See *Workers' Weekly*, No. 192, October 22, 1926 and *Report of 8th Congress C.P.G.B.*, p. 39.
[5] See E. H. Brown, "Building the Party", *Communist Review*, Vol. 7, No. 3, July 1926, and discussions that followed in subsequent numbers.

THE DISTRICTS

At the time of the Sixth Congress of the Party (mid-May 1924) there were 136 local Party organisations (embracing 51 Local Party Committees and 84 Group Leaders' Committees). By the Seventh Congress (May-June 1925) there were 162 local Party organisations (59 Local Party Committees and 103 Group Leaders' Committees).[1]

Of these the London District accounted for 29, South Wales 24, Manchester 18, Glasgow 13, Tyneside 10, Sheffield 9, Birmingham 9, Bradford 8, Liverpool 6, Fife 6, and unattached 30.[2]

Already the study of District Reports indicates that some Districts had shown characteristics (and problems) that were not just temporary. London at that time was giving the best results. From the Sixth to the Seventh Congress its membership had increased by about 300. Its work in the trade unions and Trades Councils was satisfactory, but complaints were already at that period being made that involvement in *national* work was drawing many of the most active London members away from London activity. The membership of Glasgow District was already overwhelmingly in heavy industry. From Fife it was already being reported that the "Communist spirit" was strong, but the Communist organisation weak. From South Wales, too, it was reported that members were relatively easy to win for the Party but relatively difficult to organise. Birmingham at that time was a weak district. Manchester too, was still unsatisfactory, its position having been weakened by internal dissension. The Bradford District was growing, but finding that, in this traditional stronghold of the I.L.P., there were many problems to meet. Tyneside in May 1925 was "one of the weakest" of the Party districts. Sheffield was making progress, Liverpool too. In the "outlying" areas, where districts had not yet been formed, there was progress towards a District Committee in Kent, good work at Barrow, at Brighton, and the possibility arising of a district around Dundee.[3]

A London Report of November 1925 presents an analysis of the

[1] Organising Report of Executive Committee to Seventh Congress, *Report of 7th Congress*, p. 144.
[2] Regrouping according to the current pattern (1966) of Party Districts would give London 29, S. Wales 24, Manchester and Liverpool 24, Glasgow and Fife 19, Sheffield and Bradford 17, Tyneside 10, Birmingham 9, unattached 30.
[3] See Organising Report of C.E.C. to Seventh Congress of C.P.G.B., *Report of 7th Congress*, p. 144-147. There are interesting reports of the South Wales District and of the Manchester District in the *Workers' Weekly*, No. 181, of August 7, 1925, p. 5.

position in the District. There were at the time 29 local Party Committees, about 1,000 dues-paying members; 750 considered "active", 15 Party training groups; 27 factory groups with a membership of 245 or about a quarter of the total; 20 factory papers with a total fortnightly circulation of around 8,000; nearly the total membership were members of trade unions and 200 holding trade union positions; 400–500 associated members of the National Minority Movement; members in about 30 local Labour Parties; 10 sections of the N.U.W.C.M.; 200 women members of the Party or about one-fifth, 6 women's committees of the Party with two papers.[1] It is the picture of an *extraordinarily active membership*, very many of whom were devoting almost every moment which they could find to building the Party and the working-class movement, of a Party whose members were nearly all trade unionists, firmly rooted in the Labour Movement—but also of a complexity of organisations in and around the Party, all of which could be justified on paper, all of which were aimed to form a link between Party and masses or to improve and control the organisation of the Party, but the very complexity of which could to a degree begin to do just the opposite.

By the Eighth Congress (October 1926) the relative position in the Districts had very much changed. The Executive's Report on organisation showed the following situation at mid-September 1926:[2]

	Locals	Membership
Tyneside	39	1,900
London	36	1,560
South Wales	41	1,500
Sheffield	13	1,200
Glasgow	17	1,105
Manchester	30	680
Liverpool	12	576
Fife	8	502
Birmingham	18	326
Bradford	11	250
Dundee, Edinburgh and Outlying	20	1,131
	245	10,730

[1] London Statistical Report of November 5, 1925, Party Records.
[2] Organising Report of C.E.C. to Eighth Congress, *Report of 8th Congress C.P.G.B.*, p. 39.

Tyneside, not so long before "the weakest of our Districts", now topped the list. Above all the position reflected the great influx of miners into the Party in the months that followed the General Strike. "The problem of assimilating, instructing and thoroughly organising these new members is being given serious attention" the Executive reported to Congress. But this task was not to prove so easy as it sounded.

The Party in this period of 1925-1926 was an overwhelmingly proletarian Party.[1] It was a young Party. Of the delegates to the Seventh Congress, for instance, 64 per cent were under thirty-five. It was a Party nearly all of whose members were active trade unionists. Amongst intellectual and professional people it was still extremely weak. In agriculture its influence was minimal.

PARTY PRESS

The Seventh Congress (May-June 1925) considered the position and progress of the Party press. At the end of 1923 the average weekly sale of the *Workers' Weekly* stood around 40,000. For one single issue the cherished aim of 100,000 was reached at the elections which saw the downfall of the Labour Government, but then circulation settled down around 50,000[2] of which half were regarded as regular readers. In the months that followed the General Strike, circulation mounted along with membership and by the time of the Eighth Congress (October 1926) it stood around 80,000.[3] As the sale was carried out almost entirely by the Party members themselves this was a creditable achievement.

The publication of the *Sunday Worker*, a militant and united left paper in which Party members played a considerable role, was another marked achievement of this period. The *Sunday Worker*, launched in March 1925, was an important part of and contributor to the growing movement of the Left. It was a truly united initiative in which Communists played an important part both in writing for the paper and in distributing it and raising funds.

Amongst the many shareholders, alongside Communists, were branches of the Labour Party, of the I.L.P., Co-operative Guilds,

---

[1] See speech of Arthur MacManus at Seventh Congress, *Report of 7th Congress*, p. 35.
[2] Organising Report of C.E.C. to Seventh Congress, *Report of 7th Congress*, pp. 149-150.
[3] Organising Report of Central Committee to Eighth Congress, *Report of 8th Congress*, p. 49-51.

trade union branches, especially Lodges of the Miners' Federation. Contributors included Labour and I.L.P. M.P.s and leading figures of the trade union movement. The *Sunday Worker* Campaign Committee included Communists like R. Dunstan, Helen Crawfurd, Tom Mann and S. Saklatvala, M.P., and prominent Labour and trade union figures like Alex Gossip, A. J. Cook, Fred Longden, A. MacNulty and the Rev. Malcolm MacCallum. William Paul, who wrote many of the editorials, and Walter Holmes played a major role on the journal. The first issue appeared in mid-March 1925. By the time of the Seventh Congress circulation had settled down around 100,000.[1]

The theoretical journal of the Party, the *Communist Review*, was selling around 3,000–3,500 in this period.[2] The *Labour Monthly* was going strong and becoming something of a rallying point in the Communist and Labour left.

Between the Eighth Congress there was a marked increase in publication of leaflets, pamphlets and books.[3] Over two million leaflets were distributed (apart from special election leaflets) between May 1924 and May 1925 and 18 pamphlets published with a total circulation of around 100,000. A number of the main works of Marx, Engels and Lenin were published or republished along with Stalin's *Theory and Practice of Leninism*, Bogdanoff's *Short Course of Economic Science* and a *Manual of Party Training*. Between June 1925 and October 1926 the Party published 16 books, including John Reed's *Ten Days that Shook the World*. Others included works of Marx and Lenin, J. T. Murphy's *Meaning of the General Strike*, and Trotsky's *Where is Britain Going?*. Publication of pamphlets remained on a high level (around 100,000 copies in all).

To the above, of course, should be added the hundred or so factory papers that were appearing with fair regularity, and all the bulletins and leaflets of the days of the General Strike. Again, this was no mean achievement for a small Party of 5,000–10,000 members.

PARTY TRAINING

The slogans of these years—"For a Mass Party", "Bolshevisation of the Party"—were taken to mean a Party not only larger, not only with

[1] See Statement by A. H. Hawkins, *Report of 7th Congress of C.P.G.B.*, pp. 121–124.
[2] Organising Report of C.E.C. to Seventh Congress, *Report of 7th Congress of C.P.G.B.*, pp. 149–150.
[3] See Appendix to this chapter.

better links with the people, but a Party with a high degree of socialist understanding.

In the history of the British Labour Movement there has often been a deep contradiction between a high level of organisation and a low level of political theory. The reformists claimed to be "practical men", not concerned with high-falutin' theories. In fact their studied lack of theory was itself a theory, a "theory of no theory", an iniquitous "theory", for the absence of specifically *socialist* ideas left the mind wide open for the theory of the ruling class, of capitalism.

In the British context, therefore, the Communist Party had a special, an unusually high responsibility for taking to the British working people the ideas, the science of socialism.

But how could they do this unless the *members* of the Communist Party were themselves *imbued* with socialist understanding? And that meant not just book-learned people, but people capable, in the face of all the propaganda of capitalism, of explaining in a comprehensible manner the ideas of Marxism to their workmates and to the public.

If we are to be able to help the workers to understand socialism, said Andrew Rothstein, speaking on the "Bolshevisation of the Party" at the Seventh Congress:

> "we need to be conscious socialists ourselves, educated Marxists ourselves, and be able to give the workers Marxism and Socialism."[1]

The normal Communist method of Marxist education was the holding in the localities of "classes" or "schools"—a long tradition in the Labour Movement. Soon after the Sixth Congress the Party produced a *Training Manual* along with a series of *Training Charts* (on historical events). At the time of the Seventh Congress it was estimated that there were around 90 training groups in existence with around 800 Party members receiving tuition, and that of these a half were in the London and Glasgow[2] Districts. The holding of socialist classes amongst the working class had a particularly deep tradition in the Glasgow area.

By the end of the year (December 1925) Party training was at about the same level, though South Wales was now the most active District

---

[1] See *Report of 7th Congress of C.P.G.B.*, pp. 109–112.
[2] Organising Report of C.E.C., *Report of 7th Congress of C.P.G.B.*, pp. 159–160. By March 1925 2,500 out of an edition of 3,000 had been sold of the *Party Manual* and *Training Charts*.

in this respect.[1] By the Eighth Congress (October 1926) it was estimated that roughly one-half of the Party membership had attended some or other type of educational course, and that in the previous winter about 1,000 Party members had attended classes, with London, South Wales, Manchester and Glasgow in the lead.[2]

The Communist International was in this period putting great emphasis on improving Party training in its various sections. Early in 1925 it decided to assist in this work by organising a central "Lenin School" in Moscow that could be attended by members of the leading sections of the International, including the C.P.G.B. Five students were invited from Britain (between the ages of 21–35) to be selected by the British Party, to attend the first 18-month course, and to work for the Party on their return.[3] A special Selection Committee was set up to select the British group,[4] and by the time of the Eighth Congress they were in residence at Moscow, facing a curriculum that was to say the least formidable.[5] It had been proposed at the Seventh Congress to organise a central school in Britain, with 20 students to endure a similar course, but with the arrests, the General Strike, and the campaign of solidarity with the miners, the proposition was adjourned.

THE Y.C.L. 1925–1926

In the last months of 1924 and the first months of 1925 the Young Communist League was a very small organisation. It had perhaps 500 members, and was confined to a few Districts.[6] It was at that time somewhat turned in on itself, with an *internal* life out of all proportion to its size and without sufficient contact with the working-class youth in

[1] *Workers' Weekly*, No. 150, December 18, 1925, p. 4. There were now 25 classes in South Wales, 15 in London, 13 in Manchester and 10 in Glasgow. In all Britain, around 86 classes with 795 attending.

[2] *Report of 8th Congress C.P.G.B.*, pp. 47–49.

[3] Party circular of May 9, 1925 and Tom Bell's report at Seventh Congress of C.P.G.B., *Report of 7th Congress*, pp. 124–129.

[4] Tom Bell, George Deacon and Harry Inkpin.

[5] As reported by Tom Bell it included: Historical Materialism, Political Economy, Leninism, Imperialism, Contemporary World Economy, Agrarian Question, History of Socialism, History of the Third International, History of the Russian Communist Party, Practice of the Russian Communist Party, Lessons of the October Revolution, the Italian Question, The German Revolution, and Lessons of the Hungarian Revolution.

[6] By May 1925 there were District Committees functioning in London, Glasgow, Manchester and Yorkshire. See C.E.C. Organising Report to Seventh Congress of C.P.G.B., *Report of 7th Congress*, pp. 161–163.

industry. Its composition was about 40 per cent industrial and 60 per cent recruited from outside industry.[1]

Yet, with all these weaknesses, it compared well with any other Labour youth organisation. The I.L.P. Guild of Youth and the Young People's Section of the Labour Party were only just founded, the latter grudgingly in 1924. The small Y.C.L. membership was extremely active and extremely devoted. It discussed, held classes. The first Y.C.L. week-end school was held in London at the end of February 1925.[2] It educated its members in hatred of imperialism and of militarism and colonialism, in that way pioneering the anti-colonialist struggle of the British youth. It organised activity amongst children. It had a leadership which contained young men some of whom, like William Rust, D. F. Springhall, Walter Tapsell, Ted Ainley, and Jack Cohen, were to devote their lives to the working-class movement.

It was unfortunate that, from the beginning, both Communist Party and Young Communist League took up an extremely sectarian attitude towards the youth organizations of the I.L.P. and of the Labour Party. A Party circular, for instance, of January 1925, signed jointly by A. Inkpin for the Party and W. Rust for the Y.C.L. *opposed* the formation of the Young People's Section of the Labour Party on the grounds that the Y.C.L. was "the only organisation the young workers needed" and that its application for affiliation to the Labour Party had been rejected. A "strong Labour youth organisation," it said, "will be an obstacle in the way of the development of the Y.C.L."[3] This sectarian attitude failed to see that in view of the overwhelmingly bourgeois character of the mass youth organisations in Britain, the formation of Labour Party and I.L.P. youth organisations represented a progress, whatever reformist ideas they might still hold, that until the Communist Party and Y.C.L. were of *far wider* influence it was *absurd* to see the Y.C.L. as the "only" Labour youth organisation, and that, above all, *youth organisations within the Labour Party or I.L.P., far from being reserves of reformism amongst the youth, were far more likely to become reserves of militant socialism amongst the reformists.*

At the Seventh Congress of the Communist Party in May–June, 1925, William Rust moved the resolution on the Y.C.L. It called on the League to endeavour to treble its membership, to follow the Party

[1] Ibid.
[2] *Workers' Weekly*, No. 112, March 27, 1925, p. 6. Jack Cohen was the tutor, an omen of years to come.
[3] Party circular *The Labour Youth Movement*, January 13, 1925.

example and try to develop on the basis of factory groups, to turn to mass work. The Party saw the League as "the reserve of the Communist Party".

But once again the sectarian attitude to the Labour Party and I.L.P. youth organisations was repeated, and, if anything, strengthened.[1] They were seen as reserves of reformism, formed by the right wing to divert the youth from class struggle. This might have been the intention of the right wing, but if so *they* were sadly mistaken. In fact most of the Labour Party and I.L.P. leaders were, from the beginning, scared stiff of their own youth.

The Third Congress of the Young Communist League was held at the Socialist Hall in Manchester in July 1925,[2] with 70 delegates attending, including seven representatives of Y.C.L. factory groups. Membership at that time was around 600.[3] William Rust, Secretary of the Y.C.L., introduced the Executive Committee's Report. There were discussions on "bolshevisation" and recruiting, in which stress was laid on differentiating between the Party and the Y.C.L., on the danger of the Y.C.L. imitating, taking over the political and organisational methods proper to the Party. Strong solidarity was expressed with the struggles of the Moroccan and Chinese peoples against imperialism. The campaign was outlined for solidarity with the miners. Decisions were taken on the fight against colonialism. It was agreed to work towards a national organisation of Communist children's organisations or Young Pioneers. And the call was endorsed to treble the membership. The attitude to the I.L.P. and Labour Party Youth Organisation was repeated, but at the same time an *Open Letter to the Labour Youth*, calling for unity in action was adopted.

In the 16 months between the Third Y.C.L. Congress (July 1925) and its Fourth Congress (December 1926) there were a number of positive developments.

There was a good turn to mass activity in the campaigns of solidarity with the miners both before and after the General Strike. In the General Strike, as we have seen, despite the fact that the Secretary, William

[1] W. Rust, "It is quite clear that the Y.C.L. is the only organisation the young workers need. Consequently those other organisations, the I.L.P. Guild of Youth, the Labour Party Youth Sections, are unnecessary and are assisting to split the forces of the young workers ... these organisations are being formed by the right wing of the Labour Party to create a reserve of reformism. The objective of these organisations is to lead the young workers away from the class struggle." *Report to 7th Congress C.P.G.B.*, pp. 100–102.

[2] *Workers' Weekly*, No. 128, July 17, 1925, pp. 2 and 4.

[3] E.C. Report to Fourth Congress of Y.C.L., pp. 25–26. Membership is here given at 1,800 and said to have trebled since July 1925.

Rust, was already in gaol, and the Acting-Secretary, D. F. Springhall, was early arrested, the Y.C.L. acquitted themselves well, edited the *Young Striker*, were everywhere active, though one of the weaknesses later discussed was the absence of specifically youth representatives on the Councils of Action. The Y.C.L. was extremely active in the mass campaign for the miners in the bitter months of May–November 1926 after the sell-out of the General Strike.

Though on a small scale, and often with slogans that were far too narrow to be understood by many youth, courageous work was continued against imperialism, colonialism, militarism. Amongst the leading Y.C.L.'ers there was a deep, unbreakable feeling of internationalism, a hatred of racialism, a continuous effort to make known the struggles of the colonial and semi-colonial peoples.

Though there were still sectarian approaches, considerable advance was made in contacting and co-operating with the Young People's Sections of the Labour Party and the I.L.P. Guild of Youth. In July 1925 the Y.C.L. Executive approached the I.L.P. Guild of Youth and the Young People's Section of the Labour Party asking for a joint campaign, through joint committees in districts and localities for 100 per cent trade unionism amongst the youth, a campaign for the release of William Rust, for the preparation of a young workers' delegation to visit the Soviet Union, and for the development of workers' sport. The Young People's Section, under adult "advice", ignored the call. The Guild of Youth, however, accepted.[1] On November 29 delegations of the two organisations met and revealed a large measure of agreement, particularly on the development of trade unionism amongst the youth. But a full meeting of the Guild of Youth Leadership, again with adult "advice", rejected the positions of its own delegation and unity was formally rejected.[2] In April 1926 the Y.C.L. proposal for united action was again rejected by the Guild of Youth conference, but only by a majority of 37 votes to 25. In fact, in many localities, united labour youth committees, involving Y.C.L., Guild of Youth and Labour Party Youth, began to come into existence. Without *formal* unity, Guild of Youth and Labour Party Youth worked side by side with Y.C.L.'ers in many localities to prepare the youth delegation to Russia, in support of the miners, and in aid for those imprisoned during the General Strike.

The Y.C.L. began to work well in many areas with other sections of

---

[1] *Report of Executive Committee to Fourth National Congress of Y.C.L.*, p. 31, 1926.
[2] *Workers' Weekly*, No. 148, December 4, 1925, p. 2.

the Labour Youth, but still its approaches were often sectarian, looking for differences rather than points of agreement.[1]

Progress was made by the League in its work amongst children. The Third Congress of the Y.C.L. (July 1925) had decided to bring together the different Communist children's groups that had developed in the previous 18 months or so into a national organisation under Y.C.L. auspices. Already at this time a children's paper, *The Young Comrade*, largely written by the children themselves, was being published with a circulation around 4,000.[2]

The first national Conference of these "Young Comrades Leagues" was held in Manchester in mid-February 1925, with some 70 delegates (30 of whom were children) from all over the country.[3] At this time there existed some 17 children's groups with approximately 300 members,[4] mainly in London, Manchester and Glasgow.

A general report was discussed; a constitution adopted confining membership to those between 10–14; and a programme of demands adopted including free school meals, free medical and dental treatment, establishment of children's homes and playgrounds, abolition of caning in schools, against compulsory religious teaching and against "patriotic teaching", for the maintenance of children of locked-out or striking workers. A leadership was elected composed of Y.C.L.'ers and children.[5]

Above all there was considerable progress in building the Young Communist League. Many new recruits were made, including 200 youths from the pits, in the last months of 1925, when the Y.C.L. began publicly to campaign for support for the miners.[6] But, as with the adult Party, it was following the General Strike that large-scale recruiting really began, above all in the coalfields. In May 1926, the Y.C.L.

---

[1] When the I.L.P. Guild of Youth consented, finally, to meet the delegation from the Y.C.L. Executive, the Y.C.L. sharply criticised them for the delay in answering. See E.C. Report to 4th Congress of Y.C.L., p. 16. Was it intentional, a Freudian slip or printer's sabotage that led to the section on Guild of Youth and Young People's Sections of the Labour Party in the above report being printed under the heading of "Opponent's Department"?

[2] *Workers' Weekly*, No. 128, July 17, 1925, p. 6. It was an 8-pager at ½d.

[3] Ibid., No. 160, February 26, 1926, p. 4, "First Conference of Young Comrades".

[4] E.C. Report to 4th Congress of Y.C.L., pp. 19–20.

[5] The main report was given by David Ainley. On the second day was held the children's own session, when the chair was taken by A. Campbell, the 13-year-old son of J. R. Campbell, and the resolution was introduced by Halpin, 13-year-old delegate from Openshaw. The names of the leadership elected are given in Appendix III to this chapter.

[6] *Workers' Weekly*, No. 141, October 16, 1925, p. 3.

paper, *The Young Worker*, became a weekly, and rapidly doubled its circulation. By the Fourth Congress of the League, held at the Sheffield A.E.U. Institute on December 18, 1926, the Y.C.L. had 1,800 members. It had trebled its membership since the previous Congress. And of these 75 per cent were young miners.[1]

The Fourth Congress contained an as yet unresolved contradiction between a broadening of approach to the mass of working class-youth and a continued, and even increasing, sectarian approach.[2]

The Eighth Congress of the Party (October 1926) had recognised the turn of the League to trade unionism and had praised this "first successful approach by the Y.C.L. to the mass organisations of the workers—the trade unions".[3] The mass of members who had joined the League were miners, and at its Fourth Congress (November 1926) the Y.C.L. could proclaim that its membership was overwhelmingly industrial.

It now had achieved some really good contact and co-operation with other sections of the Labour youth. There had been really effective work to prepare the youth delegation to Russia.[4] The 13 young workers who finally were elected included 5 members of the Guild of Youth (one from the leadership), 2 from the Young People's Section of the Labour Party (one a London leader), four Y.C.L.'ers, one from the trade unions and one Communist member of the London Trade Council.[5]

The organisation was larger: it had eight Districts[6] some of which, like South Wales with 26 branches, Glasgow with 12 and Manchester with 13, had greatly developed; it had a number of full-time workers, a journal, *The Young Worker*, with increasing circulation (the Fourth Congress put the target of 10,000 circulation); its leadership was active and getting younger. The average age of the 120 delegates at the Fourth

[1] E.C. Report to 4th Congress of Y.C.L., pp. 23-24.
[2] For Fourth Congress of Y.C.L. see (i) *A Congress of Young Fighters: Report of the 4th Congress of the Young Communist League of Great Britain*, 36 pp., 1927, (ii) *Report of the Executive Committee to the Fourth National Congress of the Y.C.L. of Great Britain*, 31 pp., 1926, and (iii) *Statutes and Rules of the Y.C.L. of Great Britain adopted at the 4th Congress*, Y.C.L., 1927.
[3] *Report of 8th Congress of C.P.G.B.*, pp. 75-78, resolution "On the Y.C.L."
[4] For instance, 36 delegates from Labour youth organisations met at Manchester on June 5, 1926 to discuss the delegation at a Conference called by the Manchester United Front Committee which contained representatives of *all* the Labour youth organisations. See *Workers' Weekly*, No. 173, June 11, 1926, p. 3.
[5] Resolution on the Y.C.L. adopted at Eighth Congress of C.P.G.B.
[6] London, Glasgow, Fife, Manchester, Newcastle, Sheffield, Bradford, South Wales. See *E.C. Report to 4th Congress of Y.C.L.*, p. 27.

Congress, half of whom were miners, was 20 years and 8 months. It had adopted new *Statutes and Rules*.[1]

But in contrast to these advances, the old sectarianism was still at work and, if anything, increasing. It can be seen in the continued attitude to the Guild of Youth and Labour League of Youth (by now the Young People's Sections had become the Labour League of Youth) expressed in the resolution *The Crisis in Great Britain and the Organisation of the Working Youth*.[2] It was shown, too, in the *completely negative* attitude to the mass bourgeois youth organisations like the Y.M.C.A. and Scouts, in which the bulk of the members were workers.[3] It was shown in the language of the resolutions which must have been almost incomprehensible to the great majority of working youth, in the relative disregard of the special problems and special interests of young people. It was shown in the fact that, despite several successive resolutions to this effect, there was still little difference in organisation and method of work between the Y.C.L. and the Communist Party.

The Y.C.L. at the time of the Fourth Congress was stronger in numbers,[4] stronger in the Districts, more proletarian, more in contact with other sections of Labour youth than ever before. But many of its approaches and attitudes were pulling it away from the mass of the youth, tending to isolate it.

[1] By the *Statutes and Rules* adopted at the Fourth Congress, the basic unit was henceforth the "Factory Group" and where this was not tenable the "Street Group". Membership with full voting powers was open to all youth between the ages of 14 and 25 who "accept the programme and statutes of the League and support it by taking an active part in its work as well as paying the prescribed dues". The League Congress was accepted as the supreme authority. The Executive Committee was to be composed of 25 members who had been members of the League for at least one year. The Y.C.L. was "politically subordinated to the Party, but organisationally autonomous. . . . Mutual representation shall obtain between all Committees and factory groups of the two organisations on the principle of one reciprocal delegate with full voice and vote."

[2] "At a time when the young workers are showing political interest and activity the capitalists and their reformist lackeys are redoubling their efforts to capture them. Of these attempts, those distinguished by the title of 'Labour' (The Labour League of Youth) and the I.L.P. Guild of Youth) are the most dangerous, because they seek to deflect the healthy growing class political instinct of the young workers into reformist channels." *Congress of Young Fighters*, p. 8.

[3] Resolution on *The Bourgeois Youth Movement*, ibid., pp. 29–31.

[4] The Thesis on "The International Situation" submitted to the 8th Congress of the C.P.G.B. (October 1926) speaks of "the entry of 1,500 young workers into the League since the General Strike, more than doubling its members" (*Report of 8th Congress*, p. 34). This would mean a total of around 3,000 members for the Y.C.L. towards the end of 1926. Remembering that many of the recruits made at the enthusiastic meetings after the General Strike were never really integrated in the League, I would think that the figure of 1,800 given in December by the Y.C.L. itself is a more accurate estimate of the situation at the end of 1926.

CHAPTER V—APPENDIX I

CONGRESSES OF THE COMMUNIST PARTY
1924-1926[1]

Congress	Venue	Date	Main Contents
Sixth	Manchester (Caxton Hall, Salford)	May 16–18, 1924	Attitude to Labour Government and Labour Party; Party Re-organisation
Seventh	Glasgow (St. Mungo Hall)	May 30–June 1, 1925	Preparation for Coming Offensive: Relations with Labour Party; Fight against Imperialism
Eighth	London (Battersea Town Hall)	October 16–17, 1926	Analysis of General Strike and Strategy to follow it; Solidarity with Miners; Building a Mass Party

CHAPTER V—APPENDIX II

COMMUNIST PARTY LEADERSHIP BETWEEN THE SIXTH AND EIGHTH PARTY CONGRESSES

(a) *Central Executive Committee elected at Sixth Party Congress, Manchester, May 17–19, 1924*[2]

R. Page Arnot
Tom Bell
E. H. Brown
William Brain
J. R. Campbell
Helen Crawfurd
George Deacon
R. Palme Dutt
Aitken Ferguson
William Gallacher

W. Hannington
Arthur Horner
T. A. Jackson
Arthur MacManus
J. T. Murphy
Harry Pollitt
C. M. Roebuck[3]
Robert Stewart
J. R. Wilson

Albert Inkpin (General Secretary)

[1] For first five Congress of C.P.G.B. see Appendix I to Chapter II.
[2] Organising Report of C.E.C., *Report of 7th Congress of C.P.G.B.*, pp. 141–142.
[3] Andrew Rothstein.

Substitute Members

                A. H. Hawkins   Edgar Lansbury

Representatives of Other Organisations
The following served on the C.E.C. as representatives of other organisations:

    Tom Quelch   (for Minority Movement)
    William Rust   (for Young Communist League)
    Beth Turner   (for Women's Section of Party)

(*b*) *Bureaux, Departments and Movements of Personnel from Sixth to Seventh Congresses*[1]

At its first meeting the Central Committee appointed the following to constitute the Political and Organising Bureaux:

Political Bureau
T. Bell, W. Gallacher, A. MacManus, J. T. Campbell, J. T. Murphy, H. Pollitt, C. M. Roebuck. *Substitutes:* J. R. Campbell and R. Palme Dutt.

Organising Bureau
R. Page Arnot, W. Brain, George Deacon, W. Hannington, T. Quelch, R. Stewart. *Substitutes:* E. H. Brown and R. Palme Dutt.

    A. Inkpin as General Secretary, was a member of both Bureaux.

    Shortly after the Sixth Congress, R. P. Dutt was granted an extended leave from the Executive owing to ill health. J. R. Campbell, who replaced Dutt as Editor of the *Workers' Weekly*, was co-opted on to the Political Bureau. W. Rust (Y.C.L.) and Beth Turner (Women's Section) were later brought on to the Political Bureau with consultative vote.

    During the greater part of the period the following acted as heads of the different departments:

Industrial	J. R. Campbell
Agitation and Propaganda	Thomas Bell
Editor of Workers' Weekly	J. R. Campbell
Parliamentary and Municipal	J. T. Murphy
Colonial	Thomas Bell
Co-operative	J. T. Murphy
Unemployed	W. Hannington
Youth	C. M. Roebuck

[1] Ibid.

Editor of Communist
  Review   Thomas Bell
Publications   A. H. Hawkins
Women's Section   Beth Turner

(c) *Central Executive Committee elected at Seventh Party Congress, Glasgow, May 30—June 1, 1925*[1]
(With votes out of 102 valid ballot papers)

R. P. Arnot	91	A. Inkpin	88
Thomas Bell	96	T. A. Jackson	80
E. H. Brown	49	W. Joss	68
J. R. Campbell	99	A. MacManus	78
Helen Crawfurd	76	J. T. Murphy	94
R. P. Dutt	85	H. Pollitt	101
A. Ferguson	67	C. M. Roebuck	85
W. Gallacher	97	R. Stewart	86
W. Hannington	85	Beth Turner	66
A. Horner	70	Nat Watkins	55

Substitute Members

                J. R. Wilson   47
                E. Woolley   48

(d) *Bureaux, Departments and Movements of Personnel between Seventh and Eighth Congresses*
At its first meeting (June 13-14, 1925) the new Central Committee appointed its General Secretary, Bureaux and Department Heads as follows:[2]

General Secretary: A. Inkpin (unanimously)

Political Bureau
T. Bell, J. R. Campbell, W. Gallacher, A. Inkpin, A. MacManus, J. T. Murphy, H. Pollitt, C. M. Roebuck, W. Rust (representing Y.C.L.), G. Hardy (as Substitute)

Organising Bureau
R. Page Arnot, J. R. Campbell, A. Inkpin, T. A. Jackson, T. Quelch, C. M. Roebuck, Beth Turner, N. Watkins.

---

[1] *Report of Seventh Congress of C.P.G.B.*, pp. 115-116.
[2] *Workers' Weekly*, June 19, 1925, p. 6.

Secretariat
T. Bell, J. R. Campbell, J. T. Murphy and General Secretary, A. Inkpin.

Departments

Industrial	J. T. Murphy
Parliamentary	W. Gallacher
Agit. Prop.	T. Bell
Colonial	A. MacManus
Y.C.L.	C. M. Roebuck
Workers' Weekly	As R. P. Dutt was given leave J. R. Campbell became Editor
Women's Work	Beth Turner

(e) *Changes after the Arrests of the Twelve*[1]
Following the arrest of the twelve Communist leaders, the meeting of the Political Bureau of October 22, 1925, made the following replacements:

Added to Political Bureau
E. H. Brown, T. A. Jackson, R. W. Robson.

Added to Organising Bureau
W. Joss, J. J. Vaughan.

Acting Editor of Workers' Weekly
T. A. Jackson

R. Stewart became *Acting General Secretary*

(f) *Executive Committee elected at Eighth Party Congress*

William Allan	W. C. Loeber
R. P. Arnot	A. MacManus
Thomas Bell	J. T. Murphy
Ernest Brown	Harry Pollitt
J. R. Campbell	Dave Ramsay
Tom Clark	R. W. Robson
Helen Crawfurd	A. Rothstein
R. P. Dutt	W. Rust

[1] Minutes of Political Bureau. Party Records.

Aitken Ferguson R. Stewart
W. Gallacher S. Saklatvala
A. Horner Tom Thomas
W. Hannington A. G. Tomkins
Albert Inkpin Beth Turner
T. A. Jackson Nat Watkins
W. Joss J. R. Wilson

G. Hardy (for Minority Movement)
H. Young (for Y.C.L.)

CHAPTER V—APPENDIX III

YOUNG COMMUNIST LEAGUE LEADERSHIP BETWEEN SECOND AND FOURTH CONGRESSES

(a) National Executive Committee as at May 1925[1]

Jack Cohen J. Shields
W. Duncan H. Smith
A. Pearce D. F. Springhall
J. Prothero W. Tapsell
J. Robertson D. Wilson
E. Rothstein E. Woolley
C. M. Roebuck (for Party) H. Young
W. Rust

(b) Leadership elected at Third Congress, Manchester, July 1925[2]

Central Bureau in London
Cohen, Gildersleaves, Pearce, Rust, Shuttleworth, Springhall, Tapsell, West, Wilson.

Provinces
Patterson (Glasgow), Prothero (South Wales), Robertson (Leith), Smith (Yorks), Woolley (Manchester)

Substitute Members
D. Ainley (Manchester), M. Jordan (Shipley) and W. Williams (South Wales).

[1] Organising Report of C.E.C. to Seventh Congress of C.P.G.B., *Report of 7th Congress C.P.G.B.*, pp. 161–163.
[2] *Workers' Weekly* No. 128, July 17, 1925, pp. 2 and 4.

(c) Leadership elected of the Young Comrades League, elected at First Conference, Manchester, February 13–14, 1926[1]

London Members
R. Goldman, H. Lovell, J. McFarlane, R. Shar, D. F. Springhall.

Children
W. Baker, A. Campbell, I. Greenhouse (South Wales), Iris Hardy, C. Hughes (Glasgow), H. Lee (Manchester), J. Malkin (Yorkshire).

[1] *Workers' Weekly*, No. 160 February 26, 1926, p. 4.

INDEX

Ablett, Noah, 164
Adams, Francis, 302 n.
Ahmed, Muzaffar, 303
Ainley, David, 365
Ainley, Ted, 353
Allan, William, 364
Allenby, Lord, 303
Allerdyce, Mrs. M., 261 n.
Allison, George, 325 n.
All-Russian Council of Trade Unions (A.R.C.T.O.), 14, 16, 17, 18, 23, 243, 245, 275, 287, 319, 321, 322, 324
Altogether Builders' Labourers, 119
Amalgamated Engineering Union (A.E.U.), 92, 201, 227
Amalgamated Society of Woodworkers (A.S.W.), 242, 249
Amalgamated Weavers' Association (A.W.A.), 242
Amsterdam International, see International Federation of Trade Unions
Anderson, Sir John, 40
Anglo-Russian Miners' Committee, 239
Anglo-Soviet Relations, 315-25
Anglo-Soviet Trade Union Committee, 16-21, 226, 237, 287, 318, 321, 322, 323, 324
Anglo-Soviet Trade Union Conference, 17-19, 20
Archbishop of Canterbury, 121, 123, 173
Archer-Shee, Lieutenant-Colonel Sir Martin, 37
Armstrong, Rear-Admiral, 39
Arnold, Lord, 81
Arnot, Robin Page, 68, 69, 90, 161, 162, 233, 241, 276 n., 287, 361, 362, 363, 364

Asquith, Lord, 123, 173
Associated Society of Locomotive Engineers & Firemen (A.S.L.E.F.), 29, 30, 86, 92, 234
Astbury, Mr. Justice, 123

Baker, W., 366
Baldwin, Stanley, 25, 30, 31, 38, 65, 109, 122, 128, 129, 130, 143, 146, 172, 185, 211, 215, 221, 231, 236, 239, 240, 241, 293
Balfour, Lord, 123, 145
Beacham, V., 309
Beaverbrook, Lord, 118
Bell, Tom, 67, 69, 79, 90, 291, 296, 304, 325 n., 327, 352 n., 361, 362, 363, 364
Bennett, 72
Beveridge, Sir William, 98
Bevin, Ernest, 42, 48, 50, 59, 62, 87, 110, 112, 124, 128, 177, 178 n., 180, 274
Birkenhead, Lord, 113, 236
Biron, Sir Charles, 71, 81
Bishop, Reg, 44 n.
Blakeney, Brigadier-General, 39
Bodkin, Sir Archibald, 69
Bogdanoff, 350
Boilermakers, 201
Bolton, Harry, 164
Boughton, Rutland, 101, 344
Bourne, Cardinal, 124, 126, 129, 173
Bradshaw, Mrs. Norah, 272
Brailsford, H. N., 54, 80, 82 n., 192, 197
Brain, Billy, 162 n., 345, 361, 362
Bramley, Fred, 14, 15, 16, 19, 20, 21, 316
Bright, Frank, 166, 167
British Broadcasting Corporation (B.B.C.), 117, 121, 123, 128, 130, 132, 140, 144, 151, 173, 175

British Empire Union, 39 n.
British Fascists, 38, 43, 66, 89, 97, 102, 103, 153, 201, 209, 210, 228
British Gazette, 117, 118, 119, 120, 121, 123, 139, 140, 141, 142, 144, 145, 146, 151, 173
British Worker, 119, 121, 122, 128, 139, 140, 141, 143, 144, 145, 146, 147, 151, 153, 184, 319
Brockway, Fenner, 192
Bromley, John, M.P., 14, 54, 60, 63, 82, 87, 93 n., 131, 219, 234, 238, 257, 275, 316
Brown, E. H., 90, 95, 259 n., 263, 325 n., 326 n., 346 n., 361, 362, 363, 364
Brown, Isabel, 167, 346
Brown, W. J., 60, 283
Buchanan, George, M.P., 11 n., 54
Bucharin, 73 n.
Burgess, H. G., 218
Burns, Emile, 340 n.
Buxton, Roden, 299

Campbell, A., 366
Campbell, J. R., 12, 44 n., 46 n., 67, 69, 70, 71, 73, 74, 75, 76, 82, 84, 90, 154, 258, 361, 362, 363, 364
Campbell, J. T., 362
Campbell, Stephen, M.P., 54
Cant, Ernie, 67, 69, 339
Carmichael, Duncan, 158
Cauder, Lord, 80
Chamberlain, Arthur, 256
Chandler, G. W., 272
Chang Tso-lin, 306, 310
Churchill, Winston, 24, 25, 32, 113, 123, 140, 145, 172, 175, 241, 242, 323
Citrine, Walter, 41, 84, 87, 93 n., 106 n., 113
Clark, Tom, 364
Clarke, Dr. Percival, 165
Clarke, Mr. Percival, 69
Clynes, J. R., 43, 48, 50, 62, 65, 84, 85, 121, 176, 179, 185, 197, 247, 248, 252, 254, 271, 277, 298, 300
Cohen, Jack, 353, 353 n., 365

Cole, G. D. H., 54, 82 n., 257
Cole, Margaret, 54
Colyer, W. T., 44 n., 260, 299, 303
Communist International, 70, 72, 73, 76, 171, 190, 193, 225, 226, 263 n., 264, 267, 268, 270, 287, 288, 292, 318, 321, 323, 324, 325-7, 332, 340 n., 352
Communist International, The, 287-8
Communist Party of Great Britain (C.P.G.B.):
  Arrest of the Twelve, 65, 67-79, 80-6, 94, 172, 364
  Communist International, 325-7
  Congresses—
    Sixth 1924, 335, 344, 347, 351, 361
    Seventh 1925, 11-13, 14, 19, 27, 257, 289, 290, 291, 294-5, 296, 303, 304, 314, 327, 334, 335-6, 338, 344, 347, 349, 350, 353, 361, 363
    Eighth 1926, 164, 171, 181 n., 186, 187, 190, 198 n., 219 n., 223 n., 230, 245, 262, 268, 286, 289, 291, 294-5, 311, 325, 335, 337, 340, 346, 348, 349, 350, 351, 357, 361, 363
  Differences within, 287-8
  Factory Groups, 337-40
  Imperialism, 290-304
  Left Wing Movement, the, 261-2
  Life and Organisation, 335-58
  Manifesto of May 1926, 207-8
  Press, 349-52
  Press and Publications on Imperialism, 328-30
  Records of Membership, 344-8
  Relations with the Independent Labour Party (I.L.P.), 262-71
  Relations with the Labour Party, 51-6, 66, 88-90, 255-7
  Relations with the Trade Unions, 248-50
  Statements, 88-90, 200-2, 202-5, 205-7, 209-10, 210-2, 212-8, 219-29, 330-2
Communist Party of the Soviet Union, 321, 327

Index

Communist Review, 295, 350, 363
Cook, A. J., 13, 22, 23, 26, 27, 29, 31, 34, 47, 48, 49, 54, 80, 82, 83, 85, 94, 96, 105, 113, 125, 126, 133, 178, 182, 193, 234, 235, 238, 239, 243, 245, 251, 260, 270 n., 273, 274, 276, 277, 287, 288, 315, 320, 322, 325, 350
Co-operative Guilds, 102, 104, 160, 349
Co-operative movement, 47, 48, 93, 96, 108, 110, 114, 133, 136, 138, 150, 158, 181, 182, 189, 193, 201, 207, 208, 210, 217, 225, 227, 235, 248, 274
Co-operative Union, 201, 227
Coppock, Richard, 80, 94
Councils of Action, 45, 103, 104, 108, 110, 114, 115, 119, 126, 130, 133, 136, 137, 138, 141, 142, 144, 145, 146, 147, 147-53, 154, 155, 157, 158, 159, 161, 164, 165, 169, 170, 172, 181, 182, 184, 189, 190, 193, 196, 205, 207, 208, 210, 212, 219, 221, 225, 355
Crawfurd, Helen, 83, 90, 313 n., 350, 361, 363, 364
Cramp, C. T., 50, 56, 87, 99, 131, 179, 183, 219, 234, 274, 277
Crick, Will, 59, 261 n., 266, 278
Crook, Professor Wilfred, 41, 118

Daily Chronicle, The, 15, 19
Daily Express, The, 15
Daily Herald, The, 31, 38, 67 n., 84, 94, 121, 140, 293 n.
Daily Mail, The, 15, 114
Daily News, The, 64, 321
Daily Telegraph, The, 19, 64
Dange, 303
Das Gupta, 303
Davies, Rhys, J., M.P., 283
Davies, S. O., 197
Dawes Plan, The, 24, 25, 49, 57, 88, 299, 315
Deacon, George, 352 n., 361, 362
Despard, Mrs., 313
Dobbie, W., 87
Dorritt Press, 165

Douglas, E., 325 n.
Drummond, Colonel F. Dudley Williams, C.B.E., 80
Duff, Admiral Sir Alexander, 37
Dukes, Charles, 183
Duncan, W., 365
Dunnico, Reverend H., 82
Dunstan, Dr. Robert, 256, 280, 350
Dutt, Clemens, 73 n.
Dutt, R. Palme, 25 n., 28 n., 35, 43, 65, 66, 68, 90, 91 n., 184, 271 n., 290 n., 291, 293 n., 308, 361, 362, 363, 364

Edwards, Joe, 44
Electrical Trades Union (E.T.U.), 92
Elgar, W., 84
Elsbury, Sam, 20, 252, 272, 273, 275, 276
Emergency Powers Act (E.P.A.), 111, 122, 131, 134, 136, 139, 144, 147, 166, 167, 173, 174, 175, 222, 232, 235, 273
Engels, F., 187, 350
Evening News, The, 72
Ewer, W. N., 82 n.

Falkland, Lord, 37
Ferguson, Aitken, 58, 61, 62, 90, 326 n., 361, 363, 365
Figgins, J. B., 249
Fimmen, Edo, 16
Financial Times, 64
Findlay, Alan, 14, 316
Fletcher, George, 22, 156, 157, 167, 251
Forshaw, John, 166
Fowler, F., 87
Fox, Ralph, 73
Friend, Ernest, 70

Gallacher, Willie, 44 n., 57, 67, 69, 71, 73, 74, 76, 78, 82, 90, 196, 286, 299, 301, 304, 311, 325, 325 n., 361, 362, 363, 364, 365
Garvin, J. L., 107
Geddes, Alexander, 162 n., 325 n., 346
Gibbons, John, 300
Gildersleaves, 365

Giles, G. C. T., 313 n.
Gill, T., 87
Gladstone, Mr., 302
Glasgow Herald, 19
Goldman, R., 366
Gosling, Harry, 87
Gossip, Alex, 22, 23, 54, 102, 260, 278, 280, 313, 313 n., 350
Gould, Mrs. Ayrton, 284
Granville, Lord, 302
Greenhouse, I., 366
Grey, Sir Edward, 192
Grey, Lord of Fallodon, 173
Griffiths, Ben, 79
Griffiths, Dan, 266
Guild of Youth, 353-5, 357, 358

Haldane, Lord, 59
Halket, Mr., 168
Hallsworth, J., 272
Hands Off China Campaign, 305-12, 330-2
Hannington, Wal, 22, 67, 69, 70, 78, 81, 90, 95, 102, 286, 313 n., 361, 362, 363, 365
Hardinge, Lord, of Penshurst, 37
Hardy, George, 22, 90, 95, 104, 115, 170, 326 n., 363, 365
Hardy, Iris, 366
Hastings, Detective William, 74
Havelock-Wilson, 152 n.
Hawkins, A. H., 350 n., 362, 363
Hayday, A., 87, 93 n.
Henderson, Arthur, 43, 53, 57, 60, 168, 132
Henderson, Arthur, Junior, 69
Hertzog, General, 304
Hicks, George, 16, 80, 82, 83, 85, 87, 93 n., 257, 271, 322
Hodges, Frank, 13, 244, 245, 247
Hogg, Sir Douglas, 71
Hogg, Sir Douglas McGarel, K.C., 145
Holmes, Walter, 350
Horner, Arthur, 22, 23, 26, 27, 90, 95, 100, 101, 103, 105, 108 n., 185, 233, 243, 244, 246, 247, 248, 251, 272, 276, 278, 283, 310, 324, 325, 361, 363, 365

Horrabin, J. F., 54
Horrabin, Winifred, 54
Hughes, C., 366
Humphreys, D. S., 87
Humphreys, Sir Travers, 68, 69
Hunter, E. E., 299
Hutchinson, W. H., 102

Independent Labour Party (I.L.P.), 33, 42, 61, 82, 84, 88, 107, 109, 126, 133, 148, 152, 159, 178, 181, 189, 191-2, 197, 199, 231, 233, 243, 256, 278, 282, 283, 290, 293, 310, 314, 334, 349, 354
Independent Labour Party Guild of Youth, 353-5, 357, 358
Inchcape, Lord, 58
Inkpin, Albert, 44 n., 53, 67, 69, 78, 90, 257 n., 286, 337, 345, 353, 361, 362, 363, 364, 365
Inkpin, Harry, 352 n.
International Class War Prisoner's Aid (I.C.W.P.A.), 81, 82, 83, 167, 296, 313, 314
International Co-op Alliance, 227
International Federation of Trade Unions (I.F.T.U.), 14, 15, 16, 17, 20, 207, 226, 237, 275, 276, 321, 323
International Miners' Federation, 242, 244

Jackson, Frank, 278, 282
Jackson, T. A., 90, 95, 166, 361, 363, 364, 365
Jacobs, M., 299
Jellicoe, Lord, 37
Jenkins, B. M., 87
Johnston, Tom, M.P., 54
Jones, Jack, M.P., 70
Jordon, M., 365
Joseph, G. E., 48
Joss, W., 90, 363, 364, 365
Joy, Bert, 325 n.
Joynson-Hicks, Sir William (Jix), 32, 38, 40, 72, 175

Kerrigan, Peter, 103
Keynes, J. M., 25

Kirkwood, David, M.P., 54, 244, 278, 283
Kitchener, Detective-Sergeant, 70

Labour Party, 11, 13, 16, 82, 84, 88, 93, 96, 99, 107, 109, 120, 126, 133, 148, 152, 159, 175, 177, 178, 179, 180, 181, 189, 191, 192, 199, 207, 214, 217, 222, 225, 227, 228, 231, 232, 233, 246, 248, 251, 252, 256, 257, 258, 259, 262, 272, 278, 281, 282, 283, 291, 293, 295, 297, 304, 307, 308, 310, 313, 314, 326, 349, 354
   Conference, Liverpool, 1925, 44, 51, 52, 55, 56–67, 75, 88, 183, 257, 258, 298–9, 303, 309, 313
   Conference, Margate, 1926, 131, 244, 245, 255, 260, 277–87, 299–300, 311
   League of Youth, 280, 358
   Young Peoples' Section, 353, 355, 357
Labour Women's Fund, 239, 245, 284
Lampson, Miles, 312
Lansbury, Edgar, 165, 362
Lansbury, George, M.P., 54, 65, 80, 82, 83, 84, 181, 232, 236, 257, 260, 270, 278, 280, 281, 313
Lansbury's Labour Weekly, 16, 54, 81, 164, 181, 269
Larkin, Jim, 296, 313
Lathan, George, 87
Law, Arthur, 87
Lawrence, General Sir Herbert, 98
Lawrence, Susan, 80
Lawther, Will, 161, 164, 266
Lee, H., 366
Lee, Kenneth, 98
Lee, P., 274
Lees-Smith, Professor H. B., M.P., 81
Left Wing, The, 257
Left-Wing Movement, 257–62
Lenin, V. I., 23, 120, 172, 175, 290, 320, 350
Lewes, Daniel, 166
Lewes, Isaac, 166
Lismer, Ted, 167

Little, Jack, 162 n.
Llewellyn, E. G., 261 n.
Llewelyn, Emrys, 166
Llewellyn, Evan, 80
Lloyd, Lt.-Gen. Sir Francis, 37
Lloyd George, 25, 75, 173, 190, 222, 342
Locarno Pact, 315
Loeber, W. C., 249, 272, 274, 364
London Society of Compositors, 47
Longden, Fred, 266, 350
Lovell, H., 365
Lovell, H. B., 82, 167

Macassey, Sir Lyndon, 37
MacCallum, Reverend Malcolm, 350
MacDonald, Ramsay, 19, 33, 51, 56, 58, 59, 60, 61, 62, 63, 65, 66, 76, 84, 85, 91, 96, 99, 108, 112, 121, 124, 173, 175, 176, 179, 180, 183, 184, 185, 191, 192, 197, 231, 247, 258, 262, 269, 271, 278, 284, 292, 299, 303, 317, 322
Mack, J. D., 261 n.
Maclean, Neil, M.P., 54, 82 n.
MacManus, Arthur, 68, 69, 73 n., 90, 293, 311, 325 n., 339, 344, 349 n., 361, 362, 363, 364
MacNulty, A., 350
Maitland, Sir Arthur Steel, 125
Malkin, J., 366
Manchester Guardian, 38
Mann, Tom, 22, 23, 44, 45, 82 n., 101, 251, 252, 253, 260, 350
Marchbank, J., 87
Marsh, Sam, M.P., 70
Martin, Kingsley, 180
Marx, Karl, 23, 76, 187, 350
Maxton, James, M.P., 54, 82 n., 257
McFarlane, 366
McLaughlin, J., 272, 273, 274
Miles, George, 167
Miners' Federation (M.F.G.B.), 13, 24, 28, 29, 30, 79, 82, 91, 92, 93, 104, 105, 106, 107, 112, 113, 120, 127, 130, 164, 178, 182, 200, 217, 233, 234, 236, 237, 238, 240, 241, 242, 243, 244, 245, 247, 266, 275, 283, 320, 323, 325, 350

Mining Association of Great Britain, 28, 107, 233, 242
Ministry of Transport, 117
Moffat, Abe, 26, 156, 164
Moffat, Alex, 156
Moffat, David, 156
Mond, Sir Alfred, 55
Mondism, 280
Montagu, Norman, 25
Montgomery, Sir Kerr, 161
Moody, C. J., 62, 249, 299
Morel, E. D., 257
Morning Post, 98, 121, 140, 320
Morrison, Herbert, 282, 303
Mosley, Sir Oswald, 59, 283
Murphy, J. T., 68, 69, 78, 79, 90, 156, 168, 192 *n.*, 276 *n.*, 287, 323 *n.*, 325 *n.*, 350, 361, 362, 363, 364

National Citizen's Union, 39 *n.*
National Furnishing Trades Association (N.A.F.T.A.), 250
National Guard, 39 *n.*
National Minority Movement, 11, 21–4, 44–6, 49, 50, 67, 92, 93, 97, 99, 101, 103, 104, 105, 107, 109, 115, 120, 126, 133, 137, 149, 154, 157, 164, 165, 169–70, 194, 202, 212, 224, 225, 228, 231, 233, 242, 248, 249, 250–5, 262, 272, 273, 277, 279, 286, 287, 288, 291, 308, 309, 348
  Conference of Action, March 1926 101–4
National Society of Operative Printers and Assistants (N.A.T.S.O.P.A.), 114
National Unemployed Workers Committee Movement (N.U.W.C.M.) 45, 54, 84, 96, 149, 202, 227, 251, 348
National Union of Foundry Workers, 92
Nation Union of General and Municipal Workers (N.U.G.M.W.), 248, 252

National Union of Railwaymen (N.U.R.), 30, 86, 131, 168, 201, 234, 249, 268
National Union of Vehicle Builders (N.U.V.B.), 47
New Leader, 84, 192, 197, 265, 266, 268
Newbold, Walter, 257
Noel, Reverend Conrad, 82 *n.*

Observer, The, 55, 107
O'Connor, Detective Sergeant, 70
O'Dell, G. A., 261 *n.*
Organisation for the Maintenance of Supplies (O.M.S.), 36, 37, 38, 39, 66, 89, 91, 97, 102, 111, 120, 160, 162, 172, 175, 200, 209, 210, 214, 263, 265
Oudegeest, 276
Oxford, Lord, 123

Page-Croft, Sir Henry, 320
Palmer, Sir Alfred M., 169
Parker, Chief Inspector, 68
Paper Workers' Union, 141
Patterson, 365
Paul, William, 260, 350
Pearce, A., 365
Peuple, Le, 15
Plebs League, 160
Pole, Felix J. C., 218
Pollitt, Harry, 13, 20, 23, 42, 45, 48, 49, 50, 51, 57, 58, 60, 62, 65, 67, 69, 71, 73, 74, 75, 77, 78, 82, 90, 102, 244, 253, 258, 272, 278, 282, 283, 285, 286, 290, 297, 299, 314, 315, 361, 362, 363
Pollitt, Marjorie, 83, 166
Postgate, R. W., 82 *n.*, 257
Potter, Fred, 54
Poulton, E. L., 87
Price, Phillips, 257
Prothero, J., 365
Proudfoot, David, 345
Pugh, Arthur, 93, 110, 112, 127, 183, 272, 275, 277
Purcell, A. A., 14, 16, 19, 54, 82, 83, 124, 257, 271, 277, 287, 297, 316, 322

Index

Quayle, Mary, 126 n.
Quelch, T., 90, 338, 362, 363

Railway Clerks Association, 30, 86
Rakosi, 314
Ramsay, Dave, 364
Ranfurly, Lord, 37
Reade, Arthur E. E., 327, 327 n.
Red Friday (1925), 31, 33, 34, 35, 36, 40, 44, 46, 51, 95, 100, 108, 133, 200, 201, 202-3, 205, 209, 225, 289, 344
Redgrave, H. S., 278
Red International of Labour Unions (R.I.L.U.), 14, 72, 276, 318
Redmond, John, 75
Reed, John, 350
Reith, John, 121
Richardson, W. P., 239, 283
Robertson, J., 365
Robinson, Mrs., 325 n.
Robotnik, 15, 19
Robson, R. W., 95, 158, 165, 259, 326 n., 364
Rodd, Sir Rennell, 37
Roebuck, C. M. *See* Rothstein, Andrew
Rogers, Detective William, 74
Rothermere, Lord, 279
Rothstein, Andrew, 90, 126 n., 159 n., 272, 327 n., 361, 362, 363, 364, 365
Rothstein, E., 365
Royal Commission (Samuel) on the Mines, 31, 42, 91, 97-101, 102, 104, 106, 107, 108, 110, 118, 136, 137, 172, 175, 193, 200, 202-3, 205, 206, 208, 211, 212, 214, 215, 223, 239, 274
Rust, Bill, 67, 69, 78, 90, 286, 325 n., 326 n., 353, 354, 362, 363, 364, 365

Sacco and Vanzetti, 314
Saklatvala, S., M.P., 82, 90, 122, 139, 163 n., 167, 292, 296, 304, 350, 365
Samuel, Sir Herbert, 97, 124, 125, 126, 127, 145, 146, 175, 211

Samuel Memorandum, 125, 126, 127, 128, 130, 132, 146, 175
Sassenbach, 276
Scarborough, Lord, 37
Scobell, Walter, 266
Scurr, John, 81
Scurr, Mr., 311
Selbie, R. H., 218
Sexton, James, M.P., 49
Shar, R., 366
Shaw, Bernard, 81
Shields, J., 365
Shinwell, Emanuel, 60
Shuttleworth, 365
Simon, Sir John, 123, 143, 173
Skinner, O. W., 87
Slessor, Sir Henry, M.P., 69, 71, 74
Smillie, Robert, 241, 275
Smith, E. V., 167
Smith, H., 365
Smith, Herbert, 14, 29, 34, 112, 125, 235, 240, 241, 245, 316
Snowden, Philip, 27, 84, 176, 185
Southall, Joseph, 266, 278, 280
Span, Bessie, 167
Span, Sarah, 167
Special Constables, 120, 222, 227
Spencer, George, M.P., 241, 244, 245, 246, 247
Springhall, D. F., 167, 170, 325 n., 326 n., 353, 355, 365, 366
Stack, Sir Lee, 301
Stalin, J., 323, 350
Stewart, Bob., 90, 95, 164, 165, 166, 265, 325 n., 361, 362, 363, 364, 365
Stoker, R., 166
Strachey, John, 270 n.
Strain, J., 272, 275, 315
Sunday Times, The, 43 n.
Sunday Worker, The, 39, 54, 67 n., 72, 79, 81 n., 84, 85, 115, 134, 136, 174, 207, 257, 259, 349, 350
Sun Yat-sen, 306, 331
Swales, A. B., 47, 49, 50, 54, 87, 272
Swift, Justice Rugby, 78
Symons, Madeleine, 81

Tanner, Jack, 252, 272, 273, 274

Tapsell, Walter, 353, 365
Tawney, R. H., 82 n.
Thomas, J. H., 41, 48, 50, 51, 62, 63, 65, 87, 92, 93 n., 96, 105, 107, 110, 111, 118, 125, 127, 131, 145, 146, 172, 175, 176, 178, 179, 182, 183, 184, 185, 191, 211, 219, 231, 247, 249, 250, 254, 268, 269, 271, 284, 292, 297, 317, 322, 343
Thomas, Tom, 365
Thompson, W. H., 69
Tillett, Ben, 14, 19, 81, 82 n., 87, 93 n., 284, 309, 316
Times, The, 15, 19, 38, 64, 85 n., 93, 117, 168, 173
Tomkins, A. G., 272, 273, 275, 276, 309, 365
Tomsky, 14, 15, 17, 21, 319
Trades Councils, 31, 45, 46, 47, 50, 58, 61, 66, 82, 89, 96, 101, 102, 103, 104, 108, 110, 115, 132, 148, 149, 156, 158, 159, 160, 181, 194, 201, 202, 207, 208, 226, 227, 228, 231, 235, 249, 250, 252, 254, 256, 260, 268, 274, 278, 281, 282, 311, 345, 347, 357
Trades Union Congress:
  1924 Hull, 14, 308
  1925 Scarborough, 20, 44, 46–51, 91, 105, 183, 271, 276, 287, 295, 297, 309, 315
  1926 Bournemouth, 242, 249, 251, 255, 271–7, 287, 310, 324
  1926 Special Congress, 29, 30
  General Council, 13, 14, 15, 16, 17, 18, 19, 20, 28, 29, 30, 31, 33, 41, 46, 47, 50, 66, 84, 86, 91, 92, 93, 94, 95, 96, 100, 102, 104, 105, 106, 107, 108, 109, 110, 111, 112, 113, 114, 115, 116, 117, 119, 120, 122, 123, 124, 125, 126, 127, 128, 130, 131, 132, 133, 135, 137, 138, 139, 140, 141, 142, 143, 145, 146, 148, 150, 151, 161, 173, 174, 177, 178, 180, 181, 182, 183, 184, 185, 186, 191, 192, 194, 195, 201, 202, 205, 207, 208, 210, 211, 213, 214, 215, 217, 219, 220, 222, 223, 225, 226, 227, 228, 230, 231, 233, 234, 237, 238, 239, 241, 245, 246, 248, 253, 254, 271, 272, 273, 274, 276, 283, 307, 309, 316, 319, 321, 323, 324
  Industrial Committee, 93, 106, 109, 110, 113
  Relations with Soviet Trade Unions, 318–25
Trade Unions:
  Conference of Executives, 30, 107, 108, 109–12, 201, 237, 265
  Delegations to Soviet Union, 316–8
  International Unity, 13–7, 19, 23, 104, 276
Trade Union Unity, 16
Transport and General Workers Union (T.G.W.U.), 29, 30, 86, 92, 201
Trevelyan, C. P., M.P., 81, 303
Trotsky, Leon, 321, 326
Turner, Ben, 59
Turner, Beth, 90, 362, 363, 364, 365
Turner, John, 14, 316

United Ladies Tailors Union, 250
Usmani, Shaukat, 303

Vanzetti. *See* Sacco
Varley, 245
Vaughan, Joe, 59, 60, 102, 260, 364
Volunteer Services Committee, 120
Vorwarts, 15

Wadge, F., 249
Walkden, A. G., 87, 93 n., 131, 146, 219
Walker, 93 n.
Walker, H. A., 218
Wall, A., 70
Wallace, C., 69
Wallhead, R. C., M.P., 283
Walshe, Christina, 101
Warr, Earl de la, 81
Warwick, Dowager Countess of, 81
Watkins, Nat, 45, 90, 363, 365
Webb, Harry, 167
Wedgewood, Colonel Josiah, M.P., 81, 83
Wedgewood, R. L., 218

Weekly Dispatch, 27, 65
Weekly Worker, 84
West, 365
Wheatley, John, M.P., 54, 81
Wilkinson, Ellen, M.P., 82 *n*., 272, 273
Willey, O. G., 256
Williams, Evan, 240
Williams, Robert, 81, 84, 278
Williams, W., 365
Wilson, D., 365
Wilson, Edward, 169
Wilson, J. R., 90, 325 *n*., 361, 363, 365
Wintringham, Tom, 67, 69, 110 *n*.
Women's Relief Committees, 239, 245, 284
Wood, Sir Kingsley, 161
Woolley, E., 90, 363, 365
Worker, The, 253
Workers' Bulletin, The, 134, 135, 136, 138, 139, 141, 142, 144, 145, 146, 147, 151, 158, 159, 165, 166
Workers' Daily, 111, 134, 136, 148, 166
Workers' Defence Corps, 96, 103, 110, 114, 115, 136, 149, 153, 154, 155, 193, 201, 208, 210, 214, 220, 227

Workers Industrial Alliance, 29, 92-3, 96, 105, 201
Workers International Relief (W.I.R.), 313
Workers' Weekly, 12, 27, 34, 35, 39, 42, 67, 68, 71, 76, 77, 88, 94, 100, 108, 109, 111, 154, 165, 166, 262, 295, 296, 301, 302, 304, 305, 307, 310, 312, 344, 345, 349, 362, 364
Wu Pei-fu, 306

Young, H., 365
Young, Mrs., 70
Young Communist League, 67, 69, 74, 162 *n*., 165, 166, 167, 169-70, 308, 326, 345, 352-8
Young Communist League,
 Third Congress, 354, 356, 365
 Fourth Congress, 354, 357, 358, 365
Young Comrade, The, 356
Young Striker, The, 167, 170, 355
Young Worker, The, 357

Zaghoul Pasha, 301
Zinoviev, 320